Idolatry
and the
Hardening
of the
Heart

Idolatry and the Hardening of the Heart

A STUDY IN BIBLICAL THEOLOGY

Edward P. MEADORS

t&t clark

BS
543
.M46
2006

Copyright © 2006 by Edward P. Meadors

All rights reserved. No part of this book may be reproduced, stored in a retrieval system, or transmitted in any form or by any means, electronic, mechanical, including photocopying, recording, or otherwise, without the written permission of the publisher, T&T Clark International.

T&T Clark International, 80 Maiden Lane, New York, NY 10038

T&T Clark International, The Tower Building, 11 York Road, London SE1 7NX

T&T Clark International is a Continuum imprint.

Cover design: Lee Singer

ISBN 0-567-02-5632 (Hardcover)
ISBN 0-567-02573-X (Paperback)
A catalog record of this book may be obtained from the Library of Congress.

Printed in the United States of America

06 07 08 09   10 9 8 7 6 5 4 3 2 1

"Guard yourselves from idols."
(1 John 5:21)

"Above all else, guard your heart,
for it is the wellspring of life."
(Proverbs 4:23)

Table of Contents

Acknowledgments viii

Preface ix

1. The Biblical Paradigm: Idolatry and the Hardening of the Heart 1
2. Idolatry and the Heart: Words in Context 12
3. Pharaoh's Falsehoods: Human Gods are No Gods at All 17
4. "Follow Vanity and Become Vain: Israel is Guilty Too" 37
5. Listen But Don't Perceive: The Prophetic Commission 56
   to Harden Hearts
6. Seeds, Taxes, and Mammon: Jesus and the Kingship of God 77
7. Paganism, the Temple, and the Hardening of the Heart in Acts 97
8. Exchanging God for an Image: Idolatry in Romans 1-2 105
9. God Hardens Whom He Desires: Divine Sovereignty in Romans 9 119
10. Jealousy and the Partial Hardening of Israel (Romans 10-11) 139
11. "Hardening of the Followers of the Beast": The Book of Revelation 154
12. Insidious Idols Within: Pride, Theology, and Worship 173
    Conclusions and Contemporary Applications

Bibliography 196

Index of Biblical and Other Ancient Sources 203

Index of Modern Authors 214

I AFFECTIONATELY
DEDICATE THIS BOOK TO
MY MOTHER AND FATHER

Acknowledgments

It is with great appreciation that I thank Doug Buckwalter, Howard Marshall, and Kenneth Kitchen for their constructive criticisms of this book. I am forever in debt to each of these outstanding scholars.

I also owe a debt of gratitude to Taylor University for providing a sabbatical semester to do research during the fall of 2001. The staff of Taylor's Zondervan library was and continues to be a pleasure to work with.

I also want to thank my students at Taylor and the members of the adult Sunday School classes that I have taught over the years at Upland Community Church. Both audiences have served as gracious sounding boards and constant sources of encouragement. We live in a wonderful community.

Finally, I thank my family for being everything and more that a family should be: Grandpa and Ruth McDonald, Nana and Papa Meadors, the Pointers, my brothers and sister and their families, my precious wife Kathy, and my three pride and joys—Edward Jr., Davis, and Mary Katherine.

Edward P. Meadors
July, 2006

Preface

> *"The idols of the nations are but silver and gold, the work of man's hands. They have mouths, but they do not speak; They have eyes, but they do not see; They have ears, but they do not hear; Nor is there any breath at all in their mouths."* . . . *"***Those who make them will be like them**, yes, everyone who trusts in them."*
> (Psalm 135: 15, 18)

The purpose of this book is to provide a biblical, theological answer to Isaiah's question, "Why, O Lord, do you cause us to stray from your ways, *and harden our heart from fearing you*" (Isa 63:17a)? The biblical answer is pervasive, explicit, easy to understand, and interrelated with almost every major biblical theme. The hardening of the heart is most often quite simply God's disciplinary punishment for the specific sin of idolatry. As idols have eyes but cannot see and ears but cannot hear, so idolaters lose their sensory faculties as they conform to created, inanimate objects.

This book is an exercise in biblical theology with a brief statement of contemporary application in the concluding chapter. Beginning in the Old Testament the hardened heart finds rescue in the "new covenant" promises that Isaiah, Jeremiah, Ezekiel and Hosea prophesy. In these remarkable prophesies God promises to remove Israel's idols, cleanse his people, anoint them with his Spirit, write his law upon their hearts, and turn their hearts of stone into hearts of flesh (see esp. Ezek 36:22-36). This event comprises the new covenant, which wills to restore true life and spiritual vitality to God's disabled people.

The New Testament tells how Jesus activates these promises and brings them into effect in the lives of those who respond to him in faith. Healings of the blind, lame, deaf and dumb signal Jesus' identity as Isaiah's anointed herald of salvation (Lk 7:22; Isa 61:1-4), who rescues God's people from hardening, exile, and death before leading transformed, "born again" believers into the kingdom of God. Jesus' death, the blood of the "new covenant" (Luke 22:20), activates and generates this "new covenant salvation" in the lives of believers. But for those who aggressively defy faith in Jesus out of a preference for religious tradition, the inevitable consequence is continued hardening (Mark 7:1-23).

The Apostle Paul, in turn, testified that it was his mission to explain and preach this very message. Identifying himself as a "servant of the new covenant"

(2 Cor 3:6), Paul charted both the problem of hardening (Rom 1:18-32) and its solution—the Gospel that God by his grace wills to justify, recreate, and resurrect all who profess faith in Jesus. Those who do not believe suffer intellectual blindness (2 Cor 4:3-4) by contrast to believers, who experience transformation and rebirth in union with Christ (2 Cor 3:14-18). "If any man is in Christ, he is a new creature; the old things passed away; behold, new things have come" (2 Cor 5:17).

With breathtaking closure, the book of Revelation applies this rationale to the historical context of the seven churches of Asia Minor, who lived with the agonizing temptation to compromise with the idolatry laden Roman emperor cult. Revelation's message is for those *"who have ears to hear what the Spirit says to the churches"* (Rev 2:7, 11, 17, 29; 3:6, 13, 22). Those who do not have ears to hear are idolatrous followers of the beast: *"and the rest of mankind, who were not killed by these plagues, did not repent of the works of their hands, so as not to worship demons, and the idols of gold and of silver and of brass and of stone and of wood, which can neither see nor hear nor walk"* (Rev 9:20). The sermonic "charge" of Revelation is therefore a battle command to worship God exclusively (Rev 19:10; 22:9) with perseverance and hope in anticipation of eternal citizenship in the "new heavens" and the "new earth."

Hardening is thus a striking negative foil to the saving regeneration that transforms authentic worshipers of the true living God. As the Apostle Paul affirms, *"But we all, with unveiled face beholding as in a mirror the glory of the Lord, are being transformed into the same image from glory to glory, just as from the Lord, the Spirit"* (2 Cor 3:18). A feature of creation theology, the phenomenon envisions God the creator exercising his creative power to *recreate* repentant, faithful worshipers. Sin's distortion undone, atonement with God through faith in Jesus Christ restores the *imago Dei*, the holy character that God willed for humanity in the beginning.

Climaxing Israel's remarkably unique *aniconic*[1] religious history, Jesus Christ emerges as the equally unique incarnate icon of God (2 Cor 4:4: *"hos estin eikōn tou theou"*). Against the backdrop of Israel's violated aniconism, Jesus arrives not as a product of the human imagination but as God himself incarnate. The only one of his kind (John 1:14, 18: *monogenēs*), he brought for those who would repent and believe (Mark 1:15) the healing power of God's rule, the exclusive means of regeneration from spiritual recalcitrance.

There is great hope in the true living God who wills that his people turn from idols to know union with him through the atoning, new covenant work of Jesus Christ accomplished supernaturally by the indwelling of the Holy Spirit (2 Cor 3:16-18). We sinners may indeed be born again!

---

[1] *Aniconic*—without visual images of the divine (Greek: *an* "without" + *eikōn* "image").

Chapter 1

The Biblical Paradigm: Idolatry and the Hardening of the Heart

*Why, O Lord, do you cause us to stray from your
ways, and harden our heart from fearing you?* (Isa 63:17a)

I. Introduction

How to reconcile God's love and mercy with his active, unyielding "hardening" of human hearts is a question that has fueled theological debate throughout Jewish and Christian history. Not surprisingly, in answer to this question Christians today often respond with the "determinist" or "free will" arguments inherited from theological traditions. The less traditional accept the apparent paradox as evidence of humanity's inability to comprehend fully the mind of God—we look through a glass dimly. All agree, however, that the question is important. Theologically, it affects how one understands God. And biblically, the issue surfaces with repeated prominence. From Pharaoh's hardening to Isaiah's commission, from Jesus' parables to Paul's eschatology, God "hardens" human hearts to demonstrate his supremacy and accomplish his will. The phenomenon is explicit and incontrovertible. One cannot question that God "hardened" biblical characters and people groups. He clearly did. The question, rather, is why? Was God's action arbitrary and unconditional?[1] Were the biblical recipients of hardening neutral, ordinary human beings, God hardening them purely to display his power to do so? And if such was the case, was God himself just and truly righteous as the one who hardened, so that the resulting sin exalted his glory? Would this not make God the author of sin?[2] Or did God's sovereignty define justice from one biblical episode to the next, so that, whatever God did, he was just and righteous in doing it, simply

---

[1] In American Evangelicalism this increasingly popular mindset traces its origin to Jonathan Edwards: "By the mere pleasure of God, I mean his sovereign pleasure, his arbitrary will, restrained by no obligation . . . " ("Sinners in the Hands of an Angry God"; *Selected Writings of Jonathan Edwards*, (ed. H. P. Simonson; New York: Frederick Ungar Publishing Co., 1970), 97.

[2] Which is in fact the conviction of Evangelical pastor and author John Piper: "God decrees all things, even all sins" ("Is God Less Glorious Because He Ordained that Evil Be?: Jonathan Edwards on the Decrees of God," n.p. [July, 1998]. Online: http://www.desiringgod.org/library/topics/suffering/god_and_evil.html. Similarly, Wayne Grudem, (*Systematic Theology: An Introduction to Biblical Theology* [Grand Rapids: Zondervan, 1994], 322-51); and, in biblical theology, Walther Eichrodt: " There was no other way of expressing the uncanny, overpowering, 'demonic' character of the power of sin, than by seeing this too as a work of Yahweh" (*Theology of the Old Testament* [trans. J. A. Baker; Westminster: Philadelphia, 1967], 2.180).

because he was sovereign God?[3] *And what of the individuals hardened?* Did hardening determine their eternal plight, so that it became in essence their eternal death sentence? Or was recovery possible? And if so, who would accomplish it and how would it happen?

II. Purpose and Thesis

The purpose of this book is to address these questions as they unfold in Scripture. We shall do so by examining the hardening phenomenon as it relates to the biblical axiom that worshipers *become like that which they worship*. Idolaters, those who worship created things,[4] suffer hardening and sensory depletion as they assimilate to the inanimate objects of their faith. Accordingly, as idols have eyes, ears, noses, and mouths but cannot see, hear, smell, and speak, so too do idolaters lose their sensory faculties as they conform to inanimate objects.

Psalms 115 and 135 represent the clearest expressions of the hardening paradigm in the Bible:

Ps 115:4-8	Ps 135:15-18
Their idols are silver and gold, the work of man's hands. They have mouths, but they cannot speak; they have eyes, but they cannot see; they have ears, but they cannot hear; they have noses, but they cannot smell; they have hands but they cannot feel; they have feet, but they cannot walk; they cannot make a sound with their throat. *Those who make them will become like them, everyone who trusts in them.*	The idols of the nations are but silver and gold, the work of man's hands. They have mouths, but they do not speak; they have ears, but they do not hear; nor is there any breath at all in their mouths. *Those who make them will be like them, yes, everyone who trusts in them.*

---

[3] As John J. Davis surmises: "Theologically speaking, anything God does is right on the *a priori* grounds that He is God" (*Moses and the Gods of Egypt* [Grand Rapids: Baker, 1971]), 136. Similarly, John Piper writes "it is the glory of God and his essential nature mainly to dispense mercy (but also wrath, Ex 34:7) on whomever he pleases apart from any constraint originating outside his own will. This is the essence of what it means to be God. This is his name" (*The Justification of God*, Grand Rapids: Baker [1983], 203). Similarly, G.K. Beale in support of Piper ("An Exegetical and Theological Consideration of the Hardening of Pharaoh's Heart in Exodus 4-14 and Romans 9," *TrinJ* 5 NS [1984]: 152.

[4] Yehezkel Kaufmann: "The Bible conceives of idolatry as the belief that divine and magical powers inhere in certain natural or manmade objects and that man can activate these powers through fixed rituals. These objects, upon which magical rituals are performed, are 'the gods of the nations.' The Bible does not conceive the powers as personal beings who dwell in the idols; the idol is not a habitation of the god, it is the god himself" (*The Religion of Israel: From its Beginnings to the Babylonian Exile* [trans. Moshe Greenberg; Chicago: The University of Chicago Press, 1960), 14. According to Kaufmann, "the Jewish attitude toward paganism was determined by the belief that the pagans worshiped idol-fetishes" (p. 13).

One a complaint, the other a hymn,[5] both satirically expose how "non-sentient gods reduce their worshipers to the same level of obtuseness."[6] The axiom "you become like that which you worship" is clearly present in both: *"Those who make them* (idols) *will become like them."* Committed to a worldview that seeks supernatural security in images from the natural world, idolaters fail to see the truth of God's supreme power as the true living God. Idolaters thus bring upon themselves the curse of sensory debilitation. In separation from God, the true creator, sustainer, and inspirer of life, sensory faculties diminish, so that idolaters cannot perceive God, even when his revelation stares them directly in the face.

To be sure, *idolatry is not the only cause of hardening in the Bible.* Hardening is a consequence of testing God (Ps 95:8-10) and refusing to repent (Jer 5:20-23). And yet, idolatry is rarely distant in context. As H. J. Fabry observes, "Obduracy as rejection of the call to repent (cf. Jer 5:23; 18:12: Ezek 2:4; 3:7) goes hand in hand with self-deluding idolatry (Jer 9:13 [14]; 13:10)."[7] Idolatry is the most prominent cause as a result of the heart's responsibility in worship. Thus Ezekiel is told, "Son of man, these men have set up their idols *in their hearts"* (Ezek 14:3).[8] Similarly, the Jewish Pseudepigraphical book of Jubilees (161-140 B.C.) questions much later:

> *Why do you worship* those who have no spirit in them? Because they are works of the hands, and you are carrying them upon your shoulders, and there is no help from them for you, except great shame for those who made them *and the misleading of the heart for those who worship them.* Do not worship them." (Jubilees 12:5)

Classic witnesses of this tradition, Psalms 115 and 135 contrast the reality of God's universal existence and inherent power with the impotence of idols and the non-existent deities they represent. They call for renewed trust in God and renewed commitment to undivided worship of him. For unlike idols, God can do what he promises (Pss 115:3; 135:5-12).

The allusions in Psalm 135 to the historical figures of Pharaoh, Sihon and Og, the kings of Egypt, Heshbon and Bashan (Ps 135:8-11), recalls these characters specifically as archetypal challengers of Yahweh's exclusive role as king over his people. Each actively attempted to prevent the people of Israel from receiving the covenant promise of land from Yahweh: Pharaoh by not letting the people leave Egypt; Sihon and Og by not letting the people pass through their territories on the way to the promised land (cf. Neh 9:22-23). In faithfulness to the Abrahamic covenant, Yahweh cursed and utterly devastated each monarch in keeping with his former promise to "bless those who bless you and curse those who curse you"

---

[5] Leslie A. Allen, *Psalms 101-150* (WBC 21; Waco: Word, 1983), 108, 227. However, both Psalms are somewhat eclectic in form, neither fitting neatly into a traditional psalm genre. See Richard J. Clifford, *Psalms 73-150* (AOTC; Nashville: Abingdon, 2003), 194.
[6] Mitchel Dahood, *Psalms III: 101-150* (New York: Doubleday, 1970), 141.
[7] Fabry, "לֵב *leb*; לֵבָב *lebab*," *TDOT* 7:429.
[8] See also Deut 11:16-18; 29:17-21; 30:17-18; Jer 5:19-25; 7:17-29; 17:1-2; Ezek 14:1-8; 20:16; Hos 10:1-2.

(Gen 12:3a).[9] In the case of both Pharaoh and Sihon this curse involved hardening (Exod 4:21; 7:3-4, 13-14 etc.; Deut 2:30-31).

Exemplary is the fact that these three pagan kings were idolaters. The Psalmist refers to them specifically because they served as historical examples of the phenomenon that one becomes like that which one worships (Ps 135:15-18). The "idols of the nations" (Ps 135:15) represent the forms of Ancient Near Eastern (ANE) paganism that jeopardized Israel's covenant with Yahweh—the specific idols being those of Egypt, Heshbon, and Bashan (Ps 135:8-14).[10]

As idolatrous cursers of Yahweh's covenant people, Pharaoh, Sihon and Og set in motion the curse forewarned in Gen 12:3a. By cursing God's people, these kings brought the covenant curse upon themselves. In hardening them, Yahweh illustrated the end awaiting all who would attempt to supplant him and endanger his covenant. He did this in part by allowing these opponents to play out the consequences of their fatally flawed worldviews that presupposed the power of idols and pagan deities. For in conflict with Yahweh and the people of Israel, historical evidence suggests that these kings would have consulted their gods through amulets, representative statues, sacrifices, and prayer. As they did so, Yahweh gave them over to the hardening consequences of their own idolatry. The repeated emphasis that God "hardened" them indicates that the recalcitrance intensified beyond the preexisting hardened condition. A further, deeper, perhaps more complete hardening occurred, because these men directly rejected the living God in favor of their tradition steeped, icon oriented superstition. For this reason these three villains are remembered throughout the Bible as exemplary opponents

---

[9] Note the phenomenon of the curse of Sihon and Og and their utter devastation as described in Num 21:21-35.

[10] The prominence of *iconism* (the paying of homage to divine images) in ancient Egypt is an indisputable fact due to the preponderance of amulets and other divine images that date from every period of ancient Egyptian history. The biblical evidence indicates that the ancient Israelites came to regard these icons as idolatrous and the gods they represented as incompatible with Yahwism (Exod 12:12; 18;11; see Ch. 3). Sihon and Og, on the other hand, were Amorite kings devoted to the polytheistic and syncretistic religions prevalent in the land of Canaan that the Israelites encountered in the conquest. Existing historical sources offer little information detailing the religions of Sihon and Og. It is probable, however, that they, like other Amorites (e.g., the kings of Jerusalem, Hebron, Jarmuth, Lachish, and Eglon; Josh 10:5), were devoted to multiple deities including Dagan, Hadad, Anat, one or more representations of Baal, and others. These mythical figures would have been the objects of their iconography, temple worship, prayers, and national confidence. Yahweh's defeat of Heshbon and Bashan thus signaled Yahweh's divine sovereignty over these nations and their deities and attested his continued faithfulness to his covenant with Abraham. Victories over Sihon and Og established continuity with Yahweh's defeat of Pharaoh and the gods of Egypt in the exodus, while at the same time setting a precedent for the conquest of Canaan. Instructive information and extensive bibliography on the Amorites and their religion may be found in the following: J. Finegan, *Myth and Mystery* (Grand Rapids: Baker, 1989), 119-54; G. E. Mendenhall, "Amorites," *ABD* 1.199-202; P.L. Day, "ANAT," *DDD* 36-43; J.F. Healey, "Dagon," *DDD* 216-19; J.C. Greenfield, "Hadad," *DDD* 377-82; W. Herrmann, "Baal," *DDD* 132-39.

of Yahweh.[11] Their stories provide instructive warnings for the people of Israel. Yahweh was invincible, intolerant of syncretism, and jealously committed to protecting his covenantal partner. He would act again in the same way in the future, if need should arise—even towards Israel, if his own people should commit spiritual suicide through covenant infidelity.

The severity of the conquest naturally followed. Yahweh acted decisively and comprehensively to protect his covenant with Israel by defeating Israel's political enemies and rendering impotent their pagan deities. For in the ANE it was understood that when a nation fought an opposing people, they also fought against that nation's gods.[12] Hence Yahweh's victories over Pharaoh, Sihon, and Og proved his superiority over the many gods of Egypt and the Transjordan.[13] Exodus 12:12; 18:11; Num 33:4; and Ezek 20:7 thus cite the exodus as proof of God's victory over *all* the gods of Egypt.

III. Deuteronomy 28-29

The Psalmist, of course, was not the only writer of Scripture to associate these figures with the hardening paradigm. This phenomenon also appears in the renewal of the covenant urged by Moses towards the conclusion of his "farewell discourse" in Deuteronomy 28-29, where irreverence toward God (Deut 28:58-68) results in the reversal of divine blessings. The author of Deuteronomy recounts Moses' prophecy that Israel, should she ever defect from God, would experience exile rather than deliverance, decimation rather than multiplication, anxiety rather than rest, and sensory depletion rather than divine inspiration:

> Moreover, the Lord will scatter you among all peoples, from one end of the earth to the other end of the earth; and there you shall serve other gods, wood and stone, which you or your fathers have not known. And among those nations you shall find no rest, and there shall be no resting place for the sole of your foot; but *there the Lord will give you a trembling heart, failing of eyes, and despair of soul.* (Deut 28:64-65)

This curse in turn provides the context for understanding the phenomenon of sensory deterioration that Deuteronomy 29 shares with Psalms 115 and 135.

Deuteronomy 29 locates the idolatry and hardening phenomenon firmly within the framework of Yahweh's covenant with Israel (*"These are the words of the covenant . . . "*; Deut 29:1; also vv. 9, 12-14). Typical of ancient covenants,

---

[11] Sihon and Og are referred to in the following locations: Num 21:21-35; 32:33; Deut 1:4; 2:24-3:13; 4:46-47; 29:7; 31:4; Josh 2:10; 9:10; 12:2-5; 13:10, 12, 21, 30-31; 1 Kings 4:19; Neh 9:22; Ps 135:11; 136:14-20.

[12] See Dennis J. McCarthy, *Treaty and Covenant* (Rome: Biblical Institute, 1978); G. E. Mendenhall and G. A. Herion, "Covenant," *ABD* 1.1179-1202.

[13] As Amorites, the people of Heshbon and Bashan would have been devoted to the Canaanite gods Dagan, Hadad, Anan, Baal etc., as inherited from their forefathers. As a people they therefore represented a military and religious challenge to the covenant, just as Pharaoh had. See George E. Mendenhall, "Amorites," 202.

Deuteronomy recalls the history of Yahweh's relationship with Israel, emphasizing especially Yahweh's role as savior in delivering Israel from Egypt (Deut 29:2-3). Then, abruptly, it pronounces: "*yet to this day the Lord has not given you a heart to know, nor eyes to see, nor ears to hear*" (Deut 29:4). The reference to Sihon and Og then provides historical evidence attesting the foolishness of obstructing the will of God by contrast to the blessing of being his faithful, obedient people.

After further admonishments to abide by the covenant, Moses warns the Israelites to avoid the misfortune experienced by her enemies Egypt, Heshbon (Sihon), and Bashan (Og):

> Moreover, you have seen their abominations *and their idols of wood, stone, silver, and gold*, which they had with them; lest there shall be among you a man or woman, or family or tribe, whose *heart* turns away today from the Lord our God, to go and serve *the gods of those nations*; lest there shall be among you a root bearing poisonous fruit and wormwood. And it shall be when he hears the words of this curse, that he will boast, saying, I have *peace though I walk in the stubbornness of my heart* in order to destroy the watered land with the dry. The Lord shall never be willing to forgive him, but rather the anger of the Lord and his jealousy will burn against that man, and every curse which is written in this book will rest on him, and the Lord will blot out his name from under heaven. (Deut 29:17-20)

This stark warning assured the Israelites that they would indeed face the same tragic fate as their defeated enemies, if they adopted their idolatrous ways. Like Pharaoh, Sihon and Og, Israel would develop a "stubborn heart" that would lead to utter destruction, if she should ever fall prey to idolatry (Deut 29:18-20). This would provide evidence to successive generations that Israel's exile was the consequence of her own idolatrous sin:

> And all the nations shall say, why has the Lord done thus to this land? Why this great outburst of anger? Then men shall say, because they forsook the covenant of the Lord, the God of their fathers, which he made with them when he brought them out of the land of Egypt. And they went and served other gods and worshiped them, gods whom they have not known and whom he had not allotted to them. Therefore, the anger of the Lord burned against that land, to bring upon it every curse which is written in this book; and the Lord uprooted them from their land in anger and in fury and in great wrath, and cast them into another land, as it is this day. (Deut 29:24-28)

The parallels between Deuteronomy 29 and Psalm 135 are explicit and instructive. In Deuteronomy 29 the idolater is portrayed as a breaker of the covenant, one "whose heart has turned away from the Lord," and one who walks in the stubbornness of his heart. Integral to covenantal renewal, therefore, is knowledge of the hardening paradigm and adherence to what would come to be known as the first two of the Ten Commandments (Exod 20:2-6; Deut 5:6-10). Moses' call for covenant rededication in essence sounded the same alert as Psalms 115 and 135. Conjoining the two, the hardening pattern unfolds as follows:

(1) The eventual recipient of hardening disregards Yahweh's past saving acts that he performed for the deliverance of his covenant people.
(2) The offender breaks the covenant by committing idolatry.
(3) The offender conforms to paganism and its many manifestations (political, religious, social, and ethical).
(4) Hardening of the heart, sensory depletion, and spiritual deadening occur.
(5) The offender suffers exile as God's divinely enforced punishment for defiant violation of the covenant.

Aware that Israel herself could potentially suffer this curse,[14] Deuteronomy pleads for covenantal rededication by recalling the exodus and Yahweh's successful defeats of Og and Sihon (Deut 29:16). Deuteronomy then warns that if Israel should commit idolatry, she herself would be responsible for her unfaithfulness to Yahweh, and would suffer the same hardening curse as had been experienced by Pharaoh (Exodus 7-14) and Sihon (Deut 2:30). With a hardened heart, Israel would assume a state of stubbornness that would foolishly presume peace apart from the protection of Yahweh's rule. Ironically, should this happen, Israel would become the enemy of God[15] and suffer the curses commensurate with covenantal apostasy (cf. Isa 63:8-10, 17-19). Cursed by God for forsaking the covenant, Israel, like Pharaoh, would be fully responsible for her hardened condition.

The examples of Pharaoh, Sihon and Og in Psalm 135 and in Deuteronomy 29 thus serve as eschatological warnings paradigmatic for the corporate people of Israel. If Israel conforms to polytheism and idolatry, she will lose her distinction as the people of God. She will become the object of God's curse, experience military defeat, and foreign occupation. The land of the covenant will be lost and the people of the covenant will suffer chastisement through the fires of hardening and exile.

IV. The First Two Commandments

Elsewhere in the OT we will find that hardening continues to afflict idolaters with unmistakable regularity, because idolatry makes impossible the foundational premise of the covenant—Yahweh's exclusive role as Israel's God and king. Divine retribution for idolatry therefore becomes systemic to biblical theology as Ten Commandments 1 and 2 foreshadow:

> I am the Lord your God, who brought you out of the land of Egypt, out of the house of slavery. You shall have no other gods before me. You shall

---

[14] The warning likely was precipitated by the nation's behavior at Kadesh-Barnea as described in Numbers 14.

[15] Which much later did indeed become the conviction of the Apostle Paul (Rom 5:10).

not make for yourself an idol, or any likeness of what is in heaven above or on the earth beneath or in the water under the earth. You shall not worship them or serve them; for I, the Lord your God, am a jealous God, visiting the iniquities of the fathers on the children, on the third and the fourth generations of those who hate me, but showing lovingkindness to thousands, to those who love me and keep my commandments. (Exod 20:2-6)

The importance of these words cannot be exaggerated. With the Shema (Deut 6:4-9), they provide the point of departure for identifying idolatry as the foremost challenge to Israel's unique identity as the people of Yahweh in the ancient world. Gerhard von Rad affirms: "The prohibition on serving any other divine powers is in any case *the* commandment *par excellence* for Israel, and its stringency—there is nothing else like it in the whole history of religion. It influenced to a greater or lesser degree all vital utterances on the faith of Yahweh."[16] Tryggve Mettinger's recent comparison of Israelite aniconism with religions of surrounding cultures reaches the same conclusion: "in Israel aniconism developed to its very extreme: a programmatic anti-iconic attitude. Among ancient Semitic peoples there is hardly anything of similar dimensions."[17] And still more recently, Patrick Miller has observed: "The absence of any god but Yahweh from a central place in the course of Israel's religion is matched by the absence of Yahweh from any place in the pantheons or in the cultus of any other people of the ancient Near East. While it is possible that signs of such worship may yet turn up, that fact is rather remarkable."[18]

As we shall see in Leviticus 26, the first two commandments relate the prohibition of idols directly to the self-introductory formula 'I am Yahweh your

---

[16]*Deuteronomy*, Philadelphia: Westminster (1966), 56. Compare Wisdom of Solomon 14:11-14 (1st Cent. B.C.):

Therefore there will be a visitation also upon the heathen idols, because, though part of what God created, they became an abomination, snares for human souls and a trap for the feet of the foolish. *For the idea of making idols was the beginning of fornication, and the invention of them was the corruption of life*; for they did not exist from the beginning, nor will they last forever. For through human vanity they entered the world, and therefore their speedy end has been planned.

[17]*No Graven Image? Israelite Aniconism in Its Ancient Near Eastern Context* (Stockholm: Almqvist & Wiksell, 1995), 196.

[18]*The Religion of Ancient Israel* (Louisville, Ky./London: Westminster John Knox Press/SPCK, 2000), 3. In the same volume Miller adds, "Here we come upon one of the distinctive features of the worship of Yahweh in ancient Israel—its aniconic character. The absence of images of the deity and the concomitant prohibition against representation of deity in any form of image is anomalous in the ancient Near East" (p. 15). This did not mean, of course, that orthodox, aniconic Yahwism went uncontested from without or from within Israel. And yet an enduring tenet of orthodox Yahwism from generation to generation was its call for Israel to turn away from foreign gods and their images to the true living God of the covenant. See Miller's treatment of "Orthodox Yahwism," "Heterodox Yahwism, " and "Syncretistic Yahwism" in the same volume pp. 48-62.

God,' which summarizes God's testimony to himself and his transcendent "otherness," as the only living sovereign God. Expressions of God's will and character, the Ten Commandments attempt to make Israel more like her God.[19]

When conformity to God's character did not occur, divine discipline took over. God punished not only idolaters but also their descendents: "I, the Lord your God, am a jealous God, visiting the iniquity of the fathers on the children, *on the third and the fourth generations of those who hate me*" (Exod 20:5; cf. Exod 32:19-20; 34:6-17). The foremost command thus possessed positive and negative prophetic potential that would both determine and explain the plight of Israel's descendants in the future (Num 14:17-18; Jer 32:18-19).

V. Leviticus 26

Consequently, the curse of God's judgment results in physical and spiritual degeneration and death. When immediate death does not take place, human disorientation occurs in the form of dehumanization, hardening, or what Greg Beale has described as the "sensory malfunction"[20] process. As sin distances sinners from the creator, spiritual understanding grows dull, so that sinners lead misinformed, degenerate lives.

To underestimate the importance of God's covenant is therefore disastrous, God's hardening not being arbitrary, but willed in accord with pre-designed covenant curses.[21] Leviticus 26 further illustrates:

---

[19] It appears that God's will was that Israel reflect his holiness and not human creations. Because the human mind is incapable of comprehending the transcendent mind of God (Isa 55:8-9), attempts to portray him through artistic imagery would not only be inadequate but also scandalous. Inevitably, images of God would be created in the likeness of things visible to the human eye. Humankind would replace God's revelation with human creativity and imaginative speculation. And in the process God's otherness would be compromised and his character misconstrued. To prevent this from happening, Yahweh disclosed his authentic self-revelation in instructive words that were to be transmitted conservatively—as opposed to physical manifestations that the human mind would reproduce speculatively. This distinction would set Yahweh apart from the pagan deities of the ANE, which were often represented by humanly crafted images drawn from nature and mythology. As Brevard Childs states, "Images are prohibited because they are an incorrect response to God's manner of making himself known which was by means of his word" (*The Book of Exodus*, [Philadelphia: Westminster, 1974], 407). While the Bible abounds with anthropomorphic literary representations of God, they are understood to be symbolic of God's attributes and not constructs of God's actual image—i.e., that he has a literal face, arms, etc.

[20] G.K. Beale has developed this concept in two important publications: "Isaiah VI 9-13: A Retributive Taunt against Idolatry" *Vetus Testamentum* XLI, 3 (1991): 257-78; "The Hearing Formula and the Visions of John in Revelation," in *A Vision for the Church* (ed. M. Bockmuehl and M. B. Thompson; Edinburgh: T&T Clark, 1997): 167-80. In some contexts "sensory depletion" or "sensory deterioration" is preferable to "sensory malfunction." It is not that the senses are malfunctioning; it is, rather, that they are not functioning at all (Isa 6:9-10; Jer 5:19-22).

[21] A comment such as that of Jonathan Edwards therefore opens itself up to misunderstanding: "There is nothing that keeps wicked men at any one moment out of hell,

> But if you do not obey me and do not carry out all these commandments, if, instead, you reject my statutes, and *if you should abhor my ordinances so as not to carry out all my commandments, and so break my covenant, I in turn, will do this to you: I will appoint over you a sudden terror, consumption and fever that shall waste away the eyes and cause the soul to pine away; also you shall sow your seed uselessly, for your enemies shall eat it up.* (26:14-16)
>
> *I then will destroy your high places, and cut down your incense altars, and heap your remains on the remains of your idols; for my soul shall abhor you.* (26:30)
>
> As for those of you who may be left, *I will also bring weakness into their hearts in the lands of their enemies.* (26:36)

Here we see clearly that spiritual blindness and spiritual heart failure *coincide with the covenant infraction of idolatry.* The warning begins with the recognition formula "I am Yahweh" before specifying the covenant as the object of Yahweh's protective care. The prominence of the recognition formula indicates that God performs this punitive action to defend his own name because his people have failed to represent him accurately.

VI. Isaiah 6:9-11 and Jeremiah 5:19-22

Despite the intended exclusivity of Israel's covenant with Yahweh, the hardening paradigm, with all of its ramifications, did come to pass in Israel's history. Israel tragically did abandon the covenant to pursue the gods of her pagan neighbors. The covenant did turn from blessing to curse. Israel and Judah did suffer successive military defeats. Exile did occur.[22] And God did commission his prophets to preach a message of hardening to an obstinate people that had become like the pagan nations and their gods.

---

but the mere pleasure of God. By the mere pleasure of God, I mean his sovereign pleasure, his arbitrary will, restrained by no obligation . . . " ("Sinners in the Hands of an Angry God," in *Selected Writings of Jonathan Edwards* (ed. Harold P. Simonson [New York: Frederick Ungar, 1970], 97). Edwards' intended point is biblically undeniable—God's power alone accounts for the salvation of the redeemed. However, the Bible nowhere describes God as exercising his power in an *arbitrary* manner; to the contrary, God acts in full accord with his covenant promises.

[22] For example, see Jer 32:28-30: "Therefore thus says the Lord, behold, I am about to give this city into the hand of the Chaldeans and into the hand of Nebuchadnezzar king of Babylon, and he shall take it. And the Chaldeans who are fighting against this city shall enter and set this city on fire and burn it, with the houses *where people have offered incense to Baal on their roofs and poured out libation to other gods to provoke me to anger. Indeed the sons of Israel and the sons of Judah have been doing only evil in my sight from their youth; for the sons of Israel have been only provoking me to anger by the work of their hands*, declares the Lord."

The famous commissions of Isaiah and Jeremiah are properly understood against this theological background.

> Go and tell this people: Keep on listening, but do not perceive; keep on looking but do not understand. Render the hearts of this people insensitive, their ears dull, and their eyes dim, lest they see with their eyes, hear with their ears, understand with their hearts, and return and be healed. Then I said, Lord, how long? And he answered, until cities are devastated and without inhabitant, houses are without people, and the land is utterly desolate. (Isa 6:9-11)

> And it shall come about when they say, why has the Lord our God done all these things to us? Then you shall say to them, as you have forsaken me and served foreign gods in your land, so you shall serve strangers in a land that is not yours. Declare this in the house of Jacob and proclaim it in Judah, saying, hear this, O foolish and senseless people, who have eyes, but see not; who have ears, but hear not. Do you not fear me? Declares the Lord. (Jer 5:19-22a)

As we shall see in greater detail in chapter 5, both Isaiah and Jeremiah pronounce the hardening sentence within a historical context of idolatry. Isaiah (2:6-22) and Jeremiah (1:16; 5:18-25; 7:21-34) make this explicitly clear. God's punitive action is not arbitrary or random, nor is it unconditional. It is a systemic deterioration that God permits to infiltrate those who reject, challenge, or break his covenant due to a greater confidence in idols. Symptomatic to this disease is the intensification of the hardening process in the life of the idolater who grows increasingly distant from God because of sin. The dehumanizing process intensifies as the threat to the covenant grows more and more serious. Hardening as a phenomenon is therefore fully within the covenant plan of God and as such is determined and willed by him. It also appears to be true, however, that hardened persons are fully responsible for their own hardened conditions. John Calvin thus concluded:

> A very convincing argument may be drawn from the judgments of God to the sins of men; for God is just, and never punishes any one without a just cause, and does not blind a man, unless he deserves it, and voluntarily shuts his eyes. The blame therefore lies with men alone, who have of their own accord brought blindness on themselves.[23]

---

[23]*Commentary on Isaiah*, (trans. Rev. William Pringle; Grand Rapids: Baker, 1984), 3.378.

Chapter 2

Idolatry and the Heart: Words in Context

If we had forgotten the name of our God, or extended our hands to a strange god; would not God find this out? For he knows the secrets of the heart. (Ps 44:20-21)

I. Idols/Idolatry

The Septuagint version of the Greek Old Testament (LXX) uses the Greek word *eidōlon* (idol) to describe both images of heathen deities and heathen deities themselves. The ancient Hebrews saw little distinction between idols and the gods they represented because both were equally false and equally lifeless by comparison to the true living God. This does not mean, however, that the Israelites considered idols harmless. To the contrary, the OT conceives of demonic powers working through idols to supplant Yahweh as Israel's object of worship. This transfer of devotion, should it happen, would result in Israel's defilement (Ezek 37:23) and God's wrath (Deut 32:16-21). The LXX uses *eidōlon* to translate fourteen different Hebrew words.[1] Throughout the Bible

---

[1] These references are representative, not exhaustive. Definitions are provided by W. Baumgartner and L. Koehler, *The Hebrew and Aramaic Lexicon of the Old Testament* (=*HALOT*). Hebrew terms provided by F. Büchsel, "ειδωλον," *TDNT* 2:375-78.

ʿōṣeḇ/עֹצֶב	"False god; idol": always plural in the OT—1 Sam 31:9. *HALOT* 2.865.
pāsîl/פָּסִיל	"Carved or hewn image; idols of wood, stone, metal, silver—Deut 7:5. *HALOT* 3.948.
pesel/פֶּסֶל	"Divine image carved from wood or sculpted from stone, but later cast in metal"—Exod 20:4. *HALOT* 3.949.
ṣelem/צֶלֶם	"Statue, idol, image, likeness"—Num 33:52. *HALOT* 3.1028.
tĕrāpîm/תְרָפִים	"Image, a kind of idol, object of reverence, means of divination"—Gen 31:19. *HALOT* 4.1794-1795.
ḥamān/חַמָּן	"Incense altar, sun-pillar, used in idolatrous worship"—Isa 17:8; 27:9. *HALOT* 1.329.
gilûlîm/גִלּוּלִים	"Images of gods; idols": always plural in the OT—Lev 26:30. *HALOT* 1.192.
šiqqûṣ/שִׁקּוּץ	"An object to abhor, detested thing"—1 Kings 11:5, 7. *HALOT* 4.1640.
ʾĕlîlîm/אֱלִילִים	"Pagan gods, worthless gods, idols; implying weakness"—Lev 19:4. *HALOT* 1.55-56.
heḇel/הֶבֶל	'Vapor, breath' implying the vanity, purposelessness, and transience of idols—Deut 32:21. *HALOT* 1.236-237.
ʾēlîm/אֵלִים	"Gods of the nations—idols"—Exod 15:11. *HALOT* 1.49.

idolatry takes three simple forms: (1) worship of other gods; (2) worship of created objects; (3) syncretism with paganism. In the chapters that follow we will regard each expression as idolatry.

II. The Heart in Egyptian Thought

The heart was much more than a vital organ to the peoples of the ANE.² Ancient Egyptians believed the heart was the wellspring of character and essence. It was the center of an individual's soul, will, spirit and personality—"the innermost being, on which a man's life depends."³ From the complicated and obscure world of Ancient Egyptian literature, specialists have drawn two terms for heart that apparently interrelate to such a degree that they may be considered synonymous—*ib* and *ḥ3.ty*.⁴ The hieroglyph⁵ ❦ (*ib*) compounds with other hieroglyphs to express "middle," "interior," "sense," "wisdom," "understanding," "intelligence," "disposition," "manner," "will," "wish," "desire," "mind," "courage," "lust," "self," and "joy." ⁶ With this semantic range, the heart was believed to be the place of interchange between the gods and human beings. It was the receiver of divine inspiration and instruction. "The heart was the Egyptian equivalent of the mind, a notion perhaps best seen in the so-called Memphite Theology, in which Ptah (creator god of Memphis) creates the world through heart and tongue, i.e., intellect and *logos*."⁷ "As the seat of man's reasoning the heart is in charge of the intellect—understanding, memory, consideration, planning."⁸ Moreover, emotions and character traits such as love, concern, pity, mercy, joy ("bigheartedness"), trust ("openness of heart"), and fear ("palpitation") were

---

ʾĕlōhîm/אֱלֹהִים	Gods, foreign gods: Baal of Peor; Chemosh; Molech; Ashtoreth; Milcom—Num 25:2. *HALOT* 1.53.
baʿal/בַּעַל	"Baal," special god of the Canaanites and Philistines—2 Chron 17:3. *HALOT* 1.143.
bāmāh/בָּמָה	"High place"—Ezek 16:16; "detested thing"—1 Kings 11:5, 7; translated with *bdelugma* in Dan 11:31; 12:11. *HALOT* 1.136.

² For comprehensive bibliography on the meaning of the term "heart" in Egyptology and biblical Hebrew, see Nili Shupak, *Where Can Wisdom Be Found?: The Sage's Language in the Bible and in Ancient Egyptian Literature* (Fribourg/Göttingen: University Press/Vandenhoeck & Ruprecht [1993], 299 n. 60.

³ Shupak, *Where Can Wisdom Be Found?*, 298, 304.

⁴ For a brief study of both terms and their possible subtle distinctions with accompanying bibliography see Shupak, *Where Can Wisdom Be Found?*, 297.

⁵ Greek: *hieros* (sacred) + *glyphe* (carving)

⁶ Raymond O. Faulkner, *A Concise Dictionary of Middle Egyptian* (Oxford: Oxford U.P., 1962), 14-15; Alan H. Gardiner, *Egyptian Grammar* (Oxford: Oxford U.P., 1927), 48, 456; For instructive, substantiating quotations from Egyptian sources, see N. Shupak, *Where Can Wisdom Be Found*, 297-311.

⁷ Dr. Ogden Goelet Jr., "A Commentary on the Corpus of Literature and Tradition which Constitutes The Book of Going Forth by Day," in *The Egyptian Book of the Dead: The Book of Going Forth by Day* (ed. Eva Von Dassow; trans. Raymond O. Faulkner; San Francisco: Chronicle Books, 1994), 151.

⁸ N. Shupak, *Where Can Wisdom Be Found*, 300.

believed to flow from the heart.⁹ It was thought that the heart unmasked the true ethical character of every individual, whether good or bad. Negatively, the heart housed vices such as pride, arrogance, greed, and anger. In the afterlife the ancient Egyptians believed that the god Osiris would judge the state of one's heart, the only major organ left inside the corpse, before determining an individual's eternal plight (see ch. 3). Thus, the heart "was felt to have a will and an existence of its own."¹⁰ It was "conceived as an independent and separate entity."¹¹ Ultimately, the Egyptian appraisal of the heart culminated in deification: "The heart is god. His residence is in the innards, he is pleased when the organs are rejoicing" (Priest Neb-neteru of the 22ⁿᵈ Dynasty).¹²

III. Heart in the Old Testament

Comparing the biblical concept of heart with that of the ancient Egyptians, Nili Shupak writes:

> There is an analogy between the basic meaning of the term "heart" in Egyptian and in Biblical Hebrew. In both languages "heart" is a polysemic, multifaceted term. The different meanings of the word and the expressions associated with it are remarkably similar in Hebrew and Egyptian wisdom, but this does not always attest to reciprocal influence or linkage.¹³

Like the ancient Egyptians, the authors of the OT rarely referred to the heart as a physical, anatomical organ. Rather, the term is used "for all aspects of a person: vital, emotive, noetic, and voluntative."¹⁴ Because the English word "heart" does not have the same denotations today, references to OT occurrences of lēḇ/lēḇaḇ do not always correspond with the word "heart" in translation. Thus the word "heart" is not found in all of the following references, though lēḇ/lēḇaḇ underlies each in the original Hebrew.

In the OT lēḇ/lēḇaḇ occur 853 times: lēḇ 597, lēḇaḇ 256. The terms appear to be "totally synonymous and interchangeable."¹⁵ lēḇ/lēḇaḇ represents the distinctive nature of persons individually (Ezek 13:22; Ps 22:14-15; 27:3; Prov 18:2) as well as Israel corporately (1 Kings 8:66; 2 Chron 7:10; Isa 30:29; 60:5; Zech 10:7). Like their Egyptian neighbors, the Hebrews conceived of the heart as the receiver of intimate communication both with other human beings (Gen 50:21; Judg 19:3; Ruth 2:13) and with God (Isa 40:1-2; Ezek 3:10; Hos 2:14). Lips could lie, but the

---

⁹ Heinz-Joseph Fabry, "לֵב leḇ; לֵבָב leḇaḇ," *TDOT* 7:401. Shupak, *Where Can Wisdom Be Found*, 302-03.

¹⁰ Goelet Jr., *Commentary*, 151.

¹¹ Shupak, *Where Can Wisdom Be Found*, 298.

¹² Quotation taken from Shupak, *Where Can Wisdom Be Found*, 309.

¹³ *Where Can Wisdom Be Found*, 299.

¹⁴ Fabry, *TDOT* 7:407.

¹⁵ Fabry, *TDOT* 7:407. See also Walther Eichrodt's treatment of the heart in his *Theology of the Old Testament* (trans. J. A. Baker; vol. 2; Philadelphia: Westminster, 1967), 142-45.

heart, as harbor of truth, concealed and potentially could reveal the absolute truth, as in Delilah's betrayal of Samson: "When Delilah saw that he had told her all that was *in his heart*, she sent and called the lords of the Philistines, saying, 'Come up once more, for he has told me all that is *in his heart*'" (Judg 16:18).

The ancient Hebrews viewed the heart as the vital, life-generating center of human beings. A healthy heart produced a healthy life. The heart was one's emotional center either in a positive or negative sense depending on the character of the individual.

Positively, the heart cries out to God (Ps 84:2), rejoices in God (Ps 13:5), sings to the Lord (Ps 57:7), and expresses joy in seeking God's salvation (Ps 105:3; 1 Chron 16:10; 1 Sam 2:1; Zeph 3:14). Joy and gladness of heart come only after the people wholly devote their "heart" to Yahweh, to "walk in his statutes and to keep his commandments" (1 Kings 8:61). The "waiting" heart thus rejoices in God's presence (Ps 16:9; 33:21). The Psalmist acknowledges that the law of the Lord restores the soul and gives joy to the heart (19:8; cf., 119:111-112). In this spirit, God's word becomes the joy and delight of Jeremiah's heart at the moment of his calling (Jer 15:16). Furthermore, the healthy heart is the seat of wisdom (Prov 2:10; 4:21; 7:3; 10:8; 16:21, 23; 22:17; Job 22:22; 33:3; Isa 32:4), which enables prudent decision making (Prov 22:17; Eccles 7:2; Isa 32:4; Ezek 40:4; 44:5). It retains knowledge of the promises of God (Josh 23:14) and the potential for accurately understanding God's revelatory signs and wonders (Deut 29:4; Isa 42:25). It is the memory bank that comprehends meaning in the present based on experience of the past (Isa 46:8-13; 47:7; 57:11). Hence Deuteronomy's famous call for covenant renewal occurs in acknowledgement of the heart's full responsibility in judgment before God: "But if your *heart* turns away and you will not obey, but are drawn away and worship other gods and serve them, I declare to you today that you shall surely perish" (Deut 30:17-18a).

Negatively, the heart can experience fatigue (Ps 38:10), anguish (Jer 4:19), bitterness (Ps 73:21), despair (Ps 61:2), disorientation (Ps 22:14), fear (1 Sam 24:5), sadness (1 Sam 1:8), and sickness (Prov 13:12). The corrupt heart suffers the consequences of sin. It can be the victim of sexual seduction (Prov 6:25; Ezek 16:30) and the location of exchange for harlots and idols:

> Harlotry, wine, and new wine take away the *understanding* (lit. "the heart"–*lēb*). My people consult their wooden idol, and their diviner's wand informs them; for a spirit of harlotry has led them astray, and they have played the harlot, departing from their God. (Hos 4:11-12)

The heart can also harbor lust (Job 31:9; Prov 6:25), aspiration for worldly goods (Ps 62:10), temptations (Job 31:7), bribes (Eccles 7:7), wickedness (Ps 141:4), and the aggressive pursuit of dishonest and selfish gain (Jer 22:17; Ezek 33:31).[16] Therefore, like the Egyptians, the Hebrews equated one's ethical condition with the state of one's heart. So it is that Eliphaz inquires of Job: "*Why does your heart carry you away*? And why do your eyes flash, that you should turn your spirit

---

[16] Fabry, *TDOT* 7:423.

against God, and allow such words to go out of your mouth?" (Job 15:12-13). And Jeremiah writes that Judah's sin of idolatry (17:2) "is written down with an iron stylus; with a diamond point it is engraved *upon the tablet of their heart*" (Jer 17:1).

The heart, as the compartment of sin, acts as the inhibitor of devotion to God and ethical respect for other human beings. As such it is the seat of an arrogance and pride that tragically *replaces* God with the false comfort of self-sufficiency, resulting in divine judgment and self-destruction (Deut 8:11-20; Isa 14:13-15; Jer 49:16; Hos 13:6). In this respect, the Hebrew concept of heart contrasts diametrically with that of ancient Egypt. The OT nowhere deifies the heart; it is always subject to Yahweh. And again, it is fully responsible for its sin in violation of God's will.[17]

Theologically, God knows the heart (Ps 44:21; 1 Sam 16:7), and tests it (Deut 8:2; 13:3). He infuses wisdom in the hearts of some (1 Kings 10:24; 2 Chron 9:23; Neh 7:5) but debilitates the hearts of others (Exod 4:21; 1 Sam 10:9; Dan 5:21). God's omniscience and sovereignty come to the fore in this process as he demonstrates his knowledge of the human heart and his authority to judge its condition and determine its future plight: "Sheol and Abaddon lie open before the Lord, how much more the hearts of men!" (Prov 15:11; cf. 1 Kings 8:39; Ps 7:9-10; 17:3; 26:2-3; Prov 24:12; Jer 11:20; 12:3; 17:10; 20:12). Eschatologically, God promises to circumcise the heart of his faithful people (Deut 30:6), to write the law upon their hearts (Jer 31:31), to create within them a pure heart, free of idols (Ezek 11:19; 36:26; cf. Ps 51:10), transformed from stone to flesh (Ezek 36:26). The prophets therefore anticipated that Israel would rejoice and "be glad" in heart only when Yahweh acted to forgive the nation's sin and restore the exiles to the promised land (Zech 10:7; Isa 60:4-5; 66:14-15). God's power to recreate from within was therefore the only hope for Israel's hardened heart (Ezek 36:22-27).

In conclusion, the heart defies concrete definition in the OT, because it is a living, emotive, intangible, impressionable, fickle, ontological dimension of human beings, which is prone toward complicated dysfunction. Its only hope is the saving, re-creative work of God. "The heart is more deceitful than all else and is desperately sick; who can understand it?" (Jer 17:9).

---

[17] Shupak mistakenly contrasts the Egyptian concept of heart which allows man "free choice" and the biblical concept which she claims does not: "In the Biblical wisdom the heart is no longer depicted as an organ that transmits the will of God and allows man 'free choice'" (*Where Can Wisdom Be Found*, 311). This statement, however, is misleading if taken as representative of the entire OT, where the heart frequently exercises freedom separate from divine determination—including wisdom literature (Lev 19:17; Num 15:39; Deut 14:26; 15:9; 20:8; 24:15; 29:18; 1 Kings 2:44; *2 Kings 10:31*; 2 Chron 19:3; 26:16; 29:10; 30:19; 34:27; Ps 84:2; Prov 21:4; *27:19*; 28:14; *Eccl 11:9*; Isa 14:13; 59:13; Ezek 14:4; 16:30).

Chapter 3

Pharaoh's Falsehoods: Human Gods are No Gods at All

אֵין כַּיהוָה אֱלֹהֵינוּ

"*There is none like YHWH our God*" (Exod 8:10).

For I will go through the land of Egypt on that night, and will strike down all the first-born in the land of Egypt, both man and beast; *and against all the gods of Egypt I will execute judgments—I am the Lord.* (Exod 12:12)

Exodus tells the story of what happened when a powerful pagan king challenged Yahweh's covenant with his people Israel. In this story the hardening of Pharaoh's heart is a theological phenomenon that sets in motion God's covenant promise to Abraham to "curse those who curse you" (Gen 12:3). Pharaoh's hardening and the attendant plagues against Egypt stem from Pharaoh's oppression of Israel and his refusal to let God's people go. Pharaoh's hardening also assists Yahweh's ultimate covenant purposes by prolonging the public display of his absolute power (Exod 4:21; 9:13-17; 10:1) and his commitment to preserve the covenant people (Exod 4:22-23). In this course of events Pharaoh epitomizes the consequence awaiting all human obstacles to the covenant plan of God. The plagues demonstrate the impotence of idolatry and polytheism thereby establishing the benevolent wisdom of the Ten Commandments. In the end Pharaoh emerges as the archetypal hardened sinner—a classic foil to the character of faithful obedience Yahweh desires in his people Israel.

The purpose of this chapter is to examine the story of the hardening of Pharaoh's heart against the background of ancient Egyptian religion within the context of Exodus, where Pharaoh directly challenges Yahweh's covenantal relationship with the descendants of Abraham. God acts in Exodus to defend his covenant and to inflict his designed curse for idolatry. Had he not hardened Pharaoh's heart and demonstrated publicly the impotence of Egypt's false deities, he would have proven himself unfaithful to his promises to Abraham and presided with indifference over obstinate defiance fueled by pagan confidence in Egyptian polytheism. The famous acts of God recorded in Exodus therefore emerge consistent with general biblical revelation. They need not be viewed as arbitrary acts God randomly and unconditionally performed solely to glorify himself.

Forming the skeletal outline of this chapter are five features that are foundational to the Exodus story. *First*, Exodus theologically continues the covenant story begun in Genesis (Exod 15:13-18). This truth largely explains why

God acted so decisively against Pharaoh and his empire. Pharaoh emerges as fully responsible for his hardening, when he is assessed within his historical context. *Second*, against the tendency to absolutize one cause at the expense of another, it is important to emphasize the parts played by *both* God and Pharaoh in the hardening process. Passages where God hardens Pharaoh's heart stand side by side with passages where Pharaoh hardens his own heart. As we shall see, both phenomena are understandable in light of general biblical theology and should be given equal attention. We should be careful to not prioritize one set of passages at the expense of the other. *Third*, since the exodus takes place in Egypt, its recounting fittingly unfolds in the guise and idiom of the Hebrew people submerged in *Egyptian* culture. The conceptual background for understanding the hardening phenomenon is the New Kingdom era of Egyptian history (1570-1070 B.C.), when virtually all historians agree the exodus took place. Attention to this simple observation may prevent anachronistic interpretations of Exodus fueled by systems of thought originating outside of Egypt at a much later date. *Fourth*, ancient Egyptian religion was iconic and superstitious. Ancient Egyptians and their kings believed that amulets and spells could provide help and protection both in this life and in the afterlife. Hence, it is historically valid to incorporate Exodus into our study of idolatry and the hardening of the heart. Exodus exposes as powerless *all* of Egypt's gods, including Pharaoh, through the plagues and through Pharaoh's hardening. Through plagues God displays that he alone is all-powerful and that covenant with him is the only means of true deliverance. It is in Israel's best interest to remain faithful to him, because he is the only living God. *Fifth*, Exodus establishes a pattern for God's future acts of redemption and judgment. It discloses how and why God acts as he does and how he continually expects his people to act. Yahweh saves and delivers his people when external foes like Pharaoh threaten his covenant. As he did in Egypt, so he will continue to do as long as Israel is faithful. In the same way, he will harden and render powerless all who jeopardize his covenant with Israel, even Israel herself, when her actions betray the obligations of the covenant.

I. THE COVENANTAL THEOLOGY OF EXODUS AND THE HARDENING OF PHARAOH'S HEART

The hardening of Pharoah's heart and the plagues against Egypt complement attributes of Yahweh previously discovered by the reader of Genesis. Yahweh, as creator, is still active. He preserves the power to re-create in order to heighten human perception, as he reminds Moses in Exod 4:12. Conversely, and equally true, he maintains the power to diminish sensory perception and take away life. As he did at Babel (Gen 11:6-9), Yahweh may still confuse those who attempt to usurp his authority as God: "Who has made man's mouth? Or who makes him dumb or deaf, or seeing or blind? Is it not I, the Lord?" (Exod 4:11). Similarly, Yahweh maintains his faithfulness to his former promises to Abraham, Isaac, and Jacob. He acts in defense of his people and in answer to their prayers: "So God heard their groaning; *and God remembered his covenant with Abraham, Isaac, and Jacob*. And God saw the sons of Israel, and God took notice of them" (Exod 2:23-25; see also 3:6-10, 14-15; 4:4-5; 6:3-8; 19:3-6; 32:13; 33:1).

Exodus is the story of God's acts to deliver his covenant people from their bondage as Egyptian slaves. In conflict with manmade sovereignties that compete for Israel's subservience and allegiance (Egypt, Pharaoh, the Egyptian deities), Yahweh proves his faithfulness as all-powerful living God. The covenant with Abraham endures because Yahweh, *the all-powerful living God*, sustains it against human and iconic opposition. That he does so is evidence of his faithfulness to Abraham and his love for his people.

II. THE PART PLAYED BY YAHWEH AND PHARAOH IN THE HARDENING PROCESS

That both Pharaoh and God participate in the hardening of Pharaoh's heart in Exodus is an incontrovertible fact.[1] In Exodus the hardening passages unfold as follows:

Exod 4:21: And the Lord said to Moses, when you go back to Egypt see that you perform before Pharaoh all the wonders which I have put in your power; but <u>I will harden his heart</u> (*ḥzq*; חזק) so that he will not let the people go.

Exod 7:3 But <u>I will harden</u> (*qšh*; קשה) Pharaoh's heart that I may multiply my signs and my wonders in the land of Egypt.

Exod 7:13 Yet <u>Pharaoh's heart was hardened</u> (*ḥzq*; חזק), and he did not listen to them, as the Lord had said.

Exod 7:14 Then the Lord said to Moses, <u>Pharaoh's heart is stubborn</u> (*kbd*: כבד); he refuses to let the people go.

Exod 7:22 But the magicians of Egypt did the same with their secret arts; and <u>Pharaoh's heart was hardened</u> (*ḥzq*; חזק), and he did not listen to them, as the Lord had said.

Exod 8:15 But when Pharaoh saw that there was relief, <u>he hardened his heart</u> (*kbd*; כבד) and did not listen to them, as the Lord had said. (8:11 in MT)

Exod 8:19 Then the magicians said to Pharaoh, this is the finger of God. But <u>Pharaoh's heart was hardened</u> (*ḥzq*; חזק), and he did not listen to them, as the Lord had said. (8:15 in MT)

Exod 8:32 <u>But Pharaoh hardened his heart</u> (*kbd*; כבד) this time also, and he did not let the people go. (8:28 in MT)

Exod 9:7 And Pharaoh sent, and behold, there was not even one of the livestock of Israel dead. But <u>the heart of Pharaoh was hardened</u> (*kbd*; כבד), and he did not let the people go.

Exod 9:12 <u>And the Lord hardened Pharaoh's heart</u> (*ḥzq*; חזק), and he did not listen to them, just as the Lord had spoken to Moses.

---

[1] For readers of the New Testament this is not a surprise, since the cause of hardening is both human and divine in the New Testament. See Rom 9:18; Heb 3:8, 15; 4:7; cf. 2 Thess 2:10-12.

Exod 9:34	But when Pharaoh saw that the rain and the hail and the thunder had ceased, he sinned again <u>and hardened his heart</u> (*kbd*; כבד), he and his servants.
Exod 9:35	<u>And Pharaoh's heart was hardened</u> (*ḥzq*; חזק), and he did not let the sons of Israel go, just as the Lord had spoken through Moses.
Exod 10:1	Then the Lord said to Moses, go to Pharaoh, for <u>I have hardened his heart</u> (*kbd*; כבד) and the heart of his servants, that I may perform these signs of mine among them,
Exod 10:20	<u>But the Lord hardened Pharaoh's heart</u> (*ḥzq*; חזק), and he did not let the sons of Israel go.
Exod 10:27	<u>But the Lord hardened Pharaoh's heart</u> (*ḥzq*; חזק), and he was not willing to let them go.
Exod 11:10	And Moses and Aaron performed all these wonders before Pharaoh; yet <u>the Lord hardened Pharaoh's heart</u> (*ḥzq*; חזק), and he did not let the sons of Israel go out of his land.
Exod 14:4	Thus <u>I will harden Pharaoh's heart</u> (*ḥzq*; חזק), and he will chase after them; and I will be honored through Pharaoh and all his army, and the Egyptians will know that I am the Lord. And they did so.
Exod 14:8	<u>And the Lord hardened the heart of Pharaoh</u> (*ḥzq*; חזק), king of Egypt, and he chased after the sons of Israel as the sons of Israel were going out boldly.
Exod 14:17	<u>And as for Me, behold, I will harden the hearts of the Egyptians</u> (*ḥzq*; חזק) so that they will go in after them; and I will be *honored through Pharaoh and all his army, through his chariots and his horsemen.

The three Hebrew terms for hardening in Exodus, *kbd* (כבד), *qšh* (קשה), and *ḥzq* (חזק) correlate well with an Egyptian context. As has been noted in most studies of the hardening of Pharaoh, these terms have slightly different connotations that are not fully captured by the English word "harden" or by the Greek verbs *sklērynein* and *barynein*, which the LXX translators adopted to translate each of the Hebrew verbs as they occur in Exodus chapters 7-14.

The primary meaning of *ḥzq* is to "make hard, raise objections, be obdurate, make difficulties." Positively, it may describe a strong heart that is "steadfast, unswerving in its purpose, unchanging, and courageous (Pss 27:14; 31:25[24]; Josh 11:20)."[2] Negatively, however, if the pursuit is foolish, *ḥzq* translates as "stubbornness" (Ezek 2:3-4; 3:7-9; Jer 5:3), as is obviously the case for Pharaoh in Exodus.[3] *qšh*, "hard, severe, fierce,"[4] unlike *kbd* and *ḥzq* consistently bears

---

[2] Robert R. Wilson, "The Hardening of Pharaoh's Heart," *CBQ* 41 (1979): 23.
[3] Exod 4:21; 7:13, 22; 8:19 [15], 9:12, 35; 10:20, 27; 11:10; 14:4, 8.
[4] *HALOT* 3.1152.

negative connotations of obstinacy (Exod 7:3; 13:5).⁵ Shupak notes that *qšh lēb* "is widely used in the Bible to convey stubbornness and is not at all limited to passages with an Egyptian background" (e.g., Ezek 3:7; Ps. 95:8; Prov 28:14).⁶ With a different nuance *kbd* has the primary meaning "*to be heavy*."⁷ When describing bodily organs, the term "indicates that the organ in question is not functioning normally."⁸ Thus, when appealing to his inadequacy as a speaker, Moses claims he is "heavy of tongue" (*kbd*), so that he lacks confidence speaking (Exod 4:10). Similarly, Gen 48:10 describes the eyes of the aged Jacob as "so heavy that they could not see" (*kbd*). Likewise in Isa 6:9-10; 59:1; and Zech 7:11 the "heavy" (*kbd*) ear does not hear properly. Interestingly, this "heaviness" and its associated dysfunction occurs as a result of the aging process (Gen 48:10), the failure to repent upon the hearing of the prophetic message (Zech 7:11), and God's punishment for idolatry (Isa 6:9-10).

A cursory reading of these hardening passages shows that God, Pharaoh, and Pharaoh's heart all participate in the hardening process.⁹ A culpable participant in hiding, Pharaoh's own depraved heart proves untrustworthy, as it hardens Pharaoh against God and indeed against Pharaoh's own best interests and those of his kingdom. At the same time Pharaoh hardens his own heart by disobeying God, by trusting in his own sovereignty as king, and by trusting in the power of the Egyptian deities he serves as priest. His hardening therefore is in part predicated by his own sin as Exod 9:34 makes clear, "*he sinned again* and hardened his heart." In other words, Pharaoh's heart, hardened by self-worship and cultural indoctrination, foolishly dismisses the wisdom of obeying the creator of his own life, whom the reader of the Pentateuch knows to be Yahweh. God therefore intensifies the hardening curse indicative of willful disobedience (cf. 2 Thess 2:10-12). As Pharaoh hardens in self-trust and confidence in Egyptian polytheism, God compounds the curse of hardening. Pharaoh is no longer able to perceive reality accurately—namely, that the plagues incrementally are proving the emptiness of Egyptian religion on the one hand and Yahweh's absolute sovereignty on the other. Because of this spiritual incapacitation, Pharaoh refuses to consider the wise counsel of his own magicians (Exod 8:19).

God also hardens Pharaoh for obstructing Israel's path to the promised land. Pharaoh's expressed repentance is insincere (Exod 10:17) and falls short of acknowledging, "the earth is the Lord's" (Exod 9:29). He and his people do not come to the point where they "fear the Lord God" (Exod 9:30). The book of Exodus thus maintains both Pharaoh's personal responsibility and God's absolute sovereignty. He would inevitably experience hardening (Exod 9:17) as long as he

---

[5] Deut 2:30; 10:16; 2 Kings 17:14; 2 Chron 30:8; 36:13; Neh 9:16-17, 29; Ps 95:8; Prov 28:14; Jer 7:26; Ezek 2:4; 3:7.

[6] "ḤZQ, KBD, QŠH LĒB, 398. It is Shupak's opinion that "*qšh lēb* is, thus, an independent Hebrew expression bearing no relation to the Egyptian terminology."

[7] See Robert R. Wilson, "The Hardening of Pharaoh's Heart," 22.

[8] Wilson, "Hardening of Pharaoh's Heart," 22.

[9] God (10x) 4:21; 7:3; 9:12; 10:1, 20, 27; 11:10; 14:4, 8, 17; Pharaoh (3x): 8:15, 32; 9:34; Pharaoh's heart (6x): 7:13, 14, 22; 8:15; 9:7, 35. In 14:17 God hardens not just Pharaoh but all the Egyptians.

impeded the progress of God's people, and as long as he stood confident in his superstitious stature as a god among gods—the prevailing cultural fetish concerning the Pharaohs of ancient Egypt.

III. THE EGYPTIAN BACKGROUND OF THE HARDENING OF PHARAOH'S HEART

Exodus fittingly unfolds in the guise and occasional idiom of a Hebrew people exposed to Egyptian culture. Historians have substantiated Egyptian features in Exodus like the name of Phinehas, the Egyptian respect for magic, the accurate use of the title "Pharaoh," the historicity of Egyptian midwives and birthing stools, and historical corroboration that Pharaohs of this era did in fact enslave foreigners to build public projects, etc.[10] More subtly, James Hoffmeier has proposed that the expressions "arm" of God (Exod 6:6; 15:16) and "hand" of God (Exod 3:19-20; 7:4) parody the Egyptian fetish that Pharaoh ruled Egypt with an invincible "strong hand" or "strong arm."[11] And John Currid has found comparable polemical intent behind the confrontation between the staff of Moses and the serpents of Pharaoh's magicians. That Moses' staff-turned-serpent swallowed up its Egyptian look-alikes attests Yahweh's sovereignty over Pharaoh, whose crown bore the image of Wadjet—the serpent goddess believed to be one of the divinities responsible for the protection and empowerment of the Egyptian king.[12]

In view of these phenomena, it is plausible that Pharaoh's hardening may also find its origin in an Egyptian idiom. For early Egyptian literature gave birth to the expressions "big-hearted," "great hearted," "straight hearted," "hot hearted," "inflamed heart," "sealed heart," "light of heart," "firm of heart," "lacking in

---

[10] See Nili Shupak "ḤZQ, KBD, QŠH LĒB, The Hardening of Pharaoh's Heart in Exodus 4:1-15:21 — Seen Negatively in the Bible but Favorably in Egyptian Sources," in *Egypt, Israel, and the Ancient Mediterranean World* (Studies in Honor of Donald B. Redford; ed. Gary N. Knoppers and Antoine Hirsh; Leiden–Boston: Brill, 2004), 390; J. K. Hoffmeier (*Israel in Egypt*, New York: OUP, 1996); John D. Currid (*Ancient Egypt and the Old Testament*, Grand Rapids: Baker, 1997), 83-120; Kenneth A. Kitchen, "Exodus," *ABD* 2 (1992) 700-708. Donald B. Redford disagrees, seeing little Egyptian influence on Exodus ("An Egyptological Perspective in the Exodus Narrative" in *Egypt, Israel, Sinai: Archaeological and Historical Relationships in the Biblical Period* [ed. A. F. Rainey; Tel Aviv, 1987] 137-61.

[11] J. K. Hoffmeier; "The Arm of God versus the Arm of Pharaoh in the Exodus Narratives, " *Biblica* 67 (1986): 378-87; John D. Currid, *Ancient Egypt and the Old Testament* (Grand Rapids: Baker, 1997), 83-103: "When Aaron's rod swallowed the staffs of the Egyptian magicians, Pharaonic deity and omnipotence were being denounced and rejected outright. Pharaoh's cobra-crested diadem had no power against Yahweh" (94).

[12] Currid, *Ancient Egypt*, 89-94.

heart," and "to wash the heart."[13] The concept "hard of heart" would therefore seem to befit an Egyptian background.[14]

The Hebrew portrayal of the hardening of Pharaoh's heart in Exodus may correlate with the Egyptian belief that the heart (*ib*), as the essence of a person, was the storehouse of the sin or righteousness that sealed one's fate in the afterlife. John D. Currid has argued this point by recounting the ancient Egyptian judgment of Ani, as found in spell 125 of *The Book of the Dead*.[15] As the sequence of actions unfold, the dead soul of Ani enters a divine judgment hall where his dismembered heart is weighed on a balance against a feather. If Ani's heart outweighs the feather (which represents Maat, the goddess of truth and righteousness), he is guilty of sin. This verdict would result in Ani's being gobbled up by the goddess Amemit,[16] whose unnerving image featured a crocodile's forepart, a lion's or panther's middle, and a hippopotamus's hindquarters. Understandably, the very meaning of the name Amemit, "she who gobbles up," struck fear in those who lived in trepidation that this plight might be theirs in the afterlife. But this never happens in the many extant variants. The scales balance in Ani's favor proving the purity of his heart, so that he is able to sidestep Amemit and pass on to a peaceful afterlife.[17]

Currid surmises that Yahweh's hardening of Pharaoh's heart may be "a polemic against the prevailing notion that Pharaoh's character was pure and untainted."[18] Unlike Ani's, Pharaoh's heart was ill suited for a favorable after-death verdict.

If the Egyptian judgment of Ani is a proper background for understanding the sequence of events that befall Pharaoh, we may surmise *that the heaviness or hardness of Pharaoh's heart is an idiomatic indicator of his sin and therefore his human mortality.* In combination with the successive plagues, Yahweh's hardening of Pharaoh "demythologizes" Pharaoh for the reader of Exodus, so that all sane observers may perceive the impotence of Pharaoh by contrast to the reality of Yahweh's cosmic power. In this case Pharaoh's heavy heart foreshadows his future guilt before the supernatural scales of divine judgment. Because his heart was hard, it would not, according to Egyptian legend, balance on the scale with

---

[13] See *Ancient Egyptian Literature* (trans. Miriam Lichtheim; Berkeley: University of California Press, 1973) 1: 76 n. 6; 77 n(n). 9, 16; 78 n(n). 29, 44; 79 n. 52; 80 n. 71; 107 n. 1; 178; 183 n. 20; 2: 69.

[14] There is no proof, of course, that the Hebrew concept "heart" was borrowed from its Egyptian counterpart, though Israel clearly shared with Egypt the concept that the heart was the multifunctional, multidimensional human organ that defined one's personality, essence, soul, and spirit. See ch. 2.

[15] *The Book of the Dead* is not a narrative, but a series of magical spells for the afterlife, originating in the Pyramid Texts of the 3rd millennium BC and Coffin Texts of the 2nd millennium BC, and adding fresh spells in the New Kingdom to form a new corpus that was then transmitted through the rest of Egyptian history down to Roman times.

[16] Also sometimes spelled Ammit or Amam.

[17] Currid, *Ancient Egypt*, 96-103. Also, Carol Andrews, *Amulets* (Austin: University of Texas Press, 1994), 56. This scene has many variants. In some depictions, Ani's heart is weighed against a figure of the goddess Maat in the presence of Maati-goddesses only.

[18] Currid, *Ancient Egypt*, 102.

Maat, and so he would prove to be untrue and unrighteous, and therefore unfit for a peaceful eternity. Furthermore, it could not be said that it was the Egyptian deities Osiris and Amemit who determined Pharaoh's fate. Rather, it was Israel's God who would determine Pharaoh's fate, because it was Yahweh, not the Egyptian deities, who was hardening Pharaoh's heart.

Not all scholars are persuaded that Exodus has *The Book of the Dead* as part of its conceptual background, however. Nili Shupak objects, "This idea is utterly wrong"[19] in view of the impossibility of the biblical author borrowing the expression "heavy hearted" from the Egyptian literature of the dead. She counters that the literary comparisons between the Hebrew terms and their Egyptian counterparts expose a polemic, which turns originally positive Egyptian idioms into negative Hebrew correctives.[20]

Shupak's criticisms are valid. While the Egyptian historical background cannot be fully constructed by philology alone, it is problematic that there does not appear to be a demonstrable allusion to the afterlife in any of the Exodus hardening passages. It is not entirely apparent that a polemic is at play either. Argumentative dispute between God and Pharaoh or Moses and Pharaoh simply does not occur with respect to the heart. Rather, it is in private conversation with Moses that God prophesies his hardening of Pharaoh and the Egyptians (Exod 4:21; 14:17). Elsewhere Exodus simply describes that the phenomenon did happen (Exod 7:13, 14, 22).

While one might argue that the Egyptian expectation of the judgment of the heart would be a fairly remarkable omission from the thought world of Exodus, especially in view of its polemic against Egyptian polytheism, it is important to note as a precaution that spells and vignettes from *The Book of the Dead* were not a part of popular culture within ancient Egypt. [21] *The Book of the Dead* papyri were expensive luxuries for the funerals of the well-to-do and had little impact on the peasantry slaving away in fields and pastures. Hebrew exposure to Egyptian temple ritual was minimal to non-existent due to the fact that cult practices took place privately deep inside great structures behind massive surrounding walls.[22] Similarly, amulets inscribed with Spell 30 of *The Book of the Dead* were placed over the hearts of the mummified dead within hidden tombs—they were not on public display. [23] Thus Hebrew exposure to the vignette of Ani and others like it

---

[19] "ḤZQ, KBD, QŠH LĒB, 401. See also J. R. Huddelstun, "Who is this that Rises like the Nile? Some Egyptian Texts on the Inundation and a Prophetic Trope" in *Fortunate the Eyes that See*, (ed. A. B. Beck et al.; Grand Rapids: Eerdmans, 1995), 347 n. 25.

[20] "ḤZQ, KBD, QŠH LĒB, 399.

[21] See A. I. Sadek, *Popular Religion in Egypt during the New Kingdom* (Hildesheimer ägyptologische Beiträge 27; Hildesheim: Gerstenberg, 1987).

[22] I am in debt to Kenneth Kitchen via direct correspondence for the historical clarifications of this paragraph.

[23] Spell 30, the "heart scarab formula," was believed to have the power to silence the heart in the afterlife. As Carol Andrews explains, "it (the heart scarab) would allow anyone who possessed it to live a totally reprehensible life and still enter heaven" (Andrews, *Amulets*, 56). Spell 30A: "O heart which I had from my mother, O my heart which I had upon earth, do not rise up against me as a witness in the presence of the Lord of Things; do not speak

remains uncertain and may be considered speculative until supportive evidence comes forth. Until then the connection between *The Book of the Dead* and the hardening of Pharaoh in Exodus remains a conjecture, albeit an interesting and provocative one.

What is most important in Exodus is the Hebrew theological notion that stubbornness and "sensory depletion" symptomatically follow inattention to prophetic warning and disobedience to divine command (cf. Zech 7:11).[24] This establishes the biblical axiom that Yahweh inspires and quickens the faculties of those who believe and obey him (Exod 4:11-15), while conversely acting to inhibit understanding in those who reject him because of disbelief, direct defiance, or confidence in another security (Deut 29:16-28).

(a) *The Culpability of Pharaoh*

It is unclear that ancient Egyptians held either to a rigid form of unconditional determinism or absolute free will.[25] On the one hand, Egyptologist Siegfried

---

against me concerning what I have done, do not bring up anything against me in the presence of the Great God, Lord of the West" (*The Egyptian Book of the Dead: The Book of Going Forth By Day*, (trans. Raymond O. Faulkner; ed. Eva Von Dassow; San Francisco: Chronicle Books, 1994), 103. Spell 30B: "When thou goest forth to the goodly place prepared for us yonder, make not our name to stink to the courtiers who create mankind in (his) place, that it may be well for us and well for the Hearer and that the judge may be glad. Think not up lies (against me) beside the God in the presence of the great God the lord of the west" (*The Book of the Dead Or Going Forth By Day*, (trans. Thomas George Allen; Chicago: University of Chicago Press, 1974), 40.

[24] Zech 7:11 describes a sequence of divine actions strikingly similar to that experienced by Pharaoh, who long before had ignored Yahweh and his prophet Moses--"But they refused to pay attention, and turned a stubborn shoulder and made their ears heavy from hearing. And they made their hearts like flint so that they could not hear the law and the words which the Lord of hosts had sent by is Spirit through the former prophets; therefore great wrath came from the Lord of hosts" (Zech 7:11-12). In the same way that Zechariah's audience "turned a stubborn shoulder and made their ears 'heavy from hearing,' " so Pharaoh hardened his heart against Moses, God's prophet, thereby causing his heart to "be heavy" and incapable of perceiving the reality of Yahweh behind the plagues. His disabled "heavy" heart became such, we may infer, because it was contaminated by disregard for Yahweh's word and by disobedience to Yahweh's command (Exod 5:2).

[25] Greg Beale's assertion that in Exodus "the hardening may be viewed as a polemic against the Egyptian idea of Pharaoh's deity and the belief that Pharaoh's heart was the all-controlling factor both in history and society" is conjectural ("Pharaoh's Heart in Exodus 4-14 and Romans 9," 149). The predominant ancient Egyptian worldview seems to have been that the gods were in control of world history, not the king's heart. The Memphite text Beale cites does not refer to Pharaoh's heart or Pharaoh's control of history: "There came into being as the heart and there came into being as the tongue (something) in the form of Atum. The mighty Great One is Ptah, who transmitted [*life* to all gods], as well as (to) their *ka's*, through this heart, by which Horus became Ptah, and through this tongue, by which Thoth became Ptah. (Thus) it happened that the heart and tongue gained control over [every] (other) member of the body, by teaching that he is in every body and in every mouth of all gods, all men, [all] cattle, all creeping things, and (everything) that lives, by thinking

Morenz has cited the Old Kingdom Coffin Text *"I did not command that they might do evil, [but] it was their hearts that violated what I had said"* to display the ancient Egyptian view that "man is free to act as he pleases. The evil in the world is the consequence of this freedom to forsake God's will."[26] Translator and Egyptologist Miriam Lichtheim reaches the same conclusion on the basis of *The Instruction of Ptahhotep* (from well-preserved Middle Kingdom papyri):

> The wise is known by his wisdom,
> The great by his good actions;
> His heart matches his tongue,
> His lips are straight when he speaks;
> He has eyes that see,
> His ears are made to hear what will profit his son,
> Acting with truth he is free of falsehood.
>
> He who hears is beloved of god,
> He whom god hates does not hear.
> *The heart makes of its owner a hearer or non-hearer,*
> Man's heart is his life-prosperity-health![27]

The *Ptahhotep* text exemplifies the ancient Egyptian conviction that the heart, as seat of wisdom and truth, was what enabled the eyes and ears to function properly so that a person could act wisely according to truth.

On the other hand, the *Ptahhotep* text clarifies that the inability to hear was indeed associated with one's conflict with god: *"He who hears is beloved of god, he whom god hates does not hear."* Yet the Ptahhotep text places the blame for spiritual deafness not on god but upon the human heart: *"The heart makes of its owner a hearer or non-hearer."* For this reason Lichtheim comments, "Once again the note of determinism is sounded; and it is quickly countered by the assertion that it is a man's own heart that determines his behavior."[28] Thus there seems to have been a dynamic interplay between divine causation and human responsibility in the ancient Egyptian worldview.

In Exodus the monotheistic worldview and religious outlook is radically different. There is one God and he alone determines the fate of humanity. God's activity in the hardening process is indisputable, if not unconditional. He hardens for at least four explicit reasons: to perform revelatory signs (10:1); to exact honor

---

and commanding everything that he wishes." Reproduced as found in *Ancient Near Eastern Texts* (ed. J. B. Pritchard; Princeton: Princeton University Press, 1966), 5.

[26] Siegfried Morenz, *Egyptian Religion* (trans. A. E. Keep; Ithaca, New York: Cornell, 1973), 57-58.

[27] *Ancient Egyptian Literature*, 1:73-74.

[28] *Ancient Egyptian Literature*, 2:80 n. 68. Commenting on the same document, Lichtheim adds elsewhere "the idea that the gods determine a man's character and fate was not developed to the point where it would have overwhelmed the sense of free will and personal responsibility" (77 n.23). On the Egyptian concept of fate see Siegfried Morenz, *Egyptian Religion*, 57-80.

from Pharaoh and his army (14:4, 17-18); to reveal his identity as Lord (14:4, 18); and to attest his authority to judge the state of Pharaoh's heart—evidence that it was he who was the omniscient true living God, while Pharaoh was a mere man (14:8). The dispute between Pharaoh and Yahweh is over kingship—who really is king and who really has custody of Israel?

Throughout this conflict Pharaoh is culpable for persecuting God's people. A descendant of the Egyptian king who mass murdered the first-born sons of Israel (Exod 1:16), he emerges as a "chip off the old block"—an unfair, oppressive sovereign, who enslaves God's people and forces them to do hard labor. Against the background of the covenant, Pharaoh shadows over the people of Israel as a living curse. He defies Yahweh directly and ignores his commands. Moses' first exchange with Pharaoh discloses the insubordinate condition of this Egyptian's heart toward God : "But Pharaoh said, who is the Lord that I should obey his voice to let Israel go? I do not know the Lord, and besides, I will not let Israel go" (Exod 5:1-2). With these words Pharaoh directly challenges Yahweh's covenant with Israel and Yahweh's exclusive kingship over her. He acts in confidence that he, his nation, and his gods, as dictating sovereignties, can authoritatively suppress and decisively defeat Israel and her Lord. This same confidence leads Pharaoh to later threaten Moses with the death penalty (Exod 10:28-29). As dull-witted as this action may seem to the modern reader, in its historical context Pharaoh's thinking would be perfectly understandable. For the ancient mind it was unthinkable that a serious deity could be aligned with a powerless, oppressed people—as Yahweh was with the Hebrew people before the exodus. Therefore, as king of the greatest empire of the day, Pharaoh oppressed Israel with total confidence—smirking at the thought of yielding to the foreign god of his Hebrew slaves. Why should Pharaoh negotiate with Moses? Present circumstances demonstrated *his* divine favor, not Moses'. For *he* was king. Israel, on the other hand, was an enslaved, oppressed people! How powerful could her god be?

Pharaoh thus assumed the superiority of Egypt's deities over the God of Israel, just as he assumed Egypt's sovereignty over the Israelite slaves. Exodus exclaims the futility of this assumption. The signs of Exodus 7-14 signal the message explicitly pronounced in Exod 18:11 and Num 33:4—that Yahweh is immeasurably more powerful than all the gods of Egypt put together. Hence, not only was Pharaoh's assumption false, but the opposite was true. Yahweh's victorious intervention on behalf of his people would declare in terms understandable to Egyptians and Hebrews alike the sovereignty exclusive to Yahweh and the unchanging faithfulness of Yahweh to his people Israel.

While debate continues as to the exact identity of the Pharaoh of the exodus—whether Thutmose III, Amenhotep II, or Rameses II—we can be sure that whoever the Pharaoh was, he was not *religiously* neutral. As chief priest, Pharaoh was a product and promoter of Egyptian religion as well as the chief participant in its cult. He therefore posed a direct threat to Hebrew monotheism in view of the fact that Egyptian religion was polytheistic, syncretistic, ritualistic in a pagan manner, and politically monarchial.

A brief description of each of these features of ancient Egyptian religion will enable us to better understand how Egyptian culture clashed with Israel's theology and her covenant with Yahweh. This in turn will help us to better understand why God inflicted hardening upon Pharaoh.

(b) *Egyptian Polytheism*

Ancient Egypt's deities were organized hierarchically with the creator god assuming the premier position as king of the gods.[29] Though no consensus existed as to who specifically the "king" god was, conventional thought accepted the prominence of one and the independent existence of many others.[30] Egyptian religion was thus polytheistic with multiple deities in all centers, except during Akhenaten's stark monotheism (= Amenhotep IV; 18th Dynasty).

(c) *Egyptian Syncretism*

Ancient Egyptian religion was also syncretistic — it absorbed foreign belief systems into its religious hierarchy. Egyptologist Edward F. Wente notes:

> Despite repeated assertions in royal inscriptions concerning foreigners being ignorant of god, in actuality Asiatic deities, such as Astarte, Baal, Resep, and Anat, were accepted in Egypt in the course of the New Kingdom . . . and full testimony to the power of Asiatic deities is evident

---

[29] Edward Wente ("Egyptian Religion," *ABD* 2.408) notes: "Though there have been repeated attempts to discern an underlying belief in a monotheistic god behind Egypt's pantheon, the worship of many gods was, with the exception of Akhenaten's reformation (ca. 1350 B.C.E.), never abrogated until the pagan culture ended with the gradual spread of Christianity and the final closing of the Isis temple at Philae in the 6th century C.E."

[30] The following excerpts from two independent creation myths display the phenomenon. The first comes from the 17th chapter of *The Book of the Dead* (1500-1000 B.C.). The second comes from the so-called "Shabaka Stone" (dated ca. 700 B.C., though scholars agree the text derives from an original that existed as much as 2000 years earlier). The first comes from Heliopolis, the second from Memphis. Both translations are taken from *Ancient Near Eastern Texts*, 4-5.

> "I am the great god who came into being by himself." Who is he? "The great god who came into being by himself" is water; he is Nun, the father of the gods. Another version: He is Re. "He who created his names, the Lord of the Ennead." Who is he? He is Re, who created the names of the parts of his body. That is how these gods who follow him came into being." "I am he among the gods who cannot be repulsed."

> And so Ptah was satisfied, after he had made everything, as well as all the divine order. He had formed the gods, he had made cities, he had founded names, he had put the gods in their shrines, he had established their offerings, he had founded their shrines, he had made their bodies like that (with which) their hearts were satisfied. So the gods entered into their bodies of every (kind of) wood, of every (kind of) stone, of every (kind of) clay, or anything which might grow upon him, in which they had taken form. So all the gods, as well as their *ka*'s gathered themselves to him, content and associated with the Lord of the Two Lands."

in Rameses II's treaty with the Hittites. In Egypt, Asiatic deities were worshiped by Egyptians in accordance with Egyptian cult practices.[31]

This feature of Egyptian religion may explain the willingness of Pharaoh's court magicians to credit Moses' God with the plagues of insects in Exod 8:19 and locusts in Exod 10:7. Moreover, because syncretism was inimical to Israelite monotheism, Israel's background, steeped as it was in Egyptian religion, contributed to the need for Yahweh's giving of the first two of the Ten Commandments, which warned that Israel must not adopt the syncretistic practices of her former slave masters. The golden calf episode and references to the "ornaments" that Yahweh commanded the Israelites to put away in the days immediately following the exodus (Exod 32-33; esp. 33:4-6) indicate that Israel was prone to do so.

(d) *Religious Ritual in Ancient Egypt*

Though Egyptian theology varied from Memphis to Thebes to Heliopolis, Egyptian religion found conformity in ritual and practice. Priests throughout Egypt conducted worship of local deities in temple shrines. And the leading official of this religious culture was the king himself. Christine Favard-Meeks describes the practice:

> Once the offerings had been laid before the god, purified and ready to be consumed, the doors of the naos (inner sanctum) were opened, while a chorus bid the god to rouse himself. . . . At this point, the king entered the shadowy sanctuary. In its depth was the granite shrine, behind whose double-leaved door the cult statue stood. Lighting his way with a candle, the king broke the seal that protected the god's solitude, then drew the bolt, assuring the god that he was approaching in a state of purity and as not being pursued by enemies. The god's face was unveiled the instant the sun peeked over the horizon, so that the god would awaken in harmony with the rhythms of the universe. . . . The purpose of this face-to face encounter was clearly stated: "He (the king) enters, pure, to replenish Horus's altar, to provision the table of his daily service, to offer bread, to add to his food, to carry an offering to his *ka* (vital force/personality), to worship his statue, to venerate his image, to acclaim His Majesty."[32]

Israel's exposure to Egyptian ritual would have been limited to small-scale popular cults operated by citizen groups, who modeled their religious practice

---

[31] "Egyptian Religion," 410.
[32] Dimitri Meeks and Christine Favard-Meeks, *Daily Life of the Gods* (trans. G. M. Goshgarian; Ithaca, New York: Cornell, 1996), 127; see also John J. Davis, *Moses and the Gods of Egypt*, 104; S. Morenz, *Egyptian Religion*, 86-88.

after the essentials of the great temple rites.[33] It would have been here that the Hebrews encountered the greatest Egyptian challenge to Yahwism.

Within this milieu, Egyptians viewed Pharaoh as the high priest and sole liturgist in all temples and as such he embodied the corporate personality of Egyptian society. Wente notes that "in depictions of cultic activities it is the king who is universally shown officiating, and it is to him alone that the recorded speeches of the gods are directed."[34] Pharaoh was the supreme mediator between the Egyptian gods and the Egyptian nation. Therefore the king's relationship to the gods was believed to correlate with his ability to govern. His favor before the gods, aroused by priestly ritual, was thought to result in agricultural fertility and military success. On the other hand, if the king was ineffective as priest, he would also be thought to be impotent as king and as a result be the potential cause of national catastrophe. This was in fact exactly how king Akhenaten was viewed by the author of Tutankhamen's restoration inscription. Because Akhenaten had destroyed cult images, he was blamed as the cause of Egypt's separation from her gods and the military defeat that followed. In sum, Pharaoh, the king of Egypt, as the chief mediator between the Egyptian deities and the Egyptian people, was the primary figure who determined how Egyptian deities would or would not intervene in Egyptian affairs.

This historical background sheds light on the conflict between Pharaoh and Yahweh in Exodus. Because Pharaoh's intrusive governance posed a religious threat to Israel, Yahweh intervened to display publicly the impotence of Pharaoh and his gods. For, like the nation he governed, Pharaoh was polytheistic and idolatrous and a threat to Israel's exclusive religious devotion to Yahweh.

(e) *Pharaoh as Divine Monarch*

Not only was Pharaoh king, high priest, and exclusive intercessor before the gods of Egypt, but, as we have stressed, he was also believed to be divinely related to the chief Egyptian gods Re, Horus, and Osiris. James K. Hoffmeier explains:

> From Dynasty 4 onward, the Pharaoh bore the title "Son of Re." As such, he was the god of the Egyptian state and was responsible to maintain the cosmic order (maat) on earth that had been established by Re at creation (Frankfort 1978:51-66). Because of the bond that existed between the created order and the king as the incarnate "Son of Re," he was responsible for the fertility of the land as well as for the proper function of the Nile, and because of the strong bond between the sun god, Re, and the king, he was the one who illuminated the two lands, i.e., Egypt (Frankfort 1978: 56-59).[35]

---

[33] As at Deir el-Medina.
[34] Wente, *ABD* 2:409.
[35] Hoffmeier, *ABD* 2:376-377. Citing Henri Frankfort, *Kingship and the Gods* (Chicago: University of Chicago Press, 1978), 56-59.

The plagues of Exodus 7-10 would have been understood by Pharaoh and the Egyptians as a direct assault on the king, who was responsible for the proper function of the Nile, the crops, and the sun.[36]

Christine Favard-Meeks adds:

> But the pharaoh was also the incarnation of Horus, son of Isis, the model of earthly kingship, and, as such, Osiris's heir as well. In fact, both these gods were embodied in his person. Alive, the king as Horus inherited the earthly realm from his father; dead, he gained access to the next world, becoming the ancestor par excellence. His funerary cult permitted him to be at one and the same time Osiris, sovereign of the kingdom of the dead, and the dead sun who would share the destiny of Re on his journeys.[37]

Pharaoh's identity therefore was established by a complex integration of solar and Osirian myths. As such his divine status was not only a challenge to the covenant and to Israel's religious exclusivism, but he was also an abomination before Yahweh, just as other Egyptian gods were and as Canaanite, Philistine, Assyrian, Babylonian, Persian, Greek and Roman deities would be in the future. Indeed, as the incarnation of Re and/or Horus, Pharaoh was in all respects an icon himself. Among other things, Exodus is therefore the story of how Yahweh's plagues produced chaos in nature to prove that Pharaoh was not the guarantor of natural order and balance (Maat). Pharaoh, king of Egypt, was a mortal like any other and as such even he was subject to the hardening curse of Yahweh (Exod 14:8).

(f) *Egypt and Ancient Near Eastern Covenants*

Ancient Egypt apparently did not have a native religious institution analogous to the covenants of Israel and many of the other nations of the ANE. However, Egypt was not altogether ignorant of the covenantal mindset of her neighbors. In Egypt's famous war against the Hittites, Rameses II formed an army of 20,000 soldiers that was divided into four divisions of 5000 each. Each division was named after one of the four great Egyptian gods: Amun, Re, Ptah, and Seth, the belief being that these gods would protect the Egyptian army.

Egypt's wars with the Hittites, however, proved to be unwinnable, so that Rameses agreed to the terms of a parity treaty with the Hittite king Hattusilis III (1259 BC). The treaty, which has been preserved in hieroglyphics and in Akkadian, contains six basic parts:

1) Title and preamble (including mutual royal ties)
2) Historical Prologue (including history of past relations)
3) Terms of the treaty (including reaffirmation of brotherhood)
4) Deposit of the text (as on tablets in the Hittite and Egyptian archives and

---

[36] Hoffmeier, *ABD* 2:377. It is also true, of course, that the attacks would have been seen as against the individual deities—Re, Hapi, etc.

[37] Meeks, *Daily Life of the Egyptian Gods*, 123.

Egyptian temple walls)
5) List of divine witnesses
6) Curses against infraction and blessings for compliance

The outline is noticeably similar to the suzerainty treaty or covenant between Israel and Yahweh. Most importantly, however, the treaty proves Egyptian familiarity with the religious features associated with the treaty/covenant concept that pervaded the ANE. The list of divine witnesses (section 5) invokes a thousand gods of Egypt and a thousand gods of Hatti to bear witness to the treaty. Section six then calls upon the same gods to bless those that keep the treaty and curse those who break it.[38]

This background is foundational to the supernatural dimension of the plot of Exodus. All pharaohs believed in divine support in war. Ramses II's inability to defeat the Hittites in northern Syria was evidence that the Hittite gods were equal in strength to the combined forces of the Egyptian gods Amun, Re, Ptah, and Seth. Therefore the only alternative to this unwinnable war was diplomacy and a parity treaty with the Hittites.

The Pharaoh of Exodus, however, did not relent in this way in his dealings with the Israelite slaves. Pharaoh persistently and confidently oppressed the Hebrews because he was convinced, as we may plausibly conjecture, that his many gods would in the end outdo the one god of Moses and the enslaved Hebrew people. Thus persuaded, Pharaoh trusted and believed in himself and his gods. The more these inherited convictions were challenged, the more offended and more obstinate he became.

IV. THE IDOLATRY OF ANCIENT EGYPT

On the day when I chose Israel and swore to the descendants of the house of Jacob and made myself known to them in the land of Egypt, when I swore to them, saying, I am the Lord your God, on that day I swore to them, to bring them out from the land of Egypt into a land that I had selected for them, flowing with milk and honey, which is the glory of all lands. And I said to them, cast away, each of you, the detestable things of his eyes, and do not defile yourselves with the idols of Egypt; I am the Lord your God. (Ezek 20:5-7; cf. 30:13)

The Egyptians of the New Kingdom era regarded manmade images, not as themselves deities, but usually as the receptacle in which the spirit of a deity might take up residence.[39] These images adorned temples large and small. The Egyptians saw divine images as necessary catalysts that enabled gods to direct

---

[38] Kenneth A. Kitchen, *On the Reliability of the Old Testament* (Grand Rapids: Eerdmans, 2003), 283-294. See especially tables 21 and 26 (pp. 284 and 288) and Kitchen's detailed, substantive notes 104-116 on pp. 562-564.

[39] See W. M. F. Petrie, *Amulets* (London: Constable: 1914), 1-7 and more recently Carol Andrews, *Amulets*, 14: "All such figures and reliquaries must rather have been set up as a focus for veneration."

human affairs. They played an important role in both the manifestation of deities and their intervention in human affairs. This has been demonstrated by the previously mentioned inscription of Tutankhamen that describes how the destruction of cult images under king Akhenaten, Tut's predecessor, resulted in the inability of the gods and goddesses to answer prayer and aid the kingdom's army.[40]

Against this cultural background, the ten plagues against Egypt display Yahweh's intention to destroy the visual images of Egyptian deities, which the Egyptians thought to be catalysts of economic wealth and imperial dominance. The plagues, ironically, were acts Yahweh performed in Egypt's behalf.[41] For they demonstrated that Egyptian religion was empty and false, so that discerning Egyptians could avoid disillusionment by paying homage to Yahweh the true God who could do what he promised (cf. Exod 12:38 which may include Egyptians). The Egyptian deities' failure to halt the plagues evidenced their weakness before Yahweh.[42]

Yahweh's exposure of the impotence of *all* of Egypt's gods, including Pharaoh, is emphasized by the OT. On the night of the first Passover, for example, the Lord said to Moses: "For I will go through the land of Egypt on that night, and will strike down all the first-born in the land of Egypt, both man and beast; and *against all the gods of Egypt* I will execute judgments—I am the Lord" (Exod 12:12). As the consummate plague against Egypt, the killing of the first-born signifies Yahweh's devastation of all the Egyptian deities, whether real or imagined. While Yahweh's threat in these verses refers to events surrounding the last plague and not specifically the preceding nine, it is natural to assume that the preceding nine are in view as well due to the warning of the latter part of the verse— *against all the gods of Egypt I will execute judgments.*

Careful to not exaggerate the polemic against Egyptian deities in Exodus, Kenneth Kitchen carefully surmises:

> Nevertheless, it is fair to comment that the impact of various plagues can be understood as devaluing or denying Egyptian beliefs. A massively unruly and destructive Nile flood, red in hue, bringing death, was the opposite of Hapi (deity of that flood), who was normally bringer of new life by his waters. It also embodied the revived Osiris (green) — whereas virulent red was the color that denoted his enemy and murderer, Seth! Frogs were the symbol of abundance (hence, of prosperity; personified as Heqat), but here again they brought death. The rest (again) threatened or negated the prosperity that Egypt's gods were deemed to give, while the deep darkness eclipsed the supreme sun god, Re or Amen-Re. Pharaoh

---

[40] Wente *ABD* 2:409

[41] God's benevolent interest in Egypt should not be underestimated; see Isaiah 19.

[42] Of course, like syncretism, idolatry was a feature of Egyptian religion that the Israelites would be commanded to avoid. We stress again that Yahweh prohibited the making of idols in his image, choosing, rather, to reveal his existence and intervening power through word and action alone. The creator God would not be represented by human creations. It would not and could not be said that Yahweh was Israel's creation.

was traditionally entitled "Son of Re," and his patron was made invisible, as if in an eclipse of sun or moon (treated as hostile events also). Death of so many throughout the land (here, of firstborn) would probably seem to Egyptians to have negated the power of the gods completely, and the king's personal and official key role of ensuring their favor. To go much further than this would go into the realm of unjustified subjectivity.[43]

Thus, the first nine plagues suggested what the tenth plague proved—that Pharaoh was an incapable sovereign and utterly inferior to Yahweh. The death of his son and heir climaxed the plagues by proving beyond doubt his dynasty's impotence as god-kings of Egypt. His nation was in disarray and his succession was in jeopardy. And he *would* let Israel go.

The same interpretation of the final plague is found in the interpretative statement of Moses' father-in-law Jethro (Exod 18:11) and the review of the exodus event in Numbers 33:3-4:

Blessed be the Lord who delivered you from the hand of the Egyptians and from the hand of Pharaoh, and who delivered the people from under the hand of the Egyptians. Now I know *that the Lord is greater than all the gods*; indeed, it was proven when they dealt proudly against the people. (Exod 18:11)

And they journeyed from Rameses in the first month, on the fifteenth day of the first month; on the next day after the Passover the sons of Israel started out boldly in the sight of all the Egyptians, while the Egyptians were burying all their first-born whom the Lord had struck down among them. *The Lord had also executed judgments on their gods.* (Num 33:4)

The plagues that accompanied the hardening of Pharaoh's heart therefore helped establish from history the rationale behind the primary message of Exodus as expressed in the first two of the Ten Commandments. The ten plagues revealed Yahweh's absolute supremacy over the Pharaoh whom he hardened and the Egyptian deities which he devastated.

Yet Yahweh's display of power was also benevolent and salvific. It freed Israel from foreign oppression and revealed the truth of his sovereign pre-eminence to Hebrews and Egyptians alike. As elsewhere in the Bible, Exodus correlates liberation from bondage with revelation of truth. Therefore in remembrance of the exodus, Israel was to have no other gods and she was prohibited from making idols. Should she disobey, her plight would be similar to that of Egypt and the Pharaoh of the exodus—she would experience the consequences of illusory worship—national devastation, military defeat, loss of health, and hardening of the heart (Lev 26:14-46; Deut 29:17-29).

---

[43] *On the Reliability of the Old Testament*, 253. See also James Hoffmeier, *Israel in Egypt*, 149-155; Greta Hort, "The Plagues of Egypt," ZAW vol. 69 no. 28 (1957): 84-103; vol. 70 no. 29 (1958): 48-59.

The most prominent form of idolatry in ancient Egypt was the amulet. Amulets were decorative charms or ornaments believed to empower their wearers with extraordinary ability and supernatural protection in this life and in the afterlife. They originated as early as the pre-dynastic period (*c.* 4500 B.C.– 3100 B.C.) and continued to remain a prominent component of ancient Egyptian culture through to the Greco–Roman era (332 B.C.–A.D. 323).

They bore the images of sacred creatures (e.g., hippopotamus, scorpion, crocodile, vulture, cobra, bull, cow, frog), Egyptian deities (e.g., Amen-Re, Amen-ka-mutef, Hathor, Maat, Seth), sacred symbols (regal crowns, sphinx, falcon plumes, ostrich feathers) and even human body parts (e.g., face, eye, ear, tongue, hand/fist, heart). Many amulets also bore the words of sacred spells that promised to ward off evil and protect the wearer in the afterlife. In short, amulets were very common throughout ancient Egyptian history and religiously believed in by kings and commoners alike of every era. They could allay every conceivable fear in this life and the afterlife.

Pharaoh's obstinate refusal to heed Moses' warnings may have been the result of his trust in the power of amulets. This conjecture is reasonable and calculated. Egyptians would have turned to amulets in the event of plagues and discovered their impotence in the process. And it is likely that this major Egyptian fetish was the pagan influence that occasioned God's judgment in Exodus 33:5: "Say to the sons of Israel, 'you are an obstinate people; should I go up in your midst for one moment, I would destroy you. Now, therefore, put off your ornaments from you, that I may know what I will do with you.'" As a practitioner of amulets, Pharaoh represents the premier biblical example of the fate that awaits those who place trust in pagan deities and idols. A devotee of amuletic idols and a patron and priest of idol laden temples, he thus suffered the hardening of his inner will. Therefore, in faithfulness to the Abrahamic covenant, Yahweh cursed Pharaoh, because Pharaoh challenged Israel's covenant religion, the covenant promise of land, and the covenant bond between the Hebrew slaves and their God Yahweh (Gen 12:3).

Hence, in later times of theological reflection, Pharaoh became, with Sihon and Og, a prototype of the "you become like that which you worship" sentence, as Psalm 135:8-18 explains.[44] For the warning "those who make them will be like them" (Ps 135:18a) sounds after the Psalmist's contemplation of God's judgment of Pharaoh, Sihon, and Og—the three idolatrous pagan kings whom God afflicted with hardening of the inner will.

However, it is important to note that within biblical theology it is Israel, not Egypt, who is the target of Exodus's message. Exodus was written to the covenant people of God in the Hebrew language to establish proper faith and practice for God's covenant people. Thus it is they who receive God's judgment in Exod 33:4-6 and again in Ezek 20:8: "they did not cast away the detestable things of their eyes, nor did they forsake the idols of Egypt."

---

[44] The warning "those who make them will be like them" in Psalm 135:18 is the Psalmist's conclusion after contemplating God's judgment of Pharaoh, Sihon, Og and the idols of the nations.

V. CONCLUSION: EXODUS AS A PARADIGM FOR THE FUTURE

Exodus established a paradigm for how God would act and how he would expect his people to act in the future when their covenant would be challenged by foreign aggression and attraction to other covenants, other kings, and other gods. Exodus therefore became *the* classic text fueling eschatological hope for later Jews, who would await the coming of Yahweh and his prophet like Moses (Deut 18:15) to deliver the faithful from human oppression. God would act miraculously (Exod 34:10) and decisively as he had in the exodus to defeat foreign challenges to the covenant. As he had defeated the Egyptians, so he would likewise devastate the *idolatrous* Amorites, Canaanites, Hittites, Perizzites, Hivites and Jebusites. His saving action, however, would not be without condition. He would call upon Israel to respond in mutual good faith by rejecting foreign covenants and eradicating foreign gods (Exod 23:20-33; 34:10-17). The rationale and precedent for doing so was Yahweh's display of power in Egypt. God reserved the same curse that he had inflicted upon Pharaoh for those within Israel who would not maintain the covenant in faith. For Yahweh would interpret the idolatry of the Israelites as equally direct and defiant as the hard-hearted obstinacy of Pharaoh. Israel therefore would suffer Yahweh's curse despite her privileged ethnic origin, because in the beginning the covenant promised to curse those who cursed Abraham (Gen 12:3a). In Israel's case the curse would be partially self-inflicted (Israel herself would endanger Abraham's covenant by committing idolatry) and would lead to separation from divine blessing in the form of exile and hardening (cf. Deut 29:16-28).

Chapter 4

"Follow Vanity and Become Vain: Israel is Guilty Too"

> However, they did not listen, but stiffened their neck like their fathers, who did not believe in the Lord their God. And they rejected his statutes and his covenant which he made with their fathers, and his warnings with which he warned them. *And they followed vanity and became vain*, and went after the nations which surrounded them, concerning which the Lord had commanded them not to do like them. And they forsook all the commandments of the Lord their God and made for themselves molten images, even two calves, and made an Asherah and worshiped all the host of heaven and served Baal. (2 Kings 17:14-16)

The biblical history of Israel's rise and fall in the promised land affirms Yahweh's exclusive identity as sovereign God of the universe. Israel's biblical history, replete with intriguing stories of kings, prophets, villains, and heroes, has as its chief end the authentication of the God of Abraham. A theological, "I told you so," unveils in the historical books of the Old Testament, just as Deuteronomy forewarns: "But if your *heart* turns away and you will not obey, but are drawn away and worship other gods and serve them, I declare to you today that you shall surely perish" (Deut 30:17-18a). In the end Israel's fate has nothing to do with her military, economy, ingenuity, or lack thereof, but entirely with her relationship with Yahweh. Israel's unfaithfulness to Yahweh assures her defeat and exile, so that the eventual tragedy of Israel's fall historically affirms the severe truth of God's word, both his promises and his curses. In accord with the Pentateuch, especially Deuteronomy, the pre-exilic historical books—Joshua, Judges, 1-2 Samuel, 1-2 Kings and 1-2 Chronicles—affirm through Israel's historical experience that God is the exclusive security and refuge for humankind in this world of injustice, violence, and deception.

The message is remarkably simple. Israel's life should be totally devoted to faithful, sincere, exclusive worship of Yahweh. Existentially, nothing else matters. When worship of Yahweh is pure and undefiled, every other aspect of national security is safe and strong. On the other hand, when worship is divided and fraudulent, every dimension of Israel's life suffers confusion, dysfunction, and utter breakdown. The tragic message of the Old Testament is that Israel did not heed Moses' warning, or for that matter the concerted warnings of all the prophets, and as a result came to experience historically the severity of God's curse. As Israel's allegiance shifted from Yahweh to earthly kings, foreign alliances, and pagan deities, Israel's likeness to Yahweh diminished and she became pagan just as the working paradigm of this book has led us to expect. Israel became like that which she wanted, like that which she feared, like that which she worshiped. As 2 Kings 17:15 puts it "they followed vanity and became vain."

It is for this reason that Israel as a nation died. She came to experience the very curse forewarned by Moses (Deut 29:24-28). The nation constituted by the twelve tribes of Israel divided before being forced out of the promised land by foreign invaders. United Israel literally did perish. This occurred because of idolatry—the very covenant infraction that Moses warned against: "But if your heart turns away and you will not obey, but are drawn away and worship other gods and serve them, I declare to you today that you shall surely perish" (Deut 30:17-18a). Afflicted by this curse, Israel's experience began to mirror that of her pagan neighbors and even the experience of her biblical enemies. By turning a deaf ear to the word of God and by committing sacrilege after sacrilege Israel ironically assumed the position of a people antagonistic to the fulfillment of God's covenantal promises. Israel herself actively participated in the cursing of God's people, i.e., herself (Gen 12:3). Israel persecuted authentic prophets of God. She sought security in human kings and foreign alliances. And she built high places and paid tribute to Baal, Dagon, Chemosh, Asherah, and still other pagan deities.

I. THE PRE-MONARCHY PERIOD OF ISRAEL IN PALESTINE

(a) *Joshua*

The book of Joshua tells the story of Israel's conquest of the promised land from the theological perspective of the Pentateuch, especially Deuteronomy. Joshua takes over Moses' position as spiritual and military leader of God's people, endorsing all of his predecessor's counsel. Israel's military success and failure depends entirely upon her faithfulness to Yahweh and her commitment to exercise faith with courage and strength. Though the correlation between idolatry and the hardening of the heart is not present explicitly in Joshua, the concept of the heart is portrayed in a way that complements the biblical paradigm witnessed elsewhere in the Scriptures.

Heart dysfunction afflicts indiscriminately all who endanger the carrying out of God's covenantal promises. The hearts of Israel's opponents who impeded her attainment of the promised land "melted" (Josh 2:11; 5:1) upon learning of Israel's miraculous exodus from Egypt and the power of Israel's cosmic God. Behind Israel's brutal takeover of Canaan, God ensures Israel's triumph by defeating the Canaanites. God's action is not arbitrary, indiscriminate, or according to racial preference. In the truest sense Joshua depicts holy war. The Canaanites embody all that counters God's will for humanity—polytheism, immorality, and injustice.[1] Israel's mission to destroy this people is therefore to be interpreted in the same light as the tragic story of Noah and the flood (Genesis 6-9). God is acting through

---

[1] See Jack Finegan, *Myth and Mystery*, 119-54. John Day, "Canaan, Religion of," *ABD* 1.831-37 and the bibliography found on pp. 836-37; *Molech: A God of Human Sacrifice in the Old Testament* (Cambridge: Cambridge University Press, 1989). E. Yamauchi, "Cultic Prostitution," in *Orient and Occident* (ed. H. A. Hofner; AOAT 22; Neukirchen: Neukirchen-Vluyn), 1973.

Israel's invasion to protect his relationship with his covenant people and to ensure the fulfillment of his redemptive design for humanity—that humanity live in holy, undefiled covenant with God himself.

As a people intent on preventing the progress of God's covenant and the implementation of his law (God's will for humanity), the Canaanites experience the curse of heart malfunction and military defeat, as Josh 11:20 describes: "For it was of the Lord to harden their hearts, to meet Israel in battle in order that he might utterly destroy them, that they might receive no mercy, but that he might destroy them, just as the Lord had commanded Moses" (cf. Deut 6:14-15; 7:16, 25-26). The hardening of the heart thus plays an important part in God's triumphal invasion of Canaan, just as hardening had played an important role in his leading Israel out of Egypt.

The curse the Canaanite peoples experienced is also had in part by God's own people Israel. Israel also came to know the curse of spiritual heart failure in the conquest, after an Israelite, Achan, took spoils of war banned by God. As a consequence the entire nation suffered defeat at Ai where "the hearts of the people [of Israel] melted and became as water" (Josh 7:5). The curse was therefore indiscriminate in respect to ethnicity or nationality.

In his farewell address to Israel, Joshua warns Israel that God would curse his people in a way strikingly similar to the way he had cursed Canaan, if they did not remain faithful to the covenant.

> And it shall come about that just as all the good words which the Lord your God spoke to you have come upon you, so the Lord will bring upon you all the threats, until he has destroyed you from off this good land which the Lord your God has given you. When you transgress the covenant of the Lord your God, which he commanded you, and go and serve other gods, and bow down to them, then the anger of the Lord will burn against you, and you shall perish quickly from off the good land which he has given you. (Josh 23:15-16)

A major purpose evident throughout the book of Joshua is that Yahweh has historically revealed his consistent faithfulness to his command for undivided worship. Victories and defeats, curses and blessings alike find their explanation in this truth. Israel's partial success fittingly correlates with her sporadic faith. In Joshua's conclusion we find Israelites still hampered by the gods of Egypt and of the Amorites (Josh 24:14-15). Within this context, Joshua warns Israel that if they continue on this course God will devastate them: "If you forsake the Lord and serve foreign gods, then he will turn and do you harm and consume you after he has done good to you" (24:20). Then, with this warning, Joshua commands, "Now therefore, *put away the foreign gods* which are in your midst, *and incline your hearts to the Lord*, the god of Israel" (24:23). In Joshua therefore spiritual heart malfunction and hardening afflicts God's opponents who stand in the way of the progress of the covenant and its promises. The healthy heart, by contrast, is the human condition Yahweh desires—a heart bereft of idols and committed to Yahweh alone.

(b) *Judges*

The book of Judges is structured around a cycle of events tracing Israel's rise and fall with the coming and going of each successive judge. Judges chapter 2 summarizes the basic pattern of this cycle. Fundamental is Israel's tendency to fall into spiritual complacency when things go well economically, politically, and militarily. In times of comfort Israel loses her sense of dependency on God and foolishly experiments with the enticing promises of local deities. This betrayal of God for other deities brings about national crisis generation after generation. This in turn leads the people to cry out for God's deliverance during momentary awakenings in times of repentance. God then responds faithfully to the prayers of his people by providing human judges to deliver them from their enemies.

Judges may be described as a satirical polemic against idolatry. Though capable of the heroic, the judges often display serious character flaws that have tragic consequences—Jephthah and Samson being the most notable. Indeed Judges portrays all humanity as corrupt and disoriented: "In those days there was no king in Israel; everyone did what was right in his own eyes" (Judges 21:25). In view of the preceding books of the OT, we should understand the chaos of Judges as resulting from the fact that Israel did not revere Yahweh as king during this period of her history. And in anticipation of the historical books that follow, Judges sets the precedent for the kings of Israel, many of whom similarly experience chaos and disaster when they forsake God to pursue idols and foreign support.

In Judges, Israel's idolatry coincides with national despondency and sensory malfunction. We read in chapter 2 for example,

2:11	"the sons of Israel did evil in the sight of the Lord, and served the Baals"
2:12	"they followed other gods from among the gods of the peoples who were around them, and bowed themselves down to them"
2:13	"they forsook the Lord and served Baal and the Ashtaroth"
2:17	"and yet *they did not listen* to their judges, for they played the harlot after other gods and bowed themselves down to them"
2:19-22	"But it came about when the judge died, that they would turn back and act more corruptly than their fathers, *in following other gods* to serve them and bow down to them; they did not abandon their practices or *their stubborn ways*. So the anger of the Lord burned against Israel, and he said, because this nation has transgressed my covenant which I commanded their fathers, and *has not listened to my voice*, I also will no longer drive out before them any of the nations which Joshua left when he died, in order to test Israel by them, whether they will keep the way of the Lord to walk in it as their fathers did, or not."

The Israel of Judges is therefore an idolatrous, forgetful people who have ears to hear but do not hear the words of their own judges, just as later generations of idolatrous Israelites would have ears to hear but would not hear the words of their own prophets.

A primary objective of Judges manifest throughout the book is that God's saving acts through the judges in times of national repentance prove his supremacy over pagan gods and peoples. This is particularly evident following the death of the judge Jair in Judges 10. Israel fell into idolatry of epidemic proportions with hardly a foreign god going unworshiped (Judg 10:6). God intervened in this situation with language befitting his covenantal relationship with Israel in recounting his past deliverance of Israel from the Egyptians, Amorites, Ammonites, Philistines, Sidonians, Amalekites, and Maonites. In reminding Israel of these past deeds, Yahweh not only reviewed his consistent faithfulness to Israel, but also his proven superiority over the false gods of Israel's enemies. This recounting exposed Israel's sheer stupidity in pursuing other gods. God then levied the all-important challenge: "Go and cry out to the gods which you have chosen; let them deliver you in the time of your distress" (Judg 10:14). This divine challenge communicates the primary theme of Judges: God alone is God and he alone is able to deliver his people. Catastrophe awaits everyone—Israelites and Gentiles alike—who rely on false gods.

(c) *1-2 Samuel*

The books of 1-2 Samuel tell the story of the beginning of the united monarchy of Israel. God consecrates the prophet Samuel to speak his word to Eli the priest, to Saul, Israel's first king, and to the first generation under the united monarchy. The message of 1-2 Samuel accords well with the theology of previous books of the OT.

God's actions to preserve holy worship and the stipulations of his covenant with Abraham are first seen in the tragic story of Eli and his sons Hophni and Phinehas. Though Levites and privileged sons of Eli the priest, Hophni and Phinehas are identified as "sons of worthlessness who did not know the Lord" (1 Sam 2:12). Troublemakers, Hophni and Phinehas commit cultic prostitution and disrupt proper sacrifice by demanding raw meat from the people before the fat has been properly burned as a sacrifice before the Lord (2:12-17). These tragic actions convolute proper worship and therefore make Hophni and Phinehas living obstacles to the working out of God's covenantal plan. They thus become the object of prophetic judgment and the object of God's curse:

> Therefore the Lord God of Israel declares, I did indeed say that your house and the house of your father should walk before me forever; but now the Lord declares, far be it from me—for those who honor me I will honor, and those who despise me will be lightly esteemed. Behold days are coming when I will break your strength and the strength of your father's house so that there will not be an old man in your house. (1 Sam 2:30-31; cf. Gen 12:3)

Accordingly, Hophni and Phinehas express obstinate indifference to God in the face of prophetic judgment. Their sin having made them enemies of God, despite their heritage, they incur God's punishment for defiling holy worship. 1 Samuel thus explains: "If one man sins against another, God will mediate for him; but if a man sins against the Lord, who can intercede for him? But *they would not listen* to the voice of their father, for the Lord desired to put them to death" (1 Sam 2:25). Here the God-enforced disability to listen ties directly to Hophni and Phinehas's disrespect for pure worship of Yahweh—a sin that associates them with the Pharaoh of Exodus and the later generations of Israelites that would come to suffer the hardening curse pronounced by Isaiah, Jeremiah, and Ezekiel. Their idolatry replaced obedient worship with disobedient worthlessness.

The guilt of Eli should be similarly understood. To Eli the word of God came asking, "Why do you kick at my sacrifice and at my offering which I have commanded in my dwelling, and honor your sons above me, by making yourselves fat with the choicest of every offering of my people Israel?" (1 Sam 2:29). Allowing the influence of his sons and his appetite for food to have priority over his fear of God, Eli came to experience the reversal of fortune that Moses promised would characterize those who forsake Yahweh for idols:

> And the Lord said to Samuel, behold, I am about to do a thing in Israel at which both ears of everyone who hears it will tingle. In that day I will carry out against Eli all that I have spoken concerning his house, from beginning to end. For I have told him that I am about to judge his house forever for the iniquity which he knew, because his sons brought a curse on themselves and he did not rebuke them. And therefore I have sworn to the house of Eli that the iniquity of Eli's house shall not be atoned for by sacrifice or offering forever. (1 Sam 3:11-14; cf. Deut 29:14-21)

In reaction to this sin, God commissioned an unnamed prophet and Samuel to pronounce divine judgment on Eli and his sons. The obstinacy they exhibited and the fate they experienced, death at the hands of foreigners, concurs with God's predesigned punishment for idolatry—a fate Israel would eventually experience as a nation. Thus, in anticipation of the tragic end of Eli, Hophni and Phinehas, God proclaimed to Samuel, "Behold, I am about to do a thing in Israel at which both ears of everyone who hears it will tingle" (1 Sam 3:11). The expression "ears will tingle" occurs elsewhere in 2 Kings 21:12 and Jer 19:3. In both instances it expresses the reaction to be experienced by those who hear and witness the fulfillment of God's prophetic words of judgment against idolatry.[2]

---

[2] 2 Kings 21:11-12: "Because Manasseh king of Judah has done these abominations, having done wickedly more than all the Amorites did who were before him, and has also made Judah sin with idols; therefore thus says the Lord, the God of Israel, 'Behold, I am bringing such calamity on Jerusalem and Judah, that whoever hears of it, both his ears shall tingle."
Jeremiah 19:3-5: "Hear the word of the Lord, O kings of Judah and inhabitants of Jerusalem: thus says the Lord of hosts, the God of Israel, 'Behold I am about to bring a calamity upon this place, at which the ears of everyone that hears of it will tingle. Because they have forsaken me and have made this an alien place and have burned sacrifices in it to other gods that neither they nor their forefathers nor the kings of Judah had ever known, and because they have filled this place with the blood of the innocent and have built the high

III. THE UNITED MONARCHY

Israel's demise as a nation became certain when she chose to replace God with human kings, the request being interrelated with her idolatrous history. The Scriptures are explicit on this point. When the people demand that Samuel appoint for them a king so that Israel may be like the other nations, Samuel's displeasure at the prospect leads him to seek the Lord's counsel in prayer. In response God says:

> Listen to the voice of the people in regard to all that they say to you, for they have not rejected you, but they have rejected me from being king over them. Like all the deeds which they have done since the day that I brought them up from Egypt even to this day—in that they have forsaken me and served other gods—so they are doing to you also. (1 Sam 8:7-8)

After Samuel carried out God's commission to warn the people of the severe disadvantages of human kingship (1 Sam 8:9-18), the people "refused to listen to the voice of Samuel, and they said, 'No, but there shall be a king over us, that we also may be like all the nations, that our king may judge us and go out before us and fight our battles'" (1 Sam 8:19-20). The peoples' desire, clearly, is that they have a human king who will essentially perform the responsibilities exclusively associated with the God of their covenant—to secure victory in battle and to pronounce judgment (cf. 1 Sam 12:12). The request for a human king amounts to an act of idolatry—a "wicked" and "evil" request (1 Sam 12:17-20). The peoples' *refusal to listen* to the words of Samuel thus correlates with their idolatrous request for a human king—i.e., a replacement for Yahweh. Just as their worship of pagan deities evidenced their lack of faith in Yahweh, so too did their request for a human king. Desiring to be like the nations, Israel separated herself from the God of the covenant and brought upon herself the curse of self and foreign rule. Therefore with the coming of the monarch Israel experiences a steady downward spiral that results in its fracture and eventual exile. There are upward turns during times of repentance and renewal (as promised in 1 Sam 12:14), but the story as a whole evidences the consequences of separation from God because of faithless, obstinate devotion to self-rule and compliance with paganism. As Israel becomes more and more like the nations, she becomes less and less like her God, experiencing hardening along the way, so that, blinded by human pride and idolatry, she is unable to comprehend the truth of her own prophets, who speak God's authentic word.

(a) *Saul*

Israel's first king, Saul exemplifies the deterioration the Bible portrays as symptomatic for those who conduct scandalous worship. According to 1 Samuel, Saul had everything going for him: he was tall, handsome, popular, successful, and divinely chosen and anointed by the Lord to be Israel's first king (1 Sam 15:17).

---

places of Baal to burn their sons in the fire as burnt offerings to Baal, a thing which I never commanded or spoke of, nor did it enter my mind."

Yet, of his own volition, he secured a tragic fate by usurping the priestly office to offer up a corrupt sacrifice in the absence of Samuel, the legitimate prophet/priest (1 Sam 13:9-14). His milky indifference toward God thus incurred divine wrath and the inevitable loss of his kingdom. Sparing Agag the Amalekite king and hoarding the spoils of war, Saul disregarded divine instruction for conducting battle against pagan nations (1 Sam 15:9, 18-19). To make matters worse, with pomp comparable to a Pharoah or a Caesar, he set up a monument to himself (1 Sam 15:12), ordered the murder of eighty-five priests of the Lord (1 Sam 22:17-18), and hired the services of a pagan prophetess to conjure up Samuel from the dead—a direct violation of a well-known divine prohibition (1 Samuel 28; cf. Lev 19:31).

God therefore informed Samuel "I regret that I have made Saul king, for he has turned back from following me, and has not carried out my commands" (1 Sam 15:11). Samuel then entered into an altercation with Saul that substantiates the basic argument of our book. When Saul rationalized his actions and attempted to appease Samuel with a sacrifice from the choicest of his spoils of war, Samuel responded:

> Has the Lord as much delight in burnt offerings and sacrifices as in obeying the voice of the Lord? Behold to obey is better than sacrifice, and to heed than the fat of rams. *For rebellion is as the sin of divination, and insubordination is as iniquity and idolatry.* Because you have rejected the word of the Lord, he has rejected you from being king. (1 Sam 15:22-23)

The misguided religious belief that external sacrifice can atone for covenantal apostasy is equated with *divination and idolatry!* False worship, even when conducted in an orthodox manner, is idolatry. Thus Saul came to experience God's willed punishment for idolatry. He experienced the departure of the Spirit of God and its replacement with a spirit of evil (1 Sam 16:14-15; 18:10-11). He experienced severe jealousy of David, paranoia, and what might be compared to psychological derangement (e.g., 1 Sam 18:10). Upon the departure of the Spirit of God, Saul indeed became God's adversary (1 Sam 28:16). The tragic extent of God's abandonment of Saul is seen in his death, when he commits suicide after suffering defeat at the hands of the Philistines.

Saul's story is important, for his miscalculations set the stage for the religious apostasy that would eventually topple all of Israel. As Israel committed sacrilege after sacrilege, she corporately resorted to external religious tradition and ritual worship of God. But without a repentant heart, such worship utterly failed. Israel was unable to escape God's punishment. Neither the law nor the temple were able to replace sincere worship from the heart, as the Lord instructed Samuel: "God sees not as man sees, for man looks at the outward appearance, but the Lord looks at the heart" (1 Sam 16:7).

(b) *Solomon*

Solomon's reign as king of Israel began with promise and success. As son of David, he was immediately popular with the people. He became famous for his building projects, most notably the temple, and his regal wisdom, which enabled him to judge effectively. Solomon also genuinely seems to have been committed to serving the Lord. 1 Kings 3:12 reports God saying to Solomon: "I have done according to your words. Behold, I have given you a wise and discerning heart, so that there has been no one like you before you, nor shall one like you arise after you."

Yet, despite his military, judicial, and administrative successes, and his initial faithfulness to God, Solomon's career was contaminated and essentially ruined by idolatry. 1 Kings 11 tells the story. Solomon brought multiple forms of foreign worship into his own house when he adopted the political strategy of securing foreign alliances through marriage with daughters of foreign royalty. This action, a breach of Deut 17:17 and a violation of 1 Kings 9:6-7, contaminated Solomon's heart, so that he became an idolater himself.

> Now king Solomon loved many foreign women along with the daughter of Pharaoh: Moabite, Ammonite, Edomite, Sidonian, and Hittite women, from the nations concerning which the Lord had said to the sons of Israel, you shall not associate with them, neither shall they associate with you, *for they will surely turn your heart away after their gods.* Solomon held fast to these in love. And he had seven hundred wives, princesses, and three hundred concubines and his wives turned his heart away. For it came about when Solomon was old, *his wives turned his heart away after other gods; and his heart was not wholly devoted to the Lord his God, as the heart of David his father had been.* (1 Kings 11:1-4)

With detail 1 Kings 11:5, 7 reports that Solomon "went after" Ashtoreth the goddess of the Sidonians[3] and Milcom the "detestable idol" of the Ammonites.[4] He built high places east of Jerusalem for Chemosh the "detestable idol" of Moab[5]

---

[3] Ashtoreth is the Hebrew name of the Ugaritic and Phoenician goddess Astarte. It is the feminine form of Athtar or Ashtar. Ashtoreth (Sidonian) and Ashtaroth (Hebrew) are variant spellings of the same name. Referred to in Jud 2:13; 10:6; 1 Sam 7:3-4, 12:10, 1 Kings 11:5, 33; and 2 Kings 23:13, Ashtoreth is historically well established as a war goddess. See further N. Wyatt, "Ashtoreth (Astarte)," *DDD* 109-114 and the bibliography provided on p. 114.

[4] Milcom occurs 3x in the MT as a deity of the Ammonites (1 Kings 11:5, 33; 2 Kings 23:13). In addition, Milcom is alluded to as "king" of the Ammonites in Amos 1:15 and Jer 49 (=30):3. See further E. Puech, "Milcom," *DDD*, 575-76 and the bibliography provided on p. 576.

[5] Chemosh, important in the Ebla religion, was regarded as the "subduer of his enemies" and the god of Moab (Num 21:29; Jer 48:46) and also the Ammonites (Judges 11:12, 24). Jeremiah 48:7 announces the exile of Chemosh with his priests and princes. See further H.-P. Müller, "Chemosh," *DDD*, 186-89 and the bibliography provided on p. 189.

and Molech the "detestable idol" of Ammon.[6] Then in summary 1 Kings 11:8 reports "Thus also he did for all his foreign wives, who burned incense and sacrificed to their gods."

The ill-advised "high places" Solomon built were likely of two varieties.[7] The first type were open-air hilltop places of cultic worship, equipped with altars, cultic stones, and asherim (manmade wooden cultic objects of worship). The second type were possibly constructed elevations like raised platforms or mounds, sometimes created within cities themselves.[8]

The precise identity and function of Solomon's foreign deities is a matter of debate—because of grammatical and etymological complexities, the limitations of archaeological evidence, and the reality that worship of these deities varied from place to place and from generation to generation. Though the existence and influence of these deities is certain, it remains true that indisputable reconstruction of them at the time of Solomon is impossible. At least this seems to be the scholarly consensus. For the purpose of this study, however, we may confidently observe that each of these deities was the object of cultic attention that rivaled Israel's worship of Yahweh. Priests and prophets served each deity. Each was honored with temples and shrines. They received sacrifice upon altars constructed for their religious worship. They were the recipients of prayer. Worshipers believed that ritual worship of these deities would coerce agricultural productivity and divine protection. Most importantly, these deities were believed to be defenders and protectors of the people with whom they lived in a treaty relationship. They were divine kings and queens of their respective peoples as Yahweh was the divine king of Israel. They thus directly competed for the faith of the covenant people Israel.

Faithful to his word, God therefore responded to Solomon's apostasy in judgment as he promised he would in 1 Kings 9:6-7. God raised up adversaries to Solomon (1 Kings 11:14, 23) and forewarned that Solomon's kingdom would be torn away from his sons. Thus Solomon's idolatry caused the divide within Israel's united monarchy—"because they have forsaken me, and have worshiped

---

[6] Molech is referred to 8x in the MT (Lev 18:21; 20:2-5; 1 Kings 11:7; 2 Kings 23:10; Jer 32:35) and 1x in the NT (Acts 7:43). G. C. Heider writes, "Molech emerges as a netherworld deity to whom children were offered by fire for some divinatory purpose" (585); "Most scholars, however, remain persuaded that actual sacrifice by fire was involved, especially given Num 31:23" (583). Controversy surrounds the question of how similar Canaanite worship of Molech was to that of Carthaginian, whose ritual probably included child sacrifice. See further G.C. Heider, "Molech," *DDD*, 581-85 and the bibliography provided on p. 585.

[7] The Hebrew word *bamah* "high place" occurs 100x in the OT.

[8] The most specific description of a high place in the OT is 1 Sam 9:1-10:16. However, the OT provides very little descriptive detail as to what the high places looked like or what they contained. The term high place could well be a general term referring to "small gate shrines, royal chapels dedicated to foreign gods, large public sanctuaries, and rustic local sanctuaries" (J. T. Whitney, "'Bamoth' in the Old Testament," *TynBul* 30 [1979]: 137-38). Whitney seems to represent the scholarly consensus when he says "bamoth were different things in different places at different times" (198). See further W. Boyd Barrick, "High Place," *ABD* 3.196-200 and the bibliography provided on p. 200.

Ashtoreth the goddess of the Sidonians, Chemosh the god of Moab, and Milcom the god of the sons of Ammon; and they have not walked in my ways, doing what is right in my sight and observing my statutes and my ordinances, as his father David did" (1 Kings 11:33).

Solomon's policies, therefore, caused the nation of Israel to plummet down yet another notch; further proving the tragic consequences of human kingship. Susceptible to foreign influences sanctioned by human kings, Israel's divide and collapse inevitably stemmed from her idolatrous unfaithfulness to God.

(c) *David*

Despite being guilty of adultery, murder, and an act of disobedience that resulted in the deaths of 70,000 men (2 Sam 24:15), David was innocent of idolatry. In his heart, he was a faithful worshiper of Yahweh. Because of this and because of the sincerity of his repentance, the Bible remembers David as a king after God's own heart. David was sensitive to the reality and severity of God in a way that Saul and Solomon were not. This sensitivity led him to repent in true fear of God and in full recognition of God's exclusive role as the one who would determine his fate. Indeed, with great insight, David may be the first biblical character on record to request the benefits of the new covenant when he prays, "*Create in me a clean heart, O God, and renew a steadfast spirit within me. Do not cast me from your presence, and do not take your Holy Spirit from me. Restore to me the joy of your salvation, and sustain me with a willing spirit*" (Ps 51:10-12).

III. THE DIVIDED MONARCHY

(a) *Israel's Downward Spiral toward Exile*

Unfortunately, Solomon's apostasy and not David's repentance set the point of departure for the vast majority of kings that followed in Israel and Judah's respective histories. Jeroboam, Israel's first king after the split with Judah, became infamous for his making of golden calves in Bethel and Dan, which he heralded as the gods that brought Israel up out of Egypt (1 Kings 12:28). He made high places, ordained illegitimate priests, and inaugurated alternative feasts (1 Kings 12:31-33). In so doing, he attempted to centralize power in Israel by replacing the nation's God and worship with alternative creations of his own.

Like Saul and Solomon, Jeroboam began his reign as God's appointed leader over Israel. 1 Kings attributes his failure to willful, disobedient idolatry performed with a corrupt heart unlike that of David:

> Thus says the Lord God of Israel, because I exalted you from among the people and made you leader over my people Israel, and tore the kingdom away from the house of David and gave it to you—yet you have not been like my servant David, who kept my commandments and who followed me with all his heart, to do only that which was right in my sight; you also have done more evil than all who were before you, and have gone

and made for yourself other gods and molten images to provoke me to anger, and have cast me behind your back. (1 Kings 14:7-9)

1 Kings explains that it was for this voluntary sin that God cut off the house of Jeroboam and, more importantly, threatened to take Israel into captivity: "He [God] will uproot Israel from this good land which he gave to their fathers, and will scatter them beyond the Euphrates River, because they have made their Asherim, provoking the Lord to anger" (1 Kings 14:15). Tragically, Jeroboam's personal apostasy came to represent the corporate apostasy of the entire nation he governed and the apostasy of the kings that would succeed him. His reign more than any other symbolized the low standards of government that led to Israel's collapse, and the tradition of idolatry that became the addiction of Israel's kings. All subsequent kings would be measured against his standard of evil by contrast to David's standard of faithfulness.[9] Jehu is a good example: "However, as for the sins of Jeroboam the son of Nebat, which he made Israel sin, from these Jehu did not depart, even the golden calves that were at Bethel and that were at Dan" (2 Kings 10:29). In succession, Israel's kings would fall prey to the influence of Jeroboam's idolatrous policies. It is beyond the scope of this book to recount the story of each king; however, it is important to observe that Baasha, Omri, Ahab, Ahaziah, Jehoram, Jehu,[10] Jehoahaz, Jeroboam II, Zechariah, Menahem, and Hoshea were all idolatrous Israelite kings who followed in the sins of Jeroboam. 1 King's assessment of Jeroboam's son Abijam is exemplary of each of these: "he walked in all the sins of his father which he had committed before him; and *his heart was not wholly devoted to the Lord his God, like the heart of his father David*" (1 Kings 15:3; cf. 11:4; 15:14). Implicit in this description is the biblical correlation between idolatry and the corruption of the heart.

Israel's history of flagrant idolatry culminates in 2 Kings 17 as the expressed reason for Israel's disintegration and exile.[11] Within the passage the paradigm of idolatry and the hardening of the heart is evident.

1) In the ninth year of Hoshea, the king of Assyria captured Samaria and carried Israel away into exile to Assyria. (17:6a)

2) Now this came about, because the sons of Israel had sinned against the Lord their God, who had brought them up from the land of Egypt from under the hand of Pharaoh, king of Egypt, *and they had feared other gods*. (17:7)

---

[9] 1 Kings 15:34; 16:2, 3, 7, 19, 26, 31; 21:22; 22:52; 2 Kings 3:3; 9:9; 10:31; 13:2, 6, 11; 14:24; 15:9, 18, 24; 17:22.

[10] Though Jehu eradicated many of the idols of his predecessors, he still allowed for the maintenance of the shrines in Bethel and Dan. He is thus remembered as following in the sins of Jeroboam (2 Kings 10:31).

[11] The explanation for Israel's forced exile into Assyria in 1 Chron 5:25-26 is the same: "But they acted treacherously against the God of their fathers, and played the harlot after the gods of the peoples of the land, whom God had destroyed before them. So the God of Israel stirred up the spirit of Pul, king of Assyria, even the spirit of Tilgath-pilneser king of Assyria, and he carried them away into exile."

3)	*And they served idols*, concerning which the Lord had said to them, 'You shall not do this thing. (17:12).
4)	Yet the Lord warned Israel and Judah, through all his prophets and every seer, saying, turn from your evil ways and keep my commandments, my statutes according to all the law which I commanded your fathers, and which I sent to you through my servants the prophets. (17:13)
5)	And they rejected his statutes and his covenant which he made with their fathers, and his warnings with which he warned them. (17:15a)
6)	*And they followed vanity and became vain*, and went after the nations which surrounded them, concerning which the Lord had commanded them not to do like them. (17:15b)
7)	And they forsook all the commandments of the Lord their God and made for themselves molten images, even two calves, and made an Asherah and worshiped all the host of heaven and served Baal. (17:16)
8)	So the Lord was very angry with Israel, and removed them from his sight; none was left except the tribe of Judah. (17:18)

Israel's defeat and exile was God's punishment for Israel's blatant and habitual violation of the covenant, its law, and its foundational presupposition—that Yahweh alone was always to be Israel's God and king.

One dimension of God's punishment at play here is the covenantal curse of hardening, thus ensuring the completion of his judgment of Israel in having them go into exile. The statements of 2 Kings 17:14-15, "they did not listen, but stiffened their necks like their fathers who did not believe in the Lord their God" and "they followed vanity and became vain," concur with the phenomenon of idolatry and hardening as explained in Psalms 115 and 135—"those who make them will become like them, everyone who trusts in them" (Ps 115:8; 135:18). Confirming this equation is the Hebrew root *hbl* (הבל) whose noun form *hebel* (הֶבֶל) is translated as "vanity" and whose verb form *hābal* (הָבַל) is translated "became vain" in 2 Kings 17:15. It is crucial to note that the noun form frequently refers to idols in Scriptural passages closely related in context to 2 Kings 17:15. In fact, *hebel* is a term that specifically means idol in many biblical references.[12] This means that both the context and the vocabulary of 2 Kings 17:15 infer that Israel sought after vanity/idols and became vain/like idols. The NIV thus translates, "They followed worthless idols and themselves became worthless." This phenomenon parallels Psalms 115 and 135 and affirms that hardening is a symptom and consequence of idolatry. It afflicts those who do not believe in God (2 Kings 17:14) but trust in idols (2 Kings 17:15; Pss 115:8; 135:18). As we shall

---

[12] Deut 32:21; 1 Kings 16:13, 26; Isa 57:13; Jer 2:5; 8:19; 10:8, 15; 14:22; 16:19; 51:18; Jonah 2:8; Ps 31:6.

(b) *The Moral Collapse of Judah*

Judah's national life outlasted Israel's by approximately 136 years. We may attribute Judah's longevity to Asa, Hezekiah, and Josiah, Judah's good kings whose religious reforms delayed exile. In the end, however, the Babylonian forces of Nebuchadnezzar took Judah captive and forced Judah into exile in 586(7) BC, much like Assyria had done to Israel in 722 BC. The Bible explains that Judah's fall from power occurred for the same reasons that Israel's had. Rehoboam, Solomon's son and the first king of Judah, was as unfaithful to Yahweh as Jeroboam was. 1 Kings 14:22-24:

> And Judah did evil in the sight of the Lord, and they provoked him to jealousy more than all that their fathers had done, with the sins that they committed. For they also built for themselves high places and sacred pillars and Asherim on every high hill and beneath every luxuriant tree. And there were also male cult prostitutes in the land. They did according to all the abominations of the nations which the Lord dispossessed before the sons of Israel.

The ominous statement, "they did according to all the abominations of the nations which the Lord dispossessed," anticipates that Judah too in time would be dispossessed because of her abominations. Though the cumulative sins of Judah's kings would account for her fall, the primary culprit was King Manasseh. His idolatrous policies made exile inevitable:

> Because Manasseh king of Judah has done these abominations, having done wickedly more than all the Amorites did who were before him, and has also made Judah sin with his idols; therefore thus says the Lord, the God of Israel, behold, I am bringing such calamity on Jerusalem and Judah, that whoever hears of it, *both his ears shall tingle*.[14] And I will stretch over Jerusalem the line of Samaria and the plummet of the house of Ahab, and I will wipe Jerusalem as one wipes a dish, wiping it and turning it upside down. And I will abandon the remnant of my inheritance and deliver them into the hand of their enemies, and they shall become as plunder and spoil to all their enemies. (2 Kings 21:11-14)

Particularly incriminating of Manasseh's reign is the statement that his abominations surpassed even the wickedness of the Amorites, one of the former victims of the conquest. The statement portends Judah's impending doom. The

---

[13] It is striking in fact that with *emataiōthēsan* Paul uses exactly the same form of the exact same term that is used in the LXX version of 2 Kings 17:15. Both contexts reference the sin of idolatry and describe the hardening of the heart.

[14] See footnote 1 and corresponding text.

descriptions of the reforms that took place under Asa, Hezekiah, and Josiah indicate just how bad things had gotten in Judah. 1 Kings 15:11-13 recounts that Asa put away the male cult prostitutes from Judah and removed the idols that his father Abijam had made. He also dethroned his mother Maacah as queen over Judah, because she had made an image of an Asherah. In recognition of these acts, 1 Kings 15:14 declares that "the heart of Asa was wholly devoted to the Lord all his days." As we would expect, Asa's healthy heart correlates with his intolerance for idolatry.[15]

Similarly, Hezekiah "removed the high places and broke down the sacred pillars and cut down the Asherah. He also broke in pieces the bronze serpent that Moses had made, for until those days the sons of Israel burned incense to it; and it was called Nehushtan" (2 Kings 18:4). His faithfulness to Yahweh set the stage for an exodus-like triumph for Judah.[16] Yahweh rewarded Hezekiah's faithfulness by defeating Sennacherib and killing 185,000 Assyrian soldiers. The event reiterates the basic message of Exodus—God is sovereign and will intervene to protect his covenant people and will curse those who curse his people. Most importantly, the event proved Yahweh's sovereignty over the pagan deities of Samaria (2 Kings 18:33-35; 19:12) and over Sennacherib's god Nisroch, whom Sennacherib was worshiping at the very time he was assassinated (2 Kings 19:37). As in the book of Exodus, God acts in answer to the prayers of his people for deliverance:

> Truly, O Lord, the kings of Assyria have devastated the nations and their lands and have cast their gods into the fire, for they were not gods but the work of men's hands, wood and stone. So they have destroyed them. And now, O Lord our God, I pray, deliver us from his hand that all the kingdoms of the earth may know that thou alone, O Lord, art God. (2 Kings 19:17-19)

Again, as in the case of Asa, it is important to note that Hezekiah is described as walking before God in truth and "with a whole heart" (2 Kings 20:3).

Finally, the covenantal reforms of Josiah indicate the depths of Judah's national apostasy. 2 Kings 23 recounts how Josiah ordered the burning of the vessels for Baal, the Asherah, and the host of heaven (23:4, 6). He did away with the idolatrous priests (23:5). He broke down the houses of the male cult prostitutes (23:7). He destroyed the high places (23:8). He prevented men from forcing their children to pass through the fires of Molech (23:10). He did away with horses "given to the sun" and burned "chariots of the sun" with fire (23:11). He destroyed the pagan altars built by his predecessors Ahaz and Manasseh (23:12). He destroyed the high places built by Solomon for Ashtoreth, Chemosh, and Milcom (23:13-14) and the pagan altar built by Jeroboam at Bethel (23:15). He slaughtered the priests of the high places (23:20) and removed from Judah all

---

[15] 1 Kings 15:14a implies, however, that Asa was not totally successful because the high places were not taken away.

[16] 2 Kings 19:24 explicitly parallels Hezekiah's triumph over Sennacherib with the exodus.

mediums, spiritists, teraphim, and idols to confirm the words of the law (23:24; cf. 2 Chron 34:33). For this reason 2 Kings identifies Josiah as Judah's greatest king: "and before *him there was no king like him who turned to the Lord with all his heart and with all his soul and with all his might,* according to all the law of Moses; nor did any like him arise after him" (23:25).

This is how 1-2 Kings evaluates the kings of Israel and Judah: not according to military, economic, or architectural achievements, but according to their faithfulness in following God completely according to Deut 6:4-9. The success or failure of each king is inextricably bound to their adherence to this governing principle.

Josiah's reforms, as comprehensive as they were, were not enough to prevent Yahweh's punishment of Judah for their long history of idolatry. As 2 Kings 23:26-27 reports, Yahweh remained faithful to his warnings of judgment pronounced in Deut 8:19-20; 29:17-29:

> However, the Lord did not turn from the fierceness of his great wrath with which his anger burned against Judah, because of all the provocations with which Manasseh had provoked him. And the Lord said, I will remove Judah also from my sight, as I have removed Israel. And I will cast off Jerusalem, this city which I have chosen, and the temple of which I said, my name shall be there.

Judah was therefore taken into exile by Babylon as God's punishment for her idolatry (2 Kings 24-25; 1 Chron 9:1; 2 Chron 7:17-22; 36:11-22, esp. vv. 14, 16).

Judah's history therefore further substantiates the correlation between idolatry and the hardening of the heart. Judah's good kings, Asa, Hezekiah, and Josiah, removed idolatry from Judah and were thus positively remembered for their "wholehearted" worship of God and successful reigns. In contrast, the generation of Judeans ruled by Manasseh turned a deaf ear to God's promise of permanent protection in the land, which would have been theirs if only they had obeyed all that God had commanded them: "But *they did not listen*, and Manasseh seduced them to do evil more than the nations whom the Lord destroyed before the sons of Israel" (2 Kings 21:9). Hence, Judah, like Israel, became like the nations destroyed by God in the conquest. Her preoccupation with the evil idolatries authorized by her earthly kings numbed her to the realities of God's judgment. Having ears to hear, she did not hear because she had become like her kings, like her pagan neighbors, like the idols that she worshiped. The consequence was punishment in exile—a forced exile that would verify God's faithfulness to his promise to base his blessing and curse upon faithful obedience from the heart.

In these terms 2 Chron 36:11-21 tells the story of Judah's final collapse under Zedekiah, her last king. The familiar pattern of covenantal apostasy (idolatry), hardening, and exile is clearly apparent.

> And he (Zedekiah: Judah's last king) did evil in the sight of the Lord his God; he did not humble himself before Jeremiah the prophet who spoke for the Lord. (36:12)

But *he stiffened his neck and hardened his heart* against turning to the Lord God of Israel. (36:13b)

Furthermore, all the officials of the priests and the people were very unfaithful *following all the abominations of the nations* and they defiled the house of the Lord which he had sanctified in Jerusalem. (36:14)

They continually mocked the messengers of God, despised his words and scoffed at his prophets, until the wrath of the Lord arose against his people, until there was no remedy. (36:16)

Therefore he brought up against them the king of the Chaldeans who slew their young men with the sword in the house of their sanctuary, and had no compassion on young man or virgin, old man or infirm; he gave them all into his hand. (36:17)

And all the articles of the house of God, great and small, and the treasures of the house of the Lord, and the treasures of the king and of his officers, he brought them all to Babylon. (36:18)

The Chronicler thus interprets the plight of Judah according to the theological association of idolatry, the hardening of the heart, and exile. Israel's exile was a consequence of retributive justice, which God's people actively brought upon themselves.

IV. CONCLUSION

The historical books of the OT that describe the events leading up to the exiles of Israel and Judah—Joshua, Judges, 1-2 Samuel, 1-2 Kings and 1-2 Chronicles—move in unison to substantiate the fulfillment of Moses' forewarnings about idolatry in Deuteronomy 8 and 29-30 in Israel's history. Accordingly, the idolatry of Israel and Judah caused the exiles and symbolic deaths of each nation. In choosing to serve idols, Israel and Judah chose death (Deut 30:15-20). Commensurate with each nation's demoralization and death was a growing numbness to the words of the prophets and a correlating acquiescence and gravitation to the nations and kings that surrounded them. Israel and Judah became less like their God and more and more like their pagan environment. Therefore, to protect his plan for humanity, God acted to punish his own covenant people by revealing to them the severity of what life entailed when lived in dependence upon earthly kings and in defiance of the Creator—anarchy (Judges), defeat in battle (Joshua, 1-2 Kings), moral decay and dysfunction (1-2 Kings), and total loss of the benefits of divine, covenantal rule within the kingdom of God—i.e., exile from the promised land (2 Kings, 2 Chronicles).

It is not an overstatement to say that the historical books voice a concerted polemic against idolatry. Direct statements like 1 Chron 16:26 "For all the gods of the peoples are idols, but the Lord made the heavens" (also 2 Chron 2:5b) are fleshed out by stories of Israel's national experience. The examples are many.

Illustrating the polemical thrust is the story of the devastation of Dagon within the temple of the Philistines in 1 Samuel 5. The event not only proves the superiority of Yahweh over Dagon and the Philistines, but it also displays the consequences that await idolaters and all who threaten the welfare of God's covenant people: Dagon is destroyed and the Philistines experience confusion (1 Sam 5:11) and a hardness of heart likened to that of Pharaoh and the Egyptians (1 Sam 6:6).

The story of David's defeat of Goliath has a similar thrust. David twice voices the theological question, "Who is this uncircumcised Philistine, that he should taunt the armies of the living God?" (1 Sam 17:26, 36). Against the background of biblical theology, this question fully explains how the boy was able to defeat the giant. Goliath sealed his own fate when he cursed David by the Philistine gods (1 Sam 17:43). The confrontation thus pits God against the false gods of the Philistines just as Exodus pitted God against the false gods of Egypt. The story's outcome therefore relates the Exodus message in a new context—Yahweh is still sovereign and pagan gods are still impotent. Hence God rewards David's faith with a miraculous triumph.

The great story of Elijah's contest with the pagan prophets of Baal in 1 Kings 17-18 has a similar polemical thrust. When Elijah cries out, "As the Lord, the God of Israel lives, before whom I stand, surely there shall be neither dew nor rain these years, except by my word" (17:1b), he voices a direct challenge to Baal, the Canaanite god of Jezebel thought to control nature, weather, and the fertility of the soil.[17] The event is comparable to the plagues that afflicted Egypt in Exodus. God intervenes to alter nature in order to prove his sovereignty and true existence in contrast to the powerless and lifeless pagan god Baal. God vindicates his prophet Elijah as he had Moses and proves the authority of his word. Thus on Mount Carmel all the cries, prayers, and ritual bleedings of the priests of Baal prove powerless, because their god is not real.

Elijah's prayer contains the fundamental theological message:

> O Lord, the God of Abraham, Isaac and Israel, today let it be known that you are God in Israel, and that I am your servant, and that I have done all these things at your word. Answer me, O Lord, answer me, that this people may know that you, O Lord, are God, and that you have turned their heart back again. (1 Kings 18:36-37)

God's consumption of the burnt offering and the wood, stones, dust and water dramatically proves the truthfulness of Elijah's prayer with the result that the people proclaim the very revelation God has disclosed: "The Lord, he is God; the Lord, he is God" (1 Kings 18:39; cf. v. 29).

In conclusion, the historical books of the OT substantiate the correlation of idolatry and the hardening of the heart—"they followed vanity and became vain."

---

[17] Baalism apparently pervaded the entire land of Canaan. As a god, Baal is spoken of 90x in the OT. The Ras Shamra texts (1350 BC) speak of Baal as sovereign, king, ruler of a kingdom, one who has power over the clouds, storms, and lightning, one who speaks with a thundering voice, the god of wind and weather, and the god who controls the fertility of the soil. See further W. Herrmann, "Baal," *DDD*, 132-39 and the bibliography provided there.

Idolatry-induced obstinacy is fueled by human pride (2 Chron 25:19; 26:16; 32:25). Such is the rationale for understanding the heroism of kings Asa, Hezekiah and Josiah by contrast to the tragic fates of Saul, Solomon, Rehoboam, Jeroboam and indeed corporate Israel and Judah. Israel fell because she did not adhere to the greatest commandment—she did not love the Lord her God with *all* her heart (Deut 6:4-9). Instead she betrayed God and served idols. And in doing so she hardened her heart. She thus could not understand the truth of the prophets, as Pharaoh had not been able to understand the severe truth of Moses. Hence God acted to punish Israel's apostasy and stubborn pride by humbling her in foreign exile.

But exile is not the end of Israel's story. As king Manasseh came to understand in 2 Chron 33:11-13, repentance from hardened idolatry would be possible especially in exile, where true Israel would rediscover that the Lord really is God (2 Chron 33:13).

Chapter 5

Listen but Don't Perceive: The Prophetic Commission to Harden Hearts

"Go and tell this people: 'Keep on listening, but do not perceive; keep on looking, but do not understand.' Render the hearts of this people insensitive, their ears dull, and their eyes dim, lest they see with their eyes, hear with their ears, understand with their hearts, and return and be healed." (Isa 6:9-10)

"Son of man, these men have set up their idols in their hearts, and have put right before their faces the stumbling block of their iniquity." (Ezek 14:3a)

In Isaiah 6:9-10 God instructs the prophet to stifle the eyes, ears, and hearts of his people, so that they will *not* repent and be saved. As in the case of Pharaoh in Exodus, there is no way around the conclusion that God in this context is actively hardening the human heart—an action that appears on the surface to contradict the doctrine of God's love and the whole enterprise of Christian evangelism. Why would God administer such a process when he "so loves the world"? And yet the NT writers consider Isa 6:9-10 as fully harmonious with the Christian gospel. Jesus and Paul both speak of it as being fulfilled in the lives of their contemporaries (Matt 13:14-15; Mark 4:12; Acts 28:26-27). Still more alarming than the Pharaoh episode is the fact that Isa 6:9-10 and associated passages like Jer 5:21 inflict the hardening curse upon God's covenant people themselves—the descendants of Abraham, who had received the covenant promises and the law, and who lived intimately in covenant with God in a relationship that the prophets liken to marriage. Why would he harden his own people and prevent them from repenting?

The instruction God gives Isaiah in Isa 6:9-10 is to be taken seriously. It is not a rhetorical device or expression of hyperbole used in a few exceptional cases. Its use elsewhere in the prophetic writings forces us to take the curse quite literally. In Isaiah 2:9, for example, God charges, "So the common man has been humbled, and the man of importance has been abased, *but do not forgive them.*" A similar tone surfaces in Isa 22:14, " 'Surely this iniquity *shall not be forgiven you* until you die,' says the Lord God of hosts," and in Isaiah 27:11b: "For they are not a people of discernment, therefore their maker will not have compassion on them. And their creator *will not be gracious to them.*" Similarly, Jeremiah describes God intentionally turning a deaf ear to his people: "As for you, *do not pray for this people*, and do not lift up a cry or prayer for them, and do not intercede with me; for I do not hear you" (Jer 7:16); *"Therefore do not pray for this people, nor lift up a cry or prayer for them; for I will not listen when they call to me because of their disaster"* (Jer 11:14).

It is my opinion that God's distancing of himself in these references is to be properly understood against the historical background of Israel's idolatrous sin. This chapter coheres with previous chapters of this book in explaining God's hardening the heart as correlative with the specific sin of idolatry. The paradigm we have seen develop in Psalms 115 and 135, Deuteronomy, Exodus, and the Historical Books surfaces in the writing prophets as an inherited theological axiom. They simply take for granted the phenomenon as a theological reality. As before in the OT, in the writing prophets God hardens to punish and discipline idolatrous violators of his covenant in order that they may discover what separation from their creator God entails. Hardening is not arbitrary or random, but is conditioned upon sin and has a theological purpose. After we have established this point, we shall step beyond the findings of previous chapters to probe a question not yet fully addressed in this book. Is forgiveness possible after God has inflicted the hardening curse? And what part does hardening play within the plan of God for his people—if indeed his ultimate desire is for their salvation and reconciliation? And eschatologically, what role does God play in the restoration process and what responsibility do the hardened have in their recovery, if any? Our answers to these questions will lay the foundation for the second half of the book, where we will explore the theme of idolatry and the hardening of the heart in the NT.

I. IDOLATRY AS THE STIMULUS FOR PROPHETIC JUDGMENT

The problem of idolatry is ever present in the writing prophets. Hosea, Isaiah, Jeremiah, Habakkuk, Daniel, and Ezekiel each contain major treatments on the subject, while Joel, Jonah, Amos, Micah, Nahum, and Zephaniah each admonish against it, while focusing on other issues. Examples are too many to quote.[1] The tone of the prophets' language is sometimes satirical (e.g., Jer 10), sometimes heatedly polemical (e.g., Isa 40:18-25), and sometimes very direct in the form of face to face taunts (e.g., Isa 41:21-29). The prophets portray the immorality of idolatry by portraying Israel as an adulteress, a metaphor that bespeaks the continuing covenantal relationship of Israel with God. For idolatry, the breaking of the foremost law of the Ten Commandments, is a breach of covenant that jeopardizes the continuation of the covenantal relationship between God and Israel, just as adultery jeopardizes the marriage covenant between husband and wife. Metaphorically, Israel plays the role of harlot in forsaking Yahweh to

---

[1] See, e.g., Hos 4:10-14; 8:4-7; 11:2; 13:1-2; Isa 2:7-11; 40:18-20; 41:21-24, 29; 44:6-20; 45:5-7, 16, 20-25; 46:5-9; 57:13; Jer 1:16; 2:27-28; 8:19; 10:1-5, 8-9, 14-16; Hab 2:18-20; Dan 3; Ezek 6, 8, 14, 16, 20.

engage in the worship of other deities.[2] Thus the prophets equate idolatry with covenantal apostasy and moral corruption.

The combined message of the writing prophets is that God is not indifferent to the idolatrous unfaithfulness of his people. He acts to punish his people for their sin. More than that, he acts to teach them through severe punishment that idols cannot bring the security that paganism promises. The worship of other deities will result in humiliating defeat at the hands of pagan enemies and exile from the promised land. The prophets unanimously agree that idolatry is the main crime that forces the Babylonian exile.[3] God wills that in exile, in separation from the blessings of the covenant, and without military deliverance from himself, Israel will discover the impotence and shame of idolatry.

God does not accept initial expressions of repentance from Israel because they are insincere, just as they had been for generations. Like their forefathers the Israelite contemporaries of the writing prophets were stubbornly committed to a worship divided between Yahweh and the deities of the land. God thus gave Israel over to the sacrilege of idolatry that they might discover the results of idolatry for themselves. The oracles of God reflect this mindset in the book of Jeremiah:

> Then you are to say to them, it is because your forefathers have forsaken me, declares the Lord, and have followed other gods and served them and bowed down to them; but me they have forsaken and have not kept my law. You too have done evil, even more than your forefathers; for behold, you are each one walking according to the stubbornness of his own evil heart, without listening to me. So I will hurl you out of this land into the land which you have not known, neither you nor your fathers; and there you will serve other gods day and night, for I shall grant you no favor. (Jer 16:11-13; cf. Ezek 20:39)

Exile would thus serve to *destroy the pride* of Israel and show the gods of the earth to be powerless and lifeless in order to awaken the nation from its hardened resistance to the rebukes of the prophets (Zeph 2:10-11). In exile the Judeans would come to loathe themselves for their past crimes at the same time that they came to recognize that God was indeed Lord (Jer 13:9-11; Ezek 6:11-14; 16:57-63; 20:39-43; 22:13-16; 36:24-31). Until Israel's worship was exclusively devoted to Yahweh, the hardening effects of exile would continue. Only when the refining work was complete would the remaining remnant be characterized by humility before God (e.g., Zeph 3:11-13). It may be that just as Pharaoh's hardening had

---

[2] The harlotry metaphor is the governing image of Hosea, but also appears in Isa 1:21; Jer 2:19-20; 3:1-9; 5:7; Ezek 6:9; 16:30, 38.

[3] Amos 5:26-27; Hosea 8:4-8; Isa 5:3-7, 13; 10:5-11; Jer 5:19; 9:13-16; 16:11-13; 19:13; 22:8-9; 25:3-9; 44:2-3; Ezek 5:11; 23:28-31; 36:18-19. On idolatry as the main cause of the exile, see John F. Kutsko, *Between Heaven and Earth: Divine Presence and Absence in the Book of Ezekiel*, Biblical and Judaic Studies from the University of California, San Diego 17; (Winona Lake, IN: Eisenbrauns, 2000), 25-53, who argues that in Ezekiel "idolatry is the quintessential cause of the Babylonian exile" (25).

prolonged the plagues of Egypt until all the deities of Egypt were discredited, so Israel's hardening prolonged the exile until the idols seducing her were likewise totally discredited. This would make possible Israel's true and authentic repentance, which alone could satisfy God's will, since God judges on the basis of the heart and not on the basis of external cultic observances. The prophets thus equate hypocrisy of worship with idolatry, even when external worship takes the form of God-sanctioned cultic rituals such as offerings, participation in festivals, prayer, sacrifice, and temple observance (See e.g., Isa 1:11-17; 29:13; 66:3-4; Jer 7:4-10; Amos 5:21-25; Hos 6:6).

Not until Israel was refined and fully purified by the fires of exile would she discard her idols and finally realize that Yahweh was indeed Lord, the only living God (e.g., Isa 30:22; 31:7; Ezek 11:18). Only then would God bring Israel back from captivity and reassert his rule over a reunited covenant people in the city of Zion. God's effort in this disciplining and healing process would demonstrate his love, his faithfulness, and his super-abounding mercy. The end result—the covenant would work because God sovereignly willed it and because God remained faithful to his covenantal promises given long ago to Abraham and to David.

II. IDOLATRY AND THE HARDENING OF THE HEART IN THE WRITING PROPHETS

The prophets warn that the human heart is vulnerable to contamination or even habitation by idols (Ezek 14:3-4, 7). While potentially the seat of wisdom, love, and understanding, the heart contaminated by idols falters into inevitable sensory depletion and human depravity before the holiness of God. The writing prophets therefore frequently associate stubbornness or hardness of heart with idolatry as the numerous prophetic passages cited below will testify. While a cause and effect relationship following the pattern of Psalms 115 and 135 is not overtly explained among the writing prophets, the phenomenon is indeed present, so that Jeremiah likens the idolaters of his generation to those of previous generations who "followed worthless idols and became worthless themselves" (Jer 2:5; NIV).[4] As we proceed, the reader is encouraged to observe carefully the interrelationship between idolatry and sensory depletion/hardening that exists in virtually all the passages that we cite. For here again we discover the biblical phenomenon that one becomes like that which one worships.

> And the Lord said, because they have forsaken my law which I set before them, and have not obeyed my voice nor walked according to it, *but have walked after the stubbornness of their heart and after the Baals,* as their fathers taught them, therefore thus says the Lord of hosts, the God of Israel, behold, I will feed them, this people, with wormwood and give them poisoned water to drink. And I will scatter them among the nations,

---

[4] NASB: "walked after emptiness and became empty." NEB: "pursuing worthless idols and becoming worthless like them."

whom neither they nor their fathers have known; and I will send the sword after them until I have annihilated them. (Jer 9:13-16)

For I solemnly warned your fathers in the day that I brought them up from the land of Egypt, even to this day, warning persistently, saying, listen to my voice. *Yet they did not obey or incline their ear, but walked, each one, in the stubbornness of his evil heart; therefore I brought on them all the words of this covenant, which I commanded them to do, but they did not.* Then the Lord said to me, A conspiracy has been found among the men of Judah and among the inhabitants of Jerusalem. They have turned back to the iniquities of their ancestors who refused to hear my words, *and they have gone after other gods to serve them*; the house of Israel and the house of Judah have broken my covenant which I made with their fathers. (Jer 11:7-10)

Then you are to say to them, *It is because your forefathers have forsaken me*, declares the Lord, *and have followed other gods and served them and bowed down to them; but me they have forsaken and have not kept my law.* You too have done evil, even more than your forefathers; for behold, *you are each one walking according to the stubbornness of his own evil heart, without listening to me.* So I will hurl you out of this land into the land which you have not known, neither you nor your fathers; and there you will serve other gods day and night, for I shall grant you no favor. (Jer 16:11-13; cf. Jer 23:17)

In each of these passages stubbornness or "firmness"[5] of heart correlates with the refusal to listen to God's counsel and avoid the covenantal sin of idolatry. This propensity likens Jeremiah's contemporaries to their forefathers who likewise turned a deaf ear toward God by committing idolatry and by neglecting God's law. It is important to note that Jeremiah shares with Deut 29:17-29 the association of idolatry with the hardening (or making stubborn) of the heart, covenantal apostasy, and punitive exile. Deuteronomy identifies exile and its by-products as part of the divine curse God forewarned he would inflict upon Israel as punishment for covenantal apostasy. The period of exile, therefore, represents an important phase of salvation history willed by divine decree. In this regard the prophets show remarkable continuity with the Pentateuch (see also Deut 32:16, 28; Jer 5:19-27).[6]

Ezekiel describes idolatry as virtually the setting up of idols within the human heart: *"Son of man, these men have set up their idols in their hearts, and have put right before their faces the stumbling block of their iniquity"* (Ezek 14:3; cf. CD 20 8b-10a; 1QH 12 14b-17a). Here again idolatry and sensory depletion exist in a cause and effect relationship. This rationale underlies, for example, "seeing" and "hearing" passages like Ezek 6:9 and 12:2:

---

[5] *shĕrirut*, HALOT 4.1658.
[6] On this interrelationship between Deuteronomy and Isaiah 1, see L. Rignell, "Isaiah Chapter 1," *ST* 11 (1957): 156-58; G. K. Beale, "Isaiah VI 9-13," 275-76.

> Then those of you who escape will remember me among the nations to which they will be carried captive, *how I have been hurt by their adulterous hearts which turned away from me, and by their eyes, which played the harlot after their idols*; and they will loathe themselves in their own sight for the evils which they have committed, for all their abominations. (Ezek 6:9)
>
> Son of man, you live in the midst of the rebellious house, who have eyes to see but do not see, ears to hear but do not hear; for they are a rebellious house. (Ezek 12:2)

Elsewhere the writing prophets frequently identify sensory depletion as characterizing idolaters whose harlotry against God has disabled them from perceiving God's true reality, making repentance impossible. Hosea exemplifies this perspective:

> Harlotry, wine, and new wine take away the understanding. My people consult their wooden idol, and their diviner's wand informs them; For a spirit of harlotry has led them astray, and they have played the harlot, departing from their God. (Hos 4:11-12; see also 4:13-19)
>
> Their deeds will not allow them to return to their God. For a spirit of harlotry is within them, and they do not know the Lord. (Hos 5:4)

With consistent regularity the prophets associate idolatry with this disabling condition that stifles repentance. Isaiah describes the condition as an illness (Isa 1:5-6; cf. 17:10-11), Jeremiah as sheer madness (Jer 50:38). Deeply concerned, Isaiah resorts to the prophetic taunt to awaken slumbering Judah from this comatose-like spiritual condition:

> They shall be turned back and be utterly put to shame, who trust in idols, who say to molten images, You are our gods. Hear, you deaf! And look, you blind, that you may see. Who is blind but my servant, or so deaf as my messenger whom I send? Who is so blind as he that is at peace with me, or so blind as the servant of the Lord? You have seen many things, but you do not observe them; Your ears are open, but none hears. (Isa 42:17-20)

Through satire, Isaiah further describes how God himself brings about this spiritual desensitization as his willed symptom for the self-inflicted disease of idolatry:

> *But the rest of it he makes into a god, his graven image.* He falls down before it and worships; he also prays to it and says, deliver me, for thou art my god. *They do not know, nor do they understand, for he has smeared over their eyes so that they cannot see and their hearts so that they cannot comprehend.* And no one recalls, nor is there knowledge or

understanding to say, I have burned half of it in the fire, and also have baked bread over its coals. I roast meat and eat it. Then I make the rest of it into an abomination, I fall down before a block of wood! He feeds on ashes; *a deceived heart has turned him aside.* And he cannot deliver himself, nor say, Is there not a lie in my right hand? (Isa 44:17-20)

Here the prophet mocks the entire process of idol worship by describing the absurdity of a human being worshiping a block of wood left over from the day's firewood. Isaiah explains the sheer stupidity of this act as evidence that the idolater is controlled by a deceived heart, which renders him both ignorant ("they cannot comprehend," "they do not know," "nor do they understand") and impotent ("he cannot deliver himself"). The context indicates that the malfunction is not arbitrary or unconditional; it is directly associated with the sin of idolaters, whom God "has smeared over their eyes so that they cannot see and their hearts so that they cannot comprehend." The phenomenon and God's control over it indicates that as creator, God continues to either sustain life or diminish it according to his will (Isa 44:21). This realization differentiates the divine wisdom accessible to authentic worshipers of Yahweh from the human foolishness that seeks security in idols. Jeremiah further explains:

All mankind is stupid, devoid of knowledge; Every goldsmith is put to shame by his idols, for his molten images are deceitful, and there is no breath in them. They are worthless, a work of mockery; In the time of their punishment they will perish. (Jer 51:15-18)

Therein the hardening curse discloses the essence of true wisdom—because he is creator, Yahweh is humankind's exclusive source of life and understanding (cf. Wis 15:14-17). It is not surprising therefore that Yahweh's refusal to listen to idolatrous Israel in the prophets is matched by Wisdom's refusal to answer fools (Prov 1:28), who habitually reject divine counsel (Prov 1:24-25).[7]

In this process, God seems intent on turning idolaters over to the very idols that have caused their dysfunction. God's giving Egypt over to idols in Isa 19:1-3 is exemplary:

The oracle concerning Egypt. Behold, the Lord is riding on a swift cloud, and is about to come to Egypt; *the idols of Egypt will tremble at his presence, and the heart of the Egyptians will melt within them.* So I will incite Egyptians against Egyptians; and they will each fight against his brother, and each against his neighbor, city against city, and kingdom against kingdom. Then the spirit of the Egyptians will be demoralized within them; and I will confound their strategy, so that they will resort to idols and ghosts of the dead, and to mediums and spiritists. (Isa 19:1-3)

---

[7] On the correlation between wisdom/foolishness and the hardening curse, see Rikk E. Watts, *Isaiah's New Exodus and Mark* (Tübingen: J.C.B. Mohr [Paul Siebeck] 1997), 190-194, 240-56.

Jeremiah 16:13 describes God giving Judah over to the same plight: "So I will hurl you out of this land into the land which you have not known, neither you nor your fathers; and there you will serve other gods day and night, for I shall grant you no favor." God's purpose behind this forced indulgence is an issue we will pursue later in this chapter.

This turning over extends not only to literal idolatry but also to other acts that essentially supplant God's lordship over the minds and hearts of his covenantal partner—specifically external religion:

> Then the Lord said, because this people draw near with their words and honor me with their lip service, but they remove their hearts far from me, and their reverence for me consists of tradition learned by rote, therefore behold, I will once again deal marvelously with this people, wondrously marvelous; and the wisdom of their wise men shall perish, and the discernment of their discerning men shall be concealed. (Isa 29:13-14)

Similarly, Isa 66:3-4 applies this principle to cultic sacrifices and the priestly ritual of burning incense:

> But he who kills an ox is like one who slays a man; he who sacrifices a lamb is like the one who breaks a dog's neck; he who offers a grain offering is like one who offers swine's blood; *he who burns incense is like the one who blesses an idol.* As they have chosen their own ways, and their soul delights in their abominations, so I will choose their punishments, and I will bring on them what they dread. Because I called, but no one answered; I spoke, but they did not listen. And they did evil in my sight, and chose that in which I did not delight.

Likening the burning of incense to the blessing of an idol (Isa 66:3), Isaiah condemns priests who practice mere ritual as participants in an act analogous to idolatry. For this reason, he describes these priests as suffering from the same listless despondency that plagues idolaters. Preoccupied with their cultic rites, the priests have forgotten the real purpose of their service and therefore are unable to hear and respond to God's word. This idolatry of external religiosity as represented in the above two passages opens the way for the broader application of the hardening paradigm, as we shall see it surface in the NT chapters that constitute the second half of this book.

(a) *The Example of Judah: Isaiah 6:9-10; Jeremiah 5:21*

We now turn to the specific issue of Isaiah's commission to harden the people of Judah. His vision in Isaiah 6 establishes the context for the prophet's commission to *"Go and tell this people; keep on listening, but do not perceive; keep on looking, but do not understand. Render the hearts of this people insensitive, their ears dull, and their eyes dim, lest they see with their eyes, hear with their ears, understand with their hearts, and return and be healed"* (Isa 6:9-10). The chapters preceding Isaiah 6 provide the basis for understanding this divine commission, so often wrongly understood to be a determinative pronouncement of unconditional hardening. With the loftiest of descriptions, Isaiah recounts his vision of the Lord, high and lifted up, with angels surrounding him singing of his glory and holiness. The vision is of God's transcendent holiness. It contrasts sharply with the human defilement of Isaiah himself, whose sin makes him unworthy to be in God's presence. Remarkably, Isaiah is shown mercy. By God's grace and God's grace alone, Isaiah is made clean through contact with a purifying coal from the altar of God's heavenly temple. The image is one of salvation, restoration, healing, and forgiveness.

In view of the grace shown Isaiah, it is puzzling that his commission appears so brutal and indiscriminate. Why would God desensitize *his people* through the prophet's preaching and thereby prevent their repentance?

Two important observations from Isaiah's commissioning enable us to understand God's action better. First, Isaiah does not describe the hardening condition as *permanent*. He specifically asks, "Lord, how long?" (Isa 6:11). And God replies:

Until cities are devastated and without inhabitant, houses are without people, and the land is utterly desolate, the Lord has removed men far away, and the forsaken places are many in the midst of the land. Yet there will be a tenth portion in it, and it will again be subject to burning, like a terebinth or an oak whose stump remains when it is felled. The holy seed is its stump. (Isa 6:11-13)

The duration of Judah's hardening, therefore, is to last until the exile is completed and her purification is absolute (cf. Jer 12:14-17). Isaiah's portrayal of the remnant as "a terebinth or an oak" (Isa 6:13b) satirizes Judah to be like a shrine of idolatry, which is what terebinths and oaks were in Isaiah's historical context (e.g., Isa 2:13; 44:14; Ezek 6:13; Hos 2:13; 4:13).[8]

Second, God's action is not *indiscriminate*. As the thesis of this book has led us to anticipate, the hardening stimulated by Isaiah's preaching does not come about randomly, it coheres with Israel's insincere, external abuse of worship and her outright idolatry. The hardening to be accomplished by Isaiah's preaching therefore correlates with the specific sins committed by the people of Judah and it accords fully with prophetic parallels in 2 Kings 17:15 and Amos 8:11-14.[9] *God is enforcing his willed punishment for idolatry when he commissions Isaiah to enforce the hardening curse.* The commission is thus hardly unconditional.[10]

---

[8] See the arguments of G. K. Beale referred to below.

[9] See further Craig A. Evans, *To See and Not Perceive; Isaiah 6:9-10 in Early Jewish and Christian Interpretation* (JSOTSup 64; Sheffield: Sheffield, 1989), 22.

[10] Rikk E. Watts, *(Isaiah's New Exodus and Mark*, 190-91), thus comments: "Within the present literary structure of the book, the mandate in Isaiah 6:9ff presupposes a rebellious, idolatrous, and culpably uncomprehending nation. . . . Isaiah's preaching, then, is merely to effect the verdict of the divine King by confirming his hearers in their persistent and willful ignorance and, thereby, ushering them towards the consequences of their rebellion."

Greg Beale has argued that "Isa vi 9-13 functions as a pronouncement of judgment on Israel's idolatry."[11] Beale develops four pieces of evidence to support this interpretation:

(1) Substantial verbal parallels exist between Isa 6:9-10 and Psalms 115 and 135.
(2) The threat of Isa 6:13, "Yet there will be a tenth; and it again will be burned like the terebinth and the oak," is a metaphor describing God's destruction of idols elsewhere in Isaiah, particularly Isa 1:29-31.[12]
(3) The same sensory malfunction language used in Isa 6:9-10 "appears in only four sections of Isaiah xlii-xlviii and, without exception, is applied to those who worship idols" (Isa 42:16-20; 43:8-12; 44:8-20; 47:5-11).[13]
(4) Other prophetic literature corroborates Isaiah in associating idolatry with sensory malfunction.[14]

This evidence has led Beale to conclude: "Because Israel worshipped idols, God pronounced a strict *lex talionis* judgment upon them: they were to be punished by means of their own sin by being made to resemble the lifeless character of their idols and to suffer the same destructive destiny."[15] To Beale's arguments we may simply add that the context of Isaiah 1-2, the foundation for understanding Isa 6:9-10 in its final compositional form, is a context that explicitly identifies idolatry as the covenant infraction that first evoked Isaiah's prophecy. Moreover, the historical context of king Ahaz's reign and particularly his installation of Assyrian cultic furnishings in the Temple (2 Kings 16:10-18) establishes a persuasive historical background for the prophet's condemnation of idolatry in chapters 1-6

---

[11] "Isaiah VI 9-13," 257. Beale has been followed by Rikk E. Watts (*Isaiah's New Exodus and Mark*, 191) and John Kutsko (*Between Heaven and Earth*, 137).

[12] Beale, ("Isaiah VI 9-13", 271), further explains that "the purpose of the similar portrayals of Israel being like burning, cultic trees in Isa i 29-31 and vi 13 is to link their judgment to idolatry in order to indicate emphatically that their punishment was due to their idol worship." Beale develops this point on pp. 260-272 of this article.

[13] Beale, "Isaiah VI 9-13," 272-73. Isaiah 47:5-11 does not appear as clear a parallel as the three previous references in Isaiah. However, we may add to Beale's list Isa 29:9-10: "Blind yourselves and be blind. They become drunk, but not with wine; they stagger, but not with strong drink. For the Lord has poured over you a spirit of deep sleep, he has shut your eyes, the prophets; and he has covered your heads, the seers," which occurs in a context of religious idolatry where the people have exchanged authentic worship of God for cultic tradition: "Because this people draw near with their words and honor me with their lip service, but they remove their hearts far from me, and their reverence for me consists of tradition learned by rote" (Isa 29:13; see also 29:14, which further describes Judah's divinely enforced sensory malfunction).

[14] Beale lists Jer 5:21; 7:24, 26; 11:8; 25:4; 35:15; 44:5; Ezek 12:2; 44:5 and their surrounding contexts ("Isaiah VI 9-13," 274).

[15] "Isaiah VI 9-13," 274.

and the prophecies that follow in chapters 7-8.[16] Ahaz's trust in Assyrian power together with his placement of a pagan altar within the Temple stands in direct contrast to Isaiah's exclusive trust in Yahweh. It is easy to see, therefore, that Isaiah would have judged the Judean king and his people as guilty of idolatry and worthy of divine judgment.

The following quotations from Isaiah 1-2 affirm that this was indeed Isaiah's perspective:

> What are your multiplied sacrifices to me? says the Lord. I have had enough of burnt offerings of rams, and the fat of fed cattle. And I take no pleasure in the blood of bulls, lambs, or goats. When you come to appear before me, who requires of you this trampling of my courts? *Bring your worthless offerings no longer, incense is an abomination to me.* (Isa 1:11-13a)

> *Their land has also been filled with idols; they worship the work of their hands, that which their fingers have made. So the common man has been humbled, and the man of importance has been abased, but do not forgive them.* (Isa 2:8-9)

> *In that day men will cast away to the moles and the bats their idols of silver and their idols of gold, which they made for themselves to worship*, in order to go into the caverns of the rocks and the clefts of the cliffs, before the terror of the Lord and the splendor of his majesty, when he arises to make the earth tremble. Stop regarding man, whose breath of life is in his nostrils; for why should he be esteemed? (Isa 2:20-22)

It therefore makes a lot of sense, especially in view of the association between idolatry and sensory depletion elsewhere in the OT, that Isaiah's commission to harden Judah in Isa 6:9-10 is directly related to the idolatry of Judah, which Isaiah rebukes explicitly in chapters 1-2.

Jeremiah 5:19-23, a passage that also describes Judah's sensory depletion in the context of her idolatry, further corroborates this interpretation:

> And it shall come about when they say, why has the Lord our God done all these things to us? Then you shall say to them, *as you have forsaken me and served foreign gods in your land, so you shall serve strangers in a land that is not yours. Declare this in the house of Jacob and proclaim it in Judah, saying, Hear this, O foolish and senseless people, who have eyes, but see not; who have ears, but hear not.* (Jer 5:19-21)

This oracle of Jeremiah, quoted by Jesus in Mark 8:18, shares with Isa 6:9-10 the correlation between the sin of idolatry and the punishments of exile and the

---

[16] Craig Evans, (*To See and Not Perceive*, 19-52), provides an excellent reconstruction of Isa 6:9-10 against the historical and contextual background of Isaiah as a whole.

hardening of the heart. Taken together the two passages make clear that sensory depletion stems from sin, specifically idolatry, and is thus not arbitrarily or unconditionally inflicted upon morally neutral people by God.

Isaiah's commission therefore has a purifying and chastening purpose. Hardening prevents further insincere repentance and external acts of ritual worship. It brings on an exile that will purify Judah of her idols and destroy human pride: "*So the common man will be humbled, and the man of importance abased, the eyes of the proud also will be abased*" (Isa 5:15). If Judah responded to chastisement, could she share Isaiah's experience and discover divine forgiveness and sanctification?

(b) *The Example of Nebuchadnezzar*

We illustrate the prospect of the hardened state leading to salvation with an example from the book of Daniel. Daniel's presentation of Nebuchadnezzar indicates that divinely enforced sensory malfunction serves at least in part to destroy human pride and bring about sincere repentance. Furthermore, it sets the stage for our next section by citing a biblical case of an individual who suffers divinely inflicted sensory malfunction before recovering to a healthy awareness of divine reality. Daniel does this in chapters 4-5, where God literally gives the Babylonian king Nebuchadnezzar over to animal-like behavior. Setting the stage for the bizarre account is Nebuchadnezzar's mandate that all within his kingdom worship the king's newly created sixty-cubit high golden image.

Nebuchadnezzar has a dream in which a colossal, magnificent tree is chopped down at the orders of an angelic decree. The stump of the magnificent tree remains in the ground with the angelic order that the stump share with the beasts in eating the grass of the earth. The angelic watcher further orders that the mind of the stump be changed from that of a man to that of a beast. At the dream's conclusion, the angel explains that the purpose of the command is "that the living may know the Most High is ruler over the realm of mankind, and bestows it on whom he wishes, and sets it over the lowliest of men" (4:17b).

The dream is followed by Daniel's interpretation. Daniel explains that the tree and its remaining stump both represent king Nebuchadnezzar himself. Nebuchadnezzar will be driven away from humankind and forced to dwell with the beasts of the field, where he will eat grass like cattle. Daniel then explains that Nebuchadnezzar's dehumanized condition will continue until he recognizes that "the Most High is ruler over the realm of mankind, and bestows it on whomever he wishes" (4:25).

The vision is then fulfilled literally. While boasting in the majesty of his kingdom, Nebuchadnezzar hears a voice from heaven saying, "King Nebuchadnezzar, to you it is declared: sovereignty has been removed from you, and you will be driven away from mankind, and your dwelling place will be with the beasts of the field" (4:32a). The event then happens. Nebuchadnezzar is indeed driven away from humanity and does literally sojourn with the beasts of the field, eating grass like cattle.

Hence, the story describes God's dehumanization of a king who had previously enforced idolatry and who had embodied confidence in the security of his own kingdom and sovereign power. Nebuchadnezzar embodies the phenomenon of idolatry and sensory malfunction. The idolatry consists of Nebuchadnezzar's symbolic tree being a false, insufficient substitute for the kingdom of God.

With this understanding, the story of Nebuchadnezzar's dehumanization is potentially a helpful comparison that could enable us to better understand the prophetic hearing and seeing formulas and the phenomenon of the hardening of the heart. God dehumanizes Nebuchadnezzar for the specific purpose of destroying the king's pride (4:37) thereby enabling him and all human beings (4:17) to recognize that it is God, and not human kings, who rules the earth. As Daniel 4 emphasizes, Nebuchadnezzar's reason returned to him when he recognized the sovereignty of the most high God and responded to it in humble confession and worship (4:25, 34, 36). The process of sensory malfunction thus works toward his becoming a worshiper of God. Indeed he ironically becomes a spokesman for divine truth: "Now I Nebuchadnezzar praise, exalt, and honor the king of heaven, for all his works are true and his ways just, and he is able to humble those who walk in pride" (4:37). In view of this scenario, God's hardening of Israel (Isa 6:8-10) may have the same benevolent purpose and seek the same end. As we shall see, there is significant evidence that this is indeed the case.[17]

III. THE SOLUTION TO IDOLATRY AND THE HARDENING OF THE HEART IN THE WRITING PROPHETS

(a) *Are Repentance and Salvation Possible for the Hardened of Heart?*

As we saw in Isa 6:11, the purpose of hardening and exile was not to permanently prevent repentance and salvation, but to delay it until God's purification of Judah was complete. Via the purifying fires of exile God would prove the futility of Judah's idols by contrast to his own vitality as living, sovereign Lord (Jer 16:19-21; Ezek 6:9-10). God would utterly destroy Judah's idols (Ezek 6:4-6; 22:15); then, when the purifying process ended, he would end the exile by regathering his people into the promised land. This "new exodus"[18] would coincide with the reversal of divine hardening. God would heal his people by restoring their sensory faculties and by turning their hearts of stone into hearts of flesh. In this newly created state, the exiles would "loathe" themselves in remembrance of their former sins (Ezek 20:42-44). Only by doing so they would exhibit authentic repentance.

But this would not happen immediately nor would it happen unconditionally or arbitrarily. It would happen when Judah fully understood the consequences of her idolatry and felt the shame of her adulterous apostasy. God's salvation, when it occurred, would coincide with Judah's expression of renewed exclusive faith in him, the only means of canceling Judah's covenant with death (Isa 28:16-18).

---

[17] Compare Psalm 73: "When my heart was embittered, and I was pierced within, then I was senseless and ignorant; I was like a beast before you. . . . But God is the strength of my heart and my portion forever" (73:21-22, 26b).

[18] E.g., Isa 10:26-27; 51:10-11; Jer 16:14-15; 29:11-14; 31:10-14; Ezek 20:42; 36:24; 37:14; 39:27; Amos 9:14-15.

Until this happened, God would continue to give Judah over to her idols in order that she might discover for herself the impotence of manmade deities: "Then the cities of Judah and the inhabitants of Jerusalem will go and cry to the gods to whom they burn incense, but they surely will not save them in the time of their disaster (Jer 11:12; also Isa 57:13; Jer 2:27-28; Ezek 20:39).

The potential for the salvation of hardened, exiled Judah was therefore a divine promise,[19] but it was a promise that was to be preceded by divine chastisement.[20] As Jeremiah remarks, "The anger of the Lord will not turn back until he has performed and carried out the purposes of his heart; in the last days you will clearly understand it" (Jer 23:20; 30:24). What Judah had to comprehend, but did not, was that covenantal apostasy would result in defeat, disillusionment, disgrace and death. Before the exile no form of repentance could have expressed Judah's comprehensive awareness of this truth, because she had not yet experienced it (cf. Jer 42:22). Her idols still existed and she was stilled enticed and influenced by them.

The exile, however, would break Judah's stubborn adherence to idols and a remnant at least would return to the Lord to rediscover the benefits of the covenant.

> Afterward the sons of Israel will return and seek the Lord their God and David their king; and they will come trembling to the Lord and to his goodness in the last days. (Hos 3:5)

> I will go away and return to my place until they acknowledge their guilt and seek my face; in their affliction they will earnestly seek me. (Hos 5:15)

> In those days and at that time, declares the Lord, the sons of Israel will come, both they and the sons of Judah as well; they will go along weeping as they go, and it will be the Lord their God they will seek. They will ask for the way to Zion, turning their faces in its direction; they will come that they may join themselves to the Lord in an everlasting covenant that will not be forgotten. (Jer 50:4-5; cf. Isa 57:15)

Coming to the Lord in true repentance, the remnant would voluntarily cast off their idols in disgust at their own sin (Isa 30:22; 31:7).

The determinative force, therefore, of Isaiah's commission in Isa 6:8-10 should be understood by the broader context of Isaiah and the writing prophets as a whole — by the frequent sincere prophetic calls for repentance (e.g., Isa 1:16-20; 30:15; 44:22; Jer 36:3-7; Ezek 14:6; 18:31-32; Joel 2:12-13) and, most of all, by God's stated benevolent will for his people, which envisions future reconciliation with him and the restoration of the benefits of the covenant:

---

[19] "For I will restore them to their own land which I gave to their fathers" (Jer 16:15b).

[20] "And I will first doubly repay their iniquity and their sin, because they have polluted my land; they have filled my inheritance with the carcasses of their detestable idols and with their abominations" (Jer 16:18).

> I will also turn my hand against you, and will smelt away your dross as with lye, and will remove all your alloy. Then I will restore your judges as at the beginning; after that you will be called the city of righteousness, a faithful city. (Isa 1:25-26)

> For I know the plans that I have for you, declares the Lord, plans for welfare and not for calamity to give you a future and a hope. Then you will call upon me and come and pray to me, and I will listen to you. And you will seek me and find me, *when you search for me with all your heart.* And I will be found by you, declares the Lord, and I will restore your fortunes and will gather you from all the nations and from all the places where I have driven you, declares the Lord, and I will bring you back to the place from where I sent you into exile. (Jer 29:11-14; also 24:7; 32:38-40)

In that time, as Jeremiah later writes in Jer 50:20, the remnant's authentic repentance would indeed result in her forgiveness and complete exoneration.

Judah's salvation, however, would require more than human repentance and a divine pronouncement of innocence; it would require divine healing of the malfunctions brought on by idolatry. It would involve a transformation made possible only by the re-creative, healing power of God. This is indeed the kind of salvation the prophets envisioned.

> I will heal their apostasy, I will love them freely, for my anger has turned away from them. (Hos 14:4)

> And on that day the deaf shall hear words of a book, and out of their gloom and darkness the eyes of the blind shall see. (Isa 29:18)

> And the light of the moon will be as the light of the sun, and the light of the sun will be seven times brighter, like the light of seven days, on the day the Lord binds up the fracture of his people and heals the bruise he has inflicted. (Isa 30:26)

> I have seen his ways, but I will heal him; I will lead him and restore comfort to him and to his mourners, creating the praise of the lips. Peace, peace to him who is far and to him who is near, says the Lord, and I will heal him. (Isa 57:18-19)

> For I will restore you to health and I will heal you of your wounds, declares the Lord, because they have called you an outcast, saying: It is Zion; no one cares for her. (Jer 30:17)

On that day your mouth will be opened to him who escaped, and you will speak and be dumb no longer. Thus you will be a sign to them, and they will know that I am the Lord. (Ezek 24:27; also Micah 4:6-7)[21]

(b) The New Covenant

The new covenant is God's solution to the problem of the hardened heart. While Jeremiah 31 and Ezekiel 36 stand as the classic expressions of the new covenant in the prophets, the prospect of God's future merciful intervention to re-create Judah is a hope found also in Hosea 2:16-23; Isa 42:6-9; 59:20-21; Jer 24:7; 32:40-42; 33:14-26; 50:5; Ezek 11:17-21; 16:60-63 and Ezekiel 37.

Ezekiel 36, however, speaks of this process the most clearly and comprehensively. The chapter unfolds in a pattern resembling ancient covenants though its marvelous content has no parallel outside of Scripture. The passage bears five covenant components that are critically important to our study and to any study that attempts to understand the biblical concept of salvation.

1) God recounts the history of Judah's unfaithfulness before judging her unworthy of forgiveness (36:17, 20).
2) God identifies Judah's idolatry as the cause for the exile (36:18-19).
3) God then announces that he will act among the nations to prove that Judah's wayward conduct is not an accurate reflection of his nature as Judah's covenant God. He will therefore vindicate the "holiness" of his name by proving his holiness among the nations (36:21-23).
4) God then explains that he will prove his holiness by performing five acts of salvation. *First*, he will re-gather the exiles (36:24; cf. 11:17). *Second*, he will cleanse Judah of the defilement of idolatry: "Then I will sprinkle clean water on you, and you will be clean; I will cleanse you from all of your filthiness and from all your idols" (36:25; cf. Hos 2:17; Isa 42:6-9; Ezek 11:18). *Third*, God will transform Judah's heart of stone into a heart of flesh: "Moreover, I will give you *a new heart* and put a new spirit within you; and I will remove the heart of stone from your flesh and give you a heart of flesh" (36:26; cf. Jer 24:7; 31:33; Ezek 11:19). *Fourth*, God will enable his people to keep the law: "I will put my spirit within you and cause you to walk in my statutes and you will be careful to observe my ordinances" (36:27; cf. Isa 59:21; Jer 31:33; Ezek 11:20). *Fifth*, he will restore Judah to the promised land where Israel's covenant with Yahweh will be fully reconciled: "You will live in the land that I gave to your forefathers; *so you will be my people, and I will be your God*" (36:28).
5) When this salvation was complete, God's transforming work would not only testify to the nations of his holiness and his sovereign power (36:36),

---

[21] This passage speaks about Ezekiel the prophet specifically; however, within the context of ch. 24 Ezekiel the person represents the exiles as a whole: "Thus Ezekiel will be a sign to you; according to all that he has done you will do; when it comes, then you will know that I am the Lord" (Ezek 24:24).

but it would also bring about the humility within his people that he desired. In their restored condition, God's people would remember their former sins and live in a state of perpetual repentance (36:31-32; also 16:60-63).

The vision of Ezekiel 36 thus anticipated that Judah, in her reconciled state with God, would eventually have "eyes to see" and "ears to hear" the original message of the prophets, who had beckoned her during her hardened state to put away her idols and return to the Lord. This formerly was impossible because of Judah's defiant attachment to idols. But with idols removed, pride destroyed, and the heart newly created, Judah would capably perceive the danger and shame of her former condition, so that she could truly worship God without impurity and with all of her heart in genuine repentance.[22]

IV. CONCLUSION

The phenomenon of God hardening Israel's heart because of her idolatry is a recurring theme throughout the OT writing prophets. God's word through Jeremiah that Israel "walked after emptiness and became empty" (Jer 2:5) is analogous to the "you become like that which you worship" understanding of Psalms 115 and 135, and 2 Kings 17:15. This understanding reflects the rationale behind God's commission of Isaiah to "*Go and tell this people: Keep on listening, but do not perceive; keep on looking, but do not understand. Render the hearts of this people insensitive, their ears dull, and their eyes dim, lest they see with their eyes, hear with their ears, understand with their hearts, and return and be healed*" (Isa 6:9-10). For Isaiah's commission comes directly on the heels of the prophet's harsh judgment of Judah's idolatry in chapters 1-2. The opening chapters establish the point of departure for the entire book of Isaiah in regard to the problem of Judah's sin and the need for her salvation. This means that Isaiah's commission is not arbitrary or unconditionally deterministic (as the curse in Jer 5:21 similarly stems from willful idolatry in Jer 5:19). Rather, in giving Judah over to hardening and sensory depletion, Yahweh allows Judah to experience for herself the truth of his exclusivity as the living Lord, the truth of the prophecy of Deuteronomy 28-30,

---

[22] John Kutsko has argued that Ezekiel reports this message as an adaptation of a well-known ancient Mesopotamian perception, which envisioned invading kings as exiling conquered peoples along with their manmade deities. According to the ancient understanding, once antagonism abated between the conquering king and the subjects he forced into exile, the king would call for the cleansing and repair of the exiles' native, manmade gods. Then the king would allow the exiles and their gods to return home (*Between Heaven and Earth*, 101-56, esp. pp. 122-47). Kutsko concludes: "Ezekiel describes Yahweh cleansing Israel from idolatry prior to its restoration, and he uses terminology that substitutes people for idols. Thus the rehabilitation of Israel both reveals the vanity of idols and reinforces the message that is basic to Ezekiel's theology, namely, that humans are the images of God, not the idols that humans create. Second, by substituting Yahweh as the actor in the pattern of exile, restoration, and return, Ezekiel affirms that Yahweh is sole king and creator, who controls even the affairs of nations" (p. 153).

and the real loss of life that results from separating oneself from one's creator through sin. This was God's willed curse for the covenant infraction of idolatry. To prevent the curse and allow for partial repentance to assuage divine wrath would compromise the covenant and God's own holiness as well the holiness he desires for his people.[23] Moreover, it would contradict his exclusive lordship. He alone has the power to create, sustain, and maintain life in a healthy state according to his intentions. The hardening phenomenon shows the idolater that not only do idols not improve life, but far worse, they actually take away life from those who worship them. This degeneration does not take place because of the idols' power, but because God wills that human beings discover and experience for themselves the truth that he alone is Lord. Such hardening shows the powerlessness of idols—they are unable to reverse Yahweh's curse. Those who disregard this truth inevitably experience hardening, disillusionment, and death.

The writing prophets further explain that God intended for exile and hardening to destroy Israel's pride in order to make her truly fit for repentance and reconciliation with him (e.g., Isa 2:7-11; Ezek 6:6-14). Although there was a time that God did not want his prophets to forgive Judah (e.g., Isa 2:9), a day was coming with divine forgiveness upon its wings (Isa 27:8-13; 45:22-25). *God therefore delayed forgiveness in order to perfect repentance.* Eventual divine forgiveness would occur only when God removed Judah's idols (Ezek 6:4-5; 20:37-44; Micah 5:12-15; Zeph 1:4-6; 2:11) and Judah voluntarily abandoned them (Ezek 11:17-21). Isaiah confirms:

> Although the Lord has given you bread of privation and water of oppression, he, your teacher will no longer hide himself, but your eyes will behold your teacher. And your ears will hear a word behind you, this is the way, walk in it, whenever you turn to the right or to the left. And you will defile your graven images, overlaid with silver, and your molten images plated with gold. You will scatter them as an impure thing; and say to them, be gone! (Isa 30:20-22).

Divine hardening and sensory malfunction thus prolonged the exile until the removal of idols and the dismantling of Judah's pride became comprehensive.[24]

Deliverance from the affliction of divine hardening is thus possible according to the biblical testimony. Indeed, salvation from such affliction is the hope that

---

[23] According to Craig Evans, *To See and Not Perceive*, 35, this was Isaiah's interpretation of the hardening phenomenon: "But Isaiah read these traditions quite differently. He found in them evidence of God's absolute holiness (cf. 6:3), a holiness which could not tolerate Israel's sin, nor be placated by self-serving reform. For Israel to be fully restored, God would have to purge the nation. His sovereignty not only permitted this, but required it."

[24] This divine purpose for the exile is attested in Baruch 3:30-33: "For I know that they will not obey me, for they are a stiff-necked people. *But in the land of their exile they will come to themselves, and they will know that I am the Lord their God.* I will give them a heart that obeys and ears that hear; and they will praise me in the land of their exile, and will remember my name, and will turn from their stubbornness and their wicked deeds; for they will remember the ways of their fathers, who sinned before the Lord."

climaxes the OT's testimony to the love and faithfulness of God.[25] God, the prophets promise, will heal the very ones he afflicted (e.g., Micah 4:6-7). As creator he is able to do so, for he maintains the power to re-create (Ezekiel 36), even resurrect (Ezekiel 37) his undeserving, unfaithful people in order to honor his promises to Abraham and David. This anticipated creative work envisions not a fresh start in the sense of replacing a faulty people with a new, different people, but rather the transformation of a faithless and rebellious people into a people of genuine faith and worship. Through his Holy Spirit, God will turn Israel's idolatrous heart of stone into a heart of flesh (Ezek 36:18-28). Ezekiel likens the process to a resurrection of dead bones (Ezekiel 37). Hosea, later quoted by Paul, speaks of it in terms of restoring an unfaithful wife, "I [God] will also have compassion on her who had not obtained compassion, and I will say to those who were not my people, 'You are my people!' and they will say, 'You are my God!'" (Hos 2:23; Rom 9:25-26).

This creative work involves God acting unilaterally within his covenant relationship with Israel to continue the covenant bond. Without God's intervention to recreate the hardened heart of Israel through the pouring forth of the Holy Spirit, Israel's rebirth would be impossible. Observance of the law, participation in temple ritual, appeals to Jewish heredity etc., were utterly useless in bringing about restoration with Yahweh, because Israel, in God's eyes, was dead in idolatrous, adulterous sin. In exile Israel was without land or temple. She had no eyes. She had no ears. She had no heart. As a nation, she was essentially dead.

Consistent with this truth is the qualification that Israel's rebirth would be voluntary and conditioned upon a faithful relationship with God governed by authentic repentance. God would continue to require faithfulness and obedience, just as he had originally decreed (e.g., Deut 30:15-20). Ezekiel is thus able to speak of Judah's potential collaboration with this sovereign intervention, even in the matter of recreating the heart:

> Therefore I will judge you, O house of Israel, each according to his conduct, declares the Lord God. Repent and turn away from all your transgressions, so that iniquity may not become a stumbling block to you. Cast away from you all your transgressions which you have committed, *and make yourselves a new heart and a new spirit*! For why will you die,

---

[25] My findings support Craig Evans' conclusion that "It would appear, then, that obduracy in the book of Isaiah is meant to be understood as a condition, brought on variously by arrogance, immorality, idolatry, injustice, and false prophecy, that renders God's people incapable of discerning God's will. This inability leads to judgment and calamity. However, it is also understood to be a condition that God brings about himself, as part of his judgment upon his wayward people. But Isaiah, if not the eighth-century prophet, certainly the canonical book, announces that after the judgment, there is restoration, in which perception returns (attended by righteousness, justice, and trust in God)," (*To See and Not Perceive*, 46). We would qualify that idolatry could be considered the all consuming provocation of obduracy as each of the other vices Evans mentions fall under the rubric of idolatry in the sense that each involves a substitute for God—pride, immoral appetites, selfish-ambition, and self-seeking prophecy.

O house of Israel? For I have no pleasure in the death of anyone who dies, declares the Lord God. Therefore, repent and live. (Ezek 18:30-32)

It may be important to note that the Hebrew word for "make" in Ezek 18:31 is ʿāśāh ("make or do") and not bārāh ("create as in Gen 1:1). Within this context "make yourselves a new heart" appears to be a dynamic expression for repentance and not a "new creation"—a phenomenon that would be without biblical analogy. Nevertheless, tension between God's sovereignty and human responsibility to receive salvation is a biblical phenomenon that philosophical paradigms cannot reconcile. Here it seems that biblical theology transcends philosophy to reveal metaphysical truth. The tension is an extension of the reality that God does indeed live in a real relationship with his people, who make real decisions having real consequences congruent with the divine will. Judah's responsibility in regard to salvation should be understood along the same lines as her culpability for choosing death/idols rather than life/fidelity to Yahweh (Deut 30:15-20). As Israel hardened herself in conjunction with divine hardening (Zech 7:11-14),[26] so too would it be her responsibility to collaborate relationally by responding to God's work of salvation in repentance and faith (Ezek 18:30-32).

This must be understood properly, however. The OT teaches that humanity contributes nothing to the healing and resurrection that God alone accomplishes in the vision of salvation offered by the new covenant. Only God can raise the dead. Only God can recreate the heart. God's Spirit, not man's, cleanses from idolatry, brings new life, and gives the ability to keep the law. At the same time, the biblical testimony is clear that God elects to give these gifts to those who grieve over their sinful condition, who grow to loathe the memories of their sin out of respect for God (Ezek; 16:62-63; 36:31). The beneficiaries of the new covenant are therefore not arbitrarily elected, but are chosen by God in reward for their sincere repentance and faith in God's ability to do the impossible (restore the hardened heart/raise the dead). This faith is therefore postcedent to Abraham's belief in God's ability to give life to Sarah's barren womb (Gen 18:11-19) and antecedent to Paul's pronouncement that salvation is based on the explicit belief that God raised Jesus from the dead (Rom 10:9-10). Those who resist repentance and faith, even after chastisement, will face God's judgment as a consequence.

> And I shall give them one heart, and shall put a new spirit within them. And I shall take the heart of stone out of their flesh and give them a heart of flesh, that they may walk in my statutes and keep my ordinances, and do them. Then they will be my people, and I shall be their God. *But as for those whose hearts go after their detestable things and abominations, I shall bring their conduct down on their heads,' declares the Lord God.* (Ezek 11:19-21)

---

[26] Also Zech 7:11-14: "But they refused to pay attention, and turned a stubborn shoulder and stopped their ears from hearing. And they made their hearts like flint so that they could not hear the law and the words which the Lord of hosts had sent by his spirit through the former prophets."

In light of this reality, the new covenant does not appear to override the human will. Rather, the new covenant offers, by God's grace and through faith, absolute salvation to human beings, who, after divine chastisement, forsake idols to worship God exclusively.

Thus, the stern behavior of God displayed in exile, hardening, and the delaying of forgiveness represents the strong, faithful love God has for his people. When we read the entirety of the prophets, we discover that God is just as much a God of love in the prophets as he is in the Gospel of John. Even in a context like Jeremiah 9, where God laments his people's sin and severely chastises them, the imperative is given, "but let him who boasts boast of this, that he understands and knows me, that I am the Lord who exercises lovingkindness, justice and righteousness on earth; for I delight in these things, declares the Lord" (Jer 9:24). The prophets were aware of God's abiding presence over his people during chastisement: "For I am with you. For I shall make a full end of all the nations where I have driven you, yet I shall not make a full end of you; but I shall correct you properly and by no means leave you unpunished" (Jer 46:28). And most importantly, the prophets looked beyond the period of God's refining discipline to foretell a coming day when God would consummate his covenant promises to Abraham as an expression of his love and faithfulness: "He will again have compassion on us; he will tread our iniquities under foot. Yes, you will cast all their sins into the depths of the sea. You will give truth to Jacob and unchanging love to Abraham, which you swore to our forefathers from the days of old" (Micah 7:19-20).

Knowledge of this theology is critical to a full understanding of the Bible and the interrelationship of the biblical covenants. The new covenant does not abrogate God's past promises. On the contrary, the new covenant reveals the continuity of God's plan for fallen humanity from beginning to end.

As we transition to the NT section of our study, it is instructive to observe that Ezekiel 36 presupposes the messianic promises of Ezek 34:22-23 just as Jeremiah 31 presupposes the messianic promises of Jer 30:9 and anticipates those of Jeremiah 33. Eschatological days of salvation spoken of in Jer 31:31-34 coincide with the fulfillment of the Davidic covenant (Jer 33:15, 21-22, 26) and the Abrahamic covenant (Jer 33:25-26). Moreover, the new covenant transformation that accomplishes the healing of the hardened accords fully with Isaiah's eschatological promises that anticipate end-time healing (e.g., Isa 9:2; 35:4-6; 53:5; 61:1-2), and which attribute a healing ministry to the Isaianic servant—most notably the healing of the blind (42:7; also 49:6). *The reversal of the idolater's curse is therefore a promise of the new covenant that is to be administered by the coming Anointed One. With this in view, the new covenant solution to the problem of the hardened heart anticipates Jesus' miraculous healing ministry as special agent of the new covenant* (Luke 22:20; 1 Cor 11:25).

Chapter 6

Seeds, Taxes, and Mammon: Jesus and the Kingship of God

*"And Jesus answered and said to him, it is
written, you shall worship the Lord your God
and serve him only."*
(Luke 4:8 par. Matt 4:10; Deut 6:13)

*"No one can serve two masters; for either he
will hate the one and love the other, or he will
hold to one and despise the other. You cannot
serve God and mammon."* (Matt 6:24)

Biblical concepts associating idolatry and the hardening of the heart carry over directly from the OT to the NT. Intervening history and literary tradition appears to have altered these concepts little if at all. The OT correlation between idolatry and hardening seems to have influenced, for example, the Second Temple expressions of Judaism that produced the following statements from the Dead Sea Scrolls:

> And thus (is) this judgment concerning anyone who rejects, the first and the last, who put abominations upon their heart and walk in the wantonness of their heart. They have no portion in the house of the Torah. (CD 20:8b-10a)[1]

> There is in their thoughts a root which produces poison and wormwood, with stubbornness of heart they inquire, they look for you among the idols, place in front of themselves the stumbling-block of their offences, they go to look for you in the mouth of prophets of deceit attracted by delusion. They speak to your people with stuttering lip and weird tongue to convert to folly all their deeds with tricks. (1QH 12 14b-17a[2]

The NT authors speak in terms that make plain the NT's endorsement of OT prohibitions against idolatry, though NT references are far less frequent. This

---

[1] *The Dead Sea Scrolls* (ed. James H. Charlesworth; Tübingen/Louisville: J.C.B. Mohr [Paul Siebeck]/Westminster John Knox Press, 1995), 2.35. Compare to the translation of Martinez: "for they have placed idols in their heart {and have placed} and have walked in the stubbornness of their heart. For them there shall be no part in the house of the law" (The Dead Sea Scrolls Translated *Translated* (2d ed.; Grand Rapids: Eerdmans, 1996), 46.
[2] Florentíno García Martinez, *The Dead Sea Scrolls Translated*, 334-35.

truth is foundational to the chapters that follow, where I will examine NT adaptations of the OT theme.

The few references to idolatry in the NT are important. While it is true that the word idolatry (*eidōlatria*) does not occur in the Gospels, Jesus' promotion of the Shema (Deut 6:4-9) as the single most important commandment affirms his positive commitment to preserving monotheism and thus by implication his intolerance for idolatry (Mark 12:29-33 par. Matt 22:37-40). Moreover, Jesus' citing of Isa 29:13 in Mark 7:6-8 (par. Matt 15:7-9) indicates his perspective that the Jews of his generation were guilty of replacing the commandments of God with manmade laws. Though Paul equates idolatry with covetousness as just one unethical act among many other "works of the flesh" (Col 3:5; Gal 5:19-21), he sets apart idolatry as the particular sin above all others that is responsible for human depravity (Rom 1:18-32). Although Paul teaches that idols are not real (1 Cor 8:4; 10:19), but "dumb" (1 Cor 12:2), he warns that idolatry amounts to the worship of demons (1 Cor 10:19-20; see also Rev 9:20). Despite the inherent powerlessness of idols, believers, according to Paul, should shun idols (1 Cor 10:14) as testimony to their conversion (1 Thess 1:9) and their covenantal commitment to God: "What agreement has the temple of God with idols? For we are the temple of the living God; as God said, 'I will live in them and move among them, and I will be their God and they shall be my people' " (2 Cor 6:16). Hence Paul by no means considered idolatry an antiquated danger of primitive times past.

That the first Christians wanted to avoid idolatry is apparent from their varied concerns about the potential dangers inherent in eating foods offered to idols, a problem particularly acute in Corinth where apparently most available meat was produced for idolatrous temple worship. In this context Paul allowed for eating meats offered to idols with the condition that such eating not infringe on the consciences of less mature believers, who still feared the idols they formerly worshiped before converting to Christianity (1 Corinthians 8). In a different context the author of Revelation called for the Asian churches in Pergamum and Thyatira to repent from eating foods sacrificed to idols because of association with sexual immorality (Rev 2:14, 20).

Elsewhere in the NT, Stephen in Acts identifies idolatry as the specific historical cause of the Babylonian exile (Acts 7:43). Paul recoils in disgust at the sight of the idols that adorn Athens (Acts 17:16). The Jerusalem Council recommends that Gentiles abstain "from things contaminated by idols" as one of four recommendations proposed to heal the Jew/Gentile controversy spawned by the apostolic mission (Acts 15:20, 29; 21:25). The author of 1 John simply warns "little children, beware of idols" (1 John 5:21). And Rev 9:20 ominously portrays the remainder of unregenerate humankind as those who "did not repent of the works of their hands, so as not to worship demons, and the idols of gold and of silver and of brass and of stone and of wood, which can neither see nor hear nor walk." Together these passages attest to the NT's faithfulness to the scriptural command that Israel abandon idols in order to maintain intimacy with her God.

Most important for the development of our theme, however, is the NT's classification of wealth, prestige, and external religion as potentially idolatrous attractions. Jesus' criticism of the Pharisees (Luke 16:14-15), Stephen's tirade against temple malpractice (Acts 7), and Paul's appraisal of Jewish legalism (Rom

2) exemplify the subtle forms that NT idolatry takes. In each case the idols denounced are not physical images, but potentially positive institutions that have been misappropriated into fixations wrongly thought to be essential for security and peace—i.e., devotees are rebuked for attributing ultimate worth to money, temple, and the law at the expense of authentic worship of God. As a consequence, hardening develops in each of these idolatry related contexts, just as the OT paradigm would lead us to expect. As in the OT, hardening in the NT plagues those who knowingly or unknowingly obstruct the covenantal work of God, only now this covenantal work is fulfilled by Jesus and proclaimed by the apostles. Idolatry consists of a foreclosed preference for alternative religious, financial, and traditional securities, which make Jesus' ministry superfluous or even a threat to established Jewish religion.

The NT concept of the heart (*kardia*) also corresponds very closely to that of the Hebrew scriptures. In continuity with ancient Hebrew thought, the NT appraises the heart as the "center of the inner life of man and the source or seat of all the forces and functions of soul and spirit."[3] The heart reveals one's true allegiance and standing before God and is the inner harbor of human depravity and moral corruption (Rom 1:21, 24). The NT assessment of the heart is therefore quite bleak. The heart is the seat of sorrow/pain,[4] grief,[5] pride,[6] inner evil,[7] adultery/lust,[8] betrayal,[9] unbelief,[10] and most importantly for our study, obstinacy and hardening.[11] If the new covenant brings about the creation of a new heart through faith; conversely, unbelief results in the hardening of the heart (Mark 16:14; Luke 24:38; Heb 3:12-19).

Positively, however, the heart has redemptive potential in the NT. If it is the place of corruption, it is also the place of cleansing sanctification,[12] where authentic faith resides.[13] As such the heart is the human receiver of the gospel and its saving, transforming power.[14] Once transformed by the re-creative inner work of God, the heart becomes the wellspring of joy,[15] peace,[16] contentment,[17] love,[18]

---

[3] Behm, *TDNT*, 611.

[4] John 14:1, 27; 16:6; Acts 21:13; 2 Cor 2:4.

[5] Rom 9:2.

[6] Luke 1:51.

[7] Matt 12:34; 15:18-20; Mark 7:18-23; Luke 6:45; 16:15; John 13:2; Acts 5:4; 2 Pet 2:14.

[8] Matt 5:28; Rom 1:24.

[9] Acts 7:39.

[10] Mark 16:14; John 12:40; Acts 28:24-27; Heb 3:12.

[11] Matt 13:15 par; Mark 3:5; 6:52; 8:17-21; 10:5; John 12:40; Acts 7:51; 28:27; Rom 2:5; Eph 4:18; Rev 18:7.

[12] Acts 15:9; 1 Thess 3:13; Hebr 10:22; James 4:8; 1 Peter 3:15.

[13] Rom 10:8-10; Eph 3:17.

[14] Matt 13:19; Luke 8:15; 24:32; Acts 2:37; 16:14; Gal 4:6; Eph 1:18; 2 Thess 3:5.

[15] Acts 2:26.

[16] Phil 4:7; Col 3:15.

[17] John 16:22.

[18] Mark 12:30 par. (Deut 6:5); 2 Cor 7:3; Phil 1:7; 1 Thess 2:17; 1 Peter 1:22.

honest transparency,[19] undivided singleness of purpose,[20] and the source of sincere forgiveness of others.[21] In this redeemed state, the heart becomes the dwelling place of wisdom and of the knowledge of God and Jesus Christ.[22] As promised in the new covenant, the heart becomes the domain of the Holy Spirit,[23] where the law is supernaturally emblazoned within the believer in Christ.[24] Paul therefore writes in Eph 3:14-19 that within the heart authentic faith discovers the love of Christ and the fullness of God:

> For this reason, I bow my knees before the Father, from whom every family in heaven and on earth derives its name, *that he would grant you, according to the riches of his glory, to be strengthened with power through his Spirit in the inner man; so that Christ may dwell in your hearts through faith*; and that you, being rooted and grounded in love, may be able to comprehend with all the saints what is the breadth and length and height and depth, and to know the love of Christ which surpasses knowledge, that you may be filled up to all the fullness of God.

Elsewhere in the NT the transformed heart emerges as the mark of the patient disciple who waits for Jesus' return in obedience to his pre-resurrection apocalyptic teaching. Luke passes on Jesus' instruction "Be on guard, *that your hearts may not be weighed down* with dissipation and drunkenness and the worries of life, and that day come on you suddenly like a trap" (Luke 21:34). The verb Luke adopts to express "weighted down" (*barynein*) is the verb the LXX uses in Exod 7:14 to translate the Hebrew verb *kbd*, which describes the hardened state of Pharaoh in Exod 7:14 (see chap 3). In view of the enormous influence of the Exodus story on first-century Judaism, it is plausible that Luke and Jesus explained the coming *parousia* against the background of the exodus. In doing so they identified raucous living and anxiety over earthly things as distractions which could disable the heart from recognizing the day of the Lord's visitation, just as disbelief and obstinate pride had disabled Pharaoh from recognizing the presence of the hand of the Lord in the plagues God inflicted upon Egypt. Elsewhere in Luke the probable correlation between Exod 8:19 and Luke 11:20 suggests that Jesus' miracles are also intended to be analogous to the miracles of Moses. They seem to have had the same hardening effect on Jesus' opponents, the Pharisees, that Moses' miracles had on Pharaoh. Both occur in polemical contexts, both display the presence of the Kingdom of God, and both enrage adversaries who seem predisposed toward rejecting the presence of God as manifested through the miraculous signs of his chosen prophets.

This information leads to the NT conviction that God determines the eternal plight of individuals according to the state of the individual's heart. God is able to

---

[19] 2 Cor 6:11.
[20] Acts 4:32; 11:23; Rom 6:17; Rev 17:17.
[21] Matt 18:35.
[22] 2 Cor 4:6; Col 2:2; 2 Peter 1:19.
[23] Rom 5:5; 2 Cor 1:22; 3:3.
[24] Rom 2:15; Heb 8:10; 10:16//Jer 31:33.

do this because he *knows* the true condition of the human heart,[25] whether sincere or fraudulent, and will judge accordingly. In other words, one's actual character, as attested by the heart,[26] is the object of God's final judgment (Acts 7:51). In the interim period, as Paul explains, God examines the heart to approve those whom he entrusts with the gospel: "For our exhortation does not come from error or impurity or by way of deceit; but just as we have been approved by God to be entrusted with the gospel, so we speak, not as pleasing men but God, who examines our hearts" (1 Thess 2:4). Thus, like the OT, the NT presents hardening as a phenomenon willed and enforced by God. Mark 4:10-12; John 12:37-40; and Romans 9:18 substantiate this. Yet, in agreement with the OT, the NT also judges humanity as culpable for the hardening process and fully responsible for the suffering that results from the hardened state (Matt 13:11-15; Heb 3:7-14; 4:7). The apparent contradiction between these sets of passages has led at least one scholar to attribute the former passages to the original intent of Jesus and Paul, and the latter passages to the "softening," editorial interpretations of the author of Matthew and the author of Hebrews.[27] But this distinction is more apparent than real. All indicators suggest that the NT concept of hardening furthers the OT teaching that divine enforcement and human responsibility are consistently interrelated.

I. IDOLATRY AND THE HARDENING OF THE HEART IN THE SYNOPTIC GOSPELS

In a 1996 article entitled "The Jesus-Tradition and Idolatry" Karl-Gustav Sandelin concluded that the theme of idolatry is "peripheral in the synoptic Gospels."[28] Sandelin reached this conclusion after evaluating five passages in the Synoptics that would seem to have the most potential for developing Jesus' teaching on idolatry: (1) Jesus' statement on taxes ("Render to Caesar the things that are Caesar's and to God the things that are God's"; Mark 12:13-17 and par.); (2) Jesus' apocalyptic prophecy on the 'abomination of desolation,' (Mark 13:14; Matt 24:15); (3) Jesus' pronouncement of the Shema (Deut 6:4-9) as the most important commandment (Mark 12:28-34); (4) the first line of the Lord's Prayer that requests the hallowing of God's name (Matt 6:9; Luke 11:2); and (5), Jesus' indictment of his generation as an "evil and adulterous generation" (Matt 12:39; 16:4), which,

---

[25] Luke 16:15; Acts 1:24; 15:8; Rom 8:27; 1 Thess 2:4; Heb 4:12; Rev 2:23.

[26] Matt 5:8; 6:21; Mark 7:6; Luke 6:45; Acts 2:46; Rom 2:29; 2 Cor 5:12; 6:11; Eph 6:5; Col 3:22; 1 Tim 1:5; 2 Tim 2:22; Heb 10:22; 1 Pet 3:4.

[27] Craig A. Evans, *To See and Not Perceive*, 165: "For Jesus and several New Testament writers Isa. 6.9-10, as an expression of the Old Testament obduracy idea, has played an important theological role. For them this text explained the mystery of the rejection of Jesus and the apostolic witness to him. The Gospel has been rejected, not simply because its hearers were dull, but because it was and continues to be God's will." . . . "The hermeneutic that underlies this text seems to be adopted more fully by Jesus and Paul than by other New Testament writers. ". . . "With the rest of the New Testament writers, however, the perspective has shifted."

[28] *NTS* 42.3 (July 1996): 420.

against the background of Hosea 3:1, puts Jesus' adversaries in "the same category as the idolaters of Hosea's times."[29]

In my judgment Sandelin's survey does not appreciate the full gravity of the five passages he addresses, nor does he take into consideration all of the passages that possibly relate to idolatry in the Gospels. It is my contention that the temptation narrative, the parable of the sower and the soils, and the cleansing of the temple each presumes an insidious form of idolatry, which Jesus viewed as corrupting his generation. In the discussion that follows I will further explore and develop the OT backgrounds of these and other idolatry related statements.

In the course of this study, we will also discover that in more than one instance Sandelin's observation is accurate that Jesus viewed his adversaries as being in the same category as the idolaters of prophetic times past—Jesus did indeed compare his generation to the idolatrous generation spoken of in Hos 3:1. When such is the case, it should not come as a surprise that the accompanying curses of hardening and sensory depletion are present just as they were in prophetic times past. It is with this awareness that we shall address the hearing formula, "He who has ears to hear, let him hear," the disciples' lack of understanding, and the blindness of the Pharisees. We will interact with these themes as we comment on the temptation narrative, the parable of the sower and the soils, Matt 11:4-6//Luke 7:22, Matt 11:25-27//Luke 10:21-22, and the cleansing of the temple. As we progress, our ultimate purpose will be to investigate and chart idolatry and the accompanying curse of the hardening of the heart/sensory depletion in the Synoptic Gospels.

(a) *The Temptation to Worship Satan (Matt 4:8-10//Luke 4:5-8)*

The Matthean and Lukan accounts of the temptation narrative are nearly identical except for the order in which the temptations are presented. Matthew places the temptation to worship Satan as the end of the three temptations, Luke places it second.

In each account the devil takes Jesus to a high mountain and shows him all the kingdoms of the world and their glory before tempting him with the proposition: "All these things will I give you, if you fall and worship me" (Matt 4:9//Luke 4:7). Immediately, Jesus recognizes the seriousness of this action. To worship Satan would directly violate the first of the Ten Commandments and entail a direct act of rebellion against the God of Israel, who demands exclusive worship from his people. Replacing God with Satan as recipient of worship would be idolatry. Should Jesus commit the act his mission would be ruined just as Israel's was when she and then Judah were exiled to Assyria and Babylon because of idolatrous unfaithfulness.

The setting, the nature of Jesus' exchange with Satan, and the OT background to Jesus' response all verify that a form of idolatry is in view within this temptation. First, "high places" were infamous in the OT as places of idolatrous worship (e.g., Lev 26:30; 2 Kings 12:3; Isa 65:7, 11). The fact that Satan has taken Jesus to a high place (Matt 4:8), where he can see all the kingdoms of the

---

[29] *NTS* 42.3, 419.

earth perhaps implies an idolatrous temptation. Second, it is noteworthy that Satan worship was equated with idolatry in the first-century world.[30] Third, Jesus' response "You shall worship the Lord your God, and serve him only" is a quotation of Deut 6:13, which in its original context was spoken in the midst of Moses' forewarning of what would happen should Israel betray God by committing idolatry:

> You shall fear only the Lord your God; and you shall worship him, and swear by his name. *You shall not follow other gods, any of the gods of the peoples who surround you,* for the Lord your God in the midst of you is a jealous God; otherwise the anger of the Lord your God will be kindled against you, and he will wipe you off the face of the earth. (Deut 6:13-15; see also Deut 12:30-31; ch. 13)

By resisting Satan's temptation, it is understood that Jesus did what Israel should have done long ago—he affirmed monotheism by aligning himself with Yahweh alone.

Historically, the first Christians would have seen Jesus' response as authoritative instruction on how to avoid the secular pressures of participating in pagan religion and perhaps also the emperor cult. Persuaded that historical pressure to compromise was what gave rise to the Gospel account, Gerd Theissen has boldly theorized that "the model for Satan in the Temptation story was the emperor Gaius Caligula,"[31] . . . "who was the only emperor to attempt to have himself worshiped in the temple in Jerusalem in place of the biblical God."[32] Though Theissen's elaborate theory has hardly been proven, especially as it relates to the origin of the temptation narratives, it does have the advantage of a possible parallel in the Book of Revelation, where the emperor Nero (Revelation 13) and the Roman Empire (Revelation 17) conform to the character of Satan—the dragon of Revelation 12. In any case, this temptation episode would have admonished Christians of successive generations that idolatry was unacceptable according to Jesus' life and teachings.

Jesus' refusal to worship Satan thus establishes a foundation for evaluating the theme of idolatry in the Gospels. Jesus emerges as faithful to monotheism and to Moses' instructions that aimed to protect exclusive worship of Yahweh.

(b) *The Parable of the Sower and the Soil:* Mark 4:3-20; Matt 13:3-23; Luke 8:4-15

The parable of the sower and the soils explains metaphorically the different experiences had by four kinds of people who receive the Gospel message. The emphasis of the parable is not upon the soils themselves per se, but upon the

---

[30] Birger Gerhardsson, *The Testing of God's Son (Matt 4:1-11 & Par)*, (CB, NT 2; Lund: 1966), 65.
[31] *The Gospels in Context* (Tr. Linda M. Maloney; Edinburgh: T & T Clark, 1992), 217.
[32] *The Gospels in Context*, 215.

resilience, or lack thereof, of the varying soils to outside harmful forces. The scope of the parable encompasses the entire lifecycle of the seed.

As the parable unfolds, the seed sown along the road is taken away by birds and eaten. The seed sown along the rocky soil grows up but withers in the scorching heat, because it has no depth of soil. The seed that falls among thorns is strangled by the competing thorns before it can produce a crop. Only the seed sown on the good soil has success. It grows up, increases, and yields "thirty, sixty, and a hundredfold."

Between the parable and Jesus' explanation of it, each Synoptic Gospel contains a statement by Jesus that is of great interest for our study, because it applies the sensory depletion curse of Isa 6:9 to the situation of Jesus' day. A form of the same statement is found in each. The three versions have in common the emphasis that the mystery of the kingdom of God has been granted only to the followers of Jesus. It is God's will that "outsiders" not "get it" either possessively or intuitively. For this reason, Jesus presents the kingdom of God through parables in order that the debilitating prophecy of Isa 6:9-10 may be effective in his context as it was in Isaiah's day: *"in order that seeing they may not see, and hearing they may not understand"* (Luke 8:10b). The Matthean version includes three verses not found in Mark or Luke (Matt 13:12, 16, 17) and a variant version of Isa 6:9-10, which describes the sensory depletion of the hardened as largely *self-inflicted*. According to the Matthean version, Israel's heart has become dull and they have closed their eyes willfully, leaving them blind, deaf and senseless.

In the context of Isaiah 6, we have explained this desensitizing phenomenon as the direct consequence of mere ritualistic externalized religion (Isa 1:11-15; 29:11-14) and rampant idolatry (Isa 2:6-22; see ch. 5 below). Isaiah's curse, we argued, as well as Jeremiah's (Jer 5:21), finds its rationale in Pss 115:8 and 135:18, which forewarn that idolaters will become like the idols they worship. Just as idols have eyes and ears but cannot really see and hear, so idolaters have eyes and ears but are blind and deaf to the reality of the one true God. Desensitization has occurred because worshipers have become like the inanimate idols that they worship.

In the context of the parable of the sower and the soils in Matthew, Mark, and Luke, Jesus' quotation of Isa 6:9-10 is faithful to the background of Isaiah 6, Jeremiah 5, and Psalms 115 and 135. The outsiders who receive the mystery of the kingdom of God in the form of parables are not involuntarily stupefied by Jesus' metaphors. To the contrary, they are fully responsible for their tragic condition. They are the soil along the road, the rocky soil, and the thorny soil. In contrast to the good soil which receives the gospel with "an honest and good heart, and holds it fast, and bears fruit with perseverance" (Luke 8:15), those who experience sensory depletion surrender the gospel because their faith proves inadequate. They succumb to satanic deception, they forfeit the gospel upon losing their faith in times of persecution, and they permit the worries, riches and pleasures of this life to distract them from exclusively following God (Matt 13:18-23; Mark 4:13-20; Luke 8:11-15). Abandonment of the gospel for something else is idolatrous when worship of God surrenders to satanic deception, fear of persecution, or anxieties related to wealth. Hence, the infliction of sensory depletion matches the crime of idolatry as explained and implemented in prophetic times past. Matthew 6:24 attests that Jesus was aware of such subtle forms of idolatry: "No one can serve two masters; for either he will hate the one and love the other, or he will hold to one and despise the other. You cannot serve God and Mammon" (*Mammon* = Aramaic for wealth).[33]

To understand Jesus' reformulation of Isa 6:9-10 in the parable of the sower and the soils, we must interpret it properly within the context of Jesus' overall ministry. Doing so, it becomes evident that the hardening affliction stems from rejection of Jesus' messianic ministry. In this context acceptance of Jesus reveals a heart that is properly aligned with God, while rejection of Jesus stems from another preferred allegiance.

Matthew specifically affirms that the blessing of the insiders rests exclusively in their believing acceptance of Jesus: "But blessed are your eyes, because they see; and your ears, because they hear. For truly I say to you, that many prophets and righteous men desired to see what you see, and did not see it; and to hear what you hear, and did not hear it" (Matt 13:16-17). Here what the prophets did not see and hear clearly refers to the gospel of the kingdom of God preached by Jesus the Messiah. Conversely, the curse inflicted upon the outsiders occurs entirely because of their rejection of Jesus and his gospel. Thus, just as Israel was hardened for replacing Yahweh with idols, so these "outsiders" are hardened for allowing the gospel to be replaced by external anxieties, fears, and worldly attractions.

Within this context the enigmatic 'hearing formula' "He who has ears to hear, let him hear" (Matt 13:9; Mark 4:9; Luke 8:8) has its origin.[34] The sense of the expression is that those who do *not* have ears to hear are those who have already rejected Jesus. Because of their preexisting recalcitrance, they refuse to take Jesus seriously. They have already rejected the divine origin of John the Baptist's call to repentance (Matt 11:15) and Jesus' preaching and healing ministry (Matt 13:16; cf. Mark 8:18). By contrast those who do have ears to hear express a willingness to set aside everything—family relations and wealth included—to follow Jesus wholeheartedly (Luke 14:35). The expression becomes eschatological in application in the parable of the tares among the wheat (Matt 13:43) and in the book of Revelation.[35] In the parable of the tares those with "ears to hear" are able to comprehend the future turmoil that awaits followers of Satan, i.e., those who practice and promote evil. Similarly, in Revelation those with "ears to hear" have an awareness of the salvation awaiting the followers of Jesus by contrast to the destruction awaiting the rest of the world. In each case, the "hearing formula" may be considered an idiomatic descriptor of persevering faith: "he who has ears to hear" is the semantic equivalent of "he who overcomes" in the life of Christian worship and discipleship. We arrive at this conclusion on the basis of the hearing

---

[33] Os Guinness insightfully observes "But what Jesus says in speaking of Mammon is that money is a power—and not in a vague sense, as in a "force" of words. Rather, money is a power in the sense that it is an active agent with decisive spiritual power and is never neutral. . . . As such, Mammon is a genuine rival to God" (*The Call*. W Publishing Group, 1998), 140.

[34] Also Matt 11:15; 13:9, 15, 16, 43; Mark 4:23; 7:16 (in some variants); 8:18; Luke 14:35.

[35] Rev 2:7, 11, 17, 29; 3:6, 13, 22; 13:9.

formula's presence in this parable, where Jesus calls for perseverance in the midst of temptations and distractions, and on the basis of its presence in Revelation where the hearing formula is closely associated with the risen Christ's call for perseverance—especially as it occurs in combination with the expression "he who overcomes" (e.g., Rev 2:7: "*He who has an ear, let him hear* what the Sprit says to the churches. *To him who overcomes*, I will grant to eat of the tree of life which is in the paradise of God").[36]

(c) *Matthew 11:4-6//Luke 7:22*

Within the Synoptics there are two other important sayings of Jesus that relate the seeing and hearing formula to blessing and cursing. The first is voiced in response to representatives of John the Baptist, who want to know if Jesus is the "expected one."

> And Jesus answered and said to them, go and report to John *what you hear and see*; the blind receive sight and the lame walk, the lepers are cleansed and the deaf hear, and the dead are raised up, and the poor have the gospel preached to them. And blessed is he who keeps from stumbling over me. Matt 11:4-6 (par. Luke 7:22)

Inherent to this statement is the awareness that one may discern Jesus' identity from his miracles. The raising of the dead, the healing of the blind, lame, deaf, dumb, and lepers, all within Jesus' ministry of preaching the gospel to the poor, fulfill prophetic expectations (e.g., Isa 35:5) that place Jesus on par with God, as 4Q521 seems to suggest (cf. John 5:19, 21, 36).[37] The impact of the admonition, "Blessed is he who keeps from stumbling over me," is that some cannot or will not make the connection between Jesus' works and his divine identity. It appears that those who have ears to hear are one and the same as those who keep from stumbling over Jesus (Matt 11:6//Luke 7:23).

(d) *Matthew 11:25-27//Luke 10:21-22*

The second related saying, also a parallel shared by Matthew and Luke, is Jesus' famous prayer that praises the Father for *hiding* "these things" from the wise and intelligent and revealing them to babes:

---

[36] See also Rev 2:11, 17, 26; 3:5, 12-13, 21-22; 21:7.

[37] "For the Lord will visit the Pious Ones and the Righteous will He call by name. Over the Meek will His Spirit hover, and the Faithful will he restore by His power. He shall glorify the Pious Ones on the Throne of the Eternal Kingdom. He shall release the captives, make the blind see, raise up the downtrodden. Forever will I cling [to Him . . .], and [I will trust] in His Piety" . . . "then He will heal the sick, resurrect the dead, and to the Meek announce glad tidings." Quotation of 4 Q521 taken from Robert Eisenman and Michael Wise, *The Dead Sea Scrolls Uncovered* (Rockport: Element, 1992), 21.

> I praise you, O Father, Lord of heaven and earth, that you have hidden these things from the wise and intelligent and have revealed them to babes. Yes, Father, for thus it was well-pleasing in your sight. All things have been handed over to me by my Father, and no one knows who the Son is except the Father, and who the Father is except the Son, and anyone to whom the Son wills to reveal him. (Luke 10:21-22, par. Matt 11:25-27)

In this prayer the "wise and intelligent" represent the outsiders of Mark 4:10-12 par., while "the babes" represent the insiders, who have received the mystery of the kingdom of God. Jesus thanks God that he has not alienated the underprivileged by making the kingdom of God an arduous achievement accessible only to the educated elite. To the contrary, consistent with Jesus' overall ministry to the poor, this prayer describes how the mystery of the kingdom of God has been hidden from the "wise and intelligent." It recalls God's warning to Judah in Isa 29:13-14 that he would remove the wisdom of her wise men, because they gave him lip service but not their hearts.

In the context of the Synoptic Gospels "the wise and the intelligent" are the "outsiders" who rejected Jesus' ministry out of preference for their traditional religion. They have "stumbled" over Jesus because they do not believe his signs or recognize that God has inaugurated the kingdom in him. Preferring their manmade traditions, laws, and prestigious standing before the people, they experience the hardening delusion associated with the form of idolatry spoken of in Isaiah 29. For this reason, they bear the brunt of Jesus' "woes" (Matt 6:1-18; 23:1-32). In contrast, the "insiders," the "babes," the "poor," are those who recognize their sin and subsequent need for Jesus and thus come to Jesus to discover the blessings of the kingdom of God—the blessings of the beatitudes (Matt 5:3-12//Luke 6:20-23), miraculous healings (Luke 7:22), and the revelation of Jesus' identity as the Son of God (Luke 10:21-22; Isa 9:6-7).

The "outsiders" alluded to in Mark 4:11 par. and the "wise and intelligent" referred to in Luke 10:21-22//Matt 11:25-27 refer to the religious leaders who spurned Jesus' ministry in favor of their pre-existing devotion to external religious tradition. Because tradition and legalism had disabled them from perceiving Jesus' messianic authority and the presence of God's saving power in his ministry, Jesus identified these particular scribes and Pharisees as *"blind guides"* (Matt 23:16, 24), *"blind fools and blind men"* (Matt 23:17, 19), and *"blind Pharisees"* (Matt 23:26).[38] Jesus obviously isn't speaking of physical eyesight in these passages. The Pharisees and scribes he describes as foolish and blind are such spiritually because they are oblivious to the truth of Jesus and his claims. Their commitment to tradition has caused them to suffer sensory depletion or spiritual blindness just as idols had disabled the audiences of Isa 6:9-10 and Jer 5:21, who centuries before had not responded to the severe warnings of the prophets. Unwilling to consider Jesus as a genuine representative of God, the "outsiders"

---

[38] Jesus, of course, did not classify all Pharisees and scribes in this way. His polemical remarks are directed specifically toward those who oppose him and act as stumbling blocks to his ministry.

were unable to comprehend his miracles. Jesus therefore grieved at their hardness of heart (Mark 3:5; also Matt 23:37).

Jesus' exchange with the Pharisees and scribes in Mark 7:1-23 illustrates this point well. Upon learning that Jesus' disciples had disregarded cleanliness laws, the Pharisees and scribes ask, "Why do your disciples not walk according to the tradition of the elders, but eat their bread with impure hands?"(Mark 7:5). To which Jesus responds:

> Rightly did Isaiah prophesy of you hypocrites, as it is written, this people honors me with their lips, but their heart is far away from me. But in vain do they worship me, teaching as doctrines the precepts of men. Neglecting the commandment of God, you hold to the tradition of men. He was also saying to them, you nicely set aside the commandment of God in order to keep your tradition. (Mark 7:6-9)

The prophecy Jesus refers to is Isa 29:13. It's context directly relates overemphasis of tradition to counterfeit worship and a resulting loss of spiritual discernment:

> Then the Lord said, 'because this people draw near with their words and honor me with their lip service, *but they remove their hearts far from me, and their reverence for me consists of tradition learned by rote*, therefore behold, I will once again deal marvelously with this people, wondrously marvelous; *and the wisdom of their wise men shall perish, and the discernment of their discerning men shall be concealed.* (Isa 29:13-14)

Jesus thus reapplies Isaiah's indictment of Judah to the unbelieving Pharisees and scribes of his own day, who for the sake of their tradition chose to reject the claims of his ministry. The "idolatry and the hardening of the heart" mechanism is clearly present. The replacement of God's commandments and "word" (Mark 7:8, 9, 13) with manmade tradition is idolatrous—God's word and ways are replaced by humanly constructed counterfeits. As we might expect on the basis of our study thus far, *a symptom of this guilty party is loss of understanding and corruption of the heart*—"This people honors me with their lips, but their *heart* is far from me" (Mark 7:6b//Isa 29:13; cf. Mark 7:20-23).

It is important to observe within Mark that even Jesus' disciples are not sheltered from the spiritual stupor characterizing their assailants. Jesus diagnoses the disciples' hardened condition as it relates particularly to their immature faith. Unable to comprehend that Jesus' miracles signal his messianic identity and authority, the disciples exhibit a flawed faith that exposes hardened hearts. Jesus' walking on the sea thus concludes: "He got into the boat with them, and the wind stopped; and they were greatly astonished, for they had not gained any insight from the incident of the loaves, *but their heart was hardened*" (Mark 6:51-52). Then, in Mark 7, Jesus quips at the disciples share in the Pharisees' propensity for overemphasizing external practice to the detriment of internal faith: "Are you so lacking in understanding also? Do you not understand that whatever goes into the man from outside cannot defile him; because it does not go into his heart, but into his stomach, and is eliminated?" (Mark 7:18-19, so 20-23). Then in Mark 8 the disciples' lack of mature faith provokes Jesus to contemplate their still hardened state:

> And Jesus, aware of this, said to them, why do you discuss the fact that you have no bread? *Do you not yet see or understand? Do you have a hardened heart? Having eyes, do you not see? And having ears, do you not hear? And do you not remember,* when I broke the five loaves for the five thousand, how many baskets full of broken pieces you picked up? They said to him, twelve. And when I broke the seven for the four thousand, how many large baskets full of broken pieces did you pick up? And they said to him, seven. And he was saying to them, *do you not yet understand?* (8:17-21)

Here Jesus applies to the disciples the same hardening affliction that he associates with the "outsiders" of Mark 4:10-12. Having eyes, ears, and hearts, the disciples lack the ability to see, hear, and understand the magnitude of Jesus' saving power.

Jesus' words in Mark 8:18—"Having eyes, do you not see? And having ears, do you not hear?—recall Jer 5:21 and Ezek 12:2. If the disciples do not take care they potentially will suffer the same ill effects of "the leaven of the Pharisees and the leaven of Herod," i.e., they also may suffer hardening, if they do not fully align themselves with Jesus (Mark 8:15). We emphasize once more, that like Isa 6:9-10 quoted in Mark 4:10-12, Jer 5:21 occurs in a context of explicit idolatry in the OT (see Jer 5:19), as does Ezek 12:2 (see Ezek 11:21). Therefore in projecting this warning from Jeremiah and Ezekiel upon the disciples in the context of Mark 8, the impression is given that some form of idolatry threatens to desensitize the disciples that is analogous to the hardening agents that disabled the ancient audiences of Jeremiah and Ezekiel and then later disabled the "outsiders" referred to by Jesus in Mark 4:10-12.

Within the context of the Synoptic Gospels, two subtle forms of idolatry act in this way as potential hardening agents in the lives of the disciples. The first is the anxiety and worry associated with the "thorny soil" of Mark 4:18-19 par. The disciples' capacity for worry about food comes into full view after Jesus' feeding of the five thousand (Mark 8:18; cf. Luke 21:34). The second idol is a preconceived concept of messiahship, which differs from the messianic calling of Jesus by God—that Jesus go the way of the cross (see Matt 16:13-16, 21-23 par. Mark 8:27-33). These two hardening agents, anxiety over material securities and human constructs of messiahship, combine to distract even the disciples, those closest to Jesus, from perceiving the magnitude of the Gospel and Jesus' true identity and purpose. The later hardening agent, inaccurate christological understanding, relates especially to the disciples' inability to comprehend the necessity of Jesus' suffering. Luke 24:25-26 may bear witness to this phenomenon: "*O foolish men and slow of heart to believe in all that the prophets have spoken*! Was it not necessary for the Christ to suffer these things and to enter into his glory?" (Luke 24:25-26). The disciples' failure to properly understanding Jesus further relates to the truth that Jesus' identity couldn't be fully understood apart from a post-resurrection encounter (see Luke 9:44-45a; 18:31-34).

That the disciples were susceptible to hardening should not be surprising when it is remembered that the twelve disciples represented the twelve tribes of Israel. Just as Israel had suffered hardening because of idolatry after entering into covenant with Yahweh, so the disciples experienced a loss of understanding even after becoming disciples of Jesus, when they allowed physical hunger and messianic preconceptions to distract them from loyally following Jesus as God's Son, the servant messiah.

(e) *The Cleansing of the Temple: Jesus' Application of Jeremiah 7*

Another Gospel passage that shows Jesus' reaction to idolatry is the episode of his cleansing of the temple, an event that has its conceptual background in Jeremiah. In Jer 7:1-11 the prophet Jeremiah rebukes his Judean audience for placing naïve confidence in the physical temple rather than in God.[39] Israel "trusts deceptive words"—saying, "This is the temple of the Lord, the temple of the Lord, the temple of the Lord" (Jer 7:4, 8). They believe wrongly that they may secure divine deliverance by external temple observation, even when the observers themselves are guilty of robbery, murder, adultery, false oaths and idolatry (Jer 7:9-10). Thus in the eyes of Jeremiah the temple had become a virtual amulet that falsely assured salvation even in the presence of sin. In this context the expression "den of robbers" describes the ironic habitation of the temple by sinners whose acts include these vices plus *the offering of sacrifices to Baal and the walking after other gods not previously known* (Jer 7:9). Jeremiah used the expression "den of robbers" to refer to the superstitious, hypocritical temple rituals that his contemporaries practiced.

Jeremiah's corrective message is that God cannot be manipulated by temple ritual: Israel must repent, practice ethical righteousness as constituted in the law, turn from other gods, and not trust in the temple as a security in and of itself (Jer 7:3-6). Unfortunately, Judah did not repent so that her idolatry (Jer 7:16-19, 30-31) and insincere sacrifices (Jer 7:21-22) resulted in her suffering debilitation by a stubborn, evil heart, which in turn destined her for severe punishment and exile (Jer 7:16-34; cf. Deut 32:15-35).

In the Gospels, Jesus quotes Jer 7:11 to reapply the message of Jeremiah 7 to the temple abuses of his day:

> And he entered the temple and began to cast out those who were buying and selling in the temple, and overturned the tables of the moneychangers and seats of those who were selling doves; and he would not permit anyone to carry goods through the temple. And he began to teach and say to them, is it not written, *my house shall be called a house of prayer for all the nations. But you have made it a robbers' den.* (Mark 11:15-17; par. Matt 21:12-13; Luke 19:45-46)

---

[39] Similarly, in 2 Macc 13:6-7 the noun form *hierosulia* is used in reference to Menelaus's "sacrilege" of defiling the temple altar. Here "sacrilege" takes the form of improper use of a holy institution.

The rebuke exposes the sullied commercialism of the temple and the selfish motives of its leaders. The temple's proper function as a place of prayer for all nations—*a place of authentic worship*—is being violated. Thus, in continuity with Jeremiah's polemic, Jesus applies the pejorative "den of robbers" to the temple money mongers of his day, who symbolize Judaism in the eyes of Gentile visitors to Jerusalem (Mark 11:17a).

By defiling the holy place of God, the Jerusalem establishment brought upon itself the curses of Jer 7:21-34, *which include by implication the loss of sensory perception, i.e., hardening* (Jer 7:19-34). Jesus' violent action accompanied by his strategic scriptural quotation signals the warning that God will soon act to punish and discipline his people in the manner envisioned by Jer 7:21-34. This would not be because the temple leaders were literal robbers, murderers, idolaters, etc., but because they were *replacing* sincere worship of God with profiteering. Hence, Jesus' opponents would be judged guilty of a crime equal in gravity to the vices specified in Jer 7:8-11—robbery, murder, adultery, false oaths, and idolatry.

This interpretation finds attestation elsewhere in Jesus' "Lament over Jerusalem" (Matt 23:38), which concludes with the statement "Behold, your house is being left to you desolate!" This statement, containing a possible allusion to 1 Kings 9:7 and a probable allusion to Jer 22:5, also recalls Jeremiah's prophecy of the temple's destruction—in this context as punishment for Israel's idolatry.[40] Jesus' reapplication of "your house is being left to you desolate" signals his judgment that his generation is perpetuating the sins characteristic of idolatrous generations past—a recurring theme in Jesus' ministry (cf. Luke 6:22-23; 11:47-48).

II. THE HARDENING OF THE HEART IN JOHN'S GOSPEL

In John's Gospel, Jesus turns water into wine, heals the blind, restores health to the crippled, and even raises the dead to reveal that he is the creative Word of God, who was with God in the beginning and who created everything that exists (John 1:2-3). The "signs" in John signal Jesus' divine equality with Yahweh (cf. Gen 1:1; John 5:19, 21, 36) and portray Jesus as the incarnation of God's *shekinah* glory (cf. Gen 1:1; John 1:14; 8:12). They also further explain the truth that one may be "born again" by uniting in faith with Jesus the creator, who continues to create, recreate, restore, and resurrect (John 1:13; 3:1-8). John explains that salvation is a complete rebirth, appropriated by active belief in Jesus (John 1:12; 3:16; 6:29, 47; 20:31), who is the way to eternal life (John 6:47).

It is upon this foundation that we are to understand the theme of hardening in John. Hardening is inevitable for those who reject Jesus—they remain of this "world" and are therefore separate from the kingdom of God, which John equates with "eternal life." The prologue foreshadows the world's misunderstanding of Jesus, his identity, and the meaning of his work:

> And the light shines in the darkness, and the darkness did not comprehend it. (John 1:5)

---

[40] See the contexts of 1 Kings 9:6-9 and Jer 22:5-9 (esp. v. 9).

> He was in the world, and the world was made through him, and the world did not know him. (John 1:10)

> He came to his own, and those who were his own did not receive him. (John 1:11)

John closely associates "misunderstanding" with the human inclination towards evil and the refusal to accept Jesus for who he really is—the incarnate Word of God, Son of God, Messiah, and Lamb of God who came to save the world by his sacrifice on the cross.[41] God will judge on the basis of faith: "He who believes in him is not judged; he who does not believe has been judged already, because he has not believed in the name of the only begotten Son of God" (John 3:18). Reprobation emerges as a condition that the world has brought upon itself by rejecting God in order to pursue darkness: "And this is judgment, that the light is come into the world, and men loved the darkness rather than the light; for their deeds were evil" (John 3:19).[42]

It follows therefore that in John both the disciples and the Pharisees fail to understand Jesus fully. The disciples, though they do not reject Jesus, cannot fully comprehend him as he really is (John 6:60) until the hour of his glory, when after the crucifixion, resurrection, and the "breathing" of the Holy Spirit, "doubting" Thomas proclaims, "My Lord and my God!" (John 20:28). With this statement the disciples approximate the cosmic scope of Jesus attested in the prologue. In 12:16 John explains, "These things his disciples did not understand at the first; but when Jesus was glorified, then they remembered that these things were written of him, and that they had done these things to him" (see also 2:18-22).

Jesus' opponents, by comparison, are indicted for disbelief and hostile rejection of Jesus' ministry. Acting upon their preexisting convictions, they thus exemplify those who choose darkness rather than light (John 3:19). Jesus therefore speaks of them as children of the devil (John 8:44). Hence, the "misunderstanding" motif in John is inextricably intertwined with John's emphasis on faith in Jesus as the exclusive way to eternal life. Jesus' opponents do not hear because of their disbelief and their action to impede Jesus' ministry. They criticize Jesus for performing miracles on the Sabbath (John 5:16), they conspire to kill him for calling God his father (John 5:18; 7:1; 10:31-39; 11:8, 53, 57), they "grumble" upon hearing Jesus call himself the bread of heaven (John 6:41-43), they flatly deny the truth of Jesus' witness (John 8:13), they claim Jesus has a demon (John 10:20), and they instill fear in potential disciples (John 9:22; 12:42-43; 19:38). For these reasons, the reader of John is fully aware that Jesus' opponents are culpable for their hardened state—they represent falsehood and evil to the same degree that Jesus represents "the way, the truth, and the life." For this reason they cannot hear Jesus as Pharaoh could not comprehend Moses. In a gospel where

---

[41] The "misunderstanding motif" of John is discernable in John 2:22; 6:52, 60; 7:35-36; 8:43, 47; 10:6; 12:16; 13:7; 16:3, 17-18; 20:9.
[42] See also 8:12; 12:35, 45.

"everyone who is of the truth *hears* my [Jesus'] voice" (John 18:37), it stands to reason that those who are *not* of the truth do *not* hear his voice.

With this foundational understanding of John in view, we now turn to John's most difficult hardening passage—the explicit quotations of Isa 6:10 and 53:1 in John 12:37-43:

> But though he had performed so many signs before them, yet they were not believing in him; that the word of Isaiah the prophet might be fulfilled, which he spoke, Lord, who has believed our report? And to whom has the arm of the Lord been revealed? For this cause they could not believe, for Isaiah said again, he has blinded their eyes, and he hardened their heart; lest they see with their eyes, and perceive with their heart, and be converted, and I heal them. These things Isaiah said, because he saw his glory, and he spoke of him. Nevertheless many even of the rulers believed in him, but because of the Pharisees they were not confessing him, lest they should be put out of the synagogue; for they loved the approval of men rather than the approval of God.

Like Jesus (Mark 4:10-12) and Paul (Acts 28:25-27), John applies the Isa 6:9-10 curse to contemporary opponents of the gospel. John clearly perceives the curse is willed and enforced by God. He identifies God blinding eyes and hardening hearts to prevent Jesus' opponents from converting and being healed.

John's preliminary quotation of Isa 53:1,"Lord, who has believed our report? And to whom has the arm of the Lord been revealed" (John 12:3), triggers memory of Isa 53:2-12, where the suffering servant is "despised and forsaken of men" (Isa 53:3), "smitten of God and afflicted" (Isa 53:4), "crushed for our iniquities" (Isa 53:5), oppressed and afflicted "like a lamb that is led to slaughter" (Isa 53:7). In the same chapter, Isaiah condemns his entire Israelite generation as guilty of sin: "All of us like sheep have gone astray, each of us has turned to his own way" (Isa 53:6). Israel's disobedience to God therefore makes her unable to believe Isaiah's message and comprehend the Lord's revelation (Isa 53:1). The failure to believe and understand is thus a tragic symptom and consequence of sin. Yet Isaiah 53 does not stop with a proclamation of unconditional reprobation. God in his sovereign will to save his disobedient people provides the servant as a vicarious sacrifice to forgive, heal, and justify his people:

> But he was pierced through for our transgressions, he was crushed for our iniquities; the chastening for our well-being fell upon him, and by his scourging we are healed. (Isa 53:5)

> But the Lord was pleased to crush him, putting him to grief; if he would render himself as a guilt offering. (Isa 53:10)

> As a result of the anguish of his soul, he will see it and be satisfied; by his knowledge the righteous one, my servant, will justify the many, as he will bear their iniquities. (Isa 53:11)

It is important to observe that John equates the healed and forgiven audience of Isaiah 53 with the hardened and blind audience of Isaiah 6. Thus John follows one quotation with the other to indicate that the two are interrelated in his scheme of biblical theology. Both chapters describe the predicament of sinful Israel, which is what John describes when he applies Isa 6:9-10 to Jesus' opponents and the Jewish multitudes that were visiting Jerusalem for Passover (John 12:12-13). In keeping with Isaiah 6 and 53, John portrays his audience as helplessly blind and hard, and as totally unable to perceive Jesus for who he was and is, in order that they might repent and be forgiven. The hardening phenomenon of John 12:37-40 thus accords with God's sovereign will that salvation become effective only through faith in the saving power of the Lamb's sacrifice, the offering of the suffering servant. It is for this reason that John 12 surrounds the Isaiah quotations with frequent allusions to the necessity of Jesus' death (John 12:7, 24, 32, 34).

Hence, like the disciples, the Jewish multitudes and the Pharisees were unable to perceive Jesus for who he really was, because the *hour* of Jesus' death and resurrection had not yet come. Even those that did believe did so inadequately, because "they loved the approval of men rather than the approval of God" (John 12:43; cf. Rom 2:29b). But in John's Gospel this verdict is not an eternal death sentence. Still to come would be the Holy Spirit who would convict the world of sin (John 16:8). Jesus would pray for the disciples "given him" (John 17:9) and for the future beneficiaries of the disciples' mission "that the world may believe that you have sent me" (John 17:21). Jesus, when lifted up, would draw all people to himself (John 12:32).

In conclusion, it is important to recognize that John is written from a post-resurrection perspective. Accordingly, salvation in John is a post-resurrection new birth made possible by Jesus' death and resurrection and the gift of the Holy Spirit. Therefore true "seeing" and "hearing" do not take place apart from an encounter with the risen Lord. Even Jesus' closest disciples suffer misunderstanding until the discovery of the empty tomb: "So the other disciple who had first come to the tomb entered then also, and *he saw and believed. For as yet they did not understand the Scripture, that he must rise again from the dead*" (John 20:8-9).

When Jesus says to Nicodemus, "unless one is born again, he cannot *see* the kingdom of God" (John 3:3), he is referring to the new birth that will be made possible by his death and resurrection and then implemented by the Holy Spirit. As Jesus says in John 3:5, "unless one is born of water and the Spirit, he cannot enter into the kingdom of God." Eternal life in the kingdom of God is therefore contingent upon being born again through the power of the Holy Spirit. But the Holy Spirit in John is not awarded arbitrarily. It is awarded to those who believe in the resurrected Christ. Thus in John 7:38 Jesus preaches, "*He who believes in me*, as the Scripture said, 'from his innermost being shall flow rivers of living water.'" In the next verse John explains, "But this he spoke of the Spirit, whom those who believed in him were to receive; for the Spirit was not yet given, because Jesus was not yet glorified" (John 7:39). Later in John's Gospel Jesus further explained that the Holy Spirit would enable his disciples to remember and understand his teachings after his departure (John 14:26; 16:13-15). In doing so the Spirit would guide them into all truth (John 16:13).

John's message therefore is that those who reject Jesus because of a preexisting love for this world (John 3:19) will inevitably experience hardening as the consequence of their separation from the "true light which, coming into the world, enlightens every man" (John 1:9). Hardening and the inability to see and hear is the plight of every person not transformed by the Holy Spirit into born again children of God. This was and would continue to be the inevitable plight of Jesus' opponents, because the transforming power of the Holy Spirit was to be given only to those who believe in Jesus the risen Christ and Son of God (John 20:30-31; cf. Rom 11:23).[43]

III. CONCLUSION

Though idolatry is not a constant theme in the Synoptic Gospels, Jesus' sensitivity to idolatry and his action to prevent the subtle forms it can take is clear. While Jesus was not a Zealot, neither was he a Hellenist. His charge to "render to Caesar the things that are Caesar's and to God the things that are God's" (Mark 12:17 par) allows payment of taxes to Rome, but forbids worship of Caesar. "Render to God the things that are God's" was hardly a statement of compromise in this context. It was a subtle rejection of the emperor cult and a stalwart promotion of monotheistic worship.

It is telling that the "abomination of desolation," Jesus' prediction of a future reenactment of Antiochus IV's idolatrous defilement of the temple, is one of the few visual signs that Jesus forecasts as precipitating the return of the Son of Man and the final judgment. The prophecy discloses that the Son of Man will renew and restore proper undefiled worship of God. This observation forewarns the eschatological gravity of idolatry--hardly a subject of peripheral importance.

In regard to the primary thesis of this book, the fact that the disciples suffer hardening and limited understanding of the kingdom of God prior to Jesus' resurrection (Luke 24) indicates that the softening of the heart and the opening of eyes is a salvific event accomplished only by encounter with the risen Lord. Jesus' words at the last supper, "this cup which is poured out for you is the *new covenant in my blood*" (Luke 22:20), expresses the hope that Jesus' death will activate the promises of the new covenant in the lives of those who benefit from his death. It may well be that the first petition of the Lord's Prayer, "hallowed be your name," calls for the inauguration of the same event as predicted in Ezek 36:20-38.[44] If this is the case, the Lord's Prayer calls for the removal of idols and the recreation of the heart. Jesus' petition would then instruct the disciples to pray for the actualization of God's saving work in fulfilling the promises of the new covenant in the lives of Jesus' followers. In other words, in praying the Lord's Prayer,

---

[43] It is important to emphasize, however, that not all priests and Jewish leaders fell into this category in the apostolic era. Acts 6:7 reports that "a great many of the priests were becoming obedient to the faith."

[44] Sandelin, "The Jesus Tradition and Idolatry," 418-19. See also G. Lohfink, *Jesus and Community* (trans John P. Galvin; Philadelphia/New York: Fortress/Paulist, 1984), 15-17; John P. Meier, *A Marginal Jew*. Vol 2. *Mentor, Message, and Miracles* (New York: Doubleday, 1994), 294-301.

Jesus' disciples would be praying for the complete success of Jesus' ministry as it pertained to the renewal of holy worship of God—an event that entailed the removal of idols and the recreation of hardened hearts (Ezek 36:22-29).

The "misunderstanding" motif in John is fully consonant with the "Messianic Sercret" phenomenon in the Synoptic Gospels. Like the Synoptics, John perceives that the world is incapable of comprehending the magnitude of Jesus apart from the event of Jesus' death and resurrection. Therefore the disciples and the unbelieving masses suffer varying forms of misunderstanding until the "hour of glory" occurs, which God has foreordained to be the solution to human sin. Like the Israelite generation of Isaiah 6, which experienced hardening as the God willed curse for idolatry, the Jewish audience of John 12 experiences hardening for having rejected Jesus, preferring darkness to light, and loving the approval of men rather than the approval of God. But just as the hardening curse of Isaiah 6 finds remedy in the suffering servant of Isaiah 53, so the cursed audience of John 12 potentially may find salvation in the sacrificial death of Jesus as described in John 19-20—"if they do not continue in their unbelief" (Rom 11:23). That God was making this salvation possible was evidence for John that God did indeed love the world.

Chapter 7

Paganism, the Temple, and the Hardening of the Heart in Acts

> *Being then the offspring of God, we ought not to think that the divine nature is like gold or silver or stone, an image formed by the art and thought of man.* (Acts 17:29)

We would expect Luke to emphasize Christianity's incompatibility with idolatry in telling the story of Christian origins to Gentiles like Theophilus. An invective against idolatry would seem especially appropriate in chronicling Christianity's collision with Hellenism in the Roman Empire of the first century in view of the fact that the Roman world was steeped in idolatry. Temples, altars, and images of pagan deities were not only common in places like Lystra, Ephesus, Corinth, and Athens, but, as Acts 19 recounts, pagan religion contributed heavily to the cultural makeup and civic pride of these ancient cities. Religion and culture being inextricably bound, Christianity, like Judaism, posed a threat to the cultures of the Roman provinces and their leading cities.

In the book of Acts, however, the apostles do not embark on a crusade to topple and destroy pagan idols as Muslim invaders eventually would. Their mission, rather, was to obey the instruction of the risen Jesus to be witnesses of the gospel "in Jerusalem, and in all Judea and Samaria, and even to the remotest part of the earth" (Acts 1:8). Acts quite literally displays the apostles' success in carrying out this mission as the gospel spreads from the infant Jewish church of Jerusalem in Acts 2 to the enthusiastic, multinational Christian community that receives Paul in Rome in Acts 28. Luke's emphasis along the way focuses on the now exalted status of Jesus as risen Lord, who enables the apostles' mission to succeed, despite severe opposition, through the power of the Holy Spirit.

Though the gospel's incompatibility with idolatry is not the primary emphasis of Acts, the apostles are hardly indifferent to the dangers posed by "things made by human hands" (Acts 7:41, 48; 17:24-25; 19:26). Luke's description of Paul's distress over the idols in Athens (Acts 17:16) would equally describe his reaction to publicly displayed idols in Ephesus, Corinth, and probably most of the cities that he visited. Though succinct, statements challenging idolatry in Acts are nonetheless highly descriptive of the apostles' message because they appear in summarizing, programmatic statements. Stephen's admonition to the Diaspora Jews and the Sanhedrin that "the Most High does not dwell in houses made by human hands" (Acts 7:48) is virtually repeated by Paul before the philosophers of Athens in his argument that "the God who made the world and all things in it, since he is Lord of heaven and earth, does not dwell in temples made with hands" (Acts 17:24). Thus, though a frontal assault on idolatry is not the content of the apostles' gospel in Acts, correction, if not rebuke, is a clearly articulated goal. Paul explains as much to his listeners in Lystra: "We are also men of the same nature as you, and preach the gospel to you in order that you should turn from these vain things to a living God" (Acts 14:15).

It is equally apparent that persecution of the apostles was in part a consequence of their public remarks about false deities. Stephen's reference to the temple as an idol resulted in his execution. And Paul's disrespect for manmade gods sparked the uprising in Ephesus where Demetrius the silversmith shouted: "you see and hear that not only in Ephesus, but in almost all of Asia, this Paul has persuaded and turned away a considerable number of people, saying that gods made with hands are no gods at all" (Acts 19:26). This statement, which coheres with the thrust of Paul's reasoning in Lystra (Acts 14:15) and Athens (Acts 17:24-27), suggests that corrective teaching about idolatry was a basic tenet of Paul's ministry in the Gentile world.

Paul's comments to the philosophers of the Areopagus (Acts 17:23-29) show that correction of idolatry was a necessary prelude to the proclamation of Jesus' resurrection and lordship (Acts 17:30-31):

> And Paul stood in the midst of the Areopagus and said, men of Athens, I observe that you are very religious in all respects. For while I was passing through and examining the objects of your worship, I also found an altar with this inscription, 'TO AN UNKNOWN GOD.' What therefore you worship in ignorance, this I proclaim to you. The God who made the world and all things in it, since he is Lord of heaven and earth, does not dwell in temples made with hands; neither is he served by human hands, as though he needed anything, since he himself gives to all life and breath and all things; and he made from one, every nation of mankind to live on all the face of the earth, having determined their appointed times, and the boundaries of their habitation, that they should seek God, if perhaps they might grope for him and find him, though he is not far from each one of us; for in him we live and move and exist, as even some of your own poets have said, for we also are His offspring. Being then the offspring of God, we ought not to think that the Divine Nature is like gold or silver or stone, an image formed by the art and thought of man.

Without significant alterations, Paul's words reiterate OT proclamations against idolatry (e.g., Lev 19:4; Deut 5:8; Isa 40:18-20; 44:9-20; 46:5-6; cf. Wisdom 13:5, 15). This correction was necessary in order to explain how religious homage to temples, statues, shrines, and sanctuaries in effect made God subservient to human design and ritual, a reality that Paul's audience had perhaps never considered before. The Christian message would never make sense until this worldview was corrected. Paul therefore explained the incongruity between the Athenians' idolatrous customs and their belief that they were the offspring of God (Acts 17:28). Idolatry, Paul reasoned, contradicts the doctrine of God's transcendence and his exclusive role in the creation of man, a doctrine without which the resurrection of Jesus would be impossible to comprehend.

Also programmatic within Acts is the sanctioning of fellowship between Jewish and Gentile Christians upon the condition that Gentiles "abstain from things contaminated by idols and from fornication and from what is strangled and from blood" (Acts 15:20). This verdict is repeated in Acts 15:29, where the official statement of the Jerusalem Council is "that you abstain from things sacrificed to idols," and again in Acts 21:25, where years later the Jerusalem church displays its continued dedication to the decree. That Paul fully accepted these injunctions and that they are repeated three times in Acts indicates the importance Luke placed upon them as he communicated the Christian gospel to his Gentile audience. The prohibitions should be interpreted as both ceremonial and moral. Attention to the ritual needs of other gods was obviously a breach of orthopraxy, but it was also an act of infidelity, as its frequent equation with adultery in the OT makes plain (see ch. 5). The eating of food offered to idols, though in and of itself harmless, as Paul explains in 1 Corinthians 8, could be hazardous to the gospel, if its practice was interpreted as a legitimization of pagan worship (so 1 Cor 10:14-22). If interpreted in this way, the act would be tantamount to active participation in pagan idolatry. Hence idolatry was a breach of covenant law ceremonially *and* morally.

Luke's development of the hardening theme in Acts is most evident in Stephen's speech to the Diaspora Jews and the Sanhedrin in Acts 7. Here Stephen indicts his Jewish opponents for sharing in the guilt of their ancestors, thereby echoing the words of Jesus who in his earthly life had identified his opponents as sharing in the guilt of their ancestors, specifically their ancestors who had killed the prophets (e.g., Luke 11:47-48). He accuses his assailants as guilty of infidelity toward God just like the ancient Hebrews, who had repudiated Moses by constructing the golden calf and who had turned "their hearts back to Egypt":

> And our fathers were unwilling to be obedient to him, but repudiated him and in their hearts turned back to Egypt, saying to Aaron, *make for us gods who will go before us; for this Moses who led us out of the land of Egypt — we do not know what happened to him. And at that time they made a calf and brought a sacrifice to the idol, and were rejoicing in the works of their hands.* But God turned away and delivered them up to serve the host of heaven; as it is written in the book of the prophets, it was not to me that you offered victims and sacrifices forty years in the wilderness, was it, O house of Israel? *You also took along the tabernacle of Moloch and the star of the god Rompha, the images which you made to worship them.* I also will remove you beyond Babylon. (Acts 7:39-43)

Exodus 32 provides the context for understanding the phrase "turning their hearts back to Egypt" (Acts 7:39). In the Exodus account the unfaithful among the Israelites "turned their hearts back to Egypt" not only by yearning for food and comfort but also by creating and worshiping the golden calf, an idol that bore a youthful resemblance to the many Egyptian deities visualized by the image of the bull (e.g., Apis, Buchis, Mnevis). With this allusion, Stephen implies that his opponents were again in effect committing an act of apostasy comparable to that formerly committed by the worshipers of the golden calf.

In response to Israel's idolatry, Stephen reports that God turned away from them and gave them over to the worship of the hosts of heaven (Acts 7:42). In other words, Israel's idolatry provoked God to release her so that she might discover for herself the consequences of idolatry. These consequences include exile in Babylon (Acts 7:43b) and the full discovery of what awaits those who place hope in "things made by human hands" (Acts 7:41). Stephen's words closely resemble Paul's appraisal of sin in Romans 1:24, 26, 28, where Paul explains that God gave ancient peoples over to the lusts of their hearts, because they had exchanged the glory of God for images created by man (Rom 1:24).[1] From Stephen's words we learn that hardening of the heart occurred in the wilderness when the Israelites committed idolatry, turned their hearts back to Egypt, and were then given over by God, indeed forced by God, to serve the hosts of heaven. In separation from God, Israel discovered in Babylon that idols are impotent. Not only would idols separate Israel from her covenant God and creator, but idols would bring about her corporate death in exile.

The disobedience and idolatry of the ancient Hebrews remains fresh on the listeners' minds when Stephen moments later lashes out "You men who are stiff-necked and uncircumcised in heart and ears are always resisting the Holy Spirit; you are doing just as your fathers did" (Acts 7:51). *Stephen makes the association between his opponents and their rebellious ancestors not only because they share in the guilt of persecuting God's spokespersons* (Acts 7:52-53), *but also because they share in the crime of idolatry.* To verify this charge Stephen twice quotes the persecuted prophets. The first quotation is the LXX version of Amos 5:25-27 (Acts 7:42b-43), where the prophet announces God's derision of Israel's habitual idolatry in the wilderness. The second is Stephen's quotation of Isa 66:1 (Acts 7:49-50), where God ridicules Israel's mistaken perception of the temple as the place of his dwelling. When Stephen says of his opponents "you are doing just as your fathers did" (7:51), he is charging them with flagrant idolatry—i.e., they like their ancestors are idolaters and they like their ancestors have a mistaken perception of the temple. Stephen reinforces this charge when he refers to the temple as a house "made by hands" (*cheiropoiētos*; Acts 7:48). This expression, used frequently in the LXX in reference to literal idols, finds its antecedent in the golden calf, which Stephen also refers to as "the works of their hands" (Acts 7:41). *The correlation between Acts 7:41 and 7:48 thus equates superstitious temple observance with idolatry.*

The sequence of thought in Stephen's argument seems to be that the adversaries of Moses, Amos, Isaiah, and now Stephen have had in common both a misplaced allegiance to things made with human hands and a corresponding repudiation of God's prophets. Afflicting each of these evil generations is idolatry and the hardening of the heart. Hence, Stephen's description of his opponents in Acts 7:51—"You men who are stiff-necked and uncircumcised in heart and ears"—correlates with his earlier assessment of the ancient Hebrews who repudiated Moses and "in their hearts turned back to Egypt" (Acts 7:39). The two terms Stephen uses to describe his adversaries, "uncircumcised in heart"

---

[1] So Joseph A. Fitzmyer (*The Acts of the Apostles*; AB 31; New York: Doubleday, 1998, 381): "As did Paul in Rom 1:24, 26, 28, Stephen is depicted indulging in protological thinking, as he speaks of God 'handing over' the people of Israel to idolatry."

(*aperitmētos kardiạ*) and "stiff-necked" (*sklērotrachēlos*), are both LXX terms used to describe idolaters.

"Uncircumcised in heart" occurs four times in the LXX. In Lev 26:36 it portrays a weakness of heart brought on by God as punishment for idolatry and disobedience to the law of the covenant (Lev 26:1, 30). Jeremiah 9:26 uses it to describe the condition of "the house of Israel" whose inhabitants, according to Jer 9:14, "have walked after the stubbornness of their heart and after the Baals, as their fathers taught them." Ezekiel adopts the expression in 44:7 and 44:9 to portray foreigners uncircumcised in heart and flesh who defiled the ancient house of Israel with abominations and idols (Ezek 44:6-10).

The term "stiff-necked" occurs eight times in the LXX. With the exceptions of Sirach 16:11 and Prov 29:1, each describes an obstinacy stemming from idolatry (Exod 33:3, 5; 34:9; Deut 9:6, 13; Baruch 2:30). In Exod 33:3-5 it relates to the Israelites' practice of wearing the "ornaments" that they had brought from Egypt: "For the Lord said to the children of Israel, you are a *stiff-necked people*; take heed lest I bring on you another plague, and destroy you: now *then put off your glorious apparel, and your ornaments*, and I will show you what I will do to you" (Exod 33:5 LXX). The term "ornament" in this context likely refers to Egyptian amulets—jewelry that was ubiquitous in ancient Egypt and believed to empower its wearer with power and protection. Similarly, the expression "stiff-necked" in Deut 9:6-13 relates to the stubbornness of the Israelites as particularly displayed in the idolatry of the golden calf episode: "They have gone aside quickly out of the way which I commanded them, and *have made themselves a molten image*. And the Lord spoke to me, saying, I have spoken to you once and again, saying, I have seen this people, and, behold, it is *a stiff-necked people*" (Deut 9:12b-13). With this same connotation, Baruch 2:30 portrays Israel as a "stiff-necked people" following a comprehensive assessment of Israel that describes how "every man followed the imagination of his own wicked heart, to serve strange gods, and to do evil in the sight of the Lord our God" (Baruch 1:21).

Writing in the style of the LXX and against the explicit conceptual background of the golden calf episode, Luke obviously is maintaining the idolatrous connotations of the expressions "uncircumcised in heart" and "stiff-necked" as he recounts Stephen's rebuke of his opponents in Acts 7. Stephen's depiction of his opponents as "uncircumcised in heart" and "stiff-necked" identifies his opponents as idolaters like those who had repudiated Moses on Mt. Sinai and like those who had rejected the prophets throughout the Scriptures.

The specific form of idolatry afflicting Stephen's opponents is misappropriation of the temple. As the ancient Hebrews had rejoiced "in the work of their hands," when they worshiped the golden calf (Acts 7:41), so their descendants, Stephen's opponents, rejoice in the exalted status of the temple—an institution sharply undermined by Stephen's corrective that "the Most High does not dwell in houses made by *human hands*" (Acts 7:48). That the temple was indeed a central issue of conflict between Stephen and his opponents is evident from the charges raised against him by his opponents who denounce him for incessantly speaking against the temple and the law (Acts 6:13). The expression "*made by human hands*" (*cheiropoiētos*) that refers to the temple in Acts 7:48 connotes idolatry not only in Acts 17:24 and 19:26 but also throughout the LXX, where "made with human hands" (*cheiropoiētos*) is virtually synonymous with "idol" (*eidōlon*; Lev 26:1, 30; Isa 2:18; 10:11; 16:12; 19:1; 21:9; 31:7; 46:6; Dan 5:4, 23; Judith 8:18; Wis 14:8). In Acts 7 the term bears the same connotation where it recalls the sacrilege of the golden calf and the Israelites' idolatrous worship of Moloch and Rompha (Acts 7:42-43).

Consistent with Luke's adaptation of the prophet like Moses prophecy (Acts 7:37; Deut 18:15-18), Moses serves as a precedent for Jesus, while the golden calf, cited by Luke as a recipient of sacrifices (Acts 7:41), serves as a precedent for the temple. Just as the Scriptures characterize the ancient Hebrews as stiff-necked and uncircumcised in heart because of their worship of Baal, their usage of ornaments, and their worship of the golden calf, so Stephen describes his opponents as stiff-necked and uncircumcised in heart, because they have strayed from God to serve a house made with human hands. The indictment, implying a comparison (typology?) between the golden calf and the temple, an obviously offensive comparison to the Sanhedrin, was the most likely offense that provoked the charge of blasphemy—the offense that resulted in Stephen's execution.

Conclusion

Acts narrates specific events and speeches that tell of the risen Christ's work through his apostles by the Holy Spirit. After empowering the Jerusalem church on the day of Pentecost, the risen Jesus enables the apostles to carry out his commission from Jerusalem to Rome. Within this progression of events in Acts, characters that threaten the progress of the gospel suffer death (Ananias and Sapphira, Herod Agrippa I), blindness (Elymas), and hardening (the persecutors of Stephen in ch. 7 and the opponents of Paul in 28:25-28). These tragic stories do not occur randomly or arbitrarily. Each offender suffers a tragic fate for threatening the progress of the gospel of God and the well being of the covenant people of God. God's ancient promise to Abraham, "I will bless those who bless you and curse those who curse you" (Gen 12:3) remains in effect for Luke in Acts as does the entire Abrahamic covenant (cf. Luke 1:71-75). Hardening thus afflicts those who challenge the progress of the gospel as it did Pharaoh, Sihon, and Og—ancient opponents of Israel who experienced hardening when they acted to prevent Israel's advance toward the promised land.

Luke briefly describes this phenomenon as occurring to Paul's opponents in Ephesus in Acts 19:9: "Some were becoming hardened and disobedient, speaking evil of the way before the multitude" and again at the conclusion of Acts where Paul applies the prophetic curse of Isa 6:9-10 to his opponents in Rome:

> The Holy Spirit rightly spoke through Isaiah the prophet to your fathers, saying, Go to this people and say, you will keep on hearing, but will not understand; and you will keep on seeing, but will not perceive; for the heart of this people has become dull, and with their ears they scarcely hear, and they have closed their eyes; lest they should see with their eyes, and hear with their ears, and understand with their heart and return and I should heal them. (Acts 28:25b-27)

Acts 28 does not tell us specifically why Paul projected the curse of Isa 6:9-10 upon his Jewish audience, except for the simple reason that they did not believe. It is understood, however, that Paul perceives that his Jewish opponents are guilty of a form of sin that is the equivalent to the covenant infractions performed by the evil, idolatrous generation that centuries before had opposed Isaiah. Within the scope of Luke-Acts, the reader naturally associates the group Paul admonishes in Rome with the groups rebuked by Jesus in Luke 11 and by Stephen in Acts 7. The Roman Jews who fail to believe are like the Sanhedrin, which opposed Stephen, and like the Judaizers, who constantly opposed Paul. Their blind devotion to traditional, ritualistic Judaism prevented them from considering the claims of the apostles. The opponents of Jesus, Stephen, and Paul have in common not only a determined refusal to believe the gospel, but also a common dedication to preventing its spread. Ritualistic Judaism based on ethnic origin and tradition was thus the obstacle, the idol, which closed their eyes, stopped their ears, and made their hearts obstinate. The affliction thus does not occur arbitrarily or randomly. In this context Luke clearly emphasizes the personal responsibility of the hardened for their condition by quoting the LXX version of Isa 6:10: "*And they have closed their eyes*; lest they should see with their eyes, and hear with their ears, and understand with their heart and return, and I should heal them" (Acts 28:27b). This rendering of the LXX, quoted by Luke, strengthens the basic argument of this book, which is that there is a direct correlation between human resistance to God's will and the phenomenon of divine hardening. The LXX rendering of Isa 6:9-10 transmitted by Luke accurately communicates the original message of Isaiah, which pronounced the curse of hardening upon an idolatrous people who combined traditional legalism (Isa 1:10-17) with foreign idols (Isa 2:5-11, 18, 20-22) before receiving the affliction of the hardening curse in Isa 6:9-10.

Conversely, Acts also depicts the divine alternative to the hardening curse in the event of salvation, which involves a transformation creating heightened sensory perception in the lives of those who do believe in the gospel and obey God's will. Paul's commission from the risen Lord is "*to open their eyes* so that they may turn from darkness to light and from the dominion of Satan to God, in order that they may receive forgiveness of sins and an inheritance among those who have been sanctified by faith" (Acts 26:18). It is evident within this statement that the "opening of eyes" occurs together with the turning "from darkness to light and from the dominion of Satan to God." Speaking in regard to Gentiles of the Roman Empire, this transfer of allegiance implies the act of turning from idols to the living God (cf. 1 Thess 1:9), which essentially is what the gospel required in every city Paul visited on his missionary journeys in Acts.

Implicit to this discussion is the saving possibility that those hardened can indeed be delivered from the hardening affliction. Blind eyes can regain sight. Deaf ears can hear again. Hardened hearts can be softened. In accord with the new covenant promises of Ezekiel 36 and the prayer of David in Ps 51:10, the Holy Spirit makes this transformation possible for those who obey the gospel (Acts 5:32). In accord with the theology of Paul (e.g., Rom 10:9-10), this work of the Holy Spirit, as Peter reports in Acts 15:8-9, occurs only in the lives of those who believe, whether they be Jew or Gentile: "And God, who knows the heart, bore witness to them, giving them the Holy Spirit, just as he also did to us; and he made no distinction between us and them, cleansing their hearts by faith."

Exemplifying this truth in Acts, of course, is the conversion of the apostle Paul himself, a formerly hardened, legalistic Pharisee, who had collaborated with the Sanhedrine to persecute the church—a living obstacle to the progress of the gospel (e.g. Acts 26:9-11). With Paul's adoption of the hardening curse in Acts 28 fresh on our minds, we now turn to Paul's explanation of the hardening curse in Romans.

Chapter 8

Exchanging God for an Image: Idolatry in Romans 1-2

For even though they knew God, they did not honor him as God or give thanks; but they became futile in their speculations, and their foolish heart was darkened. Professing to be wise, they became fools, and exchanged the glory of the incorruptible God for an image in the form of corruptible man and of birds and four-footed animals and crawling creatures. Therefore God gave them over in the lusts of their hearts to impurity, that their bodies might be dishonored among them. For they exchanged the truth of God for a lie, and worshiped and served the creature rather than the creator, who is blessed forever. Amen. (Rom 1:21-25)

The paradigm of idolatry and the hardening of the heart is fundamental to Paul's concept of original sin and divine wrath. Paul's placement of Rom 1:21-32 at the beginning of his most theologically comprehensive epistle demonstrates the importance of the concept for him. We begin this chapter by charting Paul's concept of idolatry and the hardening of the heart as Rom 1:21-25 clearly describes. We then attempt to demonstrate that this paradigm is foundational to Paul's assessment of the spiritual state of the audience of Romans 2. In the course of our study, we will develop our argument by addressing the following subjects in the order given:

1) The New Covenant Language of Paul
2) Idolatry and the Hardening of the Heart in Romans 1
3) The Significance of Paul's Word Choice in Romans 1
4) The Phenomenon of Idolatry and the Hardening of the Heart elsewhere in Paul's Epistles
5) Idolatry and the Hardening of the Heart in Romans 2
6) The Significance of Paul's Word Choice in Romans 2
7) Idolatry and the Robbing of Temples (Romans 2:21-24)

I. THE NEW COVENANT LANGUAGE OF PAUL

Central to our argument is the observation that in Romans Paul claims to be in the business of preaching "to bring about the obedience of faith among all the Gentiles, *for his name's sake*" (Rom 1:5). The emphasis on *his name's sake* in Rom 1:5 conveys Paul's call to participate in the working out of the new covenant as promised by Ezekiel:

> *And I will vindicate the holiness of my great name which has been profaned among the nations*, which you have profaned in their midst. . . . *I will cleanse you from all your filthiness and from all your idols. Moreover I will give you a new heart and put a new spirit within you; and I will remove the heart of stone from your flesh and give you a heart of flesh. And I will put my Spirit within you.* (Ezek 36:23, 25b-26a; cf. Ezek 11:19; Jer 31:31-34)

As a bondservant of Christ Jesus (Rom 1:1), Paul saw himself as a participant in the new covenant ministry of Jesus (Matt 26:26-29; Mark 14:24-25; Luke 22:14-20). His faithfulness to Jesus' instructions for the Lord's Supper verifies this beyond a shadow of a doubt, "This cup is the *new covenant* in my blood; do this, as often as you drink it, in remembrance of me" (1 Cor 11:25). For Paul this involved the proclamation that believers in Christ were now living recipients of the promises of Jeremiah 31 and Ezekiel 36. Paul explains that the problem of idolatrous sin (Rom 1:21-25) has found its solution in Christ. Whereas idolatry had resulted in a darkening of the heart and degrading, unnatural passions (Rom 1:21, 26), faith in Christ resulted in justification (Rom 3:21-26), regeneration of the heart by the Holy Spirit (Rom 5:5), and adoption as sons of God (Rom 8:14-15).

In 2 Corinthians Paul describes his relation to these promises in greater detail where he identifies himself and his friends in the faith as "*servants* of a *new covenant*" (2 Cor 3:6). He considers his Gentile converts in Corinth as a letter of Christ "written not with ink, but with the Spirit of the living God, not on tablets of stone, but on tablets of human hearts" (2 Cor 3:3). This language clearly recalls the new covenant of Jer 31:33, "*I will put my law within them, and on their heart I will write it*," and Ezek 36:26 (cf. Ezek 11:19), "*I will give you a new heart and put a new spirit within you; and I will remove the heart of stone from your flesh and give you a heart of flesh.*"[1] Paul testifies that he and his Corinthian converts are beneficiaries of this new covenant and as such have had their veils removed, so that they might experience the transforming power of the Holy Spirit as promised in the new covenant: "But we all, with unveiled face beholding as in a mirror the

---

[1] As R. P. Martin affirms, "It is to Ezekiel (11:19; 36:26) that we must turn for these two allusions; and clearly those vv are in Paul's mind, when he writes of a "new spirit" and "tablets of stone" set over against "tablets of flesh" (*2 Corinthians* [WBC 40; Dallas: Word, 1986], 52). Similarly, V. P. Furnish, *II Corinthians* (AB 32A; New York: Doubleday, 1984), 197-98; James M. Scott: "tablets of human [lit., 'fleshly'] hearts clearly alludes to Ezekiel 11:19 and 36:26" (*2 Corinthians*; NIBC; Peabody: Hendrickson [1998], 69; Frank J. Matera (*II Corinthians*; Louisville/London: Westminster John Knox Press [2003], 79-82; Margaret Thrall, *A Critical and Exegetical Commentary on the Second Epistle to the Corinthians* (ICC; Edinburgh: T & T Clark, 2004 ed.), 1.226. Thrall's uncertainty as to the importance of the new covenant in Paul's theology—"There remains the question of Paul's motivation in introducing the motif of the new covenant. It is uncertain whether this theme played any prominent part in his theological thinking in general"—seems to adjust as her exegesis proceeds. See, for example, her commentary on 2 Cor 6:16, where she concludes, "Paul sees these scriptural promises fulfilled in the community he has founded as the messenger of the new covenant" (477).

glory of the Lord, are being transformed into the same image from glory to glory, just as from the Lord, the Spirit" (2 Cor 3:18; cf. Rom 8:29). To share this transforming power and its message is Paul's ministry (2 Cor 4:1).[2] Indeed it is this theology that establishes Paul's famous proclamation "if any man is in Christ, he is a new creature; the old things passed away; behold, new things have come" (2 Cor 5:17). Further, in 2 Cor 6:16b-18, Paul sees the promises of Lev 26:11, Ezek 37:27, Isa 52:11, and Jer 31:9 as "fulfilled in the community he has founded as the messenger of the new covenant."[3]

By way of contrast, Paul portrays unbelieving Israel, both past and present, as characterized by a hardened mind and a veiled face (2 Cor 3:14), because Israel had not turned to the Lord (2 Cor 3:16), who alone was able to remove the veil and transform the hardened.[4]

The theology of 2 Corinthians is not foreign to Romans,[5] which Paul wrote from Greece, possibly Corinth, toward the conclusion of his third missionary journey (Rom 15:25-28; Acts 20:2-3). Paul nuances the language differently in Romans, but the theology is the same. He proclaims to Jews and Gentiles alike the gospel that faith in Jesus Christ sets in motion the gospel promised "through his prophets in the holy Scriptures" (Rom 1:1). Applying new covenant language, Paul thus describes believers as "having the work of the law written in their hearts" (Rom 2:15; cf. Jer 31:33; Ezek 36:27) and the true Jew as one who is so inwardly, whose circumcision is of the heart, by the Spirit, not by the letter (Rom 2:29; cf. Ezek 36:26). Paul writes accordingly of Spirit regeneration in Rom 8:11: "But if the spirit of him who raised Jesus from the dead dwells in you, he who raised Christ Jesus from the dead will also give life to our mortal bodies through his spirit who indwells you" (cf. Gal 4:6; Ezek 36:27; 37:13-14). In Romans 9 Paul applies to believing Gentiles the new covenant promises of Hosea 2:23 and 1:10, "I will call those who were not my people, 'my people,' and her who was not

---

[2] For a thorough treatment of Paul's understanding of the new covenant in relation to the law in 2 Cor 2:14-4:6, see F. Thielman, *Paul & the Law* (Downers Grove: Intervarsity, 1994), 108-118. In addition to the passages we have cited, Thielman argues that the concept of the new (everlasting) covenant underlies 1 Thess 4:8-9 (see pp. 76-77).

[3] M. Thrall, *2 Corinthians*, 1.477.

[4] Thielman writes that at the time of Paul "Many believed that Israel lived in a period of punishment for disobedience to the law and awaited a time when God would intervene powerfully to remake the rebellious hearts of his people, live among his people by his Holy Spirit and restore his people's fortunes. Some felt that acquittal before God on the final day would come to those who freely chose to obey God's laws; others believed humanity to be so sinful that true obedience would come only as a result of God's prior work in the human heart" (*Paul & the Law*, 68).

[5] Or Galatians where Paul writes: For neither is circumcision anything, nor uncircumcision, but a new creation" (Gal 6:15). Cf. the NIV and NRSV translations: "Neither circumcision nor uncircumcision means anything; what counts is new creation" (NIV); "For neither circumcision nor uncircumcision is anything; but a new creation is everything!" (NRSV). If Gal 6:15 was a "traditional maxim," as Longenecker and Betz suggest, the new creation idea would have been among the foundational teachings that Paul incorporated into his initial evangelistic messages. See Hans Dieter Betz, *Galatians: A Commentary on Paul's Letter to the Churches in Galatia* (Hermeneia; Philadelphia: Fortress, 1979), 319 n. 79; Richard N. Longenecker, *Galatians* (WBC 41; Waco: Word, 1990), 295.

beloved, 'beloved.' And it shall be said in the place where it was said to them, 'you are not my people,' there they shall be called sons of the living God" (9:25-26). [6] It is important to observe that Hosea foresees this transformation taking place after God has removed Israel's idols (Hosea 2:17), just as is the case in Ezek 36:25.

In view of the fact that Paul believed that God promised the gospel through the prophets in the holy Scriptures (Rom 1:2; 16:25-26), we may confidently infer that Jeremiah 31, Ezekiel 36, and Hosea 2 established the conceptual background for Paul's concept of the inward transformation of the heart. For, if not from Jeremiah, Ezekiel, and Hosea, from where did Paul get these ideas? He specifies that they came from the "holy Scriptures!"[7]

II. IDOLATRY AND THE HARDENING OF THE HEART IN ROMANS 1

If the righteousness of God is revealed in the gospel to all who believe, Jew and Greek alike, from faith to faith, *the wrath* of God is revealed from heaven through God's giving idolatrous humankind over to depravity. This depravity manifests the unnatural, unethical, and immoral consequences of the human choice to replace God with other objects of worship. Paul makes plain that this human action is evil and not to be excused as an act of unknowing ignorance. For the ones responsible knowingly "suppressed" or "held back" the truth in performing these actions (Rom 1:18). They were thus stumbling blocks for others acting as living obstacles in the way of the revelation of God's truth. The scriptural paradigm of idolatry and hardening originating in Deuteronomy 29 and Psalms 115 and 135 resurfaces in Rom 1:18-32 at the core of Paul's doctrine of sin. It unfolds in the following five-part sequence:

(1) The wrath of God is revealed:
     The wrath of God is revealed from heaven against all ungodliness and unrighteousness of men, who suppress the truth in unrighteousness. (Rom 1:18)

---

[6] Corresponding to the new covenant promises of Jeremiah and Ezekiel are Hosea's description of God removing Israel's idols (Hosea 2:17; Ezek 36:25), and God transforming those who are not his people into those who are (Hosea 2:23; Jer 31:33; Ezek 36:28), who subsequently acquire the gift of *knowing the Lord* (Hosea 2:20; Jer 31:34). Hans Walter Wolff (*Hosea*, [Hermenia trans. Gary Stensell; Philadelphia: Fortress, 1974], 51) thus plausibly writes of Hosea 2:18: "here we have the first reference to a 'new covenant' of the endtime (cf. Jer. 31:31)." For further evidence of the new covenant in Pauline theology, see J. Paul Tanner, "THE NEW COVENANT AND PAUL'S QUOTATIONS FROM HOSEA IN ROMANS 9:25-26," *Bibliotheca Sacra* 162 (January-March 2005): 95-110; Paul R. Thorsell, "The Spirit in the Present Age: Preliminary Fulfillment of the Predicted New Covenant according to Paul," *JETS* 41 (1998): 397-413.

[7] The vision of the new covenant's being appropriated through the ministry of Jesus may also underlie Paul's explanation of salvation in Gal 4:6: "God has sent forth the Spirit of his son into our hearts, crying, Abba! Father!"

(2) The objects of wrath are *without excuse*. They are responsible for the plight they find themselves in:

... because that which is known about God is evident within them; for God made it evident to them. For since the creation of the world his invisible attributes, his eternal power and divine nature, have been clearly seen, being understood through what has been made, so that they are without excuse. (Rom 1:19-20)

(3) Paul identifies idolatry and the refusal to worship as the specific sins provoking the pouring forth of God's wrath.

   a. The refusal to worship:

For even though they knew God, they did not honor him as God, or give thanks. (1:21a)

And just as they did not see fit to acknowledge God any longer. (Rom 1:28a)

   b. Idolatry:

Professing to be wise, they became fools, and exchanged the glory of the incorruptible God for an image in the form of corruptible man and of birds and four-footed animals and crawling creatures. (Rom 1:23)

For they exchanged the truth of God for a lie, and worshiped and served the creature rather than the Creator, who is blessed forever. Amen. (Rom 1:25)

(4) Paul specifies that the penalty inflicted for idolatry and the refusal to worship is divine hardening with its accompanying symptom of divinely inflicted dehumanization.

... but they became futile in their speculations, and their foolish heart was darkened. (Rom 1:21b)

Therefore God gave them over in the lusts of their hearts to impurity, that their bodies might be dishonored among them. (Rom 1:24)

For this reason God gave them over to degrading passions. (Rom 1:26a)

God gave them over to a depraved mind, to do those things which are not proper. (Rom 1:28b)

(5) Paul then catalogs the unnatural, dysfunctional activities humanity has performed against humanity in separation from God to provide

evidence that God has indeed inflicted the curse of hardening on idolatrous violators of the covenant (Rom 1:29-32).

The pattern of idolatry and the hardening of heart we have charted in this book is thus clearly evident at the beginning of Romans, where it serves as a foundational premise for Paul's doctrine of sin. Peter Stuhlmacher thus effectively sums up Rom 1:18-21 with the explanatory scriptural quotation "whoever follows after that which is nothing, becomes nothing himself (Jer. 2:5)."[8]

(a) *The Significance of Paul's Word Choice in Romans 1*

These general observations become more exact when we investigate Paul's word choice in Romans 1. In defining the hardening process, Paul incorporates LXX vocabulary that recalls OT warnings against idolatry and its hardening effect. *Mataioō*, the verb translated "became futile" (NRSV, NASB, NIV) or "became vain" (KJV) in Rom 1:21, has a related contextual background in the LXX versions of 2 Kgs 17:15 and Jer 2:5.

2 Kgs 17:15: *eporeuthēsan opisō tōn mataiōn kai emataiōthēsan*
Jer 2:5: *eporeuthēsan opisō tōn mataiōn kai emataiōthēsan*
"They followed vanity and became vain" (NASB).
"They followed worthless idols and became worthless themselves" (NIV).

It is significant that Paul uses exactly the same inflected form (*emataiōthēsan*) in Rom 1:21 as the LXX translators use in 2 Kgs and Jeremiah to describe the process whereby one becomes like that which one pursues. In 2 Kgs 17:15 the expression describes Israel's condition as precipitated by Israel's rejecting God's testimonies (*ta martyria*). The MT is more precise. It describes Israel's worthless condition as a consequence of her rejecting God's statutes and his covenant. The OT context explains that the northern tribes of Israel fell because they feared other gods (2 Kgs 17:7), built high places (2 Kgs 17:9), sacred pillars or Asherim (2 Kgs 17:10), and served idols (2 Kgs 17:12). In the process the Israelites "stiffened their necks" (2 Kgs 17:14) and rejected God's statutes and covenants (2 Kgs 17:15). Israel's spiritual recalcitrance, i.e., her "stiffneckedness," correlated directly with her idolatrous violation of the covenant as 2 Kgs 17:16 makes clear: "they forsook the commandments of the Lord their God and made for themselves molten images, even two calves, and made an Asherah and worshiped all the host of heaven and served Baals."

Similarly, in Jeremiah the phrase is expressed in the midst of a tirade against idolatry, but this time against the southern kingdom of Judah (LXX Jer 1:16; 2:7-8, 11, 20, 23, 27-30; 3:9). The two crimes God identifies in Jer. 2:13, the forsaking of him and the creation of idols, are the same as those Paul reiterates in

---

[8] *Paul's Letter to the Romans* (Tr. Scott Hafemann; Louisville: Westminster/John Knox, 1994), 36.

Rom 1:18-32. Moreover, the portrayal of Judah's "walking after vanity/emptiness" again correlates with the covenant infraction of idolatry:

> *And I will pronounce my judgments on them concerning all their wickedness, whereby they have forsaken me and have offered sacrifices to other gods, and worshiped the works of their own hands.* (Jer 1:16)
>
> *... and the prophets prophesied by Baal and walked after things that did not profit.* (Jer 2:8b)
>
> *Has a nation changed gods, when they were not gods? But my people have changed their glory for that which does not profit.* (Jer 2:11)

It is also significant that *hebel* ("vapor, breath"), the Hebrew term underlying *mataioō* in 2 Kgs 17:15 and Jer 2:5, refers to idols elsewhere in the OT. The noun form *mataios* shares the same semantic connotations.[9] "Vanity," in fact, is coterminous with idolatry in numerous passages.[10] It is used frequently either as a modifier of idols or as a synonym for idol.[11] The term is also used in reference to other nations that have taken God's place in alliance with Israel[12] and to false prophets whose predictions contradict authentic prophecy.[13] Vanity or "worthlessness," therefore, characterizes anything and everything that challenges Yahweh's covenant with Israel. In the process of transferring confidence from Yahweh to these allegiances, Israel became vain and worthless in the eyes of the biblical writers. The LXX rendering of Jer 28:17-18 (Eng. 51:17-18) describes the phenomenon clearly:

> Every man has completely lost understanding (*emōranthē*); every goldsmith is confounded because of his graven images: for they have cast false gods, there is no breath in them. They are vain works (*mataia estin erga*), objects of scorn; in the time of their visitation they shall perish.

Scriptures like this color the background of Paul's thought in Romans 1. The phenomenon, to be sure, is a premise to Paul's theology and indeed much of the theology of the NT, where every challenge to God's sovereignty is perceived as vanity (*mataios*)—including literal idols (Acts 14:15), the rationalism of the wise (1 Cor 3:20), faith not rooted in historical reality (1 Cor 15:17), disputes about the law (Titus 3:9), insincere religion (James 1:26), and inherited pagan traditions (1 Pet 1:18; cf. Jer 10:3 LXX).

Related in meaning is the verb *emōranthēsan*, "they became/were made fools," which Paul uses to describe the consequence of self-confident idolatry in

---

[9] Deut 32:21; 1 Kgs 16:13, 26; Jer 10:3, 15; 16:19-20; 51:18.

[10] Jer 8:19; 10:3, 8, 15; 14:22; Zech 10:2; Ps 31:6[7].

[11] Lev 17:7; 1 Kgs 16:13; 2 Chr 11:15; Jonah 2:8; Isa 2:20; Jer 8:19; 10:3, 15; 28:18 (51:18); Ezek 8:10.

[12] Isa 30:7; Lam 4:17.

[13] Lam 2:14; Ezek 13:9, 19; 21:29; 22:28.

Rom 1:22-23. In Jeremiah 10:14-15 (LXX), as in Romans 1, the term occurs in conjunction with the *mataioō* root form to describe the plight of idolaters:

> Every man is deprived of knowledge (*emōranthē*), every goldsmith is confounded because of his graven images; for he has cast false gods, there is no breath in them. They are vain works (*Mataia estin erga*), wrought in mockery; in the time of their visitation they shall perish. Such is not the portion of Jacob; for he that formed all things, he is his inheritance; the Lord is his name.

This is the only place in the LXX where the two terms *mōrainō* and *mataios* occur together in close proximity as Paul uses them in Rom 1:21-22. Quite possibly the Jeremiah passage forms the background for Paul's thought. When the entire context of Jeremiah 10-11 is read, the basic components of the hardening pattern become apparent:

(1) Acknowledgement of a preexistent covenantal relationship with God attendant with blessings and curses (Jer 11:2-4).
(2) Exposure to pagan idolatry and the observation of the *dehumanization* that idolatry causes (Jer 10:14-15).
(3) The divine affliction of curses in the form of exile and suffering as God's designed punitive response to idolatry (Jer 10:19-22; 11:9-17).

Quite clearly Paul's conviction is that the people of his day have contracted this curse themselves as those "who practice the same things" (Rom 2:1).

Also in Paul's thought may be the famous indictment of Jer 5:21, where Israel, because of her idolatry, is described as a "foolish and heartless people" "who have eyes, and see not," "who have ears, and hear not," who have "a disobedient and rebellious heart." Writing as an apostle whose gospel was inherited from "the prophets in the holy Scriptures" (Rom 1:2), Paul perceived the sequence of events described in Jeremiah 5 and other related biblical passages (e.g., Isa 6:9; Deut 29:4; Ps 69:22-23) as apt theological and scriptural explanations for the sin and spiritual indifference that led to the rejection of the gospel of Jesus Christ by the majority of Jews and Gentiles in his day (Romans 9-11; esp. 11:8-10). For about them he writes: "There is none righteous, not even one; *there is none who understands*, there is none who seeks for God; all have turned aside, *together they have become useless*" (Rom 3:10b-12a).

Paul therefore perceives the hardening affliction as predicated by a preexisting complacency towards God. In response to this sin, God revealed his wrath by rendering human reasoning powers futile and darkening the human heart (*emataiōthēsan en tois dialogismois autōn kai eskotisthē hē asynetos autōn kardia*; Rom 1:21b). The repeated stock phrase "God gave them over" (Rom 1:24, 26, 28) indicates that God's wrath in part consists of his simple allowance for humanity to discover for itself the awful consequences of self-rule in separation from the Creator. The result is life lived in subjection to the human appetites as manifested in the catalog of vices Paul lists in Rom 1:26-32. This being the case, humanity is fully culpable for her plight in the hardened state.

(b) *The Phenomenon of Idolatry and the Hardening of the Heart Elsewhere in Paul's Epistles*

The phenomenon of idolatry and the hardening of the heart is not unique to Rom 1:18-32 and 2 Corinthians 3 within the Pauline corpus. Galatians 4:8-11 and Eph 4:17-20 are also instructive. Galatians 4:8-10 reads:

> However, at that time, when you did not know God, you were slaves to those which by nature are no gods. But now that you have come to know God, or rather to be known by God, how is it that you turn back again to the weak and worthless elemental things, to which you desire to be enslaved all over again? You observe days and months and seasons and years.

This passage confirms that Paul perceived external religious legalism as comparable to idolatry. This is the exact comparison Paul makes when he equates the observation of days, months, seasons and years with the recipient's former subjection to "those which by nature are no gods" (Gal 4:8b). For Paul, blind allegiance to ceremonial religion is comparable if not equivalent to blind allegiance to idols.

In Ephesians 4:17-19 the phenomenon of idolatry and the hardening of the heart is the same, but the idolatry in view takes the form of sensuality rather than legalism:

> This I say therefore, and affirm together with the Lord, that you walk no longer just as the Gentiles also walk, in the futility of their mind, being darkened in their understanding, excluded from the life of God, because of the ignorance that is in them, because of the hardness of their heart; and they, having become callous, *have given themselves over to sensuality*, for the practice of every kind of impurity with greediness.

The phrase "have given themselves over to sensuality" implies that the Gentiles Paul speaks of have forsaken God to pursue immorality. They are thus "excluded from the life of God," "because of the hardness of their heart." Parallels with Rom 1:18-32 are numerous—e.g., "the futility of their mind," the "darkening of their understanding," the "giving of themselves over to sensuality." Moreover, in Ephesians 5:5 Paul equates immorality, impurity, and covetousness with idolatry specifically: "For this you know with certainty, that no immoral or impure person or covetous man, who is an idolater, has an inheritance in the kingdom of Christ and God." That Paul is here equating idolatry with immorality and not just covetousness is strengthened by the link between sexual lust and idolatry in Wis 14:12; T. Reub. 4.6; T. Jud 23.1 and by his own close association of immorality, covetousness, and idolatry in 1 Cor 5:9-11 and 6:9-10—catalogs of vices yet again resembling his language in Rom 1:18-32.[14] Romans 1:18-32, 2 Corinthians 3, Gal 4:8-11 and Eph 4:17-19; 5:5 establish the paradigm of idolatry and the hardening of the heart as a major theological construct in Paul's understanding of sin.

III. IDOLATRY AND THE HARDENING OF THE HEART IN ROMANS 2

In the transition from Romans 1 to Romans 2, Paul warns that if his contemporaries continue on the course they are going they will experience the same fate that befell the afflicted persons of 1:18-32: "And do you suppose this, O man, when you pass judgment upon those who practice such things and do the same yourself, that you will escape the judgment of God?" (Rom 2:3).[15] Paul, in other words, is saying that his contemporaries are hypocritical, because in essence they are guilty of the very same sins. Therefore, in Rom 2:1-29 Paul reprimands them for considering themselves better than other sinners. As others had committed idolatry, so too were they, and their hardened state was evidence of the fact (Rom 2:5).

But how could it be said that Paul's contemporaries were committing idolatry? Paul's implied answer to this question is that his Jewish kinsmen have replaced God with a mistaken confidence in physical circumcision and outward, custodial observance of the letter of the law. For in the process of guarding the outward Jewish ethnic markers of circumcision and the law, Paul's audience has misunderstood the true symbolic meaning of circumcision and the true purpose of the law. What matters according to Paul is obedience to the law, not professed reliance upon it (Rom 2:17), declared knowledge of the law (Rom 2:18), or pronounced boasting in the law (Rom 2:23). The authentic covenant partner attests intimacy with God through faithful, sincere adherence to the requirements of the law in obedience to God—an adherence that is made possible only by the indwelling, transforming power of the Holy Spirit. The foremost of these commands, of course, were Ten Commandments 1 and 2—those implied to have been breached by the audience of Romans 1 and 2.

The tragic consequence of this religious misappropriation, Paul argues, is disenfranchisement from the transforming power of the gospel of the new covenant (Jeremiah 31; Ezekiel 36). The contrast is simple. The cosmetic, outward Jew (Rom 2:28) had developed a self-promoting fixation on the outward ethnic markers of circumcision and the law. In so doing he contracted a stubborn and unrepentant heart of pride (Rom 2:5), which caused him to store up wrath for the day of the revelation of God's righteous judgment. The authentic true Jew (Rom 2:28), by contrast to the externally minded religious idolater, is that one, who, with a broken and repentant heart, has been forgiven and now lives in reconciliation with God in the intimacy of the new covenant. His praise comes

---

[14] This is the interpretation of Andrew T. Lincoln, *Ephesians* (WBC 42; Dallas: Word, 1990), 324-325.

[15] The time reference for those being judged includes both past and present as the change of tense between Rom 1:28 (past) and 1:32 (present) suggest. Hence the interlocutor of Paul's diatribe is portrayed as passing judgment on idolaters of past history as well as fornicators of the present time.

from God, not men, and his character signifies the presence of the blessings of the new covenant—circumcision of the heart and the indwelling of the Holy Spirit (Rom 2:29). Therefore, whereas the hardened Jew breaks the foremost commandments by elevating external legalism to the place of God, the beneficiary of the new covenant keeps the law and its foremost commands by worshipping God with undivided devotion through the power of the indwelling Holy Spirit. The former, in neglecting the love of God because of an obsession with legalism, commits idolatry and incurs hardening and divine wrath. The latter, having been freed from the curse of the law, and having responded to the gospel with authentic faith, comes to know reconciliation with God in the terms spoken of in the new covenant.

(a) *The Significance of Paul's Word Choice in Romans 2*

Having broadly described Paul's thought in Romans 2, I now move on to address the significance of the LXX background of Paul's vocabulary in Rom 2:5-8. This groundwork will substantiate further our interpretation. We turn first to Rom 2:5, where the objects of Paul's criticism are portrayed as having a "stubborn and unrepentant heart" (*kata de tēn sklērotēta sou kai ametanoēton kardian*). Fitting the context we have described, *sklērotēs*, the term translated "stubborn" (NASB, NIV) or "hard" (KJV, NRSV), is used throughout the LXX to describe the state of obstinacy associated with indifference toward God.[16] Paul uses the verb form of the same root in Rom 9:18 to assert that God "hardens whom he desires" (Rom 9:18).

Of particular importance to the context of Romans 2 are numerous LXX references where the *sklērynein* word group (*sklērynō*:[17] "make stubborn"; *sklērotēs*:[18] "stubbornness"; *sklērotrachēlos*:[19] "stiff necked"; *sklērokardia*:[20] "hard hearted") describes the hardened state of unbelieving Jews. Paul recalls and reapplies this background when he portrays his Jewish generation as debilitated by a "hardened" and "unrepentant" heart (Rom 2:5). As this hardened state was descriptive of Israel in idolatrous times past,[21] so hardening characterizes Judaism

---

[16] The verb *sklērunō* is used twelve times in the LXX to describe God's hardening of Pharaoh's heart (Exod 4:21; 7:3, 22; 8:19; 9:12, 35; 10:1, 20, 27; 11:10; 14:4, 8) and once to describe the hardening of the heart of all the Egyptians (Exod 14:7). Once it is used to describe Pharaoh's stubborn state (Exod 13:5: "*esklērunen pharaō*"). The term is not used, however, to describe the act of Pharaoh's hardening his own heart. The term *barunō* ("weigh down, burden") is used by the LXX translators for this purpose to translate the Hebrew verb *kbd* (Exod 8:28; 9:24). Elsewhere it describes God's hardening of Sihon, king of Heshbon (Deut 2:30).

[17] Deut 10:16; 2 Kgs 17:14 (4 Kgs 17:14 LXX); 2 Chr 30:8; Neh 9:16, 17, 29; Ps 95:8 (Ps 94:8 LXX) ; Isa 63:17; Jer 7:26; 17:23; 19:15.

[18] Deut 9:27.

[19] Exod 33:3, 5; 34:9; Deut 9:6, 13; Bar 2:30.

[20] Deut 10:16; Jer 4:4; Ezek 3:7.

[21] Exod 33:1-6; 34:8-16; Deut 9:6-27; 10:13-17; 2 Kgs 17:13-17; Neh 9:16-18; Isa 63:17 (cf. Isa 65:1-10; Jer 4:1-4; 7:21-31; 19:12-15; 1 Esdr 1:46-49; Bar 2:3-3:7).

in Paul's day, and for the same reasons—idolatry and the refusal to repent.[22] For as idolatry had brought on OT Israel's hardened state, and as OT Israel's hardening had made her unfit for repentance, so in Paul's eyes did the Jews of his day suffer the same curse, because they too were guilty of replacing God with another object of worship. External religious tradition took the place of genuine love of God. Religion became the object of worship and the foremost commandments were broken. This violation brought on divinely enforced hardening that made repentance impossible for the duration of the affliction. Unaddressed, the condition would culminate in punitive judgment at the time of the revelation of God's wrath (Rom 2:5, 8).

(b) *Idolatry and the Robbing of Temples: Romans 2:21-24*

We now close this chapter by turning to Rom 2:21-24 where Paul amplifies the charge of idolatry that he has constructed thus far in Romans 1-2, but here with specific reference to Jewish leaders (cf. Rom 2:17).

> You, therefore, who teach another, do you not teach yourself? You who preach that one should not steal, do you steal? You who say that one should not commit adultery, do you commit adultery? You who abhor idols, do you rob temples? You who boast in the law, through your breaking the law, do you dishonor God? For the name of God is blasphemed among the Gentiles because of you, just as it is written.

Four "accusatory rhetorical questions" underlie this admonition of Paul:[23]

(1) You who teach another do you not teach yourself?
(2) You who preach that one should not steal, do you steal?
(3) You who say that one should not commit adultery, do you commit adultery?
(4) You who abhor idols, do you rob temples?

Paul's implied answer to each rhetorical question is "yes." Yes, they indeed did do the very things they tell others not to do! In the process their hypocrisy has disgraced God before the Gentiles.

That the last question specifies *literal idolatry* is qualified by James Dunn, Douglas Moo, and Tom Schreiner due to the ambiguity of the term *hierosylein*, which in its one LXX occurrence refers to the literal robbing of a Persian temple by the infamous villain Antiochus IV (2 Macc 9:2; Jos. *Ant.* 17.163).[24] Moo

---

[22] For "hardening/stubbornness" correlates with Israel's refusal to repent in 2 Kgs 17:13-17; 2 Chr 36:13-14; Neh 9:16-18, 28-31; Jer 4:1-4 (cf. Jer 3:11-17); 7:21-31; 17:19-23; 1 Esdr 1:46-58.

[23] Cranfield, *Romans*,1.167.

[24] James D.G. Dunn, *Romans* (2 vols.; Dallas: Word, 1988), 1:114-115. Douglas J. Moo, *Romans* (Grand Rapids: Eerdmans, 1996), 163-165; Thomas R. Schreiner, *Romans* (Grand Rapids: Baker, 1998), 130-135.

asserts: "Indeed, what Paul accuses the Jew of doing is not specifically worshipping idols, but 'robbing temples.'"[25] Though Moo concedes that the robbing of temples was not characteristic of many Jews, as robbery and adultery were not, the crimes, he asserts, did represent "the contradiction between claim and conduct" that pervaded Judaism.[26]

In my opinion the literal interpretation of Rom 2:22 is not persuasive, both because 2 Macc 9:2 is an unlikely conceptual background for Rom 2:22,[27] and because there is virtually no historical evidence that Jews actually robbed temples in the first century.[28] Literal stealing and adultery were uncommon within first-century Judaism. Paul, therefore, would have convinced no one if his intent was to communicate a literal allegation against his Jewish contemporaries. The vast majority of Jews was *not* guilty of these crimes in a literal sense, and therefore would not have been threatened by allegations that they were. Paul's argument is more subtle and penetrating.

In the spirit of corrective theological argumentation, Paul charges his Jewish contemporaries in Romans 2 with a spiritual form of robbery, adultery, and idolatry. Paul thus uses *hierosylein* "to rob temples" figuratively in this context as an idiomatic expression for idolatry. The structural parallelism between the last rhetorical question (Rom 2:22b) and its three predecessors (Rom 2:21-2:22a) makes this apparent. For the fact that stealing, adultery, and idolatry are alike infractions of the Ten Commandments suggests that idolatry is the intended referent for *hierosyleis*, just as robbery is the intended referent for *klepteis* and adultery the intended referent for *moicheueis*. Therefore, *hierosylein* most likely refers to a Jewish act that is interpreted by Paul as a violation of Exod 20:3-6. Within the context of Romans 2 the most likely form this idolatry took was Paul's Jewish contemporaries' exchange of God for traditional, legalistic religion.

IV. CONCLUSION

Paul adopted the OT paradigm of idolatry and the hardening of the heart as a major premise for his doctrine of universal sin. Romans 1:18-32 thus emphasizes how God gave humanity over to depravity, because humanity worshiped the creature rather than the creator. Paul conceived that like all sinners his Jewish contemporaries were guilty of idolatry. Romans 2:22b—"you who abhor idols do you rob temples?"—specifies the spiritual form this idolatry takes—the replacement of worship of God with external observance of the law. Idolatrous

---

[25] Moo, *Romans*, 163. Similarly, Dunn, *Romans* (1.114-15) and Schreiner, *Romans*, (134).

[26] Moo (*Romans*, 164) followed by Schreiner (*Romans*, 134).

[27] Within the same document of 2 Maccabees the related noun form *hierosulia* is used in reference to Menelaus's "sacrilege" of defiling the temple altar (2 Macc 13:6-7). Here "sacrilege" takes the form of improper use of a holy institution, not merely the literal robbing of temples. This sacrilege may be analogous to the improper use of the law attacked by Paul.

[28] Of course one could counter that there is equally no evidence that the Jews weren't notorious for stealing and committing adultery in the first century. This rejoinder is valid but not persuasive in my judgment.

fixation on external law made traditionally minded Jews resistant to Paul's gospel of faith with the result that they became ineligible for the saving benefits of the new covenant, which could only be appropriated by faith in Christ.

This interpretation, of course, is not entirely new. D. B. Garlington has proposed that "for Paul *the new idol is the Torah!* The 'sacrilege' in question is *Israel's idolatrous attachment to the law itself.*"[29] Joseph Fitzmyer similarly affirms:

> Do you succumb to the idolatry of elevating the Mosaic law to a position of unwarranted devotion and of bestowing on it a permanence it was never intended to have in God's ultimate plan? For Paul, Israel's clinging to the law is the exclusion of Christ and his role in God's plan. Thus Paul uses the vb. *hierosylein* in a figurative sense and shapes to his purpose an accusation that was otherwise made against Israel in other respects.[30]

In other words, Paul viewed his Jewish contemporaries as blind to the law of faith (Rom 3:27b)—that God justifies by faith apart from works of the law—because of their devotion to a manmade "law of law" or "law of works" (Rom 3:27a), which, as a virtual idol, was unable to accomplish secure relationship with God together with the attendant blessings of the new covenant. Because the Jews targeted in Romans 2 elevated law and tradition to the place of God, Paul attributed to them the condition associated with idolatry throughout the Bible—a stubborn and unrepentant heart. This understanding of Paul and the law is not conjectural. 2 Cor 3:14-16 confirms: "But their minds were hardened (*epōrōthē*); for until this very day at the reading of the old covenant the same veil remains unlifted, because it is removed in Christ. But to this day whenever Moses is read, a veil lies over their heart; but whenever a man turns to the Lord, the veil is taken away."[31]

---

[29] "ΙΕΡΟΣΥΛΕΙΝ AND THE IDOLATRY OF ISRAEL (ROMANS 2.22)," *NTS* 36 (1990): 148 (italics his). He also states: "Thus, Israel's idolatry is her tenacious insistence that the Torah is God's definitive provision for eternal life and, therefore, her clinging to the law as an object of trust to the exclusion of Christ" (149).

[30] Joseph Fitzmyer, *Romans* (New York: Doubleday, 1992), 318.

[31] On the new covenant in Pauline theology, compare James D. G. Dunn, *The Theology of Paul the Apostle* (Grand Rapids: Eerdmans, 1998), 147-150.

Chapter 9

God Hardens Whom He Desires:

Divine Sovereignty in Romans 9

So then he has mercy on whom he desires, and he hardens whom he desires. (Romans 9:18)

I. THE THEOLOGICAL CONTEXT OF ROMANS 9-11

Paul's discussion of the purpose and plight of Israel within God's plan of salvation in Romans 9-11 conforms to the theological orientation of Romans as a whole. Non-negotiable in Paul's thought is the universal sinfulness of all human beings—including the people of Israel (Rom 2:1-3:31; 11:32). Righteousness, according to Paul, continues to be an impossible attainment for human beings, both Gentiles and Jews, apart from the righteousness God bestows upon those whom he elects to save on the basis of faith in Jesus Christ and through the atoning power of Jesus' death and resurrection (Rom 10:9-10). For this is Paul's gospel: "the power of God for salvation to everyone who believes, to the Jew first and also to the Greek. For in it the righteousness of God is revealed from faith to faith: as it is written, 'But the righteous man shall live by faith'" (Rom 1:16-17). Favor before God therefore is not an ethnic birthright or a national inheritance, "for there is no partiality with God" (Rom 2:11; 11:17-24). What matters is faith in Christ (Rom 9:30-33; 10:4-11; 11:20-23). True Israel, therefore, is composed of true Jews who believe in God inwardly and as a result have been transformed by the "new covenant" work of the Holy Spirit (Rom 2:28-29). True Israelites, true Jews, the Israel "within Israel" (Rom 9:6) are those who have hearts circumcised by the Spirit of God (Rom 2:28-29). Moreover, the truly elect recipients of the new covenant are not the biological descendants of Abraham (Rom 9:8, 24), but those who exercise Abraham-like faith that God is able to accomplish his promises, especially when the promises require faith that God can do what would be humanly impossible (Rom 10:9-10; cf. Gen 15:4-6). As Paul makes perfectly clear in Romans 4 and again in Romans 9, the original promise made to Abraham was not made according to ethnic origin or upon the condition of the keeping of the law, but on the basis of faith (Rom 4:3, 9, 13, 16; 9:6-8). Paul maintains keen focus on these truths in Romans 9-11, where he explains the predicament of unbelieving, ethnic Israel in God's plan of salvation.

Throughout Romans Paul traces the continuity between the faith of Abraham and the faith of the Jewish and Gentile believers whom he refers to as the "called of God" (Rom 8:28: 9:24). As Abraham was reckoned as righteous for believing in God's power to perform what he had promised, particularly his raising up a son to Abraham's barren wife Sarah (Rom 4:18-22), so also, Paul reasons, does God continue to reckon as righteous those who adopt Abraham-like faith in confessing Jesus as Lord and believing that God raised Jesus from the dead: "Now not for his sake only was it written, that it was reckoned to him, but for our sake also, to whom it will be reckoned, as those who believe in him who raised Jesus our Lord from the dead" (Rom 4:23-24; also 10:9-10). Paul's basic premise is that the true people of God are those who believe in God and believe that he is able to do what he has promised (Rom 4:21). Non-believers, whether Gentiles or Jews, are therefore not the people of God and will not receive the benefits of the gospel *until they do believe* (Rom 11:20-21, 23-24).

Paul's theology integrates the distinct doctrines of justification, election, sanctification, and salvation into one coherent, inseparable interrelationship that is consolidated by God's reconciling mercy made available exclusively through the substitutionary ministry of Jesus Christ. Hence, election is God's sovereign choice of believers in Christ for atonement.[1] Justification is the process whereby God exonerates sinners and makes them righteous, so that they may live with him in his kingdom. Sanctification is the process whereby God transforms redeemed sinners into his likeness as an ongoing result of authentic justification and election — the process of a sinner's transformation into a Christ-like child of God (2 Cor 5:17). And salvation, as the comprehensive summation of election, justification, and sanctification, is the intimate, loving, joyous, peaceful, eternal relationship shared by the redeemed and transformed sinner with holy and merciful creator God. This relationship with its many benefits (forgiveness, healing, peace, the calling of God, eternal life, sonship) is made possible by Jesus' vicarious death and resurrection and is appropriated exclusively in the lives of those who believe in Jesus and the power of his saving work. Paul sees all of this as evidence of God's faithfulness to his covenant promises (Rom 1:16-17).

The theology of Romans 9-11 is entirely consistent with these doctrines. For Paul there is no justification, no election, no sanctification, and no salvation apart from that accomplished by God for believers in Christ according to God's sovereign will that salvation be given exclusively to those who believe in Christ.

The primary object of Paul's analysis in Romans 9-11 concerns the *unbelieving* portion of ethnic Israel (Rom 9:6). Israel's present plight as an object of God's wrath is not evidence that God is inconsistent or that God has reneged on his covenant promises,[2] but rather Israel's present condition is the result of Israel's rejection of the gospel: "They stumbled over the stumbling stone, just as it is written, 'Behold, I lay in Zion a stone of stumbling and a rock of offense, and he who believes in him will not be disappointed' " (Rom 9:32b-33). This "stumbling stone," as Rom 10:9-11 makes clear, is Jesus Christ, the crucified Messiah of Paul's gospel (Rom 1:1-7).

This is where and why the paradigm of idolatry and the hardening of the heart enters into Romans 9-11. Unbelieving Israel has rejected God's righteousness

---

[1] Similarly, Stuhlmacher (*Romans*, 147): "In the apostle's view, God's elective grace, as it manifested itself in the history of Israel, and God's work of justification belong intimately together!"

[2] Compare Paul's sentiments to those of Ezekiel 18:25.

(Rom 10:3) by rejecting Jesus Christ and the gospel message. Not subjecting themselves to the true righteousness of God, which is revealed through the gospel (Rom 1:17), they have sought to establish a righteousness of their own (Rom 10:3). Replacement of God's righteousness with human righteousness is an act commensurate with replacing God with manmade deities and is therefore by definition idolatry. The rationale is similar to that of Gal 4:8-10:

> However at that time, when you did not know God, you were slaves to those which by nature are no gods. But now that you have come to know God, or rather to be known by God, how is it that you turn back again to the weak and worthless elemental things, to which you desire to be enslaved all over again? You observe days and months and seasons and years.

Unlike Galatians, however, where Gentile beneficiaries of the gospel have been enticed to conform to legalistic Judaism, Romans 9-11 focuses on *unbelieving* ethnic Judaism that has never accepted the gospel, because of confident religious preference for law and tradition. While the audience of Galatians has combined faith in Christ with mandatory law and tradition, the objects of Paul's comments in Romans 9-11 publicly reject the person and work of Jesus and adhere to legalism exclusively. From the beginning they have rejected the gospel due to a preference for external tradition. Hence, in Paul's thought, because God does not award righteousness on the basis of religious observance, but on the basis of faith in Christ alone, unbelieving Israel has not attained what it seeks (Rom 11:7). Only those chosen according to faith attain righteousness, while the rest are hardened.

This means that the hardened within Judaism are not hardened indiscriminately, randomly, or arbitrarily. They are idolaters who have stood in the path of God's plan of salvation and have thereby challenged the working out of God's covenantal promises: "But as for Israel he says, 'All the day long I have stretched out my hands to a disobedient and obstinate people' " (Rom 10:21; Isa 65:2). What Egyptian culture and amulets had been to Pharaoh, Jewish tradition and the law seem to have become to unbelieving Israel. Their preexisting devotion to religious observance and law blinded them from perceiving God's redemptive work in the person and work of Jesus. Hence, they, like Pharaoh, suffer the affliction of hardening (Rom 11:7-10, 25). In attempting to establish their own righteousness through the keeping of the law (Rom 10:3), they have committed idolatry and are explicitly identified as counterparts to the Baal worshippers of Elijah's day (Rom 11:2-3). Ironically, the indictment of Isa 66:3 had become an apt description for the unbelieving Israel of Paul's generation: "He who burns incense is like the one who blesses an idol."

II. PERSONS, METAPHORS, AND SCRIPTURAL ECHOES IN ROMANS 9-11

Paul's doctrinal argument in Romans 9-11 essentially explains the truth of Rom 8:28 as it applies to unbelieving Israel—"all things work together for good to those who love God and are called according to his purpose." Israel's present hardened state, Paul pleads, does not signal the defeat of God's covenantal plans and promises. On the contrary, Israel's hardening, her jealousy, and even her apparent destruction (Rom 9:20-24) have positive purposes within God's plan of salvation that aims toward "showing mercy to all" (Rom 11:32). In this section, we shall see that Paul brought together previously independent biblical characters, Jewish metaphors, and scriptural quotations to demonstrate that God's present action within unbelieving Israel was exactly what the Scriptures anticipated. An integral premise to this argument is the OT paradigm of idolatry and the hardening of the heart (Rom 9:18; 11:7-10; 11:25). In the end, Paul will help us to answer a major question that attends the governing subject of this book—*is there hope for the recipient of God's hardening?*

(a) *Israel within Israel: The Faith of Abraham Continued*

The primary object of Paul's evaluation in Romans 9-11 is the corporate nation of unbelieving Israel as is consistently and repeatedly clarified throughout this section of the epistle (Rom 9:1-7, 25-26, 30-33; 10:1-4, 19-21; 11:1-2, 7-10, 13-14; 11:26-28). Though Paul's message may be applied to individuals, his primary purpose was not to describe the eternal plight of individuals within God's providential plan of salvation and reprobation. Rather his concern was for his "kinsmen according to the flesh" (Rom 9:3), who had rejected the gospel preached to them. In every sense of the word this group more than any other was a burden to Paul throughout his ministry. Though they were his own people and he had preached the gospel to them from their own Scriptures, the Jews were the first to reject Paul and the first and most persistent to persecute him. Since the first missionary journey recorded in Acts 13-14, Paul had much time to reflect upon the puzzle of his people's rejection of their own Messiah and much time to interpret their plight against the background prophecies of the OT Scriptures and covenantal promises. Romans 9-11 discloses Paul's theological understanding of this predicament.

From the start Paul defends God's faithfulness to the covenantal promises by prophetically declaring the contemporary relevance of the covenant (Rom 4:13; cf. Gal 3:16) and by drawing attention to the distinction between "the children of the flesh" and the "children of the promise" (Rom 9:6-8; cf. Gal. 4:21-31). Paul states that God has not reneged on his former promises, that in some way his word has failed, but continues to keep them in the lives of his covenantal people (Rom 9:6). The covenant promises are still alive and active. God has not turned his back on Israel (Rom 11:1). For true Israel continues to be the recipient of God's saving mercy. It was never God's intention, Paul argues, to confer the blessing of atonement unconditionally upon ethnic Israel, the physical descendants of Abraham. On the contrary, from the beginning up to the present time, God's election accorded with his sovereign choice to save those who believe in him and live according to faith. Those whom God has so chosen have subsequently become his people; they then have assumed the covenantal responsibility of representing God's justice and proclaiming his gospel. True Israel, therefore, does not include the unbelieving portion of Abraham's biological descendants—*"For they are not all Israel who are descended from Israel"* (9:6b; cf. Matt 3:7-10).

True Israel, rather, is made up of authentic Jews (Rom 2:28-29), who have embraced the gospel and as a consequence have been transformed by the Holy Spirit into genuine children of God (Rom 8:14). These, the true Israel, are the beneficiaries of the new covenant. The children of the promise, therefore, as stressed above, are the children of faith, in keeping with the Abrahamic promise that was originally based on faith (Rom 4:13-16, 20-22).

These children of the promise, the true seed of Abraham, are the remnant Paul speaks of in Rom 9:27 and 11:5. As the remnant of Isaiah's day had resisted foreign allegiances to rely upon the Lord solely (Rom 9:27; Isa 10:20-22), and as the remnant of Elijah's day had refused to bow a knee to Baal in order to maintain faithfulness to Yahweh (Rom 11:4; 1 Kings 19:18), Paul believed that a remnant existed in his day—one chosen by God according to his grace (Rom 11:5). God chose this remnant, constituted of believers in Christ (Rom 11:20; Gal 3:26-29), in a manner entirely consistent with the original Abrahamic covenant. For according to God's sovereign choice, the remnant was composed of those who believed that God "gives life to the dead and calls into being that which does not exist" (Rom 4:17; 9:9; 10:9-10; 11:20).

(b) *Biblical Characters: Isaac–Rebekah–Esau–Jacob–Pharaoh*

Paul's reference to God's promises to Rebekah about Jacob and Esau accomplishes two purposes. First, it verifies once and for all that God's call is not according to birthright but solely according to God's choice. Second, the Isaac–Rebekah–Esau–Jacob saga illustrates that God's election is not swayed by human manipulation (Rom 9:11). God alone decides and determines whom he will and will not call and bless.

Moreover, the Rebekah citation substantiates Paul's understanding of unbelieving Israel's relationship to "the children of the promise." Paul perceives that God's promise to Rebekah prefigured unbelieving Israel's relationship to believers in Christ.[3]

God's choice of Jacob would affirm—contrary to the cultural norm that reserved the fatherly blessing for the first-born—that his blessing was exclusive to the "children of the promise," who shared Abraham's faith and his commitment to the covenant. Paul's point is that the promises of the covenant are not a birthright, so that one might inherit them by law. Rather, "it is not the children of the flesh who are children of God, but the children of the promise are regarded as descendants" (Rom 9:8). Serving as a premise to all that Paul writes in Romans 9

---

[3] In Paul's thought Jacob was to the believing remnant, especially its Gentile part, what Esau was to unbelieving Jews. For Jacob whose name means "supplanter" would acquire the birthright and the blessing of his elder brother Esau, just as believing Gentiles would acquire the birthright and blessings of Israel. The parallel is too perfect to be coincidental, especially as it anticipates Paul's conclusive contrast of unbelieving Israel with believing Gentiles in Rom 9:30-33. The Esau/Jacob relationship also anticipates the potter metaphor and the Hosea quotation (9:25-26) that follow in Paul's argument. Each in turn substantiates Paul's primary point that God's election is not according to birthright or works of the law but according to God's sovereign decision to choose for salvation those who believe in him and in the saving work of Jesus.

is Paul's argument that God has reserved the covenant promises for those who exercise faith in him: "the promise to Abraham or to his descendants that he would be heir of the world was not through the law, but through the righteousness of faith" (Rom 4:13). Esau fell short of Abraham's example in that he despised his birthright (Gen 25:34) thereby indicating his disinterest, disregard, and disrespect for the covenant—for the covenant blessings *were* his birthright. Indeed, the covenant inheritance was less valuable to Esau than a bowl of stew. The statement in Mal 1:2 (Rom 9:13), "Esau I hated," should be understood against this background (cf. Heb 12:16).[4]

Moreover, we now know from the Dead Sea Scrolls that even the deterministically minded Qumran community understood God's "hatred" of historical persons as predicated upon sin. Consider the following perspectives from columns 2 and 3 from the Cairo Damascus Document (*CD*):[5]

> For God did not choose them primordially; before they were established he knew their works. And he despised the generations (in which) they [st]ood and hid his face from the land from (. . .) until their completion. (CD 2:7-8)

> Rather, they murmured in their tents and God's anger was kindled against their congregation and their sons perished through it and their kings were cut off through it, and through it their heroes perished, and their land

---

[4] The view that God hated Esau from time eternity as an extension of his plan for unconditional reprobation forces the conclusion that God intentionally created some human beings for the purpose of hating them and then ultimately pouring forth his wrath upon them for his glory. Such a prospect, in my judgment, misrepresents canonical biblical theology (see footnote 2 below) and the extra-biblical background of the Esau tradition, where "Esau represents the godless and jealous individual who is rejected by God *because of wicked deeds and evil disposition*" (U. Hübner, "Esau," ABD II, 575); italics added for emphasis. Thus God's hatred of Esau is not an extension of theological determinism, but a consequence of Esau's indifference toward the covenant and Edom's conflict with God's people Israel. The following references are representative: "And God loved Jacob, but he hated Esau because of his deeds" (Ps Philo L.A.B. 32:5; 135 B.C.-A.D. 70). "'And Isaac said to her, ' I know and see the deeds of Jacob, who is with us, that with all his heart he is honoring us. And I first loved Esau more than Jacob because he was born first, but now I love Jacob more than Esau because he has increasingly made his deeds evil. And he has no righteousness because all of his ways are injustice and violence. . . . 'And neither he nor his seed is to be saved for they will be destroyed from the earth, and they will be uprooted from under the heaven since he has forsaken the God of Abraham and he has gone after his wives and after their defilement and after their errors, (both) he and his sons" (Jubilees 35:13-14; 161-140 B.C.). See also Philo *Leg All* III 2, 88-89, 191-93; *Sacr* 17-18, 81, 120, 135; *Ebr* 9-10; *Quod Det* 45-46; *Migr* 208; *Congr* 61, 129; *Fuga* 24, 39, 43; *Virt* 209-10; *Praem* 62; *Sobr* 26-27; *Quod Omn* 57; *b. Sabb.* 145b-147; *b. B. Bat.* 16b; *b. Sanh.* 12:a; *b. Git* 57b; *1 Clem.* 4:8; *Pre. Pet.* H II 16; *Ps-Clem.* 16:6; *Acts Thom.* 84).

[5] Charlesworth, 2.15, 17. Compare to the translation of 2.7-8 by Geza Vermes: "For from the beginning God chose them not; He knew their deeds before ever they were created and He hated their generations, and He hid His face from the Land until they were consumed" (*The Complete Dead Sea Scrolls in English*; New York: Penguin, 1997), 128.

became desolate due to it. The first ones who entered the covenant became guilty through it; and they were given up to the sword, having departed from God's covenant and chosen their (own) will, straying after the wantonness of their heart, each doing his (own) will. But out of those who held fast to God's ordinances, who remained of them, God established his covenant with Israel forever, revealing to them hidden things in which all Israel had strayed: his holy Sabbaths, the glorious appointed times, his righteous testimonies, his true ways, and the desires of his will, which a person shall do and live by them. (CD 3:10-16a)

The conditional nature of God's hatred makes perfect sense in the context of Paul's argument in Romans, where God's wrath is revealed from heaven "against all ungodliness and unrighteousness of men" (Rom 1:18), whereas the concept of unconditional hatred/wrath is indeed quite foreign (Rom 5:8).

We should also observe that Esau's identity as patriarch of Edom corresponds to Jacob's identity as patriarch of true Israel. This oft-overlooked fact would have been obvious to Paul, who viewed Esau through the lens of the scriptural history that provided the backdrop for Mal 1:2-5. Against this background, Esau/Edom provided a provocative analogy to contemporary unbelieving Israel. The Scriptures are replete with charges that Esau/Edom was responsible for collaborating in and celebrating the destruction of Jerusalem in 587 B.C.[6] Obadiah's prophetic threat is representative:

Because of violence to your brother Jacob, you will be covered with shame, and you will be cut off forever. On the day that you stood aloof, on the day that strangers carried off his wealth, and foreigners entered his gate and cast lots for Jerusalem—you too were as one of them. (Obad 10-11)

For the day of the Lord draws near on all the nations. As you have done, it will be done to you. Your dealings will return on your own head. (Obad 15)

But on Mount Zion there will be those who escape, and it will be holy. And the house of Jacob will possess their possessions. Then the house of Jacob will be a fire and the house of Joseph a flame; but the house of Esau will be as stubble. And they will set them on fire and consume them, so that there will be no survivor of the house of Esau, for the Lord has spoken. (Obad 17-18)

The people Esau/Edom, therefore, even more so than the biblical individual from whom the nation got its name, were cursed eschatologically by the prophets for being a curse to the covenant people of God (cf. Gen 12:3). This is the biblical

---

[6] Ps 137:7; Isa 34:6-8; Jer 49:7-22; Lam 4:21-22; Ezek 25:12-14; 35:3-5, 14-15; Joel 3:19; Amos 1:11-12; Obadiah; Mal 1:2-5; 1 Esdras (4th-3rd cent B.C.) goes so far as to blame the Edomites for burning the temple.

explanation for God's hatred of them (Mal 1:2), and for Paul's reference to Esau in Romans 9.[7] In challenging Judah, the people of Esau committed one of the same covenant threats against God and his people that Pharaoh committed in Exodus—Pharaoh's hardening having been explicable on the basis of his idolatrous superstition and active resistance to the emigration of God's people. Therefore Esau received prophetic threats similar to those voiced by Moses against Pharaoh—namely, threats that forecast Esau's destruction at the command of the Lord (Obad 18). It is noteworthy that Obadiah's threat accompanies the symptom of spiritual deadening: "Will I not on that day,' declares the Lord, 'destroy wise men from Edom and understanding from the mountain of Esau?' " (Obad 8).

For this reason we should not take Rom 9:13 as surface level evidence of Paul's hyper-determinism.[8] The OT, the NT, and extrabiblical Jewish and Christian literature overwhelmingly portray Esau as an archetypal sinner whose curse befits his sin.[9] Paul's reference to Esau taps into this understanding. His point is that unbelieving Israel has assumed the predicament of Esau and Pharaoh, because it has rejected the gospel and challenged the progress of the new covenant mission.[10] As active opponents of the gospel, they have brought upon themselves the curses of the covenant. Hence Israel, for the same reason, has assumed the curses that God previously inflicted upon Esau and Pharaoh. As Esau became jealous of Jacob, who usurped his birthright and blessing, so Israel will become jealous of the genuine beneficiaries of the new covenant (Rom 10:19; 11:11). This regression of Israel from God's chosen people to an object of hardening is perplexing to the modern reader, but it accurately depicts Israel's history as recounted in the OT where Israel, after being chosen by God, did commit the chief crime of Pharaoh (idolatry)[11] and therefore did suffer divine hardening (Isa 6:9-10). Indeed, rebellious Israel did become the object of God's promised wrath because of her divided worship (Isa 65:12).

It appears that God raised up Israel for the same purpose that he raised up Pharaoh—to demonstrate his power and to proclaim his name throughout the

---

[7] Many of the prophetic threats against the nations of Egypt, Edom, Tyre etc. (e.g., Isa 13-23) are theologically based on the seminal promise of Gen 12:3.

[8] If God's election of Jacob was entirely indiscriminate, then Rom 9:10-13 is a direct contradiction of Rom 4:3 and Gal 3:6, where Paul argues explicitly that God chose Abraham on the basis of Abraham's faith. The grammar of these simple sentences clearly attests that Abraham is the subject, believe is the verb, and God is the direct object. This emphasis, emphasized by Paul at these critical junctures of Romans and Galatians, clarifies that human beings elected/chosen by God to receive the benefits of salvation have the responsibility to believe in Christ as Abraham believed in God. The ongoing debate on whether to treat faith "of Christ" passages as subjective or objective genitives should be approached with awareness of the direct implications of Rom 4:3 and Gal 3:6.

[9] See the two immediately preceding footnotes.

[10] So Cranfield, *Romans*, 2:485: "The Pharaoh of the Exodus, the cruel oppressor of Israel, is here introduced as the type of those who resist God—as the prefiguration of that disobedient Israel which is now opposed to the gospel."

[11] See ch. 3.

whole earth (Exod 9:16; Rom 9:17).[12] As Pharaoh was hardened for cursing God's people, unbelieving Israel was hardened for rejecting God's revelation in Christ and for standing in the way of the progress of the gospel (Rom 10:16, 21; 11:25).[13] In Paul's eyes there is no partiality with God when it comes to judgment and salvation (Rom 2:11-12). In both cases divine hardening afflicted those who had opposed God's covenantal plan—Pharaoh, for standing in the way of the exodus; unbelieving Israel, for standing in the way of the gospel.[14] In view of this symmetry, Paul's logic in Rom 9:14 makes perfect sense—"What shall we say then? There is no injustice with God, is there? May it never be!"

(c) Divine Election: Exodus 33:19

> *For He says to Moses, I will have mercy on whom I have mercy, and I will have compassion on whom I have compassion.* (Rom 9:15; Exod 33:19)

Paul's quotation of Exod 33:19 substantiates our interpretation, if proper attention is paid to the Exodus background where God declares the sovereignty of his will immediately following the golden calf incident of Exodus 32. The declaration

---

[12] Moo, *Romans*, 595 writes: "In Pharaoh's day, the plagues on the land of Egypt and the deliverance of Israel through the "Sea of Reeds," made necessary by Pharaoh's hardened heart, accomplished this purpose (see Josh. 2:10). In Paul's day, he implies, the hardening that has come upon a 'part of Israel' (see 11:5-7, 25) has likewise led to the name of God being 'proclaimed in all the earth' through the mission to the Gentiles."

[13] This demonstration of divine power and promotion of God's name serves the dual purposes of God's revelation, which manifests itself in both salvation (Rom 1:16, where the same word δυναμις defines Paul's concept of God's power for salvation) and penal judgment (Rom 1:18; 2:5-9, where God's wrath is not unconditional, but is rendered "to every man according to his deeds"). Ultimately the proclamation of God's name (Rom 1:5) is the task to which Paul and his Roman readers are devoted as part of new covenant evangelism (Ezek 36:22-38). For further references see Cranfield, *Romans*, 2:235.

[14] Hence, in the judgment of Fitzmyer, *Romans*, 568: "The 'hardening of the heart' by God is a protological way of expressing divine reaction to persistent human obstinacy against him, a sealing of a situation arising, not from God, but from a creature that rejects divine invitation. It brings out God's utter control of human history." *Contra* Moo, *Romans*, 598: "The 'hardening' Paul portrays here, then, is a sovereign act of God that is not caused by anything in those individuals who are hardened. And 9:22-23 and 11:7 suggest that the outcome of hardening is damnation. It seems, then, that this text, in its context, provides important exegetical support for the controversial doctrine of 'double predestination': just as God decides, on the basis of nothing but his own sovereign pleasure, to bestow his grace and so save some individuals, so he also decides, on the basis of nothing but his own sovereign pleasure, to pass over others and so to damn them." By this stage of this book the reader will be aware that I respectfully but forthrightly disagree with this interpretation, which I view as out of touch with the broader context of Romans and comprehensive biblical theology. God's hardening relates directly to sin, frequently idolatry, and God's justification of sinners directly relates to faith—a faith that human beings are responsible to exercise (e.g., "Abraham believed God, and it was reckoned to him as righteousness" (Rom 4:6; Gal 3:6).

occurs in response to Moses' request for God's pity on the idolatrous Israelites: "But now if you will, forgive their sin—and if not, please blot me out from the book which you have written! And the Lord said to Moses, whoever has sinned against me, I will blot him out of my book" (Exod 32:32-33). It is not a coincidence that in Rom 9:3 Paul adopts Moses' empathetic compassion for Israel: "For I could wish that I myself were accursed, separated from Christ for the sake of my brethren, my kinsmen according to the flesh." This sacrificial empathy exists because Paul judges his unbelieving kinsmen to be just as guilty as Moses' Israelite generation, which committed the golden calf apostasy. As the Israelites had replaced God with a golden calf, so Paul's contemporaries have betrayed God's purpose for themselves (Rom 9:31-33; cf. Luke 7:30) by focusing on the law and Jewish tradition instead of believing the gospel, the exclusive revelation of God's righteousness (Rom 1:17; 10:3). As a consequence, just as there was an "Israel within Israel" at the time of Moses, so too was there an "Israel within Israel" at the time of Paul. In Moses' day the "Israel within Israel" was the portion that responded to Moses' command "Whoever is for the Lord, come to me" (Exod 3:26). The "outer Israel" was the three thousand who were struck down by the Levites for not repenting of their idolatrous worship of the golden calf (Exod 32:28). Similarly, Paul perceives that the "Israel within Israel" of his day is the remnant of Israel that has turned from other allegiances to the gospel. The Israel outside of true Israel is thus the unbelieving majority that has rejected the gospel out of a preference for another allegiance, namely the law and Jewish tradition. Hence, as God previously viewed the Israelites as "obstinate" for maintaining their idolatrous ways (Exod 33:3-5), so Paul viewed his Israelite contemporaries as obstinate for religiously conserving tradition at the expense of the gospel (Rom 10:21; Isa 65:2).

Paul's quotation of Exod 33:19 thus does not indicate that God's blessing and curse are unconditionally or indiscriminately determined. God's mercy and compassion are pronounced justly by God according to his sovereign prerogative as exemplified in the particular crisis of the golden calf episode, where his judgment was for sin (Exod 32:33-34), and where his mercy spared the lives of those who responded to the call of Moses (Exod 32:26-28), laid aside their idols (Exod 33:6), received the forgiveness of God (Exod 34:9), and rededicated themselves to the covenant in holiness before God (Exod 34:10-28). In the same way, Paul interprets the plight of his kinsmen to be the result of idolatrous sin and not a consequence of God's capricious, arbitrary will. Accordingly, it is important to note that neither Rom 9:15-16 nor Rom 9:17-19 states that God *unconditionally* hardens or shows mercy, only that in the end the hardening or mercy is a decree of God based upon his sovereign will, *which is to show mercy to those who believe in Christ and to give over to reprobation those who don't* (Rom 9:30-33; 10:4-13; 11:20-23). Thus a verse like Rom 9:16, "So then it does not depend on the man who wills or the man who runs, but on God who has mercy," should be interpreted according to the governing pre-established theology of statements like Rom 3:28: "For we maintain that a man is justified by faith apart from works of the law."

(d) *The Potter Metaphor: Romans 9:20-23*

To further explain Israel's predicament, Paul incorporated the "potter" metaphor from OT and Second Temple Jewish literature (Job 10:9; 38:14; Isa 29:16; 41:25; 45:9-10; Jer 18:1-6; Wisd 15:7; 33:13; Sir 27:5; 33:13; 38:29; *T. Naph.* 2:2; 1 QS 11:22).[15] The symbolism of this metaphor would have been obvious to Paul's Jewish readers and even to Gentiles who were familiar with the LXX. Paul intentionally recalled the metaphor to further substantiate his theological assessment of Israel. Scholars have debated rigorously the identification of the exact text Paul was alluding to, but no consensus has emerged.[16] Although it is possible that Paul combined thoughts transmitted by several of these passages, a number of general comments may be helpful in putting the question into proper perspective. Priority should be given to the canonical texts of Isaiah and Jeremiah, because the entire doctrinal argument of Romans is built upon the gospel, which Paul claims to be the fulfillment of the "prophets in the holy Scriptures" (Rom 1:1). Correspondences with the language of the extrabiblical works of Wisdom, Ben Sirach, and the Psalms of Solomon are likely to be the consequence of shared dependence on the canonical prophets, unless Paul's direct dependence on these sources can be proven. The major prophets Isaiah and Jeremiah would have been the most familiar to Paul's audience and therefore the most likely foundation for his audience's interpretation of Rom 9:20-23. Paul, self-conscious of his identity as successor to the prophets (1 Thess 2:13), would have viewed his usage of the metaphor as consistent with the same metaphor used by his prophetic forbears.[17] In

---

[15] We may eliminate from this list Job 10:9; 38:14; Isa 41:25; Sir 27:5; 38:29; *T. Naph.* 2:2 , and 1 QS 11:22, because parallels in context and meaning are not apparent. Similarly, Wisdom 15:7, though containing the contrast of the two vessels, and though familiar to Paul, as is evident from the echoes of Wisd 14:22-31 in Rom 1:24-32, is not a probable background for Paul's thought in Rom 9, because in Rom 9 the potter is God (as in Isa 29 and Jer 18), whereas in Wisdom 15 the potter is a human being. Sirach 33:13 (180-166 B.C.), "Like clay in the hand of the potter, to be molded as he pleases, so all are in the hand of their maker, to be given whatever he decides," does parallel Romans 9 in describing God's sovereign freedom in blessing and cursing his creatures. However, 33:13 does not support a doctrine of unconditional reprobation, because Sirach's theology is based on retributive justice—e.g., Sirach 15:14-17: "it was he who created humankind in the beginning, and he left them in the power of their own free choice. If you choose, you can keep the commandments, and to act faithfully is a matter of your own choice. He has placed before you fire and water; stretch out your hand for whichever you choose. Before each person are life and death, and whichever one chooses will be given. For great is the wisdom of the Lord; he is mighty in power and sees everything; his eyes are on those who fear him, and he knows every human action. He has not commanded anyone to be wicked, and he has not given anyone permission to sin." *Contra* John Piper, *The Justification of God*, 177, who argues that "In Sir 33:7-13 the potter/clay image is used to describe God's determination of individual destinies" and as such sets the stage for Paul's similar deterministic usage in Rom 9.

[16] See especially Piper, *The Justification of God*, 163-99.

[17] Similarly, Richard B. Hays (*Echoes of Scripture in the Letters of Paul* (New Haven: Yale, [1989], 14): "He saw himself as a prophetic figure, carrying forward the proclamation of

this epistle where Paul constantly quotes and alludes to the Scriptures, it is most likely that he is doing so again in this context for further Scriptural backing for his theological evaluation of unbelieving Israel. Isaiah and Jeremiah used the potter metaphor for this very purpose—to describe the manner of God's dealings with idolatrous Israel. Thus, while it is possible that "Paul's imagery is probably distilled generally from many" of the texts listed above,[18] there is much to commend the judgment that Rom 9:20-23 builds particularly upon Isa 29:16; 45:9, and Jer 18:1-6.[19]

(i) *The Potter Metaphor in Isaiah 29:16*

In Isaiah 29 the potter metaphor concludes a prophetic admonition in which the primary accusation against Judah is that her worship has become insincere:

> Because this people draw near with their words and honor me with their lip service, but they remove their hearts far from me, and their reverence for me consists of tradition learned by rote, therefore behold, I will once again deal marvelously with this people, wondrously marvelous; and the wisdom of their wise men shall perish, and the discernment of their discerning men shall be concealed. (Isa 29:13-14)

Because of insincere worship, God blinds and inebriates the people of Jerusalem with the result that even their prophets and wise men lose their understanding (Isa 29:10, 14). The distancing of their hearts from God and the replacement of authentic worship with "tradition learned by rote" is analogous to Paul's accusation that the Jews of his day misconstrued the meaning of Judaism and circumcision (Rom 2:28-29) and replaced God's righteousness with a righteousness of their own (Rom 10:3). Hence, Isa 29:9-10, 13-14 shares with Romans the association of sensory malfunction and religious idolatry. The potter metaphor in Isa 29:16 identifies God as the enforcer of this process.

The sentence, however, is not absolute. Isaiah goes on to describe a coming day when a positive, corrective transformation will occur: "the deaf shall hear the words of a book," "the eyes of the blind shall see," "the afflicted also shall increase their gladness in the Lord," "the needy of mankind shall rejoice," "the ruthless shall come to an end" (Isa 29:18-20). This saving transformation will occur in fulfillment of the Abrahamic promises and in perfect accord with the new covenant:

> *Therefore thus says the Lord, who redeemed Abraham, concerning the house of Jacob, Jacob shall not now be ashamed, nor shall his face now turn pale; but when he sees his children, the work of my hands, in his*

God's word as Israel's prophets and sages had always done, in a way that reactivated past revelation under new conditions."

[18] Moo, *Romans*, 603. But see footnote 12 above. Several of the extrabiblical references are unlikely to have influenced Paul.

[19] Hays, *Echoes of Scripture in the Letters of Paul*, 66.

> midst, they will sanctify my name; indeed, they will sanctify the Holy One
> of Jacob, and will stand in awe of the God of Israel. And those who err in
> mind will know the truth, and those who criticize will accept instruction.
> (Isa 29:22-24; cf. Ezek 36:21, 23)

The earliest Christians, including Paul, understood the healing miracles of their ministries as verification of these and other related biblical promises. They viewed their salvation as the working out of the new covenant in their midst. Unbelieving Israel's plight, by contrast, was determined by her rejection of this potential salvation, which was communicated via the preaching of the gospel and activated by faith in Christ (Rom 10:9-10). Yet Israel's plight was reversible. She could be grafted into the new covenant, if she did not continue in unbelief (Rom 11:23).

(ii) *The Potter Metaphor in Isaiah 45:9*

> Woe to the one who quarrels with his maker—an earthenware vessel
> among the vessels of earth! Will the clay say to the potter, what are you
> doing? Or the thing you are making say, He has no hands?

Within Isaiah the question "Will the clay say to the potter, 'What are you doing?'"(Isa 45:9) occurs within a context in which God declares the non-existence of other deities (Isa 45:5-7, 14b, 18, 21-22) and the utter futility of idolatry (Isa 45:16-17, 20-21; cf. 44:8). The context is similar to Romans, where Paul poses the same question in the context of a prolonged argument that addresses the foolishness and hopelessness of religious legalism (Rom 9:20). As Isaiah attributed idolaters' preferences for idols to a lack of knowledge (Isa 45:20), so Paul attributes Israel's attempt to establish her own righteousness apart from the righteousness of God to Israel's religious zeal that was "not in accordance with knowledge" (Rom 10:2-3). Furthermore, Isaiah 45:16, 20 contrasts the shame, humiliation, and ignorance of manufacturers of idols with the saving power of God (Isa 45:17, 21-22), whose *righteousness* will bring *justification* and glory to the *offspring of Israel* (Isa 45:23-25). Salvation in Isaiah 45 therefore is not unconditional but is for those who turn to God from idols—"Turn to me, and be saved, all the ends of the earth; for I am God, and there is no other" (Isa 45:22). The heart of the issue is sincere worship of God (Isa 45:23).

(iii) *The Potter Metaphor in Jeremiah 18*

In common with Rom 9:20-23, Jeremiah 18 develops the potter metaphor within a broader prophetic assessment of Israel's plight as the object of God's penal judgment (Jer 18:6). Yet, as in Romans, the metaphor in Jeremiah offers the hopeful prospect that Israel's wayward course may be altered through repentance (Jer 18:4, 7-10), so that Israel's transformation may take place (as in Rom 11:20-24). As in Romans the metaphor in Jeremiah 18 associates the phenomenon of the hardening of the heart (Jer 18:12; Rom 2:5; 9:18; 11:25) with the phenomenon of Israel's stumbling because of idolatry (Jer 18:15; Rom 11:4-5, 25). And, like Romans 9, Jeremiah 18 emphasizes directly the sovereign prerogative of the potter

(Jer 18:6; Rom 9:21), the contrast between the two kinds of vessels (Jer 18:7-10; Rom 9:21), and the merciful patience of God (Jer 18:11b; Rom 9:22-23).[20]

Most importantly, Jeremiah 18 establishes the biblical precedent that a destiny of destruction is not absolute or unconditional in the plan of God:

> Can I not, O house of Israel, deal with you as this potter does? declares the Lord. Behold, like the clay in the potter's hand, so are you in my hand, O house of Israel. At one moment I might speak concerning a nation or concerning a kingdom to uproot, to pull down, or to destroy it; if that nation against which I have spoken turns from its evil, I will relent concerning the calamity I planned to bring on it. Or at another moment I might speak concerning a nation or concerning a kingdom to build up or to plant it; if it does evil in my sight by not obeying my voice, then I will think better of the good with which I had promised to bless it. So now then, speak to the men of Judah and against the inhabitants of Jerusalem saying, thus says the Lord, behold, I am fashioning calamity against you and devising a plan against you. Oh turn back, each of you from his evil way, and reform your ways and your deeds. But they will say, it's hopeless! For we are going to follow our own plans, and each of us will act according to the stubbornness of his evil heart. (Jer 18:6-12)

Paul's portrayal of the "vessels of wrath prepared for destruction" (Rom 9:22) is consistent with this authoritative, biblical background. With similar language Paul explains in 2 Tim 2:20 that becoming a vessel of honor is conditional upon repentance: "Now in a large house there are not only gold and silver vessels, but also vessels of wood and of earthenware, and some to honor and some to dishonor. Therefore, if a man cleanses himself from these things, he will be a vessel for honor, sanctified, useful to the master, prepared for every good work."[21] The conditional language of Jeremiah 18 and then 2 Timothy 2 cautions against a hyper-deterministic interpretation of Romans 9.

Clearly Paul understands eternal destruction as a consequence that awaits Jews and Gentiles, who reject the gospel of Jesus Christ. Second Thessalonians, which relates directly to our governing subject of idolatry and the hardening of the heart, illustrates:

---

[20] One might contest that Isa 29:16 and Wis. 15:7 are closer referents owing to the linguistic parallels. Isaiah 29 and Wisdom 15 have in common with Romans 9 the words *kerameus*, *pēlos*, and *plassō* by comparison to Jeremiah 18, which has in common with Romans 9 only *kerameus* and *pēlos*. The word count, however, only indicates that Paul is adopting traditional vocabulary to draw attention to the parallels between the plight of ancient Israel and the plight of contemporary Israel. The absence of one word hardly overrides the unique parallels in context and content shared by Romans 9 and Jeremiah 18.

[21] The authorship of the Pastoral Epistles does not alter this point. If 2 Timothy was written by a member of a Pauline school, it remains significant that this anonymous protégé of Paul explained Paul's vessel language (Rom 9:21) in conditional terms. 2 Timothy 2:20 shares with Romans 9:21 the words *skeuos* (vessel), *timē* (honor), and *atimia* (dishonor) and is cited as an allusion to Romans 9:21 by *Nestle Aland 27*.

> For after all it is only just for God to repay with affliction those who afflict you, and to give relief to you who are afflicted and to us as well when the Lord Jesus shall be revealed from heaven with his mighty angels in flaming fire, dealing out retribution to those who do not know God and to those who do not obey the gospel of our Lord Jesus. And these will pay the penalty of eternal destruction, away from the presence of the Lord and from the glory of his power, when he comes to be glorified in his saints on that day, and to be marveled at among all who have believed—for our testimony to you was believed. (2 Thess 1:6-10)

The penalty of eternal destruction in this passage is conditioned upon ignorance of God, participation in the affliction of God's people, knowing disobedience to the gospel, and absence of belief. The situation is similar in 2 Thessalonians 2, where Paul warns those deceived by the "man of lawlessness" who displays "himself as being God" (2 Thess 2:4b). These, Paul explains, will perish "because they did not receive the love of the truth so as to be saved" (2 Thess 2:10b). Because they followed the deception of the "man of lawlessness" rather than the truth of the gospel, God "will send upon them a *deluding influence* so that they might believe what is false, in order that they all may be judged *who did not believe* the truth, but took pleasure in wickedness" (2 Thess 2:11-12). Hardening (delusion) here directly corresponds to the rejection of the gospel, participation in idolatry (collusion with Satan) and wickedness—particularly as wickedness manifests itself in the oppression of the people of God.

For our purposes, as we evaluate Romans 9-11, it is logical to reason that Paul had a similar understanding of the plight of the "vessels of wrath prepared for destruction" and the partial hardening experienced by Israel (as well as the 'hatred' of Esau and the hardening of Pharaoh). In each case God's wrath was revealed against those who either disrespected, challenged, or rejected the carrying out of God's covenantal plan of salvation. God reserves retribution in the form of eternal destruction for those who "do not obey the gospel" (2 Thess 1:8) and do "not believe the truth" (2 Thess 2:12). Hardening, the delusion described in 2 Thess 2:11, is the inevitable derangement afflicting all who prefer some other object of faith to God, because no other objects of faith can perform what they promise. In 2 Thessalonians this alternative takes the form of collusion with "the man of lawlessness," while in Romans the alternative is idolatry (Rom 1:18-32) and religious legalism (Romans 2; 10:3-4).

(e) *Hosea, the New Covenant, and Gentile Transformation*

Paul views the potential for transformation envisioned in Jer 18:4, 6-10 as fulfilled in the lives of those who have received the saving benefits of the new covenant through faith in the gospel. This Paul reaffirms by way of a clever composite quotation of Hos 2:23 and 1:10, which in Hosea was first voiced in reference to the ten northern tribes of Israel, but is applied by Paul to Gentile believers in Christ: "I will call those who were not my people, 'my people.' And her who was not beloved 'beloved.' And it shall be that in the place where it was said to them, 'you are not my people,' there they shall be called sons of the living God" (Rom 9:25-

26). Paul's alteration of Hosea's original "I will say" to "*I will call*" expresses the conviction that all who are called by God experience the change in identity and destiny spoken of in Hosea and Jeremiah (cf. 2 Thess 2:14). Moreover, as Karl Barth and C.E.B. Cranfield have suggested, the quotation simultaneously holds forth the hope that the ten lost tribes of Israel not only prefigure the Gentiles but also prefigure that 'other' Israel—the unbelieving majority of Paul's Jewish contemporaries.[22] The possibility of such a change silences the accusation of God's unfairness, but does not promise automatic, unconditional salvation for Jews or Gentiles, because the essential condition of faith in Christ governs the text (Rom 9:30-33 and 11:20-24).

The general implications of Hosea's prophecy are of still further relevance to the broader objectives of this book. Hosea was written as a prophetic corrective to the idolatrous people of northern Israel. He warned Israel that though she had been the chosen people of God, and Yahweh had been her God and she had been Yahweh's people, she was so no longer. From God's perspective they were "*Lo-ammi*" or "not my people" (Hos 1:9). This ruptured relationship was God's punishment for Israel's obsessive idolatry:

> Harlotry, wine, and new wine take away the understanding. My people consult their wooden idol, and their diviner's wand informs them; for a spirit of harlotry has led them astray, and they have played the harlot, departing from their God. (Hos 4:11-12)

> Since Israel is stubborn like a stubborn heifer, can the Lord now pasture them like a lamb in a large field? Ephraim is joined to idols; let him alone. Their liquor gone, they play the harlot continually; their rulers dearly love shame. The wind wraps them in its wings, and they will be ashamed because of their sacrifices. (Hos 4:16-19)

Israel's destruction was predicated upon her idolatrous opposition to God (Hos 4:12; 13:9), which was accompanied by the ever present symptoms of the rejection of knowledge (Hos 4:6), the loss of understanding (Hos 4:11; 7:11), stubbornness (Hos 4:16), spiritual drunkenness (Hos 4:11-12; 7:5), insolence (Hos 7:16), the loss of inspiration from the prophets (Hos 9:7), faithlessness and pride of heart (=hardness; 10:2; 13:6; also 7:10; Rom 2:5-9), and the prospect of national exile (Hos 8:8-10; 9:3, 17; 11:5).

Despite, however, the bleakness of Hosea's indictment, Israel's hardened state in the book of Hosea is not perceived to be necessarily permanent, nor is her plight of destruction irreversible. Hosea offers hope for a new covenant reversal, which consummates in the very words quoted by Paul:

> And it will come about in that day, declares the Lord, that you will call me Ishi and will no longer call me Baali. For I will remove the names of the Baals from her mouth, so that they will be mentioned by their names no more. In that day I will also make a covenant for them with the beasts

---

[22] Cranfield, *Romans*, 2:500. Barth, *Church Dogmatics*, II.2.231.

of the field, the birds of the sky, and the creeping things of the ground. And I will abolish the bow, the sword, and war from the land, and will make them lie down in safety. And I will betroth you to me forever, yes, I will betroth you to me in righteousness and in justice, in lovngkindness and in compassion, and I will betroth you to me in faithfulness. Then you will know the Lord. (Hos 2:16-20; cf. Ezek 36:25, 38)

I will also have compassion on her who had not obtained compassion, and I will say to those who were not my people, you are my people! And they will say, you are my God! (Hos 2:23; Rom 9:25; see also Hos 1:10-11; ch. 14)

Paul argues, quite simply, that Hosea's vision of new covenant transformation has been experienced by believing Jews and Gentiles (Rom 9:24), while, by contrast, unbelieving Jews continue to exist in the same state of deluded seduction that afflicted their Israelite ancestors. Their pursuit of righteousness by works (*hōs ex ergōn*; Rom 9:32) proved their ignorance of God's instruction for worship, i.e., that God delights "in loyalty rather than sacrifice, and in the knowledge of God rather than burnt offerings" (Hos 6:6). Nonetheless, Paul knows that the potential for reversal still exists for his unbelieving kinsmen as it did for their unfaithful ancestors—"if they do not continue in their unbelief" (Rom 11:23).

(f) *The Remnant: The Cry of Isaiah (Romans 9:27-29)*

Paul reinforces these thoughts with the corrective clarification that Scripture, if rightly understood, has always maintained that only a remnant of Israel will be saved. This observation furthers Paul's defense of God's faithfulness to his covenant promises to Israel. Paul quotes an abbreviated form of Isa 1:9 and 10:22-23, of which the first part is assimilated to Hos 1:10, to convey his conviction that Isaiah's prophecy foretold the circumstances of his day—that only a fraction of Israel would accept the gospel and enter the new covenant people of God.[23] Paul viewed Israel's external, superficial worship as falling short of God's will (Rom 2:28-29), just as Isaiah had bemoaned Israel's external rituals in the Scriptures (e.g., Isa 1:10-15). As an unauthorized alternative to authentic faith, religious ritual was tantamount to idolatry (Rom 2:1b; 11:4-5), the vice endemic to the Israel of Isaiah's day (Isaiah 2). Virtually all the OT references to the "remnant," including this one from Isaiah, explain that the non-remnant was forsaken by God because of its traitorous alliances with foreign nations and its rebellious participation in idolatry (Isaiah 1-2; 10:5-11; 2 Kings 17; 23:26-27).

It is also evident, however, that the surviving remnant was not deserving of its fortune. Its preservation was an act of divine grace (2 Kgs 21:10-15; Ezra 9:8-13; Ezek 9:8-11) performed for Israel's discipline and the continued revelation and affirmation of God's sovereignty as Lord. The clearest biblical explanation for the remnant is found in Ezek 6:8-14:

---

[23] So Cranfield, *Romans*, 2:502; Stuhlmacher, *Romans*, 151, who also views the remnant as "identical to the converted Jewish Christians who belong to the church of Christ."

> However I shall leave a remnant, for you will have those who escaped the sword among the nations when you are scattered among the countries. Then those of you who escape will remember me among the nations to which they will be carried captive, how I have been hurt by their adulterous hearts which turned away from me, and by their eyes, which played the harlot after their idols; and they will loathe themselves in their own sight for the evils which they have committed, for all their abominations. Then they will know that I am the Lord; I have not said in vain that I would inflict this disaster on them.

The remnant that Paul refers to is the eschatological remnant that God promised to transform and reconstitute into his new covenant people. This remnant, which Paul interprets as prophesied by Isa 10:20, would reenter the favor of God's covenant by means of the transforming work of the Holy Spirit. This divine work would remove the ill effects of idolatry and make possible again the holiness of God's people. Ezekiel again provides a clear expression of this promise:

> Alas, Lord God! Will you bring the remnant of Israel to a complete end? Then the word of the Lord came to me, saying, Son of man, your brothers, your relatives, your fellow exiles, and the whole house of Israel, all of them, are those to whom the inhabitants of Jerusalem have said, Go far from the Lord; this land has been given us as a possession. Therefore say, thus says the Lord God, though I had removed them far away among the nations, and though I had scattered them among the countries, yet I was a sanctuary for them a little while in the countries where they had gone. Therefore say, 'thus says the Lord God, I shall gather you from the peoples and assemble you out of the countries among which you have been scattered, and I shall give you the land of Israel. When they come there, they will remove all its detestable things and all its abominations from it. And I shall give them one heart, and shall put a new spirit within them. And I shall take the heart of stone out of their flesh and give them a heart of flesh, that they may walk in my statutes and keep my ordinances, and do them. Then they will be my people, and I shall be their God. But as for those whose hearts go after their detestable things and abominations, I shall bring their conduct down on their heads,' declares the Lord God. (Ezek 11:13b-21; see also Mic 4:6-8; Zech 8:12-23)

This passage clearly correlates idolatry/covenant infidelity and the phenomenon of the hardening of the heart. Conversely, it also correlates the removal of idols and the healing transformation of the heart. The latter saving event Paul conceives as having been activated in Jesus' redemptive work, and exclusively takes place through the transforming power of the gospel: "For the law of the Spirit of life in Christ Jesus has set you free from the law of sin and of death . . . he condemned sin in the flesh, in order that the requirement of the law might be fulfilled in us, who do not walk according to the flesh, but according to the Spirit" (Rom 8:3-4;

cf. 8:12-17). The remnant therefore is composed of Spirit transformed beneficiaries of the gospel, while the hardened non-remnant is composed of those who still live in subjection to literal idols (Rom 1:18-32) or external religion, which Paul views as tantamount to idolatry (Romans 2; 10:3-4; 11:4-5).

For this reason Paul reminds his readers that were it not for God's mercy Israel would have become like Sodom and Gomorrah. This statement too has traditional connotations that contribute to Paul's overall message. In Deuteronomy 29 God had forecasted that Israel would suffer a fate comparable to that of Sodom and Gomorrah, because Israel would forsake the covenant to worship other gods (Deut 29:23-26). Therefore God would curse Israelites who were unfaithful and stubborn of heart (Deut 29:18-19) by afflicting them with "every curse" including plagues, diseases, and exile (Deut 29:22, 27-28). This same tradition regarding Sodom and Gemorrah resurfaces in Isa 1:9 (Rom 9:29), where Isaiah perceives that Israel has indeed brought upon herself these promised curses, because of her superficial worship (Isa 1:10-15; also ch. 29) and blatant idolatry (Isa 1:29-31; 2:6-22). Elsewhere in the OT the "Sodom and Gomorrah" warning emerges consistently as a prophetic threat voiced against those who challenge the covenant either militarily or religiously.[24]

Paul's application of the insult to Israel is consistent with this biblical tradition. Like Isaiah and Amos, Paul views unbelieving Israel, past and present, as unfaithful to the covenant and religiously idolatrous. Moreover, in rejecting the gospel, Israel has become an obstacle to the covenant people. Therefore in faithfulness to Deuteronomy 29, God would be entirely just if he destroyed Israel altogether as he did Sodom and Gomorrah. God's provision of the remnant as an alternative to this tragic prospect testifies to God's patient mercy and his faithfulness to the Abrahamic covenant.

(g) *What does all of this mean? (Romans 9:30-33)*

Romans 9 should be interpreted in a way that encompasses the entirety of Paul's message in Romans and the scope of his conceptual scriptural background. Romans 9 should be understood on the basis of a careful study of how all of Romans 9 relates to Paul's explicit emphasis on faith—as he articulates at the conclusion of Romans 9 in verses 30-33. For Romans 9 climaxes with Paul's explanation of the disparity between the fortune of believing Gentiles and the tragic misfortune of unbelieving Israel. The former attained unsought righteousness as a gift by faith in Christ (Rom 9:30; 3:23), while the latter did not achieve the righteousness they strove for (Rom 9:16), because they sought it where it could not be found—in external religious observance of the law. Satisfied that potentially they could become righteous through observance of the law or were indeed righteous already as observers of the law, most of Paul's Jewish contemporaries did not sense the need for the righteousness afforded by faith in Christ (Rom 9:16, 31-32), whom, in any case, they rejected as Messiah and risen Lord. Hence, they tripped over the gospel, because of their preexisting faith in the

---

[24] Isa 13:19 (against Babylon); Jer 49:18 (against Edom); 50:40 (against Babylon); Amos 4:11 (against all Israel, particularly Bashan and Samaria).

law (2 Cor 3:14-15). Therefore Paul applies to ethnic Judaism the traditional symptoms of idolatry—the hardening of the heart (Rom 2:5; 11:25), the attribute of stubbornness (10:21; also 2:5), and the dysfunction of the senses (Rom 11:8-10). They preferred the righteousness of their own making to the righteousness of God (Rom 10:3), which God revealed exclusively in the gospel (Rom 1:16-17).

For this reason unbelieving Israel did not have access to the salvation given those who believed in Christ, the "stone of stumbling" and "rock of offense" *who would not disappoint* (Rom 9:33). That Christ is the "stone of stumbling" who does not disappoint is made certain by Rom 10:11. It is also clear why he will not disappoint—because it is he who will bless believers with the benefits of the new covenant: "Hope *does not disappoint*, because the love of God has been poured out within our hearts through the Holy Spirit who was given to us. For while we were still helpless, at the right time Christ died for the ungodly" (Rom 5:5-6; also 10:9-10). This salvation which does not disappoint entails the new creation within believers (Rom 2:28-29; 2 Cor 3:18; 5:17-18; Phil 3:21) wrought by the Holy Spirit in fulfillment of the new covenant promises (Hosea 2; Jeremiah 31; Ezekiel 36; Romans 8). It occurs as a result of the saving work of Jesus' death and resurrection (Romans 10). This salvation, Paul pleads, is accessible only for those who believe in Christ. While it is not yet active in the life of unbelieving Israel, it remains available as *the exclusive cure for Israel's hardening*—"if they do not continue in unbelief" (Rom 11:23). For the stone which Paul alludes to in Rom 9:33 (Isa 28:16) is the stone, which, if believed in, would cancel Judah's "covenant with death" (Isa 28:18). Paul's gospel is that Jesus is *that* stone and that as such he is Israel's savior who can save her from destruction.[25] God's faithfulness, righteousness, and fairness therefore abound in every respect.

Conclusion

God's bearing with much patience vessels of wrath prepared for destruction in Romans 9 is of one cloth with God's patience extended to Israel in Romans 11. God exercises patience for the accomplishment of his salvific plan. Those "called" (Rom 8:28; 9:11-12), including both Jews and Gentiles, are vessels who have been saved from destruction by God's grace accomplished by Jesus' sacrifice on the cross and appropriated by faith in Christ. Romans 9 clearly articulates a change of identity and fate on the part of the vessels of mercy prepared for glory. The Hosea quote makes this clear: "*I will call those who were not my people my people, and her who was not beloved, beloved. And it shall be in the place where it was said to them, you are not my people, there they shall be called sons of the living God*" (Rom 9:25-26). The factor determining this change of fate and identity is faith as Rom 9:30-33 makes crystal clear. Paul's emphasis on faith in chapter 9 builds upon his previous arguments in Romans 1-8 (esp. chs. 1, 3-4) to strengthen the foundation for his declarations in Rom 10:8-17 and 11:20-23 that salvation is awarded and maintained exclusively on the basis of faith in Christ.

---

[25] Within Isaiah the stone of course is God himself (Isa 8:13-14). This transfer of symbolism from God to Jesus is consistent with Paul's Christological equation of Jesus with God (Rom 9:5). See Murray J. Harris, *Jesus as God* (Grand Rapids: Baker, 1992), 143-172.

Chapter 10

Jealousy and the Partial Hardening of Israel

(Romans 10-11)

I have kept for myself seven thousand men who have not bowed the knee to Baal. In the same way then, there has also come to be at the present time a remnant according to God's gracious choice. (Rom 11:4-5)

I. ROMANS 10: SEEKING A RIGHTEOUSNESS OF THEIR OWN

Asserting that unbelieving Israelites did not subject themselves to the righteousness of God because of a preferred pursuit of a righteousness of their own (Rom 10:3), Paul makes explicit his instructions for Israel's salvation in Rom 10:9-10, with frequent recourse to OT substantiation.[1] His explanation maintains the consistent argument of Romans that God's righteousness is revealed in the gospel (Rom 1:16-17) and appropriated exclusively in the lives of those who believe in Christ (Rom 10:4). The instructions are identical to those provided Gentiles, because "the same Lord is Lord of all" (Rom 10:12). The reverse of the idolatry and the hardening of the heart phenomenon characterizes those who exercise faith in the resurrected Lord Jesus. Whereas Paul denounced the idolatrous and hypocritical Jewish audience of Romans 2 as being callused by stubborn and unrepentant hearts, he now qualifies that the saved are characterized by hearts whose belief leads to righteousness (Rom 10:10). This necessitates a process of transformation from sin to righteousness that is commensurate with the promises of the new covenant. The process fully conforms to Paul's pronouncements in Rom 2:28-29 and Romans 8. In each context Paul's gospel is that the new covenant transformation promised by Jeremiah 31 and Ezekiel 36 has been activated in the lives of those who believe in and have been saved by the redemptive work of Jesus that is furthered and maintained by the Holy Spirit. Once God has rewarded the faithful with his righteousness and begun the process of reconciliation, the accompanying transformation unfolds, i.e., the writing of the law upon the heart (Rom 2:15), the circumcision of the heart (Rom 2:28-29), the indwelling of the Spirit (Rom 2:29; 5:5; 8:11-27), the process of conformity to the image of Jesus (Rom 8:29), and the glorification of the believer (Rom 8:30). This

---

[1] Old Testament quotations and allusions saturate Romans 10-11. Peter Stuhlmacher (*Romans*, 153, 158) lists the following references: 10:5 (Lev 18:5); 10:6 (Deut 9:4 = 30:12); 10:7 (Ps 107:26; Deut 30:13); 10:8 (Deut 30:14); 10:11 (Isa 28:16); 10:13 (Joel 3:5); 10:15 (Isa 52:7; Nah 2:1); 10:16 (Isa 53:1); 10:18 (Ps 19:5); 10:19 (Deut 32:21); 10:20 (Isa 65:1); 10:21 (Isa 65:2).

salvation, Paul preaches, is still on offer to unbelieving Israel. But in order for this salvation to become real in the life of the non-remnant part of Israel, these Israelites must hear, believe, and obey the preaching of the gospel, for the Holy Spirit and the accompanying benefits of the new covenant come not through legal observance but solely through the preaching of the gospel, as Paul passionately proclaims in Rom 10:12-15 (Gal 3:2-5).

In developing this explanation, Paul portrays Christ as "the goal, the essential meaning, the real substance of the law" (Rom 10:4).[2] This relationship, however, exists between Christ and the law as God revealed it in its fullness according to his original intent as portrayed in Deut 30:10. Paul sees a distinction between this law that is good and the sin twisted legalism that blinds his contemporaries. Hence, Paul is able to maintain his positive appraisal of the law (Rom 3:31; 7:12, 14a; 8:4; 13:8-10) while lamenting unbelieving Israel's misappropriation of the law (Rom 10:2-3). For the law was not at fault, but rather it was sin's convolution of the law that was responsible for Israel's tragic state, as it had been formerly for Paul himself (Rom 7:13). Therefore in Rom 10:6-8 Paul applies to Christ phraseology that Deuteronomy 30:12-14 previously applied to the law. The effect of the transfer is Paul's message that just as the law was not hidden or "not too difficult" (Deut 30:11) for Israel at the time of Moses, because God had revealed it clearly, neither was the gospel too difficult for Israel at the time of Paul, because the gospel was being preached publicly and explicitly (as Paul himself does in the verses that follow in Rom 10:9-10).

Likewise, just as "the word" (Deut 30:14), i.e., the call for sincere love of God from the heart, promised physical life and national prosperity at the time of Moses (Deut 30:9-10, 16, 20), so also, Paul argues, does the "word of faith" (Rom 10:8) promise spiritual righteousness and salvation to those who confess Jesus as Lord and believe that God raised him from the dead (Rom 10:9-10). Corresponding to this is the misfortune that comes upon those who choose not to obey because of alternative substitute allegiances. Paul reapplies the precedent of Deut 30:17 —"But if your heart turns away and you will not obey, but are drawn away and worship other gods and serve them, I declare to you today that you shall surely perish"—to his kinsmen who are storing up wrath because of their "stubborn" and "unrepentant" hearts (Rom 2:5). Their stubbornness, according to Romans, is particularly associated with their opposition to the gospel, an opposition that is precipitated by a preexisting confidence in religious legalism. Therefore, what idols had been to Israel in Deuteronomy 30, traditional legalism became to the unbelieving Israelites of Paul's day. They sought to establish a righteousness of their own through the keeping of the law (Rom 10:3).

Paul views the non-remnant as consisting of those who "did not heed the glad tidings" (Rom 10:16). What was formerly true in the age of the prophets, continued to be true in Paul's day. As the non-remnant was once composed of those who did not believe Isaiah's glad tidings (Isa 53:1; Rom 10:16), so in Paul's day the non-remnant was composed of those who did not believe the gospel. Hence, all along faith has been God's willed condition for the choice of his elect remnant. Because all Israel had heard and knew (Rom 10:18-19), unbelieving

---

[2] Cranfield, *Romans*, 2.524.

Israel was without excuse. Remnant theology, therefore, is entirely consistent with the doctrine of justification by grace through faith in Christ. The remnant are those that hear, repent, and believe from the heart. The non-remnant, the part of Israel that is not true Israel, is the hostile portion that heard but did not respond, believe, and repent (as was the case in Deuteronomy 30).

As an experienced evangelist to Israel, Paul could personally identify with God's exasperation communicated by Isaiah: "All the day long I have stretched out my hands to a disobedient and obstinate people" (Rom 10:21; Isa 65:2). Israel's response to God's revelation was the same in his day as it was in Isaiah's: Israel still was not calling upon the name of the Lord (Isa 65:1), because her religious observance continued to be misguided and religiously idolatrous (Isa 65:3, 7). Therefore her course continued to be toward destruction (Isa 65:12).

II. ROMANS 11: IDOLATRY AND THE PARTIAL HARDENING OF ISRAEL'S HEART

The rhetorical question in Rom 11:1 continues the argument which began in Romans 9 and was further explained in Romans 10—i.e., that God has not rejected his people or forsaken his promises to them. On the contrary, God has worked mysteriously throughout Israel's history to create the opportunity for her salvation. In doing so God has chosen by his grace a remnant whose continued existence is necessary in order for Israel's life to be sustained. The Gentile portion of that remnant has a peculiar role in God's strategy for Israel. For Paul hopes that when his kinsmen observe God's saving work among Gentiles, they will grow jealous of the Gentiles for receiving the salvation that was first meant for them. Goaded by this jealousy, some of Paul's kinsmen (Rom 11:14) will regain their senses and seek reconciliation with God, so that "all Israel will be saved" (Rom 11:26).

Paul begins Romans 11 with yet another analogy to scriptural history. The present remnant, Paul explains, is like that which God reserved for himself at the time of Elijah. "In the same way" (Rom 11:5) that God had kept for himself seven-thousand men who did not bow their knees to Baal at the time of Elijah, so God was now choosing for his purposes another remnant according to grace and specifically not on the basis of works (Rom 11:6). Paul implicitly compares the remnant of his day to the seven thousand who did not bow their knees to Baal and negatively compares the non-remnant of his day to the idolatrous people of Israel, who, unlike the seven thousand, *did* bow their knees to Baal. As God had chosen the faithful seven thousand while rejecting those who worshipped Baal, God was now choosing a faithful remnant *by grace* while rejecting those who were attempting to secure righteousness on the basis of works (Rom 11:6-7). The law ironically takes the form and function of an idol, because it establishes a deceptive alternative to God's righteousness exclusively appropriated through faith in Christ. This message is not ambiguous: *what Baal was to unfaithful Israel at the time of Elijah, the law has become to unbelieving Israel at the time of Paul.*

Therefore, as this study would now lead us to expect, Paul applies to Israel the telltale symptoms of idolatry—the hardening of the heart and sensory depletion:

> But if it is by grace, it is no longer on the basis of works, otherwise grace is no longer grace. What then? That which Israel is seeking for, it has not obtained, but those who were chosen obtained it, and the rest were hardened; just as it is written, 'God gave them a spirit of stupor, eyes to see not and ears to hear not, down to this very day. And David says, let their table become a snare and a trap, and a stumbling block and a retribution to them. Let their eyes be darkened to see not, and bend their backs forever. (Rom 11:6-10)

Paul recognizes that the hardening curse fulfills scriptural prophecy as indicated by the phrase "just as it is written" (Rom 11:8) — specifically, the successive quotations coming from Deut 29:4, Isa 29:10, and Ps 69:22-23. Each passage carries contextual connotations that contribute to Paul's general explanation of Israel's present hardening. We will now analyze each of these passages and attempt to explain how they complement one another in supporting Paul's overall argument.

(a) *Deuteronomy 29:4*

Deuteronomy 29:4 (Rom 11:8), *a classic expression of the idolatry and the hardening of the heart phenomenon* (Deut 29:4, 17-19, 25-26),[3] occurs within a discourse where Moses warns of the curses that will afflict members of Israel if they betray the covenant in order to worship pagan deities:

> Moreover, you have seen their abominations and their idols of wood, stone, silver, and gold, which they had with them; lest there shall be among you a man or woman, or family or tribe, whose heart turns away today from the Lord our God, to go and serve the gods of those nations; lest there shall be among you a root bearing poisonous fruit and wormwood. And it shall be when he hears the words of this curse, that he will boast, saying, I have peace though I walk in the stubbornness of my heart in order to destroy the watered land with the dry. The Lord shall never be willing to forgive him, but rather the anger of the Lord and his jealousy will burn against that man, and every curse which is written in this book will rest on him, and the Lord will blot out his name from under heaven. (Deut 29:17-20)

Paul viewed these Mosaic curses as applicable to his own day, because they were voiced prophetically in the future tense and were intended by Moses to counsel the people of Israel to recognize that their future would be determined entirely by their faithfulness or unfaithfulness to Yahweh. In Rom 11:8 Paul simply applies these promised curses to contemporary unbelieving Jews. As Moses predicted that the nations would ask, "Why has the Lord done thus to this land? Why this great burst of anger?" (Deut 29:24), so Paul views himself as essentially answering the same question in regard to God's present estrangement from hardened, unbelieving

---

[3] See ch. 1.

Israel (Rom 11:1). Therefore, viewing his words as entirely consistent with Moses' prediction, Paul pronounces a sentence that corroborates, indeed presupposes, Moses' answer in Deut 29:25-26: *"Because they forsook the covenant of the Lord, the God of their fathers, which he made with them when he brought them out of the land of Egypt. And they went and served other gods and worshipped them, gods whom they have not known and whom he had not allotted to them."* The association harmonizes perfectly with Paul's previous identification of unbelieving Israel with idolatrous worshippers of Baal (Rom 11:4).

(b) *Isaiah 29:10*

Paul integrates with the curse of Deut 29:4 the debilitating stupor (*katanyxis*)[4] Isaiah applies to Judah (Isa 29:10; Rom 11:8). This contextualization of Deuteronomy 29 serves Paul's present argument perfectly. In Isaiah 29 the cause of hardening/sensory malfunction is not the literal worship of idols but the idolatrous replacement of authentic worship of God with a superficial substitute:

> For the Lord has poured over you a spirit of deep sleep, he has shut your eyes, the prophets; and he has covered your heads, the seers. And the entire vision shall be to you like the words of a sealed book, which when they give it to the one who is literate, saying, please read this, he will say, I cannot, for it is sealed. Then the book will be given to the one who is illiterate, saying please read this. And he will say, I cannot read. Then the Lord said, *because this people draw near with their words and honor me with their lip service, but they remove their hearts far from me, and their reverence for me consists of tradition learned by rote, therefore behold, I will once again deal marvelously with this people, wondrously marvelous; and the wisdom of their wise men shall perish, and the discernment of their discerning men shall be concealed.* (Isa 29:10-14)

Paul applies this affliction to the unbelieving Jews of his day who "cannot read" or understand the truth of the gospel of Jesus Christ because they suffer a spiritual "stupor" induced by tradition's misappropriation of the law. They, like their counterparts addressed by Isaiah, maintain a reverence for tradition that has supplanted true worship of God from the heart. They, therefore, like their historical predecessors, have been given over by God to a stupor that prevents them from perceiving the truth of the gospel (cf. Isa 6:9-10; Mark 4:11-12). Moreover, because the potter metaphor is also present in Isa 29:16, it is possible that this explanation may shed further light on Rom 9:20-24: "the vessels of wrath prepared for destruction" are those unbelieving Jews whose superficial worship Paul now reproves in Rom 11:8-10.

---

[4] The allusion is virtually certain due to the fact that *katanyxis* occurs only in Rom 11:8 in the NT and in Isa 29:10 and 60:3 in the LXX.

(c) *Psalm 69*

Psalm 69, quoted by Paul in Rom 11:9-10, is an imprecatory Psalm of David that curses David's enemies.[5] In Paul's reapplication of the curse, he puts the unbelieving Jews of his day in the place of those who formerly persecuted David, the progenitor of the Davidic covenant and the messianic line. Thus Paul also identifies hardening as an affliction that incapacitates unbelieving Jews who stand as obstacles in the way of the advancement of the gospel of Jesus Christ, whom Paul preaches as the messiah, Son of God, and "descendant of David according to the flesh" (Rom 1:3b).

This negative appraisal of unbelieving Israel accords well with 1 Thess 2:14-16 and the remarks of Jesus (Luke 6:22-23; 11:46-53; 13:34-35 and par.). More importantly, as far as the context of Romans is concerned, it explains further the hardening theme that Paul proposed in Rom 1:18-24 and developed further in Rom 2:5 and 9:18. The symptoms of hardening that Paul previously applied to idolaters (Rom 1:18-24), religious hypocrites (Rom 2:5-6) and Pharaoh (Rom 9:17-18), he now applies to Jewish adversaries of the gospel. Paul recognizes that the unbelieving Jews of his day have resisted God's will by rejecting Christ and his apostles (Rom 8:17, 36) and have committed idolatry by substituting legal tradition for faith in God.

(d) *The Jealousy Phenomenon and its Relation to Israel's Idolatry*

Paul combines the curse of hardening with the related covenantal curse of Moses cited in Rom 10:19 (Deut 32:21): "I will make you jealous by that which is not a nation, by a nation without understanding will I anger you." The jealousy theme establishes Paul's transition from the present reality of Israel's obstinacy to the proclamation of his hope for Israel's future. Deuteronomy 32, the background to the jealousy phenomenon, identifies the same transition from punishment to deliverance as God's desired will. In accord with our thesis, Israel's jealousy is God's explicit punishment for idolatry.[6] Moreover, this future jealousy, as described in Deuteronomy 32, is accompanied by an absence of spiritual understanding (cf. Rom 10:3). And yet the sentence is not absolute but is intended for Israel's discipline and ultimately as a catalyst for her repentance. The following development within Deuteronomy 32 makes this clear:

> Then he said, I will hide my face from them, I will see what their end shall be; for they are a perverse generation, sons in whom is no faithfulness. *They have made me jealous with what is not God; they have provoked me to anger with their idols.* So I will make them jealous with

---

[5] Psalm 69 is quoted or alluded to frequently in the NT where it is cited as a prophetic description of Jesus' ministry: Matt 27:34, 48; Mark 3:21; 15:23, 36; Luke 13:35; 23:36; John 2:17; 15:25; 19:29; Acts 1:20; Rom 15:3; Heb 11:26; cf. Phil 4:3; Rev 3:5; 16:1.

[6] Our thesis being that hardening is a covenantal curse God inflicts upon those who imperil the covenant people in fulfillment of Gen 12:3. The most consistent biblical form of this infraction is idolatry. The only cure for this hardening disability is the salvation extended by the new covenant activated exclusively by the sacrificial ministry of Jesus.

those who are not a people; I will provoke them to anger with a foolish nation. (Deut 32:20-21)

For they are a nation lacking in counsel, and there is no understanding in them. Would that they were wise, that they understood this, that they would discern their future! (Deut 32:28)

For the Lord will vindicate his people, and will have compassion on his servants; when he sees that their strength is gone, and there is none remaining bond or free. *And he will say, 'Where are their gods, the rock in which they sought refuge? Who ate the fat of their sacrifices, and drank the wine of their libation? Let them rise up and help you, let them be your hiding place! 'See now that I, I am He. And there is no god besides me; It is I who put to death and give life. I have wounded, and it is I who heal; and there is no one who can deliver from my hand.* (Deut 32:36-39)

Jealousy therefore ultimately serves the same purpose as God's curses of exile and hardening. It is one part of God's plan for revealing his sovereignty over and against the impotence of Israel, her idols, and her foreign alliances. It is one of God's chosen means for bringing Israel back to her senses.

Paul was not alone, of course, in attributing Israel's suffering to the well-intended discipline of God. The prospect that God's punitive discipline would lead to salvation was first ordained in Deuteronomy 32 and then subsequently taken up in Jewish texts like the apocryphal book of Baruch (150-60 B.C.). Select portions of Baruch establish that Jews of the Second Temple era had an awareness of God's benevolent purpose in the discipline of his people:

From the time when the Lord brought our ancestors out of the land of Egypt until today, we have been disobedient to the Lord our God, and we have been negligent, in not heeding his voice. So to this day there have clung to us the calamities and the curse that the Lord declared through his servant Moses at the time when he brought our ancestors out of the land of Egypt to give to us a land flowing with milk and honey. *We did not listen to the voice of the Lord our God in all the words of the prophets whom he sent to us, but all of us followed the intent of our own wicked hearts by serving other gods and doing what is evil in the sight of the Lord our God.* (Bar 1:19-22)

All those calamities with which the Lord threatened us have come upon us. Yet we have not entreated the favor of the Lord by turning away, each of us, from the thoughts of our wicked hearts. And the Lord has kept the calamities ready, and the Lord has brought them upon us, for the Lord is just in all the works that he has commanded us to do. (Bar 2:7-10)

Yet you have dealt with us, O Lord our God, in all your kindness and in all your great compassion, as you spoke by your servant Moses on the

> day when you commanded him to write your law in the presence of the people of Israel, saying, If you will not obey my voice, this very great multitude will surely turn into a small number among the nations, where I will scatter them. *For I know that they will not obey me, for they are a stiff-necked people. But in the land of their exile they will come to themselves and know that I am the Lord their God. I will give them a heart that obeys and ears that hear; they will praise me in the land of their exile, and will remember my name and turn from their stubbornness and their wicked deeds; for they will remember the ways of their ancestors, who sinned before the Lord.* I will bring them again into the land that I swore to give to their ancestors, to Abraham, Isaac, and Jacob, and they will rule over it; and I will increase them, and they will not be diminished. I will make an everlasting covenant with them to be their God and they shall be my people; and I will never again remove my people Israel from the land that I have given them. (Bar 2:27-35)
>
> Do not remember the iniquities of our ancestors, but in this crisis remember your power and your name. *For you are the Lord our God, and it is you, O Lord, whom we will praise. For you have put the fear of you in our hearts so that we would call upon your name; and we will praise you in our exile, for we have put away from our hearts all the iniquity of our ancestors who sinned against you. See, we are today in our exile where you have scattered us, to be reproached and cursed and punished for all the iniquities of our ancestors, who forsook the Lord our God.* (Bar 3:5-8)
>
> *Take courage, my people, who perpetuate Israel's name! It was not for destruction that you were sold to the nations, but you were handed over to your enemies because you angered God. For you provoked the one who made you by sacrificing to demons and not to God.* (Bar 4:5-7)

Paul shares with Deuteronomy and Baruch the understanding that Israel's present hardening/stubbornness is a symptom of her own sin and that God is fully just in carrying out against Israel the curses that he promised in the ancient Scriptures. Paul also shares the eschatological hope that God, after he has adequately punished Israel to bring about the desired result of repentance, will transform Israel by giving her people hearts to obey and ears to hear so that they might worship God in purity within a restored covenant (Deut 30:6; Bar 2:31). All of this God will do in faithfulness to his covenantal promises to Abraham and in fulfillment of the new covenant (Bar 2:35; cf. Jer 32:38-40; Ezek 36:26-29; Amos 9:15).

Paul, however, through the revelation of the gospel, is able to explain with greater precision God's actions toward Israel. For the hardening and jealousy Israel experiences in exile will erode her pride and national trust thereby leading her to reconsider the true purpose of the law and the need for the fulfillment of the messianic prophecies of Scripture. This process in turn will lead to a reevaluation of the gospel of Jesus Christ whereupon previously unbelieving Jews will discover through faith in Christ the benefits of the new covenant promised by their own prophets. This turn of events will indeed evidence "life from the dead" (Rom 11:15b) in the sense predicted by Ezekiel: "Then you will know that I am the Lord, when I have opened your graves and caused you to come up out of your graves, my people. And I will put my spirit within you, and you will come to life, and I will place you on your own land. Then you will know that I, the Lord, have spoken and done it, declares the Lord" (Ezek 37:13-14). This resurrection must take place so that the hard-hearted, non-remnant (Rom 2:5; 10:21; 11:7, 25) may become true Israel composed of true Jews whose circumcision is of the heart by the Spirit of God (Rom 2:29; Deut 30:6; Ezek 36:22-37).

This expectation is consistent with the entire book of Romans. In the future Israel's security will be conditioned upon her faith in Christ and not upon her ethnic origin or her legal observance of Jewish tradition. Indeed, in order for the non-remnant to become a part of true Israel, the non-remnant must express the faith specified by Paul in Rom 3:21-31 and Rom 10:9-10. Only by doing so can the non-remnant meet the Mosaic condition of Deut 30:1-3, 9-10. In this sense "Christ is the end of the law for righteousness to everyone who believes" (Rom 10:4), for by believing in Christ, sinners, Jews and Gentiles alike, display obedience to God's plan of salvation, authentic love for God as opposed to tradition, and an Abraham-like faith that God is able to do what he promised first to Abraham, then to Jeremiah and Ezekiel as communicated now through the gospel of the atoning work of Jesus, the Messiah—namely faith that God as creator and merciful re-creator can give life to the dead and call into being that which does not exist (Rom 4:17b).

Ethnic Israel's future salvation is not a forgone conclusion, however. The new covenant as activated by Jesus' sacrificial ministry is Paul's only hope for the reversal of Israel's hardening. Paul does not anticipate the *unconditional*, wholesale salvation of ethnic Israel, otherwise he would be compromising his own gospel of justification by faith and his corrective that there is no partiality with God (Rom 2:11). He maintains his corrective that "it is not the children of the flesh who are the children of God, but the children of the promise" (Rom 9:8). This promise pertaining to all the children of God is "the promise of the Spirit through faith" (Gal 3:14). The children of the promise are those who respond positively to the gospel, with the result that they are transformed by the Holy Spirit from hardened sinners into holy children of God (Gal 3:2; Rom 8:9-17). Hence, warnings such as those found in Deut 29:19-20 and 30:17-18 still apply for unbelieving Jews who resist the gospel to the very end. Their rejection of the gospel is a rejection of God's will and an obstruction of God's providential plan (cf. Luke 7:23, 30). Salvation in Pauline terms is impossible without the justifying, atoning, transforming, sanctifying work of Christ. Without it the sinner, whether Jew or Gentile, is still afflicted by sin and totally unfit for life with God according to the new covenant.

(e) *Pruning and Grafting: The Centrality of Faith*

In Romans 11 Paul explicitly writes that unbelieving Jews *can be grafted in again* "if they do not continue in their unbelief" (Rom 11:23). Here he continues to address the major question underlying Romans 9-11—i.e., unbelieving Israel's place within God's plan of salvation. This question, so personal to Paul because of his own Jewish heritage, found precedent in Scriptures like Jer 11:8-17, the probable point of origin for his olive tree metaphor:

> Yet they did not obey or incline their ear, but walked, each one, in the stubbornness of his evil heart; therefore I brought on them all the words of this covenant, which I commanded them to do, but they did not. Then the Lord said to me, A conspiracy has been found among the men of Judah and among the inhabitants of Jerusalem. They have turned back to the iniquities of their ancestors who refused to hear my words, and they have gone after other gods to serve them; the house of Israel and the house of Judah have broken my covenant which I made with their fathers. Therefore thus says the Lord, Behold I am bringing disaster on them which they will not be able to escape; though they will cry to me, yet I will not listen to them. Then the cities of Judah and the inhabitants of Jerusalem will go and cry to the gods to whom they burn incense, but they surely will not save them in the time of their disaster. For your gods are as many as your cities, O Judah; and as many as the streets of Jerusalem are the altars you have set up to the shameful thing, altars to burn incense to Baal. Therefore do not pray for this people, nor lift up a cry or prayer for them; for I will not listen when they call to me because of their disaster. What right has my beloved in my house when she has done many vile deeds? Can the sacrificial flesh take away from you your disaster, so that you can rejoice? *The Lord called your name, a green olive tree, beautiful in fruit and form; with the noise of a great tumult he has kindled fire on it, and its branches are worthless. And the Lord of hosts, who planted you, has pronounced evil against you because of the evil of the house of Israel and of the house of Judah, which they have done to provoke me by offering up sacrifices to Baal.*

Jeremiah adopted the olive tree metaphor to communicate God's determination to punish Israel for her idolatry and God's refusal to be manipulated by superficial prayer or sacrifice (Jer 11:14-15). In Romans Paul maintains this sentence as an accurate indictment of Jews who have been "broken off for their unbelief" (Rom 11:20). However, Paul qualifies that God has not forgotten his people and has not annulled his promises to them, because in his mercy he has created the opportunity for the reconciliation of these same Jews.

Paul perhaps chose the metaphor, because, if read in isolation, the prophecy of Jeremiah may have suggested to believing Gentiles the impossibility of unbelieving Israel's future reconciliation with God. But Paul preempts this misguided idea by reasserting "that the gospel is the power of God for salvation to everyone who believes, to the Jew first and also to the Greek" (Rom 1:16). In other words, the same gospel that effectively grafted Gentile believers into the promises of Abraham could capably re-graft converted Jews into the covenantal promises that were, after all, originally theirs before idolatrous sin separated them from God (Rom 11:23).

(f) *The 'Mystery' of the Partial Hardening of Israel that Leads to the Display of God's Mercy to All*

The mystery Paul speaks of in Rom 11:25 is the mystery of the relationship between the gospel and presently hardened unbelieving Jews. How does the gospel that Paul summarizes at the beginning of Romans (1:16-18) and again at the end of the letter (16:25-26) relate to partially hardened Israel? Within Paul's gospel that promises salvation "to everyone who believes" (Rom 1:16), he identifies hardening and jealousy as elements of God's plan for unbelieving Israel's eventual repentance and salvation "according to the revelation of the mystery which has been kept secret for long ages past" (Rom 16:25). The focal point of the "hidden mystery" is most assuredly the mystery of the coming of Christ to forgive the sins of Gentiles and Jews, so that both might be made into one people of God (Rom 11:26-27; also 3:21-26; Eph 1:9-23; 3:1-12; 6:19; Col 1:25-29; 2:1-3; 4:3). Within the unfolding of God's plan, God not only hardened the idolatrous, unbelieving part of Israel, but will cultivate jealousy within her in order to demonstrate his righteousness and 'forbearance' by passing over sins previously committed. This merciful forbearance demonstrated God's righteousness toward unbelieving Israel by extending to her the opportunity to be grafted again into the people of God. Paul shares this understanding of God's disciplinary benevolence with Baruch as we saw above and also with the Testament of Zebulon (second century B.C.):

> In the writings of the fathers I came to know that in the last days you shall defect from the Lord, and you shall be divided in Israel, and you shall follow after two kings; you shall commit every abomination and worship every idol. Your enemies will take you captive and you shall reside among the gentiles with all sorts of sickness and tribulation and oppression of soul. And thereafter you will remember the Lord and repent, and he will turn you around because he is merciful and compassionate; he does not bring a charge at wickedness against the sons of men, since they are flesh and the spirits of deceit lead them astray in all their actions. And thereafter the Lord himself will arise upon you, the light of righteousness with healing and compassion in his wings. He will liberate every captive of the sons of men from Beliar, and every spirit of error will be trampled down. He will turn all nations to being zealous for him. And you shall see [God in a human form], he whom the Lord will choose: Jerusalem is his name. You will provoke him to wrath by the wickedness of your works, and you will be rejected until the time of the end. (9:5-9)

Paul's eschatology, of course, bears explicit christological and ecclesiastical emphases that are foreign to non-Christian Second Temple Jewish writings like Baruch and the Testament of Zebulon. But he shares with the Testament of Zebulon and Baruch the identification of Israel's present suffering as a divinely ordained merciful stimulant intended for Israel's future repentance.

(g) *Romans 11:26-27: Further Appeals to Scripture*

Paul next appeals to the Septuagint texts of Isa 59:20-21 and 27:9 for scriptural confirmation of this promise in Rom 11:26-27. These passages are *crucial* to his vision of ultimate, eschatological salvation as he envisions it for "all" true Israel. Isaiah 59:20-21 describes the new covenant transformation of Israel in terms comparable to Jeremiah 31 and Ezekiel 36:

> And the deliverer shall come for Zion's sake, and shall turn away ungodliness from Jacob. And this shall be my covenant with them, said the Lord; My Spirit which is upon you, and the words which I have put in your mouth, shall never fail from your mouth, nor from the mouth of your seed, for the Lord has spoken it, henceforth and forever.

It is significant that this passage is followed in Isaiah by a detailed description of the events surrounding the eschatological day of the Lord—i.e., when the nations would be gathered to Jerusalem, God would be glorified, those who refused to serve God would perish, and all the people of God would be righteous (Isaiah 60). Isaiah goes on to mention that it is for this people that the "anointed" one would come (Isa 61:1). This "new covenant" people foreseen by Isaiah is the "all Israel" envisioned by Paul in Rom 11:26.

Paul subtly combined with this vision the prophecy of Isa 27:9, which he interpreted as referring to the same event: "Therefore shall the iniquity of Jacob be taken away; and this is his blessing, when I shall have taken away his sin; *when they shall have broken to pieces all the stones of the altars as fine dust, and their idols shall be cut off, as a thicket afar off.*" In the eschatological day of the Lord, the lifting of hardening will thus coincide with the removal of idolatry as one saving dimension of the new covenant. Within Romans and 2 Corinthians 3, this reality assumes the necessity of unbelieving Israel's turning away from legalistic religion before coming to know the salvation of the new covenant.

Paul's appeal to Isaiah therefore helps us to understand better his perception of "all Israel." As Peter Stuhlmacher has suggested, "there is already a reference to the salvation of 'all Israel' in the Hebrew text of Is. 59:20 when it says, 'He comes indeed for Zion as redeemer and for all in Jacob, who turn back from their sin.'"[7] Indeed, the Hebrew text of Isa 59:20 accords perfectly with the Septuagint rendering of Isa 27:9. The two texts together qualify that the true covenant people of God include only the repentant, not necessarily *all* ethnic Israelites. With this understanding of Rom 11:26—that "all Israel" refers to all true Israel (Rom 2:28-29)—Paul maintains consistency with his entire argument in Romans. There continues to be no discrimination among God's people (Rom 10:12-13; 3:22), for all of God's eschatological people will be former sinners (Rom 3:1-20), who will have been justified by faith in Christ (Rom 3:26; Gal 3:22-27) to become branches of one tree, members of one body, citizens of one kingdom, constituents of one covenant people, and worshippers of one God.

---

[7] Stuhlmacher, *Romans*, 171.

III. CONCLUSION

Paul defends God's righteousness and covenantal faithfulness by explaining that the gospel of Jesus Christ has been revealed as the means of salvation for *everyone* who believes—the Jew first and also the Greek (Rom 1:16-17). When this is the case, it cannot be said that God has rejected his people (Rom 11:1), for the gospel came first to the Jews, whom God alone initially blessed with his special revelation (Rom 9:4-5).

At the same time, however, Paul warns that God has also demonstrated his righteousness through the revelation of his wrath against all "who suppress the truth in unrighteousness" (Rom 1:18). This is not only true of the idolatrous nations of the world, but also unbelieving Israel who has attempted to establish her own righteousness while not subjecting herself to the righteousness of God (Rom 10:3). With this understanding the hardening suffered by unbelieving Israel is as deserved as the hardening suffered by Pharaoh or the divine hatred directed at Esau. For in rejecting the gospel because of preference for religious legalism, Israel, like Pharaoh, ignored the revelation of God to her own detriment in order to maintain faith in a manmade worldview. Like Esau, Israel despised her own birthright by rejecting the gospel of her Messiah that chronologically was revealed to her first. This phenomenon attests that there is no partiality with God (Rom 2:11).

Yet Paul does not describe Israel's hardening or jealousy as necessarily terminal. Paul knows that the curses of hardening and jealousy serve as important elements within the merciful revelation of God's wrath. They prolong the revelation of the gospel just as Pharaoh's hardening prolonged the revelation of God's signs in Egypt. As fulfillments of Scripture, they demonstrate the truthfulness of God in contrast to the impotence of idols, whether cognitive or literal. As symptoms of Israel's misinterpretation of the law, hardening and jealousy also testify that the law does not impart life (Gal 3:21) and is therefore an insufficient alternative to the righteousness promised through faith in Christ.

Hardening and jealousy therefore represent stages within Israel's ultimate rehabilitation. They facilitate God's work in shutting up "all in disobedience that he might show mercy to all" (Rom 11:32; Gal 3:22).

These afflictions assist the law by apprising unbelieving Israel (Gal 3:24) of the stark reality of her sin and her continued need for a salvation not accomplished by the keeping of the law. They will become beneficial therapies if Israel does not persist in her unbelief. We can say unequivocally, therefore, that salvation is possible for the hardened, but only through repentance and active faith in Christ.[8] Furthermore, as an interlocking tradition, Romans 11 is an important interpretive key for understanding other thematically related sayings such as Mark 4:10-12

---

[8] Some have contested the centrality of faith in Christ in Romans 11 by appealing to the fact that Paul does not explicitly refer to Christ at all in this chapter. This observation is weightless, however, because within the context of Romans as a whole Paul is clearly referring to belief or unbelief in Christ in 11:20-23. Furthermore, the forgiveness of sins Paul refers to in 11:27 is clearly a reference to the forgiveness of sins Paul has specified as having been made possible by the sacrifice of Jesus as the solution to Jewish and Gentile sin (Rom 3). See further Fitzmyer, *Romans*, 619-620.

par., which on the surface appear to rule out the possibility of unbelieving Israel's future salvation.

I agree with those who identify "all Israel" (Rom 11:26) as that body of Jews and Gentiles who have come or will come to know salvation through faith in Christ.[9] This understanding makes the most sense to me biblically. In Romans 11:17-24 Paul speaks of one olive tree, not two. The branches "cut off" refers to that part of Israel reprimanded for idolatry—as the background text of Jer 11:16-17 suggests. The "partial hardening" (Rom 11:25) of Israel refers to the hardening of that part of Israel that has not obeyed God because of idolatrous preference for other objects of faith, namely the law (2 Corinthians 3).[10] Therefore, according to Paul, the partial hardening of Israel simply continues the partial hardening that God previously inflicted upon her in the prophecies of Isa 6:9-10 and Jer 5:19-21, when all Israel was not hardened (neither the prophets, nor the remnant) but only the idolatrous majority. Paul's gospel anticipates that the salvation that promises hope to this majority is the same new covenant that has brought salvation to believing Jews like himself and also to Gentile believers. For in Christ there is neither Jew nor Greek (Gal 3:28).

Hence, Paul teaches that God's promised cure for the idolatry hardened heart of Israel (Ezek 36:22-38; Jer 31:31-34) is one and the same as that which secured the salvation of believing Gentiles, who, like the non-remnant part of Israel, also formerly lived in a state of dehumanized dysfunction (Rom 1:18-32).[11] Through the sacrificial work of Christ and the gift of the Spirit, God accomplished for Jewish and Gentile believers in Christ the new creation promised by the new covenant (Rom 3, 5, 8; 2 Cor 3; 5:17; Phil 3:20-21). As a preacher of the gospel of this new covenant (2 Cor 3:6), Paul anticipates the future incorporation of other Jews who will be grafted in again with other Jewish and Gentile believers. The event will require nothing less than the resurrection of the dead (Rom 11:15), the calling of "not my people" "my people" (Rom 9:25-26). It will be accomplished for the Jew as for the Gentile only upon the occasion of "turning to the Lord" (2

---

[9] Notable defenders of this position have included J. Calvin, J. Jeremias, R. Martin, and N.T. Wright. See the bibliographical references to these scholars provided by T. Schreiner who argues to the contrary that "all Israel" refers to ethnic Israel (*Romans*, 614 n. 7). That this interpretation requires a different meaning for Israel in vs. 26 from Paul's previous usage in vs. 25 is consistent with Paul's practice and thought. Elsewhere in Romans, Paul, using the same term, distinguishes between ethnic Jews and authentic Jews in the span of just two verses (Rom 2:28-29) and explains in Rom 9:6b, "they are not all Israel who are descended from Israel."

[10] James D. G. Dunn (*Romans*, 2.679) disagrees opting to interpret *apo merous* adverbially with *pōrōsis* so that it is the hardening and blinding that are partial rather than the hardening and blinding of "part of Israel." This way "Paul still retains a concept of Israel as a unified whole." This understanding is awkward, however, in that it presupposes that Paul and other believing Jews still suffer a partial hardening with the rest of Israel. But Paul's gospel argues to the contrary. For the veil of hardening is removed in Christ (2 Cor 3:14).

[11] Rom 1:18-32 may refer to Jewish sin as well as Gentile. Romans 1:23 in particular has a plausible precedent in the ancient Egyptian amulets and perhaps also Canaanite religious expression. These Gentile idols, however, may have been adopted by the early Israelites as suggested by Exod 33:4-6, where "ornaments" (LXX *kosmos*; MT ʿ*dy*) finds its likely historical antecedent in Egyptian amulets.

Cor 3:16). Transformation will only take place when Christ removes the veil of the law that had hardened the minds of the Jews (2 Cor 3:12-18).

Chapter 11

"Hardening and the Followers of the Beast"

The Book of Revelation

And the rest of mankind, who were not killed by these plagues, did not repent of the works of their hands, so as not to worship demons, and the idols of gold and of silver and of brass and of stone and of wood, which can neither see nor hear nor walk. (Rev 9:20)

And they worshiped the dragon, because he gave his authority to the beast; and they worshiped the beast, saying, who is like the beast, and who is able to wage war with him? . . . And all who dwell on earth will worship him, everyone whose name has not been written from the foundation of the world in the book of life of the Lamb who has been slain. **If anyone has an ear to hear, let him hear.** (Rev 13:4, 8-9)

Ancient Jewish apocalyptic writings originated in atmospheres of oppression and persecution. This was the case for the persecuted Jewish audiences of Daniel and Ezekiel and the persecuted Christian audience of Revelation. These persecuted groups adopted symbolism, the language of apocalyptic, to affirm cryptically the sovereignty of God and his Christ, while at the same time parodying the comparative impotence of earthly potentates like Pharaoh, Nebuchadnezzar, and Nero—infamous villains who sponsored persecution of faithful Jewish and Christian worshipers of God. Resurfacing here and there throughout Revelation therefore are the background stories of Exodus and Daniel. Readers are reminded that God's people have always been oppressed, if not enslaved. What Pharaoh had been to the earliest Israelites, Nebuchadnezzar was to the Jews of the exile, and Caesar was to the persecuted Christians of Asia Minor. As God had performed miraculous signs and plagues to reveal his sovereignty over Pharaoh and Nebuchanezzar, so now, through apocalyptic images God was communicating his sovereignty over Caesar to comfort his beleaguered church. Revelation discloses that in the end God alone will reign supreme and his salvation will attend all who persevere in their faith through trial and persecution to the very end. Revelation's signs thus call for repentance, the restoration of undivided commitment to the one true God and king, as the seven letters of Revelation chs. 2-3 make plain. For faithful worshipers of God this message brought security and hope, because God was promising that as he had rescued the young nation of Israel from Pharaoh's grasp, and as he had rescued Daniel from the lion's den, so he would rescue his church from all her oppressors, including Rome and ultimately the supernatural forces of evil at the end of time.

Fitting to this conceptual background, the hardening of the heart formula surfaces in Revelation where worshipers of the Beast's image obstinately refuse to repent even after witnessing first hand the plagues of the seven bowls of God's wrath (Rev 16:8-10, 21). The parallels between the plagues of the seven bowls and the plagues of Exodus indicate a correlation between the hardening of Pharaoh at the time of the exodus and the obstinacy of those who refuse to repent upon witnessing the seven bowls of God's wrath in Revelation. The hardening of the worshipers of the Beast also resembles the hardening of the idolatrous majority of Israel in Isa 6:9 and Jer 5:21 and the dehumanization of Nebuchadnezzar in Daniel 4:28-37. Together these stories convey the biblical truth that God has set in motion the curse of hardening to afflict human beings who threaten the covenant and its people by fostering idolatry.

By contrast, *those who have ears to hear* in Revelation are the faithful who have not lost sight of their first love and have persevered in their faith without being seduced by the cultural allure of the state favored emperor cult. The New Jerusalem, the New Heavens, and the New Earth are reserved for these saints as the promised land was reserved for faithful Israel and as eschatological vindication was reserved for the suffering saints of Daniel 7. Those *not* having ears to hear, the majority it appears, are those privileged to witness the apocalyptic revelations of God's wrath, but who nevertheless refuse to repent (see also Rev 9:20 and its allusion to Pss 115:4-7; 135:15-17). These, we may reasonably conjecture, are like the non-remnant Israelites of old, who despite their privileged opportunity to hear the words of the prophets, nevertheless refused to repent in order to continue worshiping Baal and other pagan deities with hardened hearts. Thus, though the word *heart* occurs only three times in Revelation (Rev 2:23; 17:17; 18:7), *the sensory depletion phenomenon occurs quite clearly in connection to idolatry and to emperor worship in particular.*

In studying the relationship between idolatry and the hardening of the heart in Revelation, we will discuss the following six subjects:

1) The Historical Situation of the Seven Churches of Asia Minor;
2) Revelation's Response to the Emperor Cult;
3) The Imperial Edict and the Seven Letters of Revelation 2-3;
4) The Form of Idolatry in Revelation;
5) The "Hearing Formula"—"He who has an ear, let him hear;"
6) Idolatry and the Hardening of the Heart in Revelation 12-18—the Dragon, the Beast from the Sea, and the Beast from the Land.

I. THE HISTORICAL SITUATION OF THE SEVEN CHURCHES

The presence of the hardening phenomenon in Revelation corresponds with the prominence of idolatry in the eastern part of the Roman empire, where the seven churches of Revelation were located. Like all of Asia Minor, the seven cities of

Revelation were devoted to pagan worship.¹ The most famous of these cities, Ephesus, was renowned for its temple dedicated to the Greek goddess Artemis, the goddess of fertility and the hunt. Acts 19 recounts the challenges Paul faced when he first preached the gospel in Ephesus, whose temple symbolized not only a conceived covenant with Artemis (Diana), but also the cultural heritage of the city. Paul's letter to the Ephesians, much like Revelation 2, encourages the Ephesians to stake confidence in the exalted, invincible sovereignty of Christ, who has subjected all things to himself (including, we may infer, Artemis). Aware of Christ's incomparable power, the Ephesians, Paul wrote, could confidently engage in spiritual warfare with the total adequacy of the armor of God. "Ephesus was also the center of the imperial cult, boasting six imperial temples, one honoring Roma and Julius Caesar, two honoring Augustus, one honoring Domitian, and two honoring Hadrian."² During the reign of Domitian, the probable emperor at the time of the writing of Revelation,³ Ephesus became *neōkoros*, the temple warden of the entire province of Asia.

The remaining six cities receiving letters in Revelation 2-3 were equally saturated with pagan religious influences. Historically, Smyrna was the home of numerous pagan temples including the temple of Asclepius.⁴ Smyrna was also the first city in Asia Minor to erect a temple for *dea Roma*, the founding deity of Rome.⁵ In A.D. 23 the emperor Tiberius permitted the building of a temple in Smyrna for Augustus before giving the city the status of temple warden for the cults of Tiberius, Livy, and the Senate in A.D. 26.⁶

Pergamum, the location of the so-called "throne of Satan" (Rev 2:13), was the site of an enormous altar dedicated to Zeus and was renowned for the worship of Asclepius, the serpent god of healing.⁷ Pergamum was also the site of the first temple dedicated to the deified emperor Augustus. Within this context Colin Hemer has concluded "that the expression 'throne of Satan' refers primarily to the emperor-cult as enforced from Pergamum at a time of critical confrontation for the church."⁸ Following Adolf Deissmann,⁹ Hemer detects a 'polemical parallelism'

---

¹ The saturation of imperial altars, temples, imperial priests, imperial cults, and non-imperial temples and theatres is impressively mapped by S.R.F. Price, *Rituals and Power: The Roman Imperial Cult in Asia Minor* (Cambridge: Cambridge, 1984), xxi-xxvi.

² David Aune, *Revelation* (3 Vols.; WBC 52A; Dallas: Word, 1997), 1.154. For detailed information on the historical information relating to these sites and those relating to the other cities of Revelation 2-3, see Price, *Rituals and Power*, 254-56 (Ephesus), 252-53 (Pergamum), 258 (Smyrna), 260 (Thyatira), 264-65 (Laodicea).

³ Irenaeus, *Adv. haer.* 5.30.3; Eusebius *Hist. eccl.* 3.18.1; 5.30.3. See G.K. Beale, *Revelation* (NIGTC; Grand Rapids: Eerdmans, 1999), 4-27. Aune (*Revelation*, 1.lvi-lxx) finds the external evidence to support a date late in the reign of Domitian and the internal evidence mixed.

⁴ Tacitus, *Annals*, 3.63.

⁵ Tacitus, *Annals*, 4.56.

⁶ Tacitus, *Annals*, 4.55-56.

⁷ Bruce Metzger, *Breaking the Code: Understanding the Book of Revelation* (Nashville, Abingdon, 1993), 34.

⁸ Colin Hemer, *The Letters to the Seven Churches of Asia in their Local Setting* (JSNTSS 11; Sheffield: Sheffield Academic Press, 1986), 87.

⁹ *Light from the Ancient East* (New York; London: Hodder and Stoughton, 1910), 342ff.

between Christ and Caesar in which "the claims of Caesar are viewed by John as a Satanic parody of those of Christ."[10]

Thyatira, while not producing archaeological artifacts comparable to those of Ephesus, Smyrna, or Pergamum, is warned by the risen Christ in Revelation of the harmful influence of a certain Jezebel (Rev 2:20). The name Jezebel associates an anonymous false prophetess in Thyatira with the infamous Jezebel of the OT. Biblical Jezebel, the Sidonian wife of Israelite king Ahab, was a notorious villainess in the OT. Among other atrocities, she influenced Ahab to worship Canaanite gods (1 Kings 16:31), sponsored 850 prophets of Baal and Asherah (1 Kings 18:19), and threatened the livelihood of the true prophets of Yahweh (1 Kings 18:4; 19:1-3). Whoever this opponent to the Thyatiran church was, it is clear that *like* the Jezebel of the OT Scriptures, who attempted to integrate Baal worship with Yahwism, her ambition was to forcefully integrate pagan faith and culture with Christian faith and orthodoxy. She was thus a leader bent on spreading some form of idolatry in the church of Thyatira.

Sardis, Philadelphia, and Laodicea were exposed to similar local and imperial influences. Sardis, a former capitol of the Seleucid kingdom (281-190 B.C.), was the home of many temples including one dedicated to Artemis and another to Augustus.[11] Philadelphia became 'Philadelphia Flavia' under the Flavian emperor Vespasian (A.D. 69-79), though her height as a center for the imperial cult did not climax until A.D. 241, when she became temple warden under Caracalla. Laodicea, the wealthiest city in the region of Phyrgia, was the home of an imperial temple and a mint that produced coins that symbolized the sovereignty of the emperor. Thus there is little doubt that the Christians of the seven cities that received the letters of Revelation knew well the challenge of pagan religion, particularly the emperor cult.

Though the exact historical situation of the seven churches of Asia Minor cannot be reconstructed confidently with detail, Revelation clearly attests that the churches were suffering persecution (Rev 1:9) at the hands of an empire certain to be Rome. The fate of Antipas (Rev 2:13) and the occasional mention of Christian martyrs (6:9-11; 11:7; 20:4) indicate that actual executions had taken place. Greg Beale categorizes the persecution in Revelation as "selective" (Rev 1:9; 2:3, 9, 13; 3:8; 6:9 [?]; ch. 13), "imminent, systematic oppression" (Rev 6:9 [?]; ch. 13; 17:6; 18:24; 19:2), qualifying that each of these references "could refer to persecution already underway."[12] Within this situation the primary theological message of Revelation is that God is all powerful (*ho pantokratōr*), not Rome or her deities, and that Jesus Christ, not Caesar, is the ruler of the kings of the earth (Rev 1:5).

II. REVELATION'S RESPONSE TO THE EMPEROR CULT

Evidence of Revelation's reaction to the emperor cult is concentrated in chs. 11-13 and 17-18, where the dragon represents Satan, the first beast is the Roman empire, the second beast is the imperial priesthood, and the harlot Babylon symbolizes the

---

[10] Hemer, *The Letters to the Seven Churches*, 87.
[11] Aune, *Revelation*, 1.218.
[12] Beale, *Revelation*, 12 n. 65.

city of Rome. Together these demonically empowered forces oppose and persecute the people of God:

> And the great dragon was thrown down, the serpent of old who is called the devil and Satan, who deceives the whole world. (Rev 12:9)

> The beast that comes up out of the abyss will make war with them, and overcome them and kill them. (Rev 11:7)

> And it was given to him to make war with the saints and to overcome them; and authority over every tribe and people and tongue and nation was given to him. (Rev 13:7)

> And I saw the woman drunk with the blood of the saints, and with the blood of the witnesses of Jesus. (Rev 17:6)

These metaphors most assuredly extend beyond Roman history to prefigure the last days of persecution before God's final victory and the vindication of his faithful people. It is clear, however, that within the churches of Asia Minor the first readers of Revelation would also have interpreted these figures where possible within their own historical context—persecution at the hands of the provincial officials in Asia who represented Rome and the Roman emperor.

Historical evidence supporting emperor worship in Asia Minor at the time of Domitian (A.D. 81-96) is stronger in my judgment than that attested by some recent scholarship, which has challenged the traditional view that depicts Domitian as a tyrant persecutor of Christians. Here I write in reference to Leonard L. Thompson's influential book *The Book of Revelation: Apocalypse and Empire*.[13] My findings suggest that we should not be too hasty to dismiss the testimony of the Roman historians to follow a new perspective on Domitian that has significant problems of its own. It is significant, for example, that the Roman historian Dio

---

[13] New York: Oxford University Press, 1990. According to Thompson the records of the Roman historians Tacitus, Pliny the Younger, Dio Chrysostom, Juvenal, Suetonius, Dio Cassius, Philostratus, and Martial (in part) are all (with the exception of Martial) inaccurate after the fact misrepresentations of Domitian contrived in order to flatter Domitian's successor, the emperor Trajan. While Thompson is probably partially correct, he overstates his case. He does not consider the obvious motives for silence among Domitian's contemporaries. Had they sharply criticized Domitian during his lifetime their very lives would have been endangered. Most importantly, the reports of the above historians, while no doubt embellished in part, are too numerous to be entirely without substance. Thompson's thesis strangely depends upon a problematic correlation between Revelation and 1 Tim 2:2. With this presupposition he envisions "the seer and his audience did not live in a world of conflict, tension, and crisis. Christians lived quiet lives, not much different from other provincials" (95; cf. 132). This appraisal lacks support either in the primary source material or in the internal evidence of Revelation. For a full-length criticism of Thompson's perspective, see Thomas B. Slater, "On the Social Setting of the Revelation to John," *NTS* 44 (1998): 232-56. See also K. A. Strand, "Review of Thompson, L. L., *The Book of Revelation. Apocalypse and Empire*. New York and Oxford: Oxford University Press, 1990," AUSS 29 (1991): 188-90; Beale, *Revelation*, 10-12.

Cassius wrote that Domitian "insisted upon being regarded as a god and took vast pride in being called 'master' and 'god.' These titles were used not merely in speech but also in written documents."[14] Suetonius recounts that Domitian began a circulatory letter with the words, "Our Lord and God instructs you to do this!" Suetonius then adds "'Lord and God' became his (Domitian's) regular title both in writing and conversation."[15] We add parenthetically that it is possible that the praises of the twenty-four elders in Rev 4:11 intentionally parody these counterfeit claims, when the twenty-four cry out to the one sitting on the throne, "Worthy are you, *our Lord and our God*, to receive glory and honor and power." Also evidencing the divine claims of the emperor, Pliny the Younger, in a letter written to the emperor Trajan, tells of apostate Christians who acquiesced to Roman sovereignty "twenty-five years ago" (when Domitian was emperor?):

> Those who denied they were, or had ever been, Christians, who repeated after me an invocation to the Gods, and offered adoration, with wine and frankincense, to your image, which I had ordered to be brought for that purpose, together with those of the Gods, and who finally cursed Christ—none of which acts, it is said, those who are really Christians can be forced into performing—these I thought it proper to discharge. Others who were named by that informer at first confessed themselves Christians, and then denied it; true, they had been of that persuasion but they had quitted it, some three years, others many years, and a few as much as twenty-five years ago. They all worshipped your statue and the images of the Gods, and cursed Christ.

It is uncertain that those referred to by Pliny as having "quitted" Christianity "twenty-five years ago" did so to take up the emperor cult, nor is there conclusive evidence that the persecution of Christians during the reign of Domitian was as severe as that inflicted during the later reign of Trajan—though Trajan's reign, following Nerva, began a mere two years after the death of Domitian. However, it is probable, as Thompson himself concedes, that Trajan continued the policy toward Christians previously implemented by Domitian.[16] Indeed, the historical development of the emperor cult with its pre-Domitian phases of intensification under Caligula and Nero, and then its later heightened intensification under Trajan establishes a historical trajectory that makes the testimonies of Suetonius, Tacitus, Dio Cassius, Dio Chrysostom, and Pliny quite plausible.[17]

The fact that these Roman historians wrote their negative assessments of Domitian after his death does not disqualify the historicity of their accounts. They may have protected themselves by doing so. For as Thompson notes both Pliny and Tacitus "had friends and/or relatives who were either exiled or executed by

---

[14] Dio Cassius, LXVII 5,7.

[15] Suetonius, *Domitian* 13.

[16] Thompson, *Revelation*, 110.

[17] Thompson (*Revelation*, 97): "These sources paint Domitian as evil, almost without qualification."

Domitian."[18] Moreover, historians have always taken significant time before writing reflective assessments of political leaders. After all their profession is historiography, not reporting news.

It is also likely that persecution of Christians during Domitian's reign in the eastern provinces (including Asia Minor) went largely undocumented, because Roman historians focused most of their attention on Rome. But from the inception of the emperor cult under Julius Caesar, Augustus, and Tiberius, the eastern provinces had always promoted the emperor cult with more energy than Rome itself did in the west. It is likely that persecution of Christians in the eastern province of Asia Minor occurred even when persecution was not severe in Rome. Roman historians gave little attention to this persecution because their interest was Rome, not the provinces.

Whether the participants truly believed that the emperor was a god is impossible to tell. Some historians prefer to describe observance of the emperor cult as *homage* rather than worship—a public avowal of allegiance rather than an act of religious devotion. But for Christians this issue was to some degree moot. It was the act that mattered not the reality of its object or the sincerity of its observance. The religious heritage of Christianity, which stemmed from the Jewish Scriptures and Second Temple Judaism, condemned forced compliance to any deity or its image as virtually equivalent to voluntary idolatry. Biblical Daniel and the Hasmonean patriarch Mathias had established refusal and resistance as the policy to follow in this situation. The contrasting fortunes of the followers of the Beast and the followers of Christ in Revelation make clear Revelation's understanding that the following of Daniel's example was conceived as an unconditional requirement for safe passage through the immanent judgment of God (Rev 14:9-10!). True faith, in other words, would be authenticated by an unwillingness to bow before the Beast, even under the severest forms of persecution. Those with 'ears to hear' would understand this and would persevere to the end in anticipation of the salvation that would be theirs at the time when Jesus would intervene to vindicate his true followers (Rev 14:9-13). Thus the historicity of the persecution spoken of in Rev 1:9; 2:3, 9, 13; 3:8; 6:9; ch. 13; 17:6; 18:24; 19:2 should be taken seriously.

III. THE IMPERIAL EDICT AND THE SEVEN LETTERS OF REVELATION 2-3

David Aune, following G. Rudberg, has argued persuasively that the recurring features of the seven letters of Revelation 2-3 loosely resemble the genre of ancient imperial edicts.[19] Enough parallels exist to establish the probability that

---

[18] See Slater, "On the Social Setting of the Revelation to John," 235.

[19] Aune, *Revelation*, 1.126-130. Seven features are generally recognized as constituting the letters: (1) a greeting; (2) a title of the risen Christ; (3) a section head "I know, " introducing praise for what is good in the churches (except in the case of Laodicea); (4) a criticism of the church (except in the cases of Smyrna and Philadelphia; (5) a warning; (6) the exhortation "He that hath an ear let him hear"; and (7) a promise. Aune associates these features with the following elements of Roman imperial edicts: (1) the *proemium*; (2) the

late first-century Roman subjects would have recognized that the letters of Revelation 2-3 put the exalted Jesus in the place where imperial edicts usually put the emperor. As Aune explains: "The author's use of the royal/imperial edict form is part of his strategy to polarize God/Jesus and the Roman emperor, who is but a pale and diabolical imitation of God. In his role as the eternal sovereign and king of kings, Jesus is presented as issuing solemn and authoritative edicts befitting his status."[20] In doing so the seven letters establish the point of departure for the rest of Revelation, where the apocalyptic warning is sounded again and again that true eternal salvation is exclusive to those whose faith in God and the Lamb perseveres without compromising to the demands of human or demonic regimes. Conveying this message, the seven letters parody the imperial edicts by identifying Christ, not the emperor, as final judge in matters that pertain to life and death.

The expression, "he who has an ear let him hear what the Spirit says *to the churches,*" exhorts each of the seven and indeed virtually all churches to read and obey each of the letters out of respect for the sovereignty of the risen Christ. The prescription is for perseverance in the midst of persecution with the foreknowledge that Christ will reward faithfulness with citizenship in the paradise of God. Though the exact historical context of Revelation is debated, the seven letters clearly portray a crisis situation within the churches. Orthodoxy is challenged by "evil men" referred to as "false apostles" (Rev 2:2). False teachers identified as Nicolaitans threaten to corrupt the church's doctrine (Rev 2:6, 15). The church in Smyrna suffers "tribulation and poverty" (Rev 2:9), while engaging in conflict with a synagogue of Satan "who say they are Jews and are not" (Rev 2:9; also 3:8-9). It is anticipated that soon some will face death following severe testing and tribulation (Rev 2:10; cf. 3:10). Indeed, in Pergamum martyrdom had already been suffered by a certain Antipas, who was killed among those "where Satan dwells" (Rev 2:13).

IV. THE FORM OF IDOLATRY IN REVELATION

Amidst this situation a subtle, portentous form of idolatry jeopardizes the repentance of the church. Some within the church in Pergamum have been persuaded by Balaam, while others in Thyatira foolishly tolerate the teachings of Jezebel. Both of these characters of course derive their names from their OT counterparts. Just as Jezebel had attempted to enforce Baalism upon Israel at the time of Ahab and Elijah (1 Kings 16:31), so Balaam had counseled Israelites "to trespass against the Lord in the matter of Peor" (Num 31:16), an allusion to Israel's sacrifices to Moabite gods and collusion with Baal of Peor (Num 25:1-3). The consequence of both infidelities had been the pouring forth of God's wrath—a plague which killed 24,000 Israelites in the case of Balaam (Num 25:9) and the eventual Assyrian exile of Israel in the case of Jezebel. The general message of Revelation is the same. Offenses against God promoted by the dragon, the two

---

promulgatio; (3) the *narratio*; (4) the *dispositio*; and (5) the *sanctio*. See Aune for further definition of these features and their parallels to Rev 2-3.
[20] Aune, *Revelation*, 1.129.

beasts, and collaborators with them will be repaid with the plagues of God's wrath that constitute the seven seals, the seven trumpets, and the seven bowls.

The crimes promoted by Balaam in Pergamum and Jezebel in Thyatira are the same—to eat things sacrificed to idols and to commit acts of immorality (Rev 2:14, 20). It is clear from the context that the eating of things sacrificed to idols is a graver offense than that appraised by Paul at the beginning of 1 Corinthians 8, where Paul affirms monotheism and the nonexistence of gods represented by idols.[21] The situation that endangers the churches in Pergamum and Thyatira is closer to that addressed in 1 Cor 8:10 and in 1 Corinthians 10, where Paul warns of the harmful effects of *eating in an idol's temple*: "the things which the Gentiles sacrifice, they sacrifice to demons, and not to God; and I do not want you to become sharers in demons. *You cannot drink the cup of the Lord and the cup of demons*" (1 Cor 10:20-21). As in 1 Cor 10:7-8, where Paul combines an allusion to the golden calf episode of Exod 32:4 with an allusion to the Peor catastrophe of Num 25:1-9, the crimes encouraged by Balaam and Jezebel associate sexual immorality with the eating of foods offered to idols. This association between idolatry and sexual immorality has a long OT history that Revelation envisages as resurfacing in the form of a dangerous threat to the churches of Asia Minor. The eating of foods sacrificed to idols, whether or not accompanied by literal fornication, was interpreted as an act of infidelity by which the partaker implied the legitimacy of the deity being sacrificed to. In the OT worship of idols was equated with adultery, because idolatry represented an unfaithful breach of Israel's covenant with Yahweh. Idolatry explicitly broke Israel's covenant vow to worship God alone. Thus the OT likens idolatry to "playing the harlot." The essence of immorality, idolatry was viewed essentially as infidelity, adultery, and prostitution (e.g., Hosea).

Historically it is probable that Balaam and Jezebel were influences who were attempting to coerce Christians to integrate the emperor cult with orthodox Christian worship. This compromise would take the form of eating of foods sacrificed to idols in the environment of pagan temple ritual, where observers would interpret the meal as symbolic of the eater's endorsement of what the temple or shrine stood for—polytheism, the imperial cult, or both. In reaction to this practice the message of Revelation is identical to that of Paul—"you cannot partake of the table of the Lord and the table of demons" (1 Cor 10:20). Or as John might put it, one cannot partake of the table of the Lord and the table of the Beast.

For those who found Christianity and paganism an agreeable mixture, Revelation came as a stark corrective, which would settle for nothing less than absolute repentance. The imperial cult was not a gray area, it was wrong, diametrically opposed to God's will. It was no less a form of idolatry than that which had precipitated the downfall and exile of Israel in the OT Scriptures.

---

[21] Contra Thompson (*Revelation*, 123), who likens the teaching opposed by John in Revelation to the Pauline form of liberty described in 1 Cor 8:13-9:7. This view apparently was originally proposed by the Tübingen school; see R.H. Charles, *A Critical and Exegetical Commentary on the Revelation of St. John* (2 vols.; Edinburgh: T & T Clark [1920], 1.50).

Therefore in continuity with the example of Israel whose idolatry resulted in sensory malfunction and exile, the churches of Revelation are warned that their carefree adaptation to Roman imperialism is making them insensitive to the realities of God. The risen Lord, attempting to reverse this process, therefore rebukes the church in Sardis saying, "I know your deeds, that you have a name that you are alive, but *you are dead*" (Rev 3:1). To the church in Laodicea whose wealth may well correlate with spiritual compromise, he admonishes: "Because you say, 'I am rich, and have become wealthy, and have need of nothing,' and *you do not know that you are wretched and miserable and poor and blind and naked*, I advise you to buy from me gold refined by fire" (Rev 3:17-18a). These revelations of the Lord attest to the spiritual sickness that the churches in Sardis and Laodicea have contracted from their pagan cultures. Complacency within a paganized form of Christianity has effectively anesthetized compromisers from perceiving the horrors awaiting adversaries of God.

Revelation attempts to rouse the church from this stupor. The seven seals, the seven trumpets, the seven signs, the seven bowls, and the final triumph of God display God's sovereignty over the pagan, demonic world and God's intolerance of divided worship. The foreseen apocalyptic demise of the opponents of God serves as a warning to Christian collaborators with pagan ritual and worship. Compromising Christians would become more and more like the pagans with whom they worshiped, if they did not repent and return to their first love. If they further adopted the pagan mindset, they would become less able to repent—even in the presence of supernatural displays of God's wrath. The situation would parallel that of ancient Israel, who had become more and more like the pagan nations that surrounded her, so that when God spoke she could not perceive the message of her own prophets (Isa 6:9-10).

Being spiritually dead (Rev 3:1), and spiritually poor, blind, and naked (Rev 3:17), some within the church were well on their way toward the kind of obstinacy characterizing the survivors of the sixth trumpet:

> And the rest of mankind, who were not killed by these plagues, did not repent of the works of their hands, *so as not to worship demons, and the idols of gold and of silver and of brass and of stone and of wood, which can neither see nor hear nor walk*; and they did not repent of their murders nor of their sorceries nor of their immorality nor of their thefts. (Rev 9:20-21)

Following the paradigm this book has charted, both of these groups—compromising Christians and unrepentant pagans—are assessed as suffering the hardening affects of idolatry. They become like the idols that they worship, just as Pss 115 and 135 forewarn (to which Rev 9:20 alludes), and they become more and more resistant to the call to repent, just as anticipated by Isa 6:9 and Jer 5:21. Should this continue the plight of the church would become comparable to the plight of Israel. As the promised land was taken from unrepentant, idolatrous Israel, so the lampstand would be removed from unrepentant, idolatrous Christians (Rev 2:5; also 3:16).

V. THE HEARING FORMULA IN REVELATION

The 'hearing formula' "He who has an ear let him hear what the Spirit says to the churches" occurs at the end of each of the seven letters (Rev 2:7, 11, 17, 29; 3:6, 13, 22). The related exhortations: "Here is wisdom. Let him who has understanding calculate the number of the beast" (Rev 13:18) and "Here is the mind which has wisdom. The seven heads are seven mountains on which the woman sits" (Rev 17:9), indicate that wisdom and sensory perception in Revelation relate directly to one's ability to identify accurately the Roman emperor and the Roman empire for what they really are—temporary diabolical competitors for God's divine authority.

The probable OT conceptual background for the hearing formulas in Revelation is Ezekiel where John's apocalyptic predecessor received the commission from God: "But when I speak to you, I will open your mouth, and you will say to them, thus says the Lord God. He who hears, let him hear; and he who refuses, let him refuse; for they are a rebellious house" (Ezek 3:27; also 2:4-5, 8; 3:7, 11). Ezekiel 3:27, also echoed in Rev 22:11, may be the specific background for the hearing formula in Revelation, just as Ezekiel 1-3 was a prominent conceptual background for the book of Revelation as a whole: e.g., the four living beings (Ezek 1:5-13; Rev 4:6-8), the comparison of the voice of the Almighty to the sound of many waters (Ezek 1:24; Rev 1:15), the likening of the glory of the Lord to a rainbow (Ezek 1:28; Rev 4:3), and the prophet's eating of a scroll (Ezek 2:8-3:3; Rev 10:8-11). This list would greatly increase of course if we were to take into account all of the correspondences between Ezekiel and Revelation.

For our purposes, however, the influence of Ezekiel 1-3 on Revelation satisfactorily heightens the probability that the same scriptural passages established the repository for John's hearing formula. This being the case, we may say that John was to the churches of Asia Minor what Ezekiel had been to the Jewish exiles in Babylon. In the tradition of Ezek 3:27, John uses the hearing formula to clarify that upon the hearing of John's revelation, the churches were now responsible for their own fate (Ezek 3:18-21), whether in repentance resulting in salvation or in complacency resulting in the wrath of God. Those with understanding would recognize Caesar for the beast that he was (Rev 13:18) and would perceive the inherent evil behind Rome's attempt to usurp the worship of God and the Lamb. Once he had made the divine disclosures of Revelation, John perceived that his work as prophet to the churches was complete, so that just as God had commissioned Ezekiel with the words "He who hears, let him hear; and he who refuses, let him refuse," so John cries out, "Let the one who does wrong, still do wrong; and let the one who is filthy, still be filthy; and let the one who is righteous, still practice righteousness; and let the one who is holy, still keep himself holy" (Rev 22:11). For if the readers of Revelation had not repented by ch. 22 nothing more could be said or done to make them do so. Hence, the formula expresses God's permission for his people to respond freely to his word in obedience or disobedience, but with awareness of what the consequences will be—either in salvation or judgment. What had been the case for God's people among the exiles in Ezek 3:27 was now again the case for God's people among the churches of Asia Minor in Revelation.

Complementing this interpretation is the corollary to the hearing formula found in Jesus' words in the Synoptic Gospels: "If any man has ears to hear, let him hear" (Matt 11:15; 13:9, 43; Mark 4:9, 23; Luke 8:8). As we saw in chapter 6 of this book, within the context of the Parable of the Sower and the Soils the synoptic expression exhorts listeners to avoid the consequences befalling the seeds planted beside the road, on the rocky soil, and among the thorns. Like the churches of Asia Minor which were in danger of having their "lampstand taken away" because of compliance to pagan and particularly Roman influences, so Jesus' parable warns of the danger of losing the benefits of the gospel because of Satanic deception (Mark 4:15), persecution (Mark 4:17), and the deceitfulness of riches (Mark 4:19). It is notable for our purposes that between this parable (Mark 4:3-9) and its explanation (Mark 4:13-20) is Jesus' quotation and contextualization of Isa 6:9: "but those who are outside get everything in parables, in order *that while seeing, they may see and not perceive; and while hearing, they may hear and not understand lest they return and be* forgiven (Mark 4:11-12). In the context of Jesus' teaching in Mark 4, as in Isaiah 1-6 and Jer 5:21, it is important to observe yet again that the hardening curse is not arbitrary or unconditional but correlates with human infidelity and carelessness, which in turn are influenced by Satanic deception, outside persecution, and the allurement of earthly riches. It is probably not a coincidence that Revelation identifies each of these same dangers as threats to the lasting security of the Asian churches. Hence, the risen Christ in the book of Revelation warns the churches with virtually the same exhortation that the earthly Jesus had voiced to the disciples in the Synoptic Gospels. In each context the Lord warns that recipients of the gospel will lose their spiritual perception when they allow for outside allegiances to encroach upon their absolute devotion to Jesus and the gospel. This correlation between hardening and the replacement of Jesus with another allegiance is yet another biblical expression of the phenomenon of idolatry and the hardening of the heart.

VI. IDOLATRY AND THE HARDENING OF THE HEART IN REVELATION CHAPTERS 12-18: THE DRAGON, THE BEAST FROM THE SEA, AND THE BEAST FROM THE LAND

Reference to the Roman emperor cult and its oppression of Christians is clearest in Revelation chs. 12-18. Here the reader encounters the great red dragon, the seven-headed, ten-horned beast from the sea, the two-horned beast from the land, the great whore who sits over many waters, and the scarlet beast full of blasphemous names. These creatures recall the oppressions of past evil empires, especially Egypt and Babylon, and present them as now symbolizing Roman rule.

The apocalyptic monsters of these chapters all interrelate in Revelation's coherent portrayal of evil. In the dragon, the two beasts of chapter 13, and the scarlet dragon of chapter 17, we see, as Bruce Metzger describes, "several mirrors in which the same objects are reflected from different sides, so that the reader cannot fail to take note of them."[22] Such is true for the woman who sits over many waters in Revelation 17 and the image of Babylon in Revelation 18. Both

---

[22] Metzger, *Breaking the Code*, 83.

represent Rome. It thus appears legitimate within Revelation's apocalyptic expression for two or more symbols to represent the same thing. This mechanism occurs frequently in the Bible, where Jesus is the referent of multiple metaphors that do not always appear consistent—lamb, lion, door, key etc. That the same practice occurs in reference to evil entities in Revelation 17-18, where the great harlot and Babylon both refer to Rome, should then not come as a surprise.

Mindful of these guiding principles, we read of three conflict scenes in Revelation 12: (1) the conflict of a great red dragon and a woman "clothed with the sun," who gives birth to a son that is to rule all the nations with a rod of iron (Rev 12:1-6); (2) the war in heaven between the archangel Michael and his angels against the dragon (Rev 12:7-9); and (3), the dragon's pursuit and persecution of the woman and her offspring (Rev 12:10-17).

The dragon's identification as Satan is explicit (Rev 12:7-9). The manifestation of Satan envisioned, however, is one particularly associated with imperial power bent on repudiating God and persecuting God's people. This is suggested by OT and Second Temple Jewish writings that depict Pharaoh, Babylon, and the Roman empire as dragons.[23] The dragon here represents Satan's rule of the earth as administered by historical regimes that oppress God's people. The dragon's seven heads, ten horns, and seven diadems further amplify this impression, though Revelation does not explain these features for us in any kind of explicit historical detail. Against the background of Daniel 7:7, 20, 24 and in anticipation of Rev 17:12, the ten horns most likely symbolize ten kings or the totality of a kingly dynasty. Seven being the numerical symbol of absoluteness and the diadem being symbolic of royalty, the seven diadems symbolize absolute, royal power. The seven heads, which have no clear parallel in the OT,[24] may correlate with the seven heads of the beast in Rev 17:3 and therefore would also symbolize Roman kingship, as we will explain shortly.[25] Fitting to the symbolic nature of apocalyptic literature, Revelation 12 does not provide historical identification for the heads or the horns, probably because these images symbolize Satan's oppressive rule in general throughout history, which afflicted saints of successive eras through the oppressive and sometimes idolatrous policies of pagan empires.

In chapter 13, the *idolatrous* nature of Satan's deception becomes fully evident. At the dragon's bidding, a beast from the sea comes forth who elicits both worship of the dragon and worship of himself:

And the whole earth was amazed and followed after the beast; and they *worshiped* the dragon, because he gave his authority to the beast; and they

---

[23] Ezek 29:3 (Pharaoh); *Pss. Sol* 2:29-30 (Rome); Jer 51:34 (Babylon); see also Pss. 73[74]:13-14; 89:10; Isa. 30:7; 51:9; Ezek 32:2-3, where Pharaoh is likened to a dragon. See further Beale, *Revelation*, 632-33.

[24] See, however, Beale (*Revelation*, 635) who considers the possibility that the seven heads of Revelation 12 could allude to a compilation of the heads of the three beasts mentioned in Dan 7:4, 5, 7 plus the four heads of the third beast described in Dan 7:6.

[25] Aune (*Revelation*, 2.683) contends that originally the symbolism was more than general: "the conclusion is inescapable that each of the diademed heads must, at least originally, have symbolized a ruler."

worshiped the beast, saying, who is like the beast and who is able to wage war against him? (Rev 13:3b-4)

And all who dwell on the earth will *worship* him, everyone whose name has not been written from the foundation of the world in the book of life of the Lamb who has been slain. If anyone has an ear, let him hear. (Rev 13:8-9)

This beast that comes up from the sea, the ancient symbol of the domain of evil and death (cf. Rev. 21:1, 4), has ten horns and seven heads that parallel the features of the dragon, because the beast is the earthly administrator of the dragon's will. Revelation 13:2b recounts how "The dragon gave him [the beast] his power and his throne and great authority." Therefore, having the power, throne, and authority of the dragon (Satan), the beast from the sea (Rome) is portrayed as having dragon-like heads, horns, and diadems. The beast also appears to be the conglomeration of the features of the four beasts of Dan 7:2-7. The seven horns symbolize the totality of the beast's evil power, while the ten diadems symbolize the royalty of the beast and the universal sovereignty that he claims to possess. The blasphemous names written on the heads of the beast may correspond to the blaspheming boasts of the "little horn" of Dan 7:8.

For our purposes, it is striking that the exhortation, "If anyone has an ear, let him hear," occurs in the context of this demonically inspired idolatry. The implication is that all who worship the beast do so because they do not have ears to hear and they do not have minds to comprehend the beast's true identity and the true origin of his power. In turn the blindness and ignorance of the worshipers of the beast correlate with active idolatry that disables spiritual awareness of demonic as well as divine reality. They have eyes but they cannot see, they have ears but cannot hear, they have minds but cannot perceive; they have become like the foolish entities that they now worship (Rev 9:20; Psalms 115 and 135).

The beast who comes up from the land bears two horns and speaks like a dragon. His work is to officiate over and enforce worship of the first beast.

And he exercises all the authority of the first beast in his presence. And he makes the earth and those who dwell in it to *worship* the first beast, whose fatal wound was healed. (Rev 13:12)

And he deceives those who dwell on the earth because of the signs which it was given him to perform in the presence of the beast, telling those who dwell on the earth to make an image to the beast who had the wound of the sword and has come to life. And there was given to him to give breath to the image of the beast, that the image of the beast might even speak and cause as many as do not *worship* the image of the beast to be killed. (Rev 13:14-15)

Speaking with the voice of the dragon, the second beast represents priestly officials who facilitated and enforced civilian allegiance to the first beast, who in turn represented both the emperor and his empire. The second beast does this by way of visual deception and sensational manipulation of "images of the beast"—i.e., idols. "The command to perform idolatry alludes partly to the pressure placed on the populace and the churches of Asia Minor to give homage to the image of Caesar as a divine being."[26] Hence, followers of the beast lack "eyes to see" the fraudulent nature of the object that they worship. For this reason explanation has to be given for a proper identification of the beast: "Here is wisdom. Let him who has understanding calculate the number of the beast, for the number is that of a man; and his number is six hundred and sixty-six" (Rev 13:18). In other words, the truly wise in John's estimation, are those who are able to see beyond the second beast's deception to identify accurately the first beast for who he really is—a *man* of specific identity (Rev 13:18). John's explicit statement that the beast is a man corroborates the association of 666 with the Roman emperor.

This symbolic message, as many scholars have explained, has a coherent historical correspondence to the Roman Empire contemporary with Revelation's writing. The first beast that comes forth from the sea is Rome. The blasphemous names that adorn the heads of the beast are the blasphemous names assumed by deified Roman emperors. Historical writings and Roman coins of the era affirm that these names include Lord, God, and Savior—titles that when applied to human beings would have directly challenged Jewish and Christian concepts of monotheism.[27]

The second beast with the two horns and the voice of the dragon represents the imperial priesthood that presided over emperor worship in the eastern provinces of the Roman Empire. This priesthood, composed probably of both provincial government officials and emperor cult priests, was the probable enforcer of the persecution of Christians alluded to throughout the book of Revelation. Historically one of its methods for securing allegiance to the emperor cult was the kind of visual deception described in Rev 13:14-15. Steven J. Scherrer has confirmed that the signs spoken of in Rev 13:14-15 had historical counterparts in the trickery prominent among magicians of the day. The emperor cult would have used these, Scherrer reasons, to demonstrate the reality of the cult's claims.[28] Acting on the supposition that opposition to the emperor cult was tantamount to opposition to Roman rule, these officials would have treated uncompromising Christians with the same disdain that they treated suspected enemies of the state.

Coherent with this historical interpretation is the mysterious number 666 cited in Rev 13:18. Richard Bauckham has substantiated persuasively the centuries old

---

[26] G. K. Beale, *Revelation*, 710.

[27] The application of divine names to the Roman emperors is widely documented. Most importantly, as far as Revelation is concerned, these titles would have been particularly offensive to Christians who exclusively attributed these same titles to God and his messiah. See especially Sr. Dominique Cuss, *Imperial Cult and Honorary Terms in the New Testament* (Fribourg: The University Press, 1974), 52. Giving rise to the offense, no doubt, were inscriptions in the Hellenistic East that identified as "Savior of the World" Julius Caesar, Augustus, Claudius, Vespasian, and Titus (71).

[28] Steven J. Scherrer, "Signs and Wonders in the Imperial Cult: A New Look at a Roman Religious Institution in the Light of Rev 13:13-15," *JBL* 103/4 (1984): 599-610.

association of 666 with Caesar Nero.²⁹ Applying the ancient coding method of gematria, which correlates numbers with alphabet characters, the name Caesar Nero adds up to a total of 666, when transliterated into Hebrew: (נרון קסר/Nero Caesar: נ (50) + ר (200) + ו (6) + ן (50) + ק (100) + ס (60) + ר (200) = 666. It is also likely, as many have argued, that the name Nero stands behind the number 616, which occurs in early variant readings of Rev 13:18. If the Latin form Nero is transliterated into Hebrew without the final ן the resulting total is 616.³⁰

It is unlikely in my judgment that this association is coincidental, especially when we consider the symbolic nature of Revelation and its historical context in Asia Minor. Nor is it likely to be coincidental that the Greek word *thērion*/θηρίον (beast), when transliterated into Hebrew as *tryon*/תריון, has the numerical value 666 (ת = 400 + ר = 200 + י = 10 + ו = 6 + ן = 50).³¹ The number thus simply conveys the message that Nero is the beast. As Bauckham argues, "The gematria does not merely assert that Nero is the beast: it demonstrates that he is. Nero's very name identifies him by its numerical value as the apocalyptic beast of Daniel's prophecy."³² In sum, then, the beast is the Roman Empire as personified by Nero in particular. When John exhorts, "Here is wisdom. Let him who has understanding calculate the number of the beast" (Rev 13:18), he reasons that resilient Christians who have not lost their minds to the emperor cult will size up or calculate Caesar for what he really is—a Satan possessed human despot of a tyrannical empire.

Coupled with this message is the image of the fatally wounded head that comes back to life (Rev 13:3, 14)—an allusion to Nero resurrected from the dead, perhaps in the person of the emperor Domitian. The image combines two popular Roman myths. One legend maintains that Nero didn't actually commit suicide but secretly fled Rome to Parthia, where he planned to amass an army to retake the Roman Empire. The second legend is the same except that it depicts Nero suffering death before resurrecting prior to his departure for Parthia. The resemblances of Nero in the life and policies of Domitian apparently led some to associate the "Nero Redux or Redivivus Legend" with Domitian. This image

---

²⁹ Richard Bauckham, *The Climax of Prophecy* (Edinburgh: T & T Clark, 1993), 384-452 esp. 387. Chapter 11 explains the gematria phenomenon in detail.

³⁰ Bauckham has effectively dismissed the two major objections to this explanation—(1) that it depends on the defective spelling קסר (*qsr*) instead of קיסר (*qysr*) and (2) that John would not have done his gematria in Hebrew when he was writing to a Greek audience. To the first objection, Bauckham responds by citing an Aramaic papyrus document from the second year of Nero that uses the very same defective spelling. Its usage was therefore not altogether unfamiliar and effectively accommodated John's purposes perfectly as he attempted to equate the Beast with Nero by means of gematria. To the second objection, Bauckham responds that John was a Jewish Christian himself who would have expected some within the churches of Asia to know Hebrew (*Climax of Prophecy*, 388). Further, we must not forget that apocalyptic expression is cryptic by design. It may also be added that the other major example of gematria in the NT (Matthew's reference to the number 14 in Matt 1:17) is also performed on the Hebrew name David (דוד) despite the fact that Matthew almost certainly wrote in Greek for a Greek speaking audience.

³¹ Bauckham, *Climax of Prophecy*, 389.

³² Bauckham, *Climax of Prophecy*, 389.

signals the message that the ruling emperor at the time of Revelation's writing was oppressing Christians in a manner that recalled Nero's persecution decades before. The beast was Nero 666 and he was incarnate in the present ruling emperor, probably Domitian. The popular association that identified Domitian as a second Nero would have provided a current and lasting rationale for the equation of these two emperors (Juvenal 4:38; cf. Martial 11:33).[33]

Before describing the final defeat of the enemies of God, John contrasts the blessings and curses that await the followers of the Lamb and the followers of the Beast in chs. 16-18 and 20. The criterion for judgment is *worship*: "Fear God, and give him glory, because the hour of his judgment has come; and worship him who made the heaven and the earth and sea and springs of water" (Rev 14:7). Once again therefore the divine decree is not arbitrarily or unconditionally pronounced. God awards salvation to faithful, persevering worshipers, while cursing disobedient idolaters. The contrast is simple and complete.

The Worshipers of the Beast	The Worshipers of the Lamb
If anyone *worships* the beast and his image, and receives a mark on his forehead or upon his hand, he also will drink of the wine of the wrath of God, which is mixed in full strength in the cup of his anger; and he will be tormented with fire and brimstone in the presence of the holy angels and in the presence of the Lamb. And the smoke of their torment goes up forever and ever; and they have no rest day and night, those who *worship* the beast and his image, and whoever receives the mark of his name. (Rev 14:9b-11)	And I saw as it were, a sea of glass mixed with fire, and those who had come off victorious from the beast and from his image and from the number of his name, standing on the sea of glass, holding harps of God. And they sang the song of Moses the bond-servant of God and the song of the Lamb. (Rev 15:2-3a)
And the first angel went and poured out his bowl into the earth; and it became a loathsome and malignant sore upon the men who had the mark of the beast and who *worshiped* his image. (Rev 16:2)	And I saw thrones, and they sat upon them and judgment was given to them. And I saw the souls of those who had been beheaded because of the testimony of Jesus and because of the word of God, and those who had not worshiped the beast or his image, and had not received the mark upon their forehead and upon their hand; and they came to life and reigned with Christ for a thousand years. (Rev 20:4)

The curses plaguing the worshipers of the beast foretell the horrible consequences awaiting those who unfaithfully compromise worship of God because of mortal fear of the beast. Those with understanding, John explains, recognize the eternal

---

[33] For extensive primary and secondary historical documentation of the Nero legends, see Bauckham, *The Climax of Prophecy*, 414-50; Aune, *Revelation*, 2.737-740; H. B. Swete, *Apocalypse of John* (3rd ed. London: Macmillan, 1908), 221.

gravity of one's choice of allegiances. Those with understanding, those "who have ears to hear," are able to perceive both the identity and the fate of the beast and his followers. That the mediation of this wisdom is a major purpose of John is apparent from his progressive development of the theme (Rev 13:4, 8, 12, 15-18; 14:9-13; 16:2; 19:20; 20:4).

Painting the background of the judgment scene of Revelation 16 is once again the story of Exodus. In ch. 15 those "who had come off victorious from the beast *and from his image* and from the number of his name" worship God by singing "the song of Moses" (Rev 15:3). Historically, of course, the Song of Moses in Exodus was sung after the exodus in celebration of Yahweh's defeat of Egypt. The seven bowl plagues in Rev 16:2-21 thus appropriately recall in varying degrees the plagues God reigned on Egypt in the exodus. The plague of sores (Rev 16:2) afflicting those who had received the brand of the first beast and worshiped his image recalls the sixth plague of Exod 9:9. The turning of the sea, rivers, and wells into blood (Rev 16:3-4) recalls the first (Exod 7:20-21). The image of the sun scorching the inhabitants of the earth (Rev 16:8-9) partially recalls the fire from heaven in the seventh plague (Exod 9:22-24). And the darkening of the throne of the Beast (Rev 16:10) recalls the darkness God brought upon Egypt (Exod 10:21).

Within this context John maintains the exodus comparison by describing a form of recalcitrance among the worshipers of the beast that strongly resembles the hardened state of Pharaoh and the people of Egypt at the time of the exodus.[34]

> And men were scorched with fierce heat; and they blasphemed the name of God who has the power over these plagues; and they did not repent, so as to give him glory. (Rev 16:9; cf. Exod 7:22-23; 8:15)

> And the fifth angel poured out his bowl upon the throne of the beast; and his kingdom became darkened; and they gnawed their tongues because of pain, and they blasphemed the God of heaven because of their pains and their sores; and they did not repent of their deeds. (Rev 16:10-11)

> And men blasphemed God because of the plague of the hail, because its plague was extremely severe. (Rev 16:21)

These references draw a direct link between obstinacy and idolatry (Rev 2:21; 9:20-21), just as we have seen elsewhere in the Bible. The blasphemers who obstinately refuse to repent are one and the same as those who have the mark of the beast and worship his image. This association simply reiterates the association between idolatry and obstinacy forewarned in John's recycle of Pss 115:4-7 and 135:15-17 in Rev 9:20-21:

> And the rest of mankind, who were not killed by these plagues, did not repent of the works of their hands, so as not to worship demons, and the idols of gold and of silver and of brass and of stone and of wood, which

---

[34] Aune, *Revelation*, 2.889.

can neither see nor hear nor walk; and they did not repent of their murders nor of their sorceries nor of their immorality nor of their thefts.

VII. CONCLUSION

Revelation is essentially a call to undivided worship. Its comprehensive parody reduces the Roman Empire, the Roman emperor, and the emperor cult to weak, demonic imitations of the kingdom of God, Christ, and authentic Christian prophecy. Revelation sternly warns that compromise with Roman worship is an immoral, idolatrous act that God will punish severely. Steeped in the tradition of the OT, Revelation equates the emperor cult with idolatry and therefore portrays the followers of the emperor cult as suffering from the curse of divine hardening. Correspondence between Rev 9:20-21 and Pss 115:4-7 and 135:15-17 evidences John's awareness of the "you become like that which you worship" tradition and his adaptation of it. Compromise with Roman worship in Revelation is therefore interpreted as idolatry and brings with it the accompanying symptom of hardening. With this rationale the Book of Revelation defines ultimate wisdom by elaborately contrasting the curses awaiting worshipers of the Beast with the fortunes awaiting worshipers of the Lamb. The truly wise are those who worship the one God who alone will determine the fate of all creation. The condition of the wise is therefore the opposite of the condition that debilitates worshipers of the Beast. The wise are those who have "eyes to see" and are alert to supernatural reality. Those who do not have eyes to see are those without eternal perspective. They are followers of the Beast, whose seductions have blinded them from the immortal reality of God's rule. The former distinguish God from Caesar to reject idolatry in its many forms, even in the face of martyrdom. The latter attempt to evade persecution by complying with government policy, but in doing so suffer the consequence of rejecting the one true God and creator of the universe. They thus forfeit the salvation God has prepared for those who persevere to the end in obedient faith. Citizenship in the new heavens and the new earth is reserved for those who worship God and the Lamb exclusively.

Chapter 12

Insidious Idols Within: Pride, Theology and Worship

Conclusions and Contemporary Application

Then I will sprinkle clean water on you, and you will be clean; I will cleanse you from all your filthiness and from all your idols. Moreover, I will give you a new heart and put a new spirit within you; and I will remove the heart of stone from your flesh and give you a heart of flesh. (Ezek 36:25-26)

CONCLUSIONS

We began this book by asking three questions: Is the hardening of human hearts an unconditional, indiscriminate act on God's part, or is it an act that human beings bring upon themselves? Why does God harden human hearts? And is salvation possible for those whom God hardens? Our study having come to a close, we will now synthesize our answers and conclude with three relevant contemporary applications.

(1) *Is God's hardening of human hearts in the Bible an arbitrary, unconditional, indiscriminate act?*

The answer to this question is clearly no. Nowhere in the Bible does God randomly harden an individual or a people group. Hardening occurs in reaction to sin as a consequence of idolatry and volitional rebellion against God. Paul describes this phenomenon with great clarity in Rom 1:18-32 (see ch. 8 above), and the author of Hebrews explicitly warns of its danger, "But encourage one another day after day, as long as it is still called today, *lest any one of you be hardened by the deceitfulness of sin*" (Heb 3:13).

Sin caused hardening is evident throughout the OT. God hardened Pharaoh for oppressing Israel and for trusting in the power of Egypt and her many gods (see ch. 3). God similarly hardened the later Israelites who "went after vain idols and became vain" (2 Kings 17:15). Then, consonant with the curses of Deut 28:58-68 and 29:17-29, Isaiah and Jeremiah pronounce hardening curses upon idolatrous, morally indifferent Judah (see ch. 5; Isa 6:9-10; Jer 5:19-21).

The NT simply continues the theme. God hardens the opponents of Jesus and the apostles for rejecting the Gospel due to a preference for law, tradition, temple, and ethnicity. Guilty of a religious form of idolatry, the hardened inherit the Isaiah 6:9-10 curse from their idolatrous ancestors (John 12:36-40; Acts 7:51-53; Acts

28:25-27), who had rejected the prophets as their descendents were now rejecting Jesus and the apostles.

More literally, the worshipers of the beast suffer sensory depletion in the book of Revelation. They acquire ears that are unable to hear, because they persecute the church and worship the Beast (Rev 9:20-21; 13:8-9, 11-18; see ch. 11 above).

In light of this biblical tradition, the Abrahamic promise "I will bless those who bless you, and curse those who curse you" (Gen 12:3; Deut 30:7) is programmatic for God's punishment of adversaries who impede the progress of the Gospel, God's new covenant plan.

God thus inflicts hardening upon willful sinners who defy his covenant plan. Biblical hardening is not indiscriminate and the recipients of hardening are not spiritually neutral.

(2) Why does God harden hearts?

In review we may infer at least four reasons for divine hardening.

First, hardening is a this-worldly consequence of divine judgment. As Jesus explained, "For judgment I came into this world, that those who do not see may see; and that those who see may become blind" (John 9:39). Similarly, Paul prefaced his treatise of idolatry and the hardening of the heart (Rom 1:18-32) stating, "For the wrath of God is revealed from heaven against all ungodliness and unrighteousness of men, who suppress the truth in unrighteousness" (Rom 1:18).[1]

Second, hardening and sensory depletion are symptoms that diagnose the presence of idolatrous sin. When idols supplant God, they fail to inspire and sustain life as the only true living God can. Therefore, in separation from God, idolaters suffer hardening, sensory depletion, and spiritual death. It is in this respect that human beings are dead in sin prior to being born again through union with the risen Christ.

Third, hardening prolongs the duration of God's revelatory acts, so that final judgment and deliverance take place only after God has comprehensively accomplished his disciplinary and revelatory purposes. Exodus establishes this understanding by describing how Pharaoh's hardening intensified stage by stage in accord with each successive plague, before finally culminating in God's comprehensive defeat of Egypt and her gods (Exod 18:11). Each plague successively demonstrates the falsehood of Egypt's idolatrous religion in contrast to the truth of God's supremacy over man and nature. The exodus event then climaxes with God declaring, "I will harden the hearts of the Egyptians so that they will go in after them; and I will be honored through Pharaoh and all his army, through his chariots and his horsemen. *Then the Egyptians will know that I am the Lord*" (Exod 14:17b-18a).

---

[1] As we emphasize in ch. 8, the kernel of the hardening paradigm is found in Rom 1:21-23: "For even though they knew God, they did not honor him as God or give thanks; but they became futile in their speculations, and *their foolish heart was darkened*. Professing to be wise, *they became fools, and exchanged the glory of the incorruptible God for an image* in the form of corruptible man and of birds and four-footed animals and crawling creatures."

Isaiah's commission to harden the idolatrous people of Judah (Isa 6:9-10) similarly prolongs divine punishment for God's revelatory purposes: "Then I said, Lord, how long? And he answered, *until* cities are devastated and without inhabitant, houses are without people, and the land is utterly desolate, the Lord has removed men far away, and the forsaken places are many in the midst of the land" (Isa 6:11-12). Accordingly, the hardening affliction symptomatic of the idolatry lamented in Isaiah 1-2 continues unabated until Judah's military defeat and corporate exile achieve their chastising purposes—Judah's awakening to the reality of the impotence of idols, the futility of covenants with foreign kings, the truth of Isaiah's prophecy (cf. Deut 28:64-65), and Judah's desperate, existential need for God.[2]

Consistent with this purpose, Paul explains in the NT that God's partial hardening of Israel will mysteriously prolong the era of the preaching of the Gospel *until* God's plan of salvation reaches its climax: "For I do not want you, brethren, to be uninformed of this mystery, lest you be wise in your own estimation, that a partial hardening has happened to Israel *until* the fullness of the Gentiles has come in" (Rom 11:25-26).[3] Thus God hardens to prolong his revelation until *his* chosen time for final judgment and salvation.

Fourth, hardening and sensory depletion are forms of chastisement that aim to provoke repentance and destroy pride. The blinding effects of self-aggrandizement and manmade religion render worship little more than empty ritual—lip service at best. Nebuchadnezzar is exemplary:

> The king reflected and said, is this not Babylon the great, which I myself have built as a royal residence by the might of my power and for the glory of my majesty? While the word was in the king's mouth, a voice came from heaven, saying, King Nebuchadnezzar, to you it is declared: sovereignty has been removed from you, and you will be driven away from mankind, and your dwelling place will be with the beasts of the field. You will be given grass to eat like cattle, and seven periods of time will pass over you, until you recognize that the most high is ruler over the realm of mankind, and bestows it on whomever he wishes. Immediately the word concerning Nebuchadnezzar was fulfilled; and he was driven away from mankind and began eating grass like cattle, and his body was drenched with the dew of heaven, until his hair had grown like eagles'

---

[2] Ezekiel communicates the same message affirming that Israel will know that Yahweh is the Lord, after it has experienced the nauseating results of idolatry and rediscovered, by contrast, the holiness of her God: "As for you, O house of Israel, thus says the Lord God, go serve everyone his idols; but later, you will surely listen to me, and my holy name you will profane no longer with your gifts and with your idols" (Ezek 20:39).

[3] Peter Stuhlmacher comments: "When the full number of Gentiles have entered into the city of God and have been led into the community of salvation, the partial hardening of Israel will be taken away. In accordance with the biblical promise, Israel too, in its entirety, will thus be redeemed from its sins through the Christ who appears from Zion and likewise be led into the community of salvation. It is primarily this salvation of all Israel from the hardening of unbelief that is the goal of salvation history, and not the fact that the Gentiles are already obtaining salvation" (Romans, 173).

feathers and his nails like birds' claws. But at the end of that period I, Nebuchadnezzar, raised my eyes toward heaven, and my reason returned to me, and I blessed the most high and praised and honored him who lives forever; for his dominion is an everlasting dominion, and his kingdom endures from generation to generation. And all the inhabitants of the earth are accounted as nothing, but he does according to his will in the host of heaven and among the inhabitants of earth; And no one can ward off his hand or say to him, what have you done? *At that time my reason returned to me.* And my majesty and splendor were restored to me for the glory of my kingdom, and my counselors and my nobles began seeking me out; so I was reestablished in my sovereignty, and surpassing greatness was added to me. Now I Nebuchadnezzar praise, exalt, and honor the King of heaven, for all his works are true and his ways just, *and he is able to humble those who walk in pride.* (Dan 4:30-37)

The humbling of King Nebuchadnezzar's pride by sensory malfunction is analogous to the corporate hardening Israel experienced as a nation. Like Nebuchadnezzar, Israel finally laments her sin only after God rescues her from her hardened state. It is important to observe, therefore, that while human repentance is a necessary condition for salvation, it is God who does the healing, restoring, and recreation. Ezekiel, Baruch (150–60 B.C.), and the Testament of Zebulon (250 B.C.– Maccabean period) further substantiate this point:

Moreover, I will give you a new heart and put a new spirit within you; and I will remove the heart of stone from your flesh and give you a heart of flesh. . . . *Then you will remember your evil ways and your deeds that were not good, and you will loathe yourselves in your own sight for your iniquities and your abominations.* (Ezek 36:25-26, 31; see also Ezek 16:60-63)

For I know that they will not obey me, for they are a stiff-necked people. But in the land of their exile they will come to themselves, and they will know that I am the Lord their God. *I will give them a heart that obeys and ears that hear; and they will praise me in the land of their exile, and will remember my name, and will turn from their stubbornness and their wicked deeds; for they will remember the ways of their fathers, who sinned before the Lord.* (Baruch 2:30-33; cf. Jubilees 1:22-25; Tobit 14:5-6)

In the writings of the fathers I came to know that in the last days you shall defect from the Lord, and you shall be divided in Israel, and you shall follow after two kings; you shall commit every abomination and worship every idol. Your enemies will take you captive and you shall reside among the gentiles with all sorts of sickness and tribulation and oppression of soul. *And thereafter you will remember the Lord and repent, and he will turn you around because he is merciful and compassionate.* (T. Zeb. 9:5-7)

Hardening and exile thus work together to stimulate repentance, the erosion of human pride. When these forms of chastisement complete the purposes for which God intended them, the new covenant promises of salvation come into effect in the lives of those who respond in repentance and faith.

(3) *Is salvation possible for those whom God hardens?*

Deuteronomy 29-30 forecasts that hardening and exile (Deut 30:1) will eventually give way to God's regathering of the exiles and his circumcision of the hearts of his people (Deut 30:1-9). Thus salvation from hardening is indeed a biblical expectation for the people of God.

This prospect establishes another rationale for understanding Isaiah's commission to harden the hearts of the idolatrous Judeans in Isa 6:8-13. As emphasized above, like Deuteronomy 29-30, Isaiah 6 anticipates an end to the curse: "Then I said, Lord, how long? And he answered, *until* cities are devastated and without inhabitant, houses are without people, and the land is utterly desolate, the Lord has removed men far away" (Isa 6:11-12).[4]

But this is not the end of the story. God comes to the rescue as Israel's savior and Lord.

> Listen to me, you stubborn-minded, who are far from righteousness. I bring near my righteousness, it is not far off; and my salvation will not delay. And I will grant salvation in Zion, and my glory for Israel. (Isa 46:12-13; also 49:14-23; 51:12-22)

> For a brief moment I forsook you, but with great compassion I will gather you. In an outburst of anger I hid my face from you for a moment; but with everlasting lovingkindness I will have compassion on you, says the Lord your redeemer. (Isa 54:7-8; cf. 44:21-23; 45:21-25)

> Because of the iniquity of his unjust gain I was angry and struck him; I hid my face and was angry, and he went on turning away, in the way of his heart. I have seen his ways, but I will heal him. (Isa 57:17-18a; see the context of idolatry in 57:13)

> For in my wrath I struck you, and in my favor I have had compassion on you. (Isa 60:10; also Isa 55:7)

Prolonged hardening and exile followed by divine restoration fulfills God's ancient prophecy to prove his singular existence as Savior and God—the only living God able to reinvigorate, save, and deliver:

---

[4]Isaiah continues beyond chapter 6 to portray Israel as suffering from a spiritual despondency that is commensurate with idolatrous apostasy (Isa 44:17-20; also Isa 42:18-20, 25; 48:3-5; 63:17-19).

> Bring out the people who are blind, even though they have eyes, and the deaf, even though they have ears. All the nations have gathered together in order that the peoples may be assembled. Who among them can declare this and proclaim to us the former things? Let them present their witnesses that they may be justified, or let them hear and say, it is true. You are my witnesses, declares the Lord, and my servant whom I have chosen, in order that you may know and believe me, and understand that I am he. Before me there was no God formed, and there will be none after me. I, even I, am the Lord; and there is no savior besides me. It is I who have declared and saved and proclaimed, and there was no strange god among you; so you are my witnesses, declares the Lord, and I am God. (Isa 43:8-12; see also Isa 44:21-23; 45:21-25; 46:12-13; 49:14-23; 51:12-22; 54:7-8; 55:7; 60:10)[5]

The reversal of the hardened, exiled condition is thus a major feature of biblical salvation. Indeed the new covenant promises a reversal of fortune that synthesizes with the covenant of David (Isa 55:3), coincides with the coming of a redeemer to Zion (Isa 59:20), and inaugurates with the anointed one who will bind up the "broken hearted" (Isa 61:1, 8).

Jeremiah 31, 33 and Ezekiel 36-37 have this event in view. The problem of sin that Jer 17:1 describes, "the sin of Judah is written down with an iron stylus; with a diamond point it is engraved *upon the tablet of their heart*," finds its corrective in the new covenant promise of Jer 31:33, "But this is the covenant which I will make with the house of Israel after those days, declares the Lord, I will put my law within them, and *on their heart I will write it*; and I will be their God, and they shall be my people." Strikingly, the reversal of the hardened state occurs in conjunction with the fulfillment of the Davidic promises. The correspondence between Jer 31:31-34 and Jer 33:14-16 and between Ezek 36:24-28 and Ezek 37:24-28 indicates that Jeremiah and Ezekiel each expect a descendent of David to implement the new covenant promises of restoration and healing.

> Behold, I will take the sons of Israel from among the nations where they have gone, and I will gather them from every side and bring them into their own land; and I will make them one nation in the land, on the mountains of Israel; and one king will be king for all of them; and they will no longer be two nations, and they will no longer be divided into two kingdoms. And they will no longer defile themselves with their idols, or with their detestable things, or with any of their transgressions; but I will deliver them from all their dwelling places in which they have sinned, and will cleanse them. And they will be my people, and I will be their God. And my servant David will be king over them, and they will all have one

---

[5] See also Psalm 73:21-24: "When my heart was embittered, and I was pierced within, then I was senseless and ignorant; I was like a beast before you. Nevertheless I am continually with you; you have taken hold of my right hand. With your counsel you will guide me, and afterward receive me to glory."

shepherd; and they will walk in my ordinances, and keep my statutes, and observe them. (Ezek 37:21-24; see also Jer 33:14-16)

These Scriptures in turn provide the conceptual background for the salvation of the hard of heart in the New Testament, where Jesus comes forth as the messiah anointed by the Holy Spirit to preach the gospel to the poor and to restore health to the afflicted—including sight, hearing, and speech (e.g., Matt 15:29-31; 11:2-4 par. Luke 7:22). Prior to his death, Jesus celebrates Passover with his disciples, testifying, "this cup which is poured out for you is the *new covenant* in my blood" (Luke 22:20b).[6] These acts attest to Jesus' aim to forgive sins and reverse the consequences of the broken covenant. Whereas idolatry had brought about the loss of sensory perception, Jesus' ministry was restoring it. Hence, in the Last Supper Jesus explained that his work, now about to culminate in his death, was making possible the realization of the new covenant promises. Against the background of Jeremiah 31 and Ezekiel 36, this meant the cleansing of the heart, the writing of the law upon the heart, and the heart's transformation from stone to flesh, so that recipients of Jesus' atoning work would become the people of God.

The potential for this transformation lies at the heart of Jesus' parable of the Prodigal Son (Luke 15:11-32). The parable, as N.T. Wright has argued, tells the story of God's merciful desire to reconcile with his rebellious covenant people Israel.[7] The recalcitrance of the prodigal correlates with Israel's past rebellion against God. The son's separation from the father parallels Israel's exile. The son's hardheaded debauchery corresponds to Israel's ethical deterioration and hardening. When suffering brings the son back "*to his senses*" (Luke 15:17), and he returns to his father in sincere humility with minimal expectations, he then discovers the limitless grace, mercy, and love of his father, who has run to embrace him. The message of the story is that God, as Israel's father, does desire to restore his people Israel from exile and hardening. When this happens, Israel will awaken from her obstinacy and come to her senses (Luke 15:17). She will come to life again, after having been spiritually dead (Luke 15:24, 32; cf. Ezekiel 37). Then God's restoration of his relationship with Israel will culminate in a lavish banquet where sadness will be turned into rejoicing (Luke 15:32). The reader of Luke is aware that this reconciliation with God is taking place through the ministry of Jesus, who eats with tax collectors and sinners (Luke 5:30-32; 7:34) and who preaches of the kingdom of God—the consummate salvation event

---

[6] The Matthean and Markan versions of the Lord's Supper (Matt 26:28; Mark 14:24) imply what the Lukan and Pauline (1 Cor 11:25) versions make explicit, "Jesus interpreted his death as the establishment of the new covenant predicted in Jeremiah 31:31 and understood the blood shed in his death as analogous to the blood that, according to Exodus 24:8, Moses sprinkled on the people at the establishment of the Sinaitic covenant," (See Thielman, *Paul and the Law*, 105).

[7] N.T. Wright, *Jesus and the Victory of God* (Minneapolis: Fortress, 1996), 125-131. Wright's interpretation of the parable of the Prodigal Son against the background of Israel's history coheres with the backdrop found in Jesus' parable of the Vineyard and the Vine Growers (Mark 12:1-12 par.). See N. T. Wright, *The New Testament and the People of God* (Minneapolis: Fortress, 1992), 74-77.

when God will feast with his forgiven people (Luke 13:29; 14:16-24; cf. Isa 25:6-9). Yes, this parable proclaims, salvation is possible for the hardened.

Elsewhere in the NT, Paul writes as self-proclaimed servant of the new covenant (2 Cor 3:6) that transformation from the sin hardened state takes place when one believes in Jesus—in an anticipatory fashion in the present (2 Cor 3:2-6, 15-18) and consummately in the future (Phil 3:20-21). For Gentiles and Jews, Paul's solution to the degenerating effects of idolatry is justification by God's grace through faith in Christ (Rom 1:18-3:31). In the case of Israel, Paul holds out hope that partially hardened Israel will some day believe and come to know salvation. The partially hardened may indeed be re-grafted in, if they do not continue in their unbelief (Rom 11:23-27).

It is important to observe that the Israelites who have the potential to be grafted in again in Rom 11:23 are one and the same as Paul's unbelieving Jewish kinsmen in Rom 9:3-4, whom Paul describes as being vessels of wrath prepared for destruction (Rom 9:22). The potential for divine deliverance from otherwise inevitable destruction in Romans 9-11 echoes the conceptual background of the potter image in Jeremiah 18, where God pronounces, "if that nation against which I have spoken turns from its evil, I will relent concerning the calamity I planned to bring on it" (Jer 18:8).[8] Paul writes with this conviction "as an apostle, set apart for the Gospel of God, *which he promised beforehand through his prophets*" (Rom 1:1b-2a).

Paul thus viewed his teaching as fully consistent with the writings of Scripture that he quoted and alluded to regularly. The God of Romans 9-11 is the same God who speaks in Jeremiah 18. Paul, following in the footsteps of Jeremiah and the prophets of old, contextualizes the prophetic message with Christian refinement but without contradiction. The unbelieving, hardened part of Israel that is destined for destruction may still find salvation, if its jealousy of saved Gentiles brings about repentance and a turning to Christ in faith (Rom 11:7-27).

It is apparent, therefore, that hardening has an important role within God's eschatological plan of salvation. Within this plan Israel will suffer a partial hardening until "the fullness of the Gentiles has come in" (Rom 11:25b). From the perspective of biblical theology, it is within this phase of salvation history that John 12:37-40 is best understood:

> But though he had performed so many signs before them, yet they were not believing in him; that the word of Isaiah the prophet might be fulfilled, which he spoke, Lord, who has believed our report? And to whom has the arm of the Lord been revealed? For this cause they could not believe, for Isaiah said again, he has blinded their eyes, and he hardened their heart; lest they see with their eyes, and perceive with their heart, and be converted, and I heal them.

This audience, which clearly receives the full force of the Isa 6:9-10 curse, represents the unbelieving multitude of Jews who rejected Jesus out of a preference for preexisting Jewish traditions. They thus experienced hardening and

---

[8] See Richard B. Hays, *Echoes of Scripture in the Letters of Paul*, 66.

remained unfit for repentance for the duration of their punishment, as the precedent of Isaiah's prophecy suggests, and as Romans 9-11 explains. But when Isa 6:13 anticipates an eventual end to the hardening curse,[9] which Isaiah specifically[10] describes (Isaiah 42:14-22; 43:8-13; 44:9-23; ch. 48; 57:14-18; cf. Jer 12:14-17), and when Paul specifies an eventual end to the partial hardening of Israel (when unbelieving Jews would be grafted in again: Rom 11:23), it is consistent with general biblical theology to surmise that the hardening spoken of in John 12:37-40 is also a potentially temporary affliction that aids God's ultimate plan of salvation. Such an interpretation fully coheres with the OT background that John 12:37-40 quotes. Transposing John 12:37-40 onto the eschatological timeline of Romans 11, the hardened Jews of John 12:37-40 represent the unbelieving Jews whom Paul contemplated could be grafted in again, if they did not continue in their unbelief.

The NT explains therefore that while hardening continues to afflict unbelievers (2 Cor 4:4; Heb 3:12-13, 18-19), God recreates life within those who exercise faith in Christ. Those who believe in Jesus may be born again (John 3:3-8, 16). Thus, if idolatry and the hardening of the heart is an axiom of sin, rebirth and newness of life is an axiom of faith in Christ. God reverses the curse of idolatry and the hardening of the heart in the lives of those who have faith in Christ.[11] Vessels of wrath become vessels of glory. Those who were not God's people become "sons of the living God" (Rom 9:25-26; Hosea 2:23; 1:10).

CONTEMPORARY APPLICATIONS

There are more idols than realities in the world;
that is my 'evil eye' for this world; that is also my 'evil ear.'
(Friedrich Nietzsche, *Twilight of the Idols*)

On the subject of idolatry, Nietzsche was right. The world is full of idols that vie to supplant God in the hearts of contemporary human beings. Indeed contemporary idols are too numerous and too subjective for us to identify and

---

[9] "Because the so-called memorial introduced by ch. 6 ends in a word of hope (cf. 8.17), God's answer envisages the end of the hardening and the possibility given with it of a new beginning to his history," (Otto Kaiser, *Isaiah 1-12* [trans. J. Bowden; 2d ed.; Philadelphia: Westminster, 1983], 132).

[10] In Isaiah 42-43 it is very clear that the blind and deaf are one and the same as those whom God blesses with eschatological salvation: "Hear you deaf! And look, you blind, that you may see. Who is blind but my servant, or so deaf as my messenger whom I send? Who is so blind as he that is at peace with me, or so blind as the servant of the Lord? You have seen many things, but you do not observe them; your ears are open, but none hears" (Isa 42:18-20). It is quite clear within the context of the entire book of Isaiah that the afflicted audience of Isa 42:18-20 is the same as that which receives the curse of Isa 6:9-10. The latter chapters of Isaiah specify that this hardened, senseless audience will indeed have the opportunity for reconciliation with God, because of the mercy and grace which God himself will provide in expression of his love for his covenantal partner.

[11] As Jonah 2:8 (2:9 MT) explains: "Those who regard vain idols forsake their faithfulness."

analyze effectively in a brief conclusion.[12] The scope of this closing section is more modest. I shall briefly discuss three contemporary idols that I consider serious threats to the spiritual health of contemporary Christians and the health of the church at large. These three idols are pride, errant theology, and worship.

(1) Pride

> "We have set up our idols in our hearts; and to these we bow down, and worship them; we worship ourselves, when we pay that honor to ourselves, which is due to God only. Therefore all pride is idolatry; it is ascribing to ourselves what is due to God alone."
> John Wesley (*Sermon on Original Sin*)

We usually do not think of pride as an idol. And yet the inclination to place one's self in the place of God is endemic to human nature. All human beings have the natural inclination to think a lot more about themselves than they think about God. It is therefore true that human beings *in practice* think and act as if they themselves are more important than God. Thus, if thinking and acting are valid indicators, human beings attribute more worth to themselves than to God. And since the attribution of ultimate worth to someone or something *is worship* by definition, humanity is indeed prone toward idolatry of self.

C.S. Lewis was not exaggerating when he wrote that pride "is the complete anti-God state of mind."[13] In the act of pride human beings construct a mental image of themselves, which they promote *ritually* and *religiously*. It is an *image* and as such it is an idol that human beings existentially cultivate, cosmetically make up, and apologetically defend. It is the human ego. Many of the ambitions and phobias of the proud relate to the enhancement or destruction of this self-image that exists in the proud individual's mind. Ambitions aspire to "build up"

---

[12] For readers desiring such an attempt, I defer to the following important books: Herbert Schlossberg, *Idols for Destruction*, Wheaton: Crossway, 1990; Os Guinness and John Seel, *No God but God: Breaking with the Idols of Our Age*, Chicago: Moody Press, 1992; Vinoth Ramachandra, *Gods that fail: Modern Idolatry and Christian Mission*, Downers Grove: InterVarsity, 1997; Bruce Ellis Benson, *Graven Ideologies: Nietzsche, Derrida & Marion on Modern Idolatry*, Downers Grove: InterVarsity, 2002; Douglas R. Sharp, *No Partiality: The Idolatry of Race & The New Humanity*, Downers Grove: InterVarsity, 2002. Schlossberg proposes that history, humanity, materialism, nature, power, and religion have become contemporary idols that have distracted contemporary cultures (especially American culture) from true, authentic worship of God. *No God but God* is a valuable symposium with chapters on contemporary idols by eight different Christian authors. Ramachandra makes many of the same arguments from an international perspective. Benson addresses philosophy and theology as potential idols through an analysis of Nietzsche, Derrida, and Marion. Sharp explores the interesting thought that racism is a potentially idolatrous construct. See also Os Guinness (*The Call*, W Publishing Group, 134-143), who analyzes idolatrous features of capitalism, especially the intoxication of making money.

[13] *Mere Christianity*, (Rev. ed.; New York: Simon and Schuster, 1996), 110.

this self-image by way of accomplishing perceived feats of success. Leaders aspire to leave behind positive legacies—a permanent praiseworthy, positive image.

Fears stemming from pride relate to the awareness that the self's false image cannot go undetected forever. If the true self becomes public—a self that is less admirable than the false image presented—the result will be public shame, disgrace, and ignominious isolation. Hence, pride breeds intense insecurity.

For these reasons pride is an idolatrous convolution of reality that may systemically harden human beings, just as physical idols hardened the hearts of biblical characters. Focusing energy on creating and protecting their image, the proud do not really find their security in God—even if they profess faith. In reality their security is not in God, but in themselves, or more accurately, in their image of themselves. They deceive themselves into believing that they are self-sufficient, secure beings. Self-deceived in this way, the proud may worship God in word and appearance, despite the fact that most of their thoughts and energies are focused on promoting their own interests and not those of God or his gospel. Their ultimate goal is not worship of God but self-promotion after the manner that Paul laments in Phil 2:21: "for they all seek after their own interests, not those of Christ Jesus." Integrally related is the quest of the proud for the approval of others, which affirms, vindicates, and inflates the self's image.

Because this quest is contrary to that of Christian discipleship, Jesus admonished his audience: "How can you believe, when you receive glory from one another, and you do not seek the glory that is from the one and only God?" (John 5:44). Paul taught that a true member of God's covenant people, a true Jew, was one whose praise was "not from men, but from God" (Rom 2:29). These correctives arise from the reality that pride supplants God and effectively distances the proud from God, so that sensory depletion results—a false security that prevents the proud from recognizing the illusion of their self-image and their truly desperate need for the God who created them. As long as humanly constructed self-images remain in tact, based as they are on human measures of success and security, the proud feel secure even though their relationship with God is immature and their true character very different from Christ's.

The hardening that results from pride is easily observed in human relationships that sever and evolve into grudges, because one party in the relationship has offended the other's pride. Grudges evidence a form of hardening that selfishly refuses to forgive because the parties at fault consider their respective selves more important than the preexisting relationship. Asking forgiveness would necessitate the letting go of pride, which for proud people is terribly hard to do. Pride, therefore, is often times the cause of division and prolonged separation, just as idolatry separated Israel from God in the Scriptures.

Competition, as C.S. Lewis again astutely observed, is another aspect of idolatrous human pride.[14] Human beings have a natural inclination to promote their image by outdoing others. Security and self-confidence are gained in this way by outperforming others financially, materially, educationally, in popularity, in the success of children, even in the visibility of one's religious zeal and apparent

---

[14] *Mere Christianity*, 110.

spiritual maturity. Stimulated by pride, these forms of competition lead to division, resentment, the severing of relationships, and ultimately to insecurity. For these reasons, there is no place for competition within the body of Christ (Phil 2:1-4).

The only solution to human pride is the new covenant—a new relationship with God that transforms the believer through the blood of Christ and the anointing of the Holy Spirit. The new covenant that Jesus' death established (Luke 22:20) in fulfillment of Jeremiah 31 and Ezekiel 36 became the gospel that Paul served (2 Cor 3:6). It makes possible restored relationships both with God and with other people who have been "born again." This restoration occurs through the Holy Spirit's transformation of the pride/idol hardened heart into a Spirit regenerated heart of flesh (Ezek 36:25-27). This salvation involves the destruction of idolatrous self-images and a turning to the true living God, who created individuals as they really are. Recognizing this reality, Blaise Pascal aptly commented, "Not only do we know God through Jesus Christ, we only know ourselves through Jesus Christ."

Repentance thus occurs out of an awareness that one's true value and worth is only discovered in a peaceful and honest relationship with one's Creator and not from servitude to one's own creation—whether material or mental. In the restored relationship the promises of Ezekiel 36 become real and the believer discovers the bliss of God's new creation power. Aroused from the hardened state, the once proud of heart take on a heart of flesh and are spiritually born again to serve God and not their self-images. For those whose sin is pride, this "new birth" is salvation.

(2) Theology

> "Wrong ideas about God are not only the
> fountain from which the polluted waters of
> idolatry flow; they are themselves idolatrous.
> The idolater simply imagines things about God
> and acts as if they were true."
> A.W. Tozer (*The Knowledge of the Holy*)

Theology—thinking, studying, writing, and speaking about God, is an awe-inspiring privilege. Performed in the power of the Holy Spirit, it is an act of worship that heightens intimacy with God. For God desires to be known and understood in the special ways that he has revealed himself.

When wrongly construed, however, theology misrepresents God by conforming him to human speculation. And where human speculation creates gods, theological/philosophical idolatry is the result. As J. I. Packer admonishes: "To follow the imagination of one's heart in the realm of theology is the way to remain ignorant of God, and to become an idol-worshiper—the idol in this case being a false mental image of God, made by one's own speculation and imagination." [15] Misrepresentations of this kind either assign God attributes that

---

[15] *Knowing God*, Downers Grove: InterVarsity, 1993, 48.

the Scriptures do not specify, or they absolutize as preeminent one attribute that, when forced to be all-encompassing, unbalances God's comprehensive nature.

Students of the "quest" of the historical Jesus have long been aware of the seemingly unavoidable human tendency to recreate Jesus after the historian's own worldview and philosophy. The supposed "historical Jesus" throughout the history of Jesus research has invariably become the replication of the historian's own self-image. The same human inclination is ever present in the discipline of theology.[16] As an extension of the self and the self's tradition and heritage, theology can and often does become a form of pride and self-worship. Human beings have an innate tendency to create God in their own image. The basest form of this phenomenon became apparent after September 11, 2001, when Osama Bin Laden attributed his own terrorist activities to his god Allah. Obviously Bin Laden's Allah was an Allah very much like Bin Laden himself; that is, one who takes delight in indiscriminate terrorism.

The only sure preventative to theological idolatry of this kind is scrupulous appeal to the *entirety* of biblical revelation. Rather than conforming God to inherited biases or to humanly constructed philosophies by picking and choosing the Scriptures that fit a preconceived system of thought, the honest, truly dedicated *biblical* theologian worships God comprehensively as God reveals himself in the entirety of the Bible, allowing for mystery to remain where there is mystery, with the awareness that God has not willed to reveal everything to us—"For now we see in a mirror dimly" (1 Cor 13:12). By lessening this mystery, theological idolatries shorten the distance between humanity and God, so that the theologian's humanly constructed philosophical theology confidently and even in some cases dogmatically explains God with terms and limitations preconceived by the theologian's system of thought prior to the reading of Scripture. The result is that the theologian's theology suffers an irreparable methodological flaw—that of conforming Scripture to a preconceived system of theology, when the working method should be that of extracting theology from God's self-revelation in all of Scripture. This faulty process, especially when clothed in dogmatism, misrepresents the true magnitude, grandeur, and glory of the sovereign God who maintains: "My thoughts are not your thoughts, neither are your ways my ways,' declares the Lord. For as the heavens are higher than the earth, so are my ways higher than your ways, and my thoughts than your thoughts" (Isa 55:8).

The contemporary climate of theology in American evangelicalism exemplifies the phenomenon we are describing. *Extreme* expressions like "Totally Reformed" theology and "Open Theism" construct contemporary gods from partial, exegetically flawed biblical theologies.[17] Prioritizing select passages that

---

[16] A.W. Tozer's comment has proven prophetic: "Among the sins to which the human heart is prone, hardly any other is more hateful to God than idolatry, for idolatry is at bottom a libel on His character. The idolatrous heart assumes that God is other than He is—in itself a monstrous sin—and substitutes for the true God one made after its own likeness. Always this God will conform to the image of the one who created it and will be base or pure, cruel or kind, according to the moral state of the mind from which it emerges" (*The Knowledge of the Holy*; New York: Harper & Row, 1961, 11).

[17] I direct these comments toward respected colleagues and students, past and present, who advocate the theistic determinism I am describing. This extreme position has become

on the surface seem to substantiate their preexisting systems, they each turn their prioritized texts into governing hermeneutical keys for interpreting the entire Bible—and indeed all reality.

Upon investigation of the Bible, one concludes that this has to be the case; otherwise these extreme positions could never be reached. On the one hand, the glory of God and the sovereignty of God are indeed cherished absolutes of biblical theology and indisputable biblical truths, when properly understood. And it *is* true that today in some sectors God's righteousness, justice, and sovereignty are not fully understood within American Evangelicalism, so that churches suffering this weakness virtually mirror secular society. However, the practice of defining God's sovereignty as theistic determinism, i.e., that God is the first cause of everything that happens, is an unbiblical prescription for rectifying weak theology and practice. This is because God's sovereignty is not defined in Scripture as theistic determinism. Etymologically, the word sovereignty does not equate with determinism in the English language, where sovereignty means supremacy not cause and effect determinism. God's sovereignty, biblically understood, is God's kingship, power, and dominion—that God is above all others supreme. The Bible in its entirety testifies to this truth. The message is not that Satan, Pharaoh, Nebuchadnezzar and others have no power, but rather that God as creator and sustainer of the universe has immeasurably more power and therefore is the only real hope for deliverance from evil and its consequences in this world. And thus it is that the focal point of Jesus' ministry is the kingdom of God (Matt 6:33) and not a hope in theistic determinism. The gospel focuses squarely on God the Father who is alive and active within creation, expressing his love for the world through his prophets and apostles and ultimately through the sacrifice of his son.

"Totally Reformed" theology essentially equates God's sovereignty with the philosophy of theistic determinism—that God is the first cause of everything. It thereby subordinates God's love, mercy, freedom, grace, justice, righteousness, glory and especially holiness to the dogma of divine cause and effect. The odd result is that it is not God who is actively sovereign, but rather the deified philosophy of theistic determinism that is. Because God is the first cause of everything, God must will everything that happens—whether or not that event conforms to the character of God as revealed in Scripture.

"Totally Reformed" theologians are now aggressively arguing that God is indeed the first cause of evil. The equation of God's sovereignty with theistic determinism is for this reason understandably disturbing to most Christians, for the inevitable conclusion is that God himself is responsible for the breaking of his own

---

common in recent years among students and professionals influenced by the Reformed movement within American Evangelicalism. It represents an expression of Reformed theology, sometimes referred to as hyper-Calvinism, which does not represent the entire Reformed tradition, whose contributions to orthodox Christian theology, piety, and worship have been monumental. The Reformed movement within Evangelicalism has brought many positive correctives, most notably a restored vision of God's sovereign glory as the purpose of human history (explicitly supported by Ezek 38:23). However, like eyeglasses too powerful for the wearer, extreme theistic determinism is an over-correction to the vision of American Evangelicalism. Like all Christian traditions, it will draw closer to correct vision as it becomes more comprehensively biblical.

law—that God is therefore self-contradictory. Yet, this view is hardly a caricature. It has a firm grip on the minds of a growing number of Evangelicals, who argue that the view has solid biblical support.[18]

Mark Talbot, for example, argues that the Joseph story and the crucifixion of Jesus display God's work in evil to accomplish ultimate good.[19] He understands Joseph's statement "you meant evil against me, but God meant it for good" (Gen 50:20) to be analogous to all forms of evil, which God ultimately intends for good (Rom 8:28). Following Jonathan Edwards, he reasons that if God intended the crucifixion, the worst evil ever accomplished, for good, then the same must be true of all lesser evils. Influential pastor and theologian John Piper[20] makes the same argument, citing as biblical substantiation God's collaboration with Satan (Job 1), God's inciting David to the census that resulted in the deaths of 70,000 Israelites (2 Sam 24:1), and multiple other texts that witness God's inflicting "evil" on human beings (e.g., Judges 9:23; 1 Sam 16:14-16; 18:10; 19:9; 2 Sam 12:11; 1 Kings 9:9; 21:21; 21:29; 22:23; 2 Kings 6:33; Neh 13:18). Of the same conviction, systematic theologian Wayne Grudem writes, "Scripture repeatedly gives examples where God in a mysterious, hidden way somehow ordains that people do wrong, but continually places the blame for that wrong on the individual human who does wrong and never on God himself."[21]

Upon investigation, however, these examples are more superficial than substantive. The Joseph story is in truth not analogous to sensational evils like ethnic cleansing, rape, child sacrifice, bestiality etc. The Hebrew word for evil in Gen 50:20 (ra‛ah; רָעָה), which bears the weight of this argument, is a word that has a broad range of meanings in Hebrew including misery, adversity, distress, injury etc.—meanings different in denotation from "evil" as most people think of it today

---

[18] See, for example, Wayne Grudem, *Systematic Theology: An Introduction to Biblical Theology* (Grand Rapids: Zondervan, 1994), 322-51.

[19] "TRUE FREEDOM: THE LIBERTY THAT SCRIPTURE PORTRAYS AS WORTH HAVING" in *Beyond the Bounds* (ed. John Piper, Justin Taylor, and Paul Kjoss Helseth; Wheaton: Crossway, 2003), 77-109.

[20] Piper follows Jonathan Edwards in concluding, "God decrees all things, even all sins." For Piper's rationale and claims for biblical support, consult http://www.desiringgod.org/library/topics/suffering/god_and_evil.htm, "Is God Less Glorious Because He Ordained that Evil Be?: Jonathan Edwards on the Decrees of God," n.p. [July, 1998]. See also Piper's devotional "TO SHOW THAT THE WORST EVIL IS MEANT BY GOD FOR GOOD" in *The Passion of Jesus Christ* (Wheaton: Crossway, 2004), 118-119, and his chapter "WHY I DO NOT SAY, "GOD DID NOT CAUSE THE CALAMITY, BUT HE CAN USE IT FOR GOOD" in *Life as a Vapor* (Oregon: Multnomah, 2004), 122-126. In the latter Piper infers from Eph 1:11 that God caused the destruction of the World Trade Towers on Sept. 11, 2001. Piper's exegesis, in my judgment, is flawed by circular reasoning. His autobiographical comments in the prologue of *The Justification of God* (Grand Rapids: Baker, 1983) are self-indicting in this respect: "As soon as my doctoral studies were completed in 1974, I devoted myself to write a book on Romans 9. The God of Romans 9 took me captive while I was yet in seminary. No other picture of God ever commended itself to me as more true to what the Creator must be. If there is a God, he must be the God of Romans 9."

[21] *Systematic Theology*, 343.

in English.[22] *To be sure*, the Hebrew word can mean "evil" in the horrible sense we're familiar with, but the context is determinative. In the context of Gen 50:20, it is the misfortune of Joseph's being sold into slavery that results in the accomplishment of God's "good" plan to preserve a people in fulfillment of the Abrahamic covenant (Gen 50:20b). This context is of course very different from that of pornography, rape, child-sacrifice etc., which the Bible, of course, never identifies as positive contributions to God's plan of salvation. In their applications, Talbot and Piper extrapolate a *universal* application from a special, *unique* act of God—an intent foreign to the context of Genesis and OT theology.

The analogy to the crucifixion is equally forced. This argument betrays the fact that the NT never describes the crucifixion with the word *ponēros* (evil). To the contrary, the NT preaches the cross as Good News—the ultimate expression of God's *love*— "*For God demonstrates his own love toward us in that while we were yet sinners Christ died for us*" (Rom 5:8; cf. John 3:16). Unlike the *unwilling* rape victim or the defenseless casualties of the Holocaust, Jesus obediently and willingly sacrificed his life as a *voluntary* expression of God's love, it being the case that his death was God's means of salvation: "For this reason the Father loves me, because I lay down my life that I may take it again. No one has taken it away from me, but I lay it down on my own initiative" (John 10:17-18a).[23] To say that human sin has a similar purpose, even on a much lesser plane, is a theological hypothesis foreign to NT theology. Jesus' voluntary, benevolent self-sacrifice contrasts categorically with radical forms of evil such as child sacrifice, child pornography, ethnic cleansing, etc., especially in view of passages such as Jer 19:4-5; 32:35. Why God, who created the wonders of the ever expanding glorious universe, would require human evil to substantiate his glory is counterintuitive and a strange construal of Scripture.

Similar exegetical and logical flaws undermine the remaining arguments Talbot, Grudem, and Piper cite. Job's complex poetic wisdom does not simply equate reality with divine cause and effect. The image of Satan as God's right hand man who serves a positive role in testing the sincerity of Job's commitment, which one might construct on the basis of Job 1 in isolation, does not take into consideration Satan's disobedience to God in Genesis 3, or Jesus' description of Satan as a murderer and a liar who speaks on his own initiative (John 8:44), or Satan's battle against Michael and his subsequent expulsion from heaven in Revelation 12. Job certainly contributes to our understanding of Satan, but Job's testimony should be qualified by its poetic genre and by the rest of the Bible, which portrays Satan as an insidious opponent of God and his people.

---

[22] Koehler and Baumgartner provide the following range of semantic equivalents for *ra'ah* in the OT: wicked, evil, sad, bad, of little worth, poor (in quality), not beneficial, contemptible, of an evil disposition, morally depraved, reprobate, malicious, injurious, sinister, bringing misfortune, badly disposed, ill-disposed, heavy, sullen, 'evil in contrast to good' (Ludwig Koehler and Walter Baumgartner, *The Hebrew and Aramaic Lexicon of the Old Testament*; Tr. M. E. J. Richardson [Leiden: E. J. Brill, 1996], 3.1250-1253.

[23] See also Romans 8:32 where Paul again describes Jesus' death as God's gracious sacrifice: "He who did not spare His own Son, but delivered Him up for us all, how will He not also with Him freely give us all things?" Nowhere in the context does Paul remotely intimate that God's gracious gift is evil—in any respect.

David's census, willed as it is by God, occurs within the context of David's moral erosion and Israel's spiritual decline. The introductory clause of 2 Sam 24:1, "Now again the anger of the Lord burned against Israel," evokes recollection of biblical precedents where God's anger is always predicated upon Israel's sin.[24] The context makes clear that God is not acting arbitrarily.

Similarly, appeals to God's inflicting *evil* upon Abimelech, Saul, Ahab etc., suffer the same methodological flaw exposed above. The Hebrew word translated as "evil" in these passages is once again *ra^c* with the same range of meaning—*distress, injury, misery, calamity, and adversity*.[25] Evil therefore should be understood in the light of this semantic range within each particular biblical context. When this is understood, it becomes apparent that in these contexts God is not randomly or unconditionally inflicting horror as modern connotations of the word "evil" would suggest; rather, he is inflicting wrath, i.e., divinely willed punishment for sin.

Moreover, the argument that the Bible equates divine sovereignty with theistic determinism is not an accurate representation of the Bible as a whole. Deuteronomy 30, Jeremiah 18, Romans 11, and John 3 express clearly that human beings have a real responsibility to repent, obey, and believe in order to benefit from God's saving grace. Piper's opinion that "free will is an unbiblical notion"[26] flies directly in the face of the biblical doctrines of sin and repentance (e.g., Deut 30:15-20; Isa 66:3-4; Eccl. 7:29) and blindly ignores the rigorous logical arguments of notable contemporary Christian philosophers Alvin Plantinga, William Lane Craig, J.P. Moreland, and Richard Swinburne.[27] Most importantly, the Bible is very clear that God *does not* will sin or evil. Jeremiah, for example, reveals that it "never entered God's mind" that human beings should commit radical sin:

> Because they have forsaken me and have made this an alien place and have burned sacrifices in it to other gods that neither they nor their forefathers nor the kings of Judah had ever known, and because they have filled this place with the blood of the innocent and have built the high places of Baal to burn their sons in the fire as burnt offerings to Baal, *a thing which I never commanded or spoke of, nor did it ever enter my mind*. (Jer 19:4-5; also 7:31-32; 32:35; 44:4; 2 Chron 28:4-5)

---

[24] Biblical precedents for God's anger include Exod 4:14; 32:11, 22; 34:6; Num 11:1, 10, 33-34; 12:9; 14:18; 25:4; 32:13-14; Deut 4:25; 6:15; 7:4; 9:18-19; 11:17; 13:17; 29:20, 23-29; 31:29; Joshua 7:1, 26; 23:16; Judges 2:12, 14, 20; 3:8-9; 10:7; 2 Sam 6:7; 24:1. Elsewhere in the Bible it remains true that God's anger is never unprovoked or arbitrary.
[25] See "רע," *BDB*, 948b.
[26] "A Response to J. I. Packer On the So-Called Antinomy Between The Sovereignty of God and Human Responsibility." Online: http://www.desiringgod.org/library/topics/doctrines_grace/packer.html.
[27] Alvin Plantinga, *God, Freedom and Evil*. New York: Harper & Row, 1974; J. P. Moreland & William Lane Craig, *Philosophical Foundations for a Christian Worldview*. Downers Grove: IVP, 2003, 536-54; Richard Swinburne, *Providence and the Problem of Evil*, Oxford: OUP, 1998.

This passage may be dismissed as anthropomorphism, but the truth of its message remains whether interpreted literally or figuratively. The rest of Scripture is equally clear. Isaiah warns "woe to those who call evil good, and good evil" (Isa 5:20; cf. 66:4b; Micah 3:2). The Psalmist commands, "Hate evil you who love the Lord" (97:10). Proverbs teaches, "The fear of the Lord is to hate evil; pride and arrogance and the evil way, and the perverted mouth, I hate" (8:13). Amos commands, "Hate evil, love good" (5:15). The Lord admonishes through Zechariah, "let none of you devise evil in your heart against another, and do not love perjury; for all these are what I hate" (8:17). David prays, "You are *not* a God who takes pleasure in wickedness; *no* evil dwells with you" (Ps 5:4). And John explicitly professes that God is not the first cause of sin. To the contrary, "God is light, and in him there is no darkness at all" (1 John 1:5); "in him there is no sin" (1 John 3:5).

Thus "hyper Calvinism" may rightly be deemed a *misrepresentation* of the God of Scripture. As such, it is a theological idol that blinds its advocates from the fullness of God's comprehensive nature.

Totally Reformed extremism elucidates another dimension of the idolatry and the hardening of the heart phenomenon. Not only do we become like that which we worship, but the converse is equally true. What we worship *becomes like us*, unless the object of worship is God himself. For in attributing evil to God, Totally Reformed theologians have constructed a god in the image of sinful man and even in the image of Satan. For the Bible reveals that sin entered the world through man (Rom 5:12), having been seduced and misled by Satan (Genesis 3) in direct defiance of God (Rev 12:7-9; Gen 3:9-19).[28] In making God the first cause of evil, theistic determinists have made God more like us.

Theistic determinism, however, is not the only theological idol at large today. The contemporary school of thought known as "open theism" is also, in my judgment, a distortion of the revelation of God. In a justified attempt to amend the extremes of theistic determinism, open theists configure a god that is subject to the limitations of time and thus cannot exhaustively know the future.[29] Conceding that God cannot exhaustively know the future without exhaustively determining it, open theists argue that God does neither—that is, exhaustively know the future or

---

[28] Grudem's concession that "Calvinists must say that they do not know the answer" as to "Exactly how God can ordain that we do evil willingly, and yet God not be blamed for evil" and "Exactly how God can cause us to choose something willingly" (*Systematic Theology*, 350) unnecessarily blurs the lucid revelation of Scripture that God ordained freedom with the necessary consequence of sin, which sinners would be fully responsible for.

[29] A good entry point for the study of open theism is *JETS* Volume 45, No. 2 (June, 2002), which includes articles by Clark H. Pinnock, John Sanders, and Greg A. Boyd, the leading proponents of open theism, and Bruce A. Ware, Stephen J. Wellum, Ron Highfield, and Michael S. Horton, who judge open theism to be unbiblical. A more philosophical appraisal may be found in *Divine Foreknowledge: Four* Views (eds., James K. Beilby and Paul R. Eddy: Downers Grove: InterVarsity, 2001), 13-64, which includes a chapter on divine foreknowledge by Greg Boyd followed by responses from David Hunt (representing the simple foreknowledge view), William Lane Craig (the Middle-Knowledge view), and Paul Helm (the Augustinian-Calvinist view). The open theists, to their credit, are not naïve to the difficulties of their theology.

exhaustively determine it. "God knows the future partly as a realm of possibilities, not exclusively as settled facts."[30] The price for this concession is the natural reading of passages of Scripture which declare divine knowledge of the future acts of free nations and individuals (E.g., Deut 29:22-29; 31:14-22; 1 Kings 13:1-2; Isa 45:1; 48:8; Dan 11:36-45; Mark 14:30; John 13:19-21). Difficult for open theism, for example, is God's prediction of the apostasy of Israel well before the event (Deut 31:20; cf. 29:22-29). According to the open theist, God only knows those future events that he himself plans to determine; he does not foreknow events other free creatures will cause. With this premise, the open theist must either conclude that Deuteronomy was written after the fact or that God planned to determine Israel's apostasy and was therefore responsible for Israel's sinful idolatry—one major conclusion open theism seeks to amend (that God is responsible for evil). Moreover, the premise contradicts the seemingly clear biblical message that God does indeed foreknow the evil thoughts of free creatures (see, for example, Ezek 38:10: "Thus says the Lord God, it will come about on that day, that thoughts will come into your mind, and you will devise an evil plan").[31]

The open theist also has difficulty explaining the NT doctrine of predestination: "Open theism's denial of exhaustive divine foreknowledge renders it impossible for God to have foreknown and chosen those who would be saved in Christ—in either the Calvinist or Arminian understanding of these doctrines—before the foundation of the world" (see Rom 8:29; Eph 1:4).[32] Failure to adequately explain the foreknowledge passages above together with the failure to explain the incontrovertibly biblical doctrine of predestination exposes open theists to the same criticism that cripples hyper-Calvinism. Both force the entire Bible to conform to a singular interpretation of a select group of passages. Just as hyper-Calvinism absolutizes passages that are on the surface deterministic to force very unnatural interpretations of John 3:16, 1 Tim 2:6, 4:10, 1 John 2:2 etc., so too does open theism absolutize "dialogue" passages to force very unnatural interpretations of Romans 8:29-30; Eph 1:4-5, 11 etc. Arguably, both extremes misrepresent the comprehensive message of the Bible and in so doing misrepresent God.

Another shortcoming is open theism's limited range of positions regarding God's relation to time—a dauntingly complex, metaphysical subject. If, as open theists argue, God does not exhaustively know the future, then God is subject to time. Limiting God to the dimension of time makes God subject to his own creation (that is the physical realities that determine time as human beings know it). This limitation reverses the created order the Bible reveals, where God creates the material world and with it the dimension of time. Hence, to deny God's exhaustive knowledge of the future limits God's eternal nature and his sovereignty over his creation. This in turn may raise the question of God's sovereignty in

---

[30] Beilby and Eddy, *Divine Foreknowledge*, 9.
[31] "Thoughts" in this translation of Ezek 38:10 is a rendering of the Hebrew word *dĕbarim*, which is usually translated "words." In this context, however, words processed in one's mind clearly means thoughts.
[32] Bruce A. Ware, "Defining Evangelicalism's Boundaries Theologically: Is Open Theism Evangelical?" *JETS* 45/2 (June, 2002): 204.

regard to salvation: for if God is partially subject to time, then God may also be limited in his power to save people from the ill effects of time.

These observations lead to the suspicion that open theists have a speculative view of God and time. Comprehensive reading of the Bible suggests that this is indeed the case. God *does* have foreknowledge of events that people perform of their own volition—both sinful disobedience and obedient faith. Yet, it is also true that a comprehensive reading of the Bible reveals that God does *not* will that sinful evil occur. These two observations taken together render the conclusion that God foreknows things that he himself does not determine. Such a conclusion is impossible only if God is subject to time in the way that human beings are. However, if God, as an immortal being, is transcendent and free from the constraints of time, and yet fully cognizant of temporal reality and its history, then God's knowledge of future events that he himself does not cause is conceivable. John's description of Jesus' foreknowledge of the free choices of his listeners may well point toward such a conclusion: "For Jesus knew from the beginning who they were who did not believe, and who it was that would betray him" (John 6:64b).

This is hard, if not impossible, for mortal human beings to understand. But eternal God's relation to time is exceptional. Time is one dimension of God's creation that is beyond human comprehension, because human beings are mortal, while God is immortal. In subjecting God to time, open theists assimilate God to human limitations.

From a biblical theological perspective, what appears impossible to practitioners of metaphysics may well be possible for God—like God's future knowledge of the free actions of human beings. A similar incomprehension led the early Gnostics to render impossible the incarnation. The Gnostics could not conceive that a spiritual god could become incarnate in a fleshly body. Yet apostolic witness passionately affirms this truth (2 John 7). We should be slow to assume, therefore, that anything is impossible for God. Logic itself is a human invention and as such is limited in its ability to appraise supernatural reality fully. The Gospels attest that "the things impossible with men *are* possible with God" (Luke 18:27; also 1:37). Indeed, salvation is dependent upon this very hope (Matt 19:26; Mark 10:27). When we think of God, we include the comprehensible and the logical, but we also transcend into the realm of the incomprehensible. This reality should occasion humility and worship in the hearts and minds of those genuinely searching after God.

Anointed by the Spirit to understand what God *has* revealed in *all* of Scripture, and humbled by an awareness of humanity's incomplete knowledge of God (*God's ways are not our ways, his thoughts are not our thoughts*: Isa 55:8-9; 1 Cor 13:12), our challenge is to acknowledge all of God's attributes revealed in Scripture without misconstruing a single one. In this theological pilgrimage of worship, we are dependent on the comprehensive revelation of Scripture, the revelation of God in Jesus Christ, the inner working of the Holy Spirit, and the best efforts of the human mind to think prayerfully, objectively, deeply, and broadly about God. A rigid, closed theology that isolates one facet of God's nature as all encompassing in and of itself is a theological idol, which leads to spiritual pride that refuses to look beyond one's philosophical, manmade "system."

In my judgment open theists no less than theistic determinists have created a theological idol to accommodate a philosophical worldview. By assimilating Scripture to preexisting theologies/philosophies, by forcing unnatural interpretations of disagreeable passages, and by absolutizing preferred passages, practitioners of theistic determinism and open theism ironically share the same flawed methodology that historically has beleaguered radical liberal exegesis—the necessary creation of multiple hypotheses to maintain an originally flawed presupposition. Blessed is the theologian whose god *is* God as he really is.

(3) *Worship*

"We should be careful that the music that we use to worship doesn't become the music that we worship." (Don Hustad)

"Because this people draw near with their words and honor me with their lip service, but they remove their hearts far from me, and their reverence for me consists of tradition learned by rote, therefore behold, I will once again deal marvelously with this people, wondrously marvelous; And the wisdom of their wise men shall perish, and the discernment of their discerning men shall be concealed." (Isa 29:13-14; See also Isa 1:11-16; 66:3-4; Jer 7:4-11)

The Bible excoriates hypocritical external expressions, orthopractic rituals, stale traditions, secularized places of worship, and dead legalism. Indeed religious idolatry characterizes the hardening of the heart of each successive biblical generation.

The same danger threatens the health of the contemporary church. The "worship wars" of recent times bear evidence that significant numbers of contemporary Christians prioritize worship form and style over content and practice. As a result, Christian social expression has become insipid. Ron Sider's *The Scandal of the Evangelical Conscience* documents the tragic disconnect between evangelicalism's reproachable moral failure and her evangelical façade. Vibrant worship and appeals to the inerrancy of Scripture ring hollow as evangelical marriages break down at a rate comparable to that of secular society, as evangelical charitable giving continues to go down as incomes go up, as irresponsible sexual promiscuity is commonplace, and as racial prejudice is systemic.[33] These tragic realities are signals of false worship, just as they were in Isaiah and Jeremiah's generations (Isa 1:11-15; 29:13-14; Jer 7:4-11).

---

[33] Sider summarizes: "To say there is a crisis of disobedience in the evangelical world today is to dangerously understate the problem. Born-again Christians divorce at about the same rate as everyone else. Self-centered materialism is seducing evangelicals and rapidly destroying our earlier, slightly more generous giving. Only 6 percent of born-again Christians tithe. Born-again Christians justify and engage in sexual promiscuity (both premarital sex and adultery) at astonishing rates. Racism and perhaps physical abuse of wives seems to be worse in evangelical circles than elsewhere. This is scandalous behavior for people who claim to be born-again by the Holy Spirit and to enjoy the very presence of the Risen Lord in their lives" ("The Scandal of the Evangelical Conscience," *Books and*

How can we restore our moral integrity? Sider argues that: "We need to rethink our theology. We need to ask, "Are we really biblical?"[34] He's right. Authentic worship presupposes communion with a holy God, who calls disciples to holiness—Jesus' standards of morality (Matt 5:27-28), fidelity (Matt 5:31-32), ethics (Luke 10:30-37), and generosity (Luke 18:18-27). This in part is what it means to be the salt of the earth and the light of the world—the visible body of Christ—*distinctive*.

Positively, the biblical, theological prescription for healing is unsophisticated and faultless. It resides in the biblical axiom "you become like that which you worship." Just as idolaters negatively *deform* to the likeness of idols, so too do repentant worshipers of the living God *conform* to the true character of God: "But we all, with unveiled face beholding as in a mirror the glory of the Lord, are being transformed into the same image from glory to glory, just as from the Lord, the Spirit" (2 Cor 3:18). This, of course, includes conformity to the *holiness* of Christ.

In our generation preoccupation with style has impaired communion with Christ wherever human performance has taken the place of genuine worship of the risen Lord. It is not surprising, therefore, that contemporary preoccupation with worship style has resulted in bitterness, division, and the hardening of hearts. In the face of this unfortunate reality, Don Hustad wisely admonishes that we should be careful that the music that we use to worship doesn't become the music that we worship.[35] What Hustad says in regard to music can be applied validly to every other worship expression. God is the end, not eloquent prayer, ecstatic praise, entertainment oriented preaching, charismatic gifts, pop theology, external religiosity, etc., which invariably extol human expression and not God himself.

In the face of this challenge, we may be thankful for the corrective that the Bible itself provides. Responding to the Bible's clear teaching, the Christian church for the most part has become aware of the danger of "worship worship" in recent years and has responded with renewed commitment to singular worship of God.[36] This is as it should be. True worship, the Scriptures remind us, is to love the Lord our God with all our heart, soul, mind, and strength, and to love our neighbor as ourselves. When we do so, God relates to us as our God and we relate to him as his people. Communion occurs. By believing him, obeying him, thanking him, acknowledging his truth, and our total dependence upon him, we love the Lord with all our heart, soul, mind, and strength. Aware of our weakness, we find that indeed the true sacrifices of God are "a broken and a contrite heart" (Ps 51:17a). What the Lord requires is that we do justice, love kindness, and walk humbly with our God" (Micah 6:8). Corporately as "a chosen race, a royal priesthood, a holy nation, a people for God's own possession," it is our calling in worship to proclaim the excellencies of him who has called us out of darkness into his marvelous light (1 Peter 2:9). Our true religion, as James reminds us, is to visit

---

Culture, Jan/Feb 2005, 39; excerpted from *The Scandal of the Evangelical Conscience* [Grand Rapids: Baker Book House, 2005).
[34] Stan Guthrie, "The Evangelical Scandal," *CT* (April 2005): 72.
[35] *True Worship: Reclaiming the Wonder & Majesty* (Carol Stream: Hope, 1998), 160.
[36] See Marva J. Dawn, *How Shall We Worship? Biblical Guidelines for the Worship Wars* (Wheaton: Tyndale House, 2003), 47-57; Terry W. York, *America's Worship Wars* (Peabody, Mass: Hendrickson, 2003), xiv, 54, 58.

orphans and widows in their distress, and to keep ourselves unstained by the world (James 1:27). Thereby we contribute to the ministry of Jesus and discover the pleasure of the true living God who desires worship "in spirit and truth" (John 4:24).

In the body of Christ, therefore, true worship now is consistent with what true worship will always be. With the 24 elders of Rev 4:11, we now cast aside our ephemeral accolades to worship him who lives forever, believing, if not expressly saying, "worthy are you, our Lord and our God, to receive glory and honor and power; for you have created all things, and because of your will they existed, and were created" (Rev 4:11). Recognizing that God has exercised this creative power to recreate us that we might be "born again," and recognizing that God has demonstrated his love for us by sacrificing Jesus, our true worship resounds with the myriads of angels of Rev 5:12-13 who cry out, "worthy is the Lamb that was slain to receive power and riches and wisdom and might and honor and glory and blessing." Therefore, in true worship, we pronounce in word and deed what all creation will one day declare, "to him who sits on the throne, and to the Lamb, be blessing and honor and glory and dominion forever and ever" (Rev 5:13). Knowing this as the "Gospel truth," we resist conformity to this world, performing our "spiritual service of worship" (Rom 12:1), praising God in proof of what his will is for his people—"that which is good and acceptable and perfect" (Rom 12:2). And in the end, having worshiped God, we discover that we have become more like him (2 Cor 3:18) expectantly awaiting the transformation of "the body of our humble state into conformity with the body of his glory" (Phil 3:21). We find that we have become more like the true living God that we worship. This is an important feature of the inheritance of the saints, the goal of the prize of the higher calling of God in Christ Jesus.

> "Therefore, my beloved, flee from idolatry."
> 1 Corinthians 10:14
>
> "Worship God."
> (Revelation 19:10; 22:9)
>
> "Know that the Lord himself is God;
> It is he who has made us and not we ourselves."
> (Psalm 100:3a)

Bibliography

Allen, Leslie A. *Psalms 101-150.* Word Biblical Commentary 21. Waco: Word, 1983.
Allen, Thomas George. *The Book of the Dead Or Going Forth By Day.* Studies in Ancient Oriental Civilization, 37. Chicago: Chicago University Press, 1974.
Andrews, Carol. *Amulets.* Austin: University of Texas Press, 1994.
Aune, David. *Revelation.* Word Biblical Commentary 52 A-C. 3 vols. Dallas: Word, 1997-98.
Barrick, W. Boyd. "High Place." Pages 195-200 in vol. 3 of *The Anchor Bible Dictionary.* Edited by D. N. Freedman. 6 vols. New York: Doubleday, 1992.
Barth, Karl. *Church Dogmatics.* Edinburgh: T & T Clark, 1936-69.
Bauckham, Richard. *The Climax of Prophecy.* Edinburgh: T & T Clark, 1993.
Beale. G. K. "An Exegetical and Theological Consideration of the Hardening of Pharaoh's Heart in Exodus 4-14 and Romans 9." *Trinity Journal* 5 (1984): 129-154.
____. "Isaiah VI 9-12: A Retributive Taunt against Idolatry." *Vetus Testamentum* XLI 3 (1991): 257-78.
____. *Revelation.* The New International Greek Testament Commentary. Grand Rapids: Eerdmans, 1999.
____. "The Hearing Formula and the Visions of John in Revelation." Pages 167–80 *in A Vision for the Church.* Edited by Markus Bockmuehl and Michael B. Thompson. Edinburgh: T & T Clark, 1997.
Beilby, James K. and Paul R. Eddy, eds. *Divine Foreknowledge: Four Views.* Downers Grove: InterVarsity, 2001.
Benson, Bruce Ellis. *Graven Ideologies: Nietzsche, Derrida & Marion on Modern Idolatry.* Downers Grove: InterVarsity, 2002.
Betz, Hans Dieter. *Galatians: A Commentary on Paul's Letter to the Churches in Galatia.* Hermeneia. Philadelphia: Fortress, 1979.
Botterweck, G. J. and H. Ringren, eds. *Theological Dictionary of the Old Testament.* Translated by J. J. Willis. Grand Rapids: Eerdmans, 1974-.
Brown, Francis, S. R. Driver and C. A. Briggs. *A Hebrew and English Lexicon of the Old Testament.* Translated by Edward Robinson. Oxford: Clarendon, 1907.
Calvin, John. *Commentary on Isaiah.* Translated by Reverend William Pringle. Grand Rapids: Baker, 1984.
Charles, R. H. *A Critical and Exegetical Commentary on the Revelation of St. John.* 2 vols. Edinburgh: T & T Clark, 1920.
Charlesworth, James H, ed. *The Dead Sea Scrolls.* Tübingen/Louisville: J.C.B. Mohr [Paul Siebeck] / Westminster John Knox Press, 1995.
Childs, Brevard. *The Book of Exodus.* Philadelphia: Westminster, 1974.
Clifford, Richard J. *Psalms 73-150.* Abingdon Old Testament Commenataries. Nashville: Abingdon, 2003.

Cranfield, C. E. B. *Romans*. The International Critical Commentary. 2 vols. Edinburgh: T & T Clark, 1975-79.

Currid, John D. *Ancient Egypt and the Old Testament*. Grand Rapids: Baker, 1997.

Cuss, Sr. Dominique. *Imperial Cult and Honorary Terms in the New Testament*. Fribourg: The University Press, 1974.

Dahood, Michel. *Psalms*. Vol. 3. Anchor Bible 17A. Garden City: Doubleday, 1970.

Dassow, Eva Von, ed. *The Egyptian Book of the Dead: The Book of Going Forth By Day*. Translated by Raymond O. Faulkner. San Francisco: Chronicle Books, 1994.

Davis, John J. *Moses and the Gods of Egypt*. Grand Rapids: Baker, 1971.

Dawn, Marva J. *How Shall We Worship? Biblical Guidelines for the Worship Wars*. Wheaton: Tyndale House, 2003.

Day, John. "Canaan, Religion of." Pages 831-37 in vol. 1 of *The Anchor Bible Dictionary*. Edited by D.N. Freedman. 6 vols. New York: Doubleday, 1992.

____. *Molech: A God of Human Sacrifice in the Old Testament*. Cambridge: Cambridge University Press, 1989.

Day, P. L. "ANAT." Pages 36-43 in *Dictionary of Deities and Demons in the Bible*. Edited by K. van der Toorn et al. Leiden: Brill, 1999.

Deissmann, Adolf. *Light from the Ancient East*. New York; London: Hodder and Stoughton, 1910.

Dunn, James D. G. *Romans*. Word Biblical Commentary 38 A-B. 2 vols. Dallas: Word, 1988-91.

____. *The Theology of Paul the Apostle*. Grand Rapids: Eerdmans, 1998.

Edwards, Johathan. "Sinners in the Hands of an Angry God." Pages 96-113 in *Selected Writings of Jonathan Edwards*. Edited by Harold P. Simonson. New York: Frederick Ungar, 1970.

Eichrodt, Walter. *Theology of the Old Testament*. Translated by J. A. Baker. Philadelphia: Westminster, 1967.

Eisenmann, Robert and Michael Wise. *The Dead Sea Scrolls Uncovered*. Rockport: Element, 1992.

Evans, Craig A. *To See and Not Perceive; Isaiah 6:9-10 in Early Jewish and Christian Interpretation*. Journal for the Study of the Old Testament: Supplement Series 64. Sheffield: Sheffield Academic Press, 1989.

Fabry, H. J. "לֵב *leb*; לֵבָב *lebab*." Pages 399-437 in vol. 7 of *Theological Dictionary of the Old Testament*. Edited by G. T. Botterweck. Translated by David E. Green. Grand Rapids: Eerdmans, 1995.

Faulkner, Raymond O. *A Concise Dictionary of Middle Egyptian*. Oxford: Oxford University Press, 1962.

Finegan, Jack. *Myth and Mystery*. Grand Rapids: Baker, 1989.

Fitzmyer, Joseph A. *The Acts of the Apostles*. Anchor Bible 31. New York: Doubleday, 1998.

____. *Romans*. Anchor Bible 33. New York: Doubleday, 1992.

Frankfort, Henri. *Kingship and the Gods*. Chicago: University of Chicago Press, 1978.

Furnish, Victor Paul. *II Corinthians.* Anchor Bible 32A. New York: Doubleday, 1984.
García Martínez, Florentino. *The Dead Sea Scrolls Translated.* 2d ed. Translated by Wilfred G. E. Watson. Leiden: Brill, 1996.
Gardiner, Alan H. *Egyptian Grammar.* Oxford: Oxford University Press, 1927.
Garlington, D. B. "ΙΕΡΟΣΥΛΕΙΝ AND THE IDOLATRY OF ISRAEL (ROMANS 2.22)." *New Testament Studies* 36 (1990): 142-51.
Gerhardsson, Birger. *The Testing of God's Son (Matt 4,1-11 and Par): An Analysis of an Early Christian Midrash.* CB. NT 2. Lund, 1966.
Goelet Jr., Ogden. "A Commentary on the Corpus of Literature and Tradition which Constitutes The Book of Going Forth by Day." Pages 137-171 in *The Egyptian Book of the Dead: The Book of Going Forth by Day.* Edited by Eva Von Dassow. Translated by Raymond O. Faulkner. San Francisco: Chronicle Books, 1994.
Greenfield, J. C. "Hadad." Pages 377-82 in *Dictionary of Deities and Demons in the Bible.* Edited by K. van der Toorn et al. Leiden: Brill, 1999.
Grudem, Wayne. *Systematic Theology: An Introduction to Biblical Theology.* Grand Rapids: Zondervan, 1994.
Guinness, Os. *The Call.* W Publishing Group. 1998.
Guinness, Os. and John Seel. *No God but God: Breaking with the Idols of Our Age.* Chicago: Moody Press, 1992.
Guthrie, Stan. "The Evangelical Scandal." *Christianity Today,* (April 2005): 70-73.
Harris, Murray J. *Jesus as God.* Grand Rapids: Baker, 1992.
Hays, Richard B. *Echoes of Scripture in the Letters of Paul.* New Haven: Yale, 1989.
Healey, J. F. "Dagon." Pages 216-19 in *Dictionary of Deities and Demons in the Bible.* Edited by K. van der Toorn et al. Leiden: Brill, 1999.
Heider, George C. "Molech." Pages 581-85 in *Dictionary of Deities and Demons in the Bible.* Edited by K. van der Toorn et al. Leiden: Brill, 1999.
Hemer, Colin. *The Letters to the Seven Churches of Asia in their Local Setting.* Journal for the Study of the New Testament: Supplement Series 11. Sheffield: Sheffield Academic Press, 1986.
Herrmann, W. "Baal." Pages 132-39 in *Dictionary of Deities and Demons in the Bible.* Edited by K. van der Toorn et al. Leiden: Brill, 1999.
Hoffmeier, James K. "The Arm of God versus the Arm of Pharaoh in the Exodus Narratives." *Biblica* 67 (1986): 378-87.
____. *Israel in Egypt: The Evidence for the Authenticity of the Exodus Tradition.* New York: Oxford University Press, 1996.
Hort, Greta. "The Plagues of Egypt." Zeitschrift für die Alttestamentliche Wissenschaft 69 no. 28 (1957): 84-103; 70 no. 29 (1958): 48-59.
Huddelstun, J. R. "Who is this that Rises like the Nile? Some Egyptian Texts on the Inundation and a Prophetic Trope." *Fortunate the Eyes that See.* Edited by A. B. Beck et al. Grand Rapids: Eerdmans, 1995.
Hübner, Ulrich. "Esau." Pages 574-575 in vol. 2 of *The Anchor Bible Dictionary.* Edited by D. N. Freedman. 6 vols. New York: Doubleday, 1992.

Hustad, Donald. *True Worship: Reclaiming the Wonder & Majesty.* Carol Stream: Hope, 1998.

Kaiser, Otto. *Isaiah 1-12.* Translated by John Bowden. 2d ed. Philadelphia: Westminster, 1983.

Kaufmann, Yehezkel. *The Religion of Israel: From its Beginnings to the Babylonian Exile.* Translated by Moshe Greenberg. Chicago: The University of Chicago Press, 1960.

Kitchen, Kenneth A. "Exodus." Pages 700-708 in vol. 2 of *The Anchor Bible Dictionary.* Edited by D.N. Freedman. 6 vols. New York: Doubleday, 1992.

_____. On the Reliability of the Old Testament. Grand Rapids: Eerdmans, 2003.

Kittel, G. and G. Friedrich, eds. *Theological Dictionary of the New Testament.* Translated by G.W. Bromiley. 10 vols. Grand Rapids: Eerdmans, 1964-1976.

Koehler, Ludwig and Walter Baumgartner, eds. *The Hebrew and Aramaic Lexicon of the Old Testament.* Translated by M.E.J. Richardson. 5 vols. Leiden: E. J. Brill, 1994.

Kutsko, John F. *Between Heaven and Earth: Divine Presence and Absence in the Book of Ezekiel..* Biblical and Judaic Studies from the University of California, San Diego 17.Winona Lake, IN: Eisenbrauns, 2000.

Lewis, C. S. *Mere Christianity.* Revised Edition. New York: Simon and Schuster, 1996.

Lichtheim, Miriam. *Ancient Egyptian Literature.* 3 vols. Berkeley and Los Angelos: University of California Press, 1973-1980.

Lincoln, Andrew T. *Ephesians.* Word Biblical Commentary 42. Dallas: Word, 1990.

Lohfink, Gerhard. *Jesus and Community.* Translated by John P. Galvin. Philadelphia/NewYork: Fortress/Paulist, 1984.

Longenecker, Richard N. *Galatians.* Word Biblical Commentary 41. Waco: Word, 1990.

Martin, Ralph P. *2 Corinthians.* Word Biblical Commentary 40. Dallas: Word, 1986.

Martinez, Florentino Garcia. *The Dead Sea Scrolls Translated.* 2nd Edition. Grand Rapids: Eerdmans, 1996.

Matera, Frank J. *II Corinthians.* Louisville/London: Westminster John Knox Press, 2003.

McCarthy, Dennis J. *Treaty and Covenant.* Rome: Biblical Institute, 1978

Meeks, Dimitri and Christine Favard-Meeks. *Daily Life of the Gods.* Translated by G. M. Goshgarian. Ithica, New York: Cornell, 1996.

Meier, John. *A Marginal Jew: Rethinking the Historical Jesus.* Vol. 2. *Mentor, Message, and Miracles.* New York: Doubleday, 1994.

Mendenhall, G. E. "Amorites." Pages 199-202 in vol. 1 of *The Anchor Bible Dictionary.* Edited by D. N. Freedman. 6 vols. New York: Doubleday, 1992.

Mendenhall, G. E. and Gary A. Herion. "Covenant." Pages 1179-1202 in vol. 1 of *TheAnchor Bible Dictionary.* Edited by D. N. Freedman. 6 vols. New York: Doubleday, 1992.

Mettinger, Tryggve N. D. *No Graven Image? Israelite Aniconism in Its Ancient Near Eastern Context.* Stockholm: Almqvist & Wiksell International, 1995.

Metzger, Bruce. *Breaking the Code: Understanding the Book of Revelation*. Nashville: Abingdon, 1993.
Miller, Patrick D. *The Religion of Ancient Israel*. Louisville, Ky./London: Westminster John Knox Press/SPCK. 2000.
Moo, Douglass. *Romans*. The New International Commentary on the New Testament. Grand Rapids: Eerdmans, 1996.
Morenz, Siegfried. *Egyptian Religion*. Translated by A. E. Keep. Ithaca, New York: Cornell, 1973.
Moreland, J. P. and William Lane Craig, *Philosophical Foundations for a Christian Worldview*. Downers Grove: IVP, 2003.
Müller, Hans-Peter. "Chemosh." Pages 186-89 in *Dictionary of Deities and Demons in the Bible*. Edited by K. van der Toorn et al. Leiden: Brill, 1999.
Packer, J. I. *Knowing God*. Downers Grove: InterVarsity Press, 1993.
Petrie, W. M. F. *Amulets*. London: Constable, 1914.
Piper, John. "A Response to J. I. Packer On the So-Called Antinomy Between The Sovereignty of God and Human Responsibility." Online: http://www.desiringgod.org/library/topics/doctrines_grace/packer.html.
____. "Is God Less Glorious Because He Ordained that Evil Be?: Jonathan Edwards on the Decrees of God," n.p. [July, 1998]. Online: http://www.desiringgod.org/library/topics/suffering/god_and_evil.html.
____. *Life as a Vapor*. Oregon: Multnomah, 2004.
____. *The Justification of God*. Grand Rapids: Baker, 1983.
____. The Passion of Jesus Christ. Wheaton: Crossway, 2004.
Plantinga, Alvin. *God, Freedom and Evil*. New York: Harper & Row, 1974.
Price, S. R. F. *Rituals and Power: The Roman imperial cult in Asia Minor*. Cambridge: Cambridge University Press, 1984.
Pritchard, J. B., ed. *Ancient Near Eastern Texts Relating to the Old Testament*. 3d ed. Princeton: Princeton University Press, 1969.
Puech, Emile. "Milcom." Pages 575-76 in *Dictionary of Deities and Demons in the Bible*. Edited by K. van der Toorn et al. Leiden: Brill, 1999.
Ramachandra, Vinoth. *Gods that Fail: Modern Idolatry and Christian Mission*. Downers Grove: IVP, 1997.
Redford, Donald B. "An Egyptological Perspective in the Exodus Narrative." Pages 137-161 in *Egypt, Israel, Sinai: Archaeological and Historical Relationships in the Biblical Period*. Edited by A. F. Rainey. Tel Aviv, 1987.
Rignell, L. "Isaiah Chapter 1." Studia theologica 11 (1957): 140-58.
Ruben, S. Ben. "And He Hardened the Heart of Pharaoh." *Beth Mikra* 97/2 (1984): 112-113.
Sadek, A. I. *Popular Religion in Egypt during the New Kingdom*. Hildesheimer ägyptologische Beiträge 27. Hildesheim: Gerstenberg, 1987.
Sandelin, Karl-Gustav. "The Jesus-Tradition and Idolatry." *NTS* 42.3 (July 1996): 412-420.
Scherrer, Steven J. "Signs and Wonders in the Imperial Cult: A New Look at a Roman Religious Institution in Light of Rev 13:13-15." *The Journal of Biblical Literature* 103/4 (1984): 599-610.
Schlossberg, Herbert. *Idols for Destruction*. Wheaton: Crossway, 1990.
Schreiner, Thomas R. *Romans*. Grand Rapids: Baker, 1998.

Scott, James M. *2 Corinthians.* New International Biblical Commentary; Peabody: Hendrickson, 1998.

Sharp, Douglas R. *No Partiality: The Idolatry of Race & The New Humanity.* Downers Grove: InterVarsity Press, 2002.

Shupak, Nili. "ḤZQ, KBD, QŠH LĒB, THE HARDENING OF PHARAOH'S HEART IN EXODUS 4:1-15:21 — SEEN NEGATIVELY IN THE BIBLE BUT FAVORABLY IN EGYPTIAN SOURCES." Pages 389-403 in *Egypt, Israel, and the Ancient Mediterranean World.* Edited by Gary N. Knoppers and Antoine Hirsh. Leiden–Boston: Brill, 2004.

_____. *Where Can Wisdom Be Found? : The Sage's Language in the Bible and in Ancient Egyptian Literature.* Orbis Biblicus et Orientalis 130; Fribourg/Göttingen: University Press/Vandenhoeck & Ruprecht, 1993.

Sider, Ronald J. "The Scandal of the Evangelical Conscience." *Books and Culture.* (January/February, 2005): 8-9, 39.

_____. *The Scandal of the Evangelical Conscience.* Grand Rapids: Baker Book House, 2005.

Slater, Thomas B. "On the Social Setting of the Revelation to John." *New Testament Studies* 44 (1998): 232-56.

Strand, K. A. "Review of Thompson, L. L. , *The Book of Revelation. Apocalypse and Empire.* New York and Oxford: Oxford University Press, 1990." *Andrews University Seminary Studies* 29 (1991): 188-90

Stuhlmacher, Peter. *Paul's Letter to the Romans.* Translated by Scott Hafemann. Louisville: Westminster/John Knox, 1994.

Swete, H. B. *The Apocalypse of John.* 3d ed. London: Macmillan, 1908.

Swinburne, Richard. *Providence and the Problem of Evil.* Oxford: OUP, 1998.

Talbot, Mark. "TRUE FREEDOM: THE LIBERTY THAT SCRIPTURE PORTRAYS AS WORTH HAVING." Pages 77-109 in *Beyond the Bounds: Open Theism and the Undermining of Biblical Christianity.* Edited by John Piper, Justin Taylor, and Paul Kjoss Helseth. Wheaton: Crossway, 2003.

Tanner, J. Paul. "THE NEW COVENANT AND PAUL'S QUOTATIONS FROM HOSEA IN ROMANS 9:25-26." *Bibliotheca Sacra* 162 (January-March 2005): 95-110.

Theissen, Gerd. *The Gospels in Context.* Translated by Linda M. Maloney. Edinburgh: T & TClark, 1992.

Thielman, Frank. *Paul & the Law.* Downers Grove: Intervarsity, 1994.

Thompson, Leonard L. *The Book of Revelation: Apocalypse and Empire.* New York: Oxford University Press, 1990.

Thorsell, Paul R. "The Spirit in the Present Age: Preliminary Fulfillment of the Predicted New Covenant according to Paul." *Journal of the Evangelical Theological Society* 41 (1998): 397-413.

Thrall, Margaret. *A Critical and Exegetical Commentary on the Second Epistle to the Corinthians.* International Critical Commentary. Edinburgh: T & T Clark, 2004 ed.

Tozer, A. W. *The Knowledge of the Holy.* New York: Harper & Row, 1961.

Vermes, Geza. *The Dead Sea Scrolls in English.* London: Penguin, 1990.

von Rad, Gerhard. *Deuteronomy.* Translated by Dorothea Barton. Philadelphia: Westminster, 1966.

Ware, Bruce A. "Defining Evangelicalism's Boundaries Theologically: Is Open Theism Evangelical?" *Journal of the Evangelical Theological Society* 45/2 (June 2002): 129-212.
Watts, Rikk E. *Isaiah's New Exodus and Mark.* Wissenschaftliche Untersuchungen zum Neuen Testament. Tübingen: J. C. B. Mohr (Paul Siebeck), 1997.
Wente, Edward. "Egyptian Religion." Pages 408-411 in vol. 2 of *The Anchor Bible Dictionary.* Edited by D. N. Freedman. 6 vols. New York: Doubleday, 1992.
Whitney, J. T. " 'Bamoth' in the Old Testament." *Tyndale Bulletin* 30 (1979): 125-47.
Wilson, Robert R. "The Hardening of Pharaoh's Heart." *CBQ* 41 (1979): 18-36.
Wolff, Hans Walter. *Hosea.* Hermenia. Translated by Gary Stensell. Philadelphia: Fortress, 1974.
Wright, N. T. *Jesus and the Victory of God.* Minneapolis: Fortress, 1996.
Wyatt, Nicholas. "Ashtoreth (Astarte)." Pages 109-14 in *Dictionary of Deities and Demons in The Bible.* Edited by K. van der Toorn et al. Leiden: Brill, 1999.
Yamauchi, E. "Cultic Prostitution." Pages 213-22 in *Orient and Occident.* Edited by H. A. Hofner. Alter Orient und Altes Testament 22. Neukirchen: Neukirchen-Vluyn, 1973.
York, Terry W. *America's Worship Wars.* Peabody, Mass: Hendrickson, 2003.

Index of Biblical and Other Ancient Sources

I. Old Testament

Genesis						
		8:10	115, 171 17	32:19-20 32:22	9 189	
1:1	75, 91	8:15	19	32:28	128	
ch. 3	188	8:19	19, 20, 21,	32:32-34	128	
3:9-19	190		29, 80, 115	33:1	18	
chs. 6-9	38	8:28	115	33:3-5	101, 115, 128	
11:6-9	18	8:32	19	33:4-6	29, 35, 128,	
12:3	4, 17, 36, 38,	9:7	19		152	
	102, 126, 144,	9:9	171	33:19	127, 128	
	174	9:12	19, 20, 115	34:6-28	9, 36, 36,	
15:4-6	119	9:13-17	17, 21, 127,		101, 115, 128,	
18:11f.	75	9:20-24	115, 171		189	
25:34	124	9:29-30	21	36:22-29	96	
31:19	12	9:34-35	20, 21, 115			
48:10	21	10:1	17, 20, 115	*Leviticus*		
50:20	188	10:7	29			
50:21	14	10:17	21	18:5	139	
		10:20	20, 115	18:21	46	
Exodus		10:21	171	19:4	12, 98	
		10:27	20, 115	19:17	16	
1:16	27	10:28-29	27	19:31	44	
2:7	20	11:10	20, 115	20:2-5	46	
2:23-25	18	12:12	4, 5, 17, 33	ch. 26	8-10, 101	
3:6-10	18	12:38	33	26:1	102	
3:14-15	18	13:5	21, 115,	26:11	107	
3:19-20	22	14:4-17	20, 21, 24,	26:30	12, 82,	
3:26	128		27, 31, 115,		101-102	
4:4-5	18		189			
4:10-12	18, 21	14:17-18	174	*Numbers*		
4:11-15	25, 189	15:11	12			
4:21	4, 16-20, 24,	15:13-18	17, 22	ch. 11	189	
	115	18:11	4, 5, 27, 34,	12:9	189	
4:22-23	17		174	ch. 14	7	
5:1-2	25, 27	19:3-6	18	14:17-18	9, 189	
6:3-8	18, 22	20:2-16	7-9, 12, 117	15:39	16	
7-14	7, 27	23:20-33	36	21:21-35	4, 5	
7:3-4	4, 19, 21, 22,	24:8	179	25:1-9	13, 161-	
	115,	32-33	29, 127		162, 189	
7:13-14	4, 19, 20, 24,	32:4	162	31:16	161	
	80	32:11	189	31:23	46	
7:20-23	19, 20, 24,	32:13	18	32:13-14	189	

32:33	5		191	**Ruth**	
33:3-4	5, 27, 34	ch. 30	141, 147, 177		
33:52	12	30:6	16, 146-147	2:13	14
Deuteronomy		30:7	174	**1 Samuel**	
1:4	5	30:9-10	140, 147		
2:24-3:13	5	30:12-14	139, 140		
2:30-31	4, 7, 21	30:15-20	53, 74-75, 140, 189	1:8	15
4:25	189			2:1	15
4:46-47	5	30:17-18	3, 15, 37-38, 147	2:12-17	41
5:6-10	7, 98,			2:22	41
6:4-9	8, 52, 55, 78, 81	31:4	5	2:25	42
		32:14-22	12, 49, 60, 111, 139, 144, 145, 191	2:29	42
6:13-15	39, 77, 83, 189			2:30-31	41
				3:11-14	42
7:4	189	31:29	189	5:11	54
7:5	12	32:28	60, 145	6:6	54
7:16	39	32:36-39	145	7:3-4	45
7:25-26	39			8:7-18	43
8:2	16			8:19-20	43
8:11-20	16	**Joshua**		9:1-10:16	46
9:4	139			10:9	16
9:6	101, 115	2:10	5, 127	12:10	45
9:13	101	2:11	38	12:12	43
9:18-19	189	5:1	38	12:14	43
9:27	115	7:1	189	12:17-20	43
10:13-17	115	7:5	39	13:9-14	44
10:16	21, 115	7:26	189	15:9-12	44
11:16-18	3, 189	9:10	5	15:17	43
12:30-31	83	10:5	4	15:18-19	44
13:3	16	11:20	20, 39	15:22-23	44
13:17	189	12:2-5	5	16:7	16, 44
14:26	16	13:10-12	5	16:14-16	44, 187
15:9	16	13:21	5	17:26	54
17:17	45	13:30-31	5	17:36	54
18:15-18	36, 102	23:14-16	15, 39, 189	17:43	54
20:8	16	24:14-15	39	18:10-11	44, 187
24:15	16	24:20, 23	39	19:9	187
27:17-29	173			22:17-18	44
28-29	5-7			24:5	15
28-30	72	**Judges**		28:16	44
28:58-68	5, 173, 175,	2:11-22	40, 189	31:9	12
ch. 29	7, 25, 137, 177	3:8-9	189		
		9:23	187	**2 Samuel**	
29:2-4	6, 15, 112, 142, 143	10:6	41		
		10:7	189	12:11	187
29:7	5	10:14	41	24:1	187, 189
29:9-16	6, 7	11:12, 24	45	24:15	47
29:17-29	3, 6, 16, 34, 36, 60, 142-143, 147, 189	16:18	15	30:8	21, 115
		19:3	14		
		21:25	40		

Index of Biblical and Other Ancient Sources

1 Kings

2:44	16
3:12	45
4:19	5
8:61	15
8:66	14
9:6-9	45, 46, 91, 187
10:24	16
11:1-4	45, 48
11:5-7	12-13, 45-46
11:8	46
11:14	46
11:23	46
11:33	45, 47
12:28	47
12:31-33	47
13:1-2	191
14:7-9	48
14:15	48
14:22-24	50
15:3	48
15:11-13	51
15:14	48, 51
15:34	48
16:2-3	48
16:7	48
16:13	49
16:19	48
16:26	48-49
16:31	48, 157, 161
17-18	54
18:4	157
18:19	157
18:39	54
19:1-3	157
19:18	123
21:21	187
21:22	48
21:29	187
22:23	187
22:52	48

2 Kings

3:3	48
6:33	187
9:9	48
10:29	48
10:31	16, 48
12:3	82
13:2	48
13:6	48
13:11	48
14:24	48
15:9	48
15:18	48
15:24	48
16:10-18	65
ch. 17	48
17:5	38
17:7-23	54, 110, 72, 111, 115-116
17:12-18	21, 37, 49, 50
17:22	48
18:4	51
18:33-35	51
ch. 19	51
20:3	51
21:9	52
21:10-15	42, 50, 135
ch. 23	51-52
23:10	46
23:13	45
23:26-27	135
chs. 24-25	52

1 Chronicles

5:25-26	48
9:1	52
16:10	15
16:26	53

2 Chronicles

2:5	53
7:10	14
7:17-22	52
9:23	16
17:3	13
19:3	16
25:19	55
26:16	16, 55
28:4-5	189
29:10	16
30:19	16
32:25	55
33:11-13	55
34:27	16
36:11-22	21, 52-53, 116

Ezra

9:8-13	135

Nehemiah

7:5	16
9:16-18	21, 115, 116
9:22-23	3, 5
9:28-31	115-116
13:18	187

Job

ch. 1	187-188
10:9	129
15:12-13	15-16
22:22	15
31:7-9	15
33:3	15
38:14	129

Psalms

5:4	190
7:9-10	16
13:5	15
16:9	15
17:3	16
19:5	139
19:8	15
22:14-15	14-15
26:2-3	16
27:3	14
27:14	20
31:6-7	49, 111
31:25	20
33:21	15
38:10	15
44:20-21	12
51:10-12	16, 47, 103
51:17	194
57:7	15
61:2	15
62:10	15
ch. 69	144
69:22-23	112, 142
73:13-14	166
73:21-24	15, 68, 178

84:2	15-16	*Isaiah*		29:22-24	131
89:10	166			30:7	111, 166
95:8	21	chs. 1-2	65-66	30:15	69
97:10	190	1:5-6	61	30:20-22	59, 69, 73
100:3	195	1:9-21	58-59, 69,	30:26	70
105:3	15		84, 103,	30:29	14
ch. 115	7, 57, 59,		135, 137,	31:7	69, 102
	72, 84, 108,		193	32:4	15
	155, 167,	1:25-26	70	35:4-6	76
	171-172	1:29-31	65, 137	40:1-2	14
115: 4-8	2, 49, 84	2:5-22	11, 56-57,	40:18-25	57, 98
119:111-112	15		73, 84,	41:21-29	57, 129
ch. 135	6-7, 57, 59,		102, 103,	42:6-9	71, 76
	72, 84, 108,		111, 137	42:14-22	61, 65, 177,
	155, 167,	5:3-7	58		181
	171-172	5:13-15	58, 67	42:25	15, 177
135:8-18	4-5, 35, 49	5:20	190	43:8-13	65, 178, 181
135:15-18	2, 4	ch. 6	84, 96	44:6-23	57, 62, 65,
136:14-20	5	6:8-11	9-11, 21,		69, 98,
141:4	15		56, 63-69,		177, 178,
			84-85, 87,		181
			93-94, 102-	45:1	191
Proverbs			103, 112,	45:5-25	57, 73, 129-
			126, 143,		130-131,
			152, 155,		177, 178
			173, 175, 180	46:5-9	57, 98, 102,
1:24-25	62	6:11-13	64-65, 175,	46:8-13	15, 177, 178
1:28	62		177	47:5-11	15, 65
2:10	15	8:13-14	138	ch. 48	181
4:21	15	9:2	76	48:3-8	177, 191
6:25	15	9:6-7	87	49:6	76
7:3	15	10:5-11	58, 102, 135	49:14-23	177-178
8:13	190	10:20-23	123, 135-	51:9-22	68, 166,
10:8	15		136		177-178
13:12	15	10:26-27	68	52:7-11	107, 139
15:11	16	13:19	137	53:1-12	76, 93-94,
16:21-23	15	14:13-15	16		139-140
18:2	14	16:12	102	54:7-8	177-178
21:4	16	17:8-11	12, 61	55:3	178
22:17	15	ch. 19	33, 62, 102	55:7-9	9, 177-178,
24:12	16	21:9	102		185, 192
27:19	16	22:14	56	57:11-19	15, 49, 57,
28:14	16, 21	25:6-9	180		69-70, 177,
29:1	101	27:8-13	12, 56		181
		28:16	139	59:1	21
Ecclesiastes		29:9-10	65, 130,	59:13	16
			142-143	59:20-21	71, 150, 178
		29:11-14	59, 63, 65,	60:4-5	14, 16, 143
7:2	15		84, 87-88,	60:10	177-178
7:7	15		130, 193	61:1-2, 8	76, 150,
7:29	189	29:16	129-130		178
11:9	16	29:18	70	63:8-10	7

Index of Biblical and Other Ancient Sources

63:17-19	1, 7, 115, 117	14:22	49, 111	51:34	166
65:1-11	82, 115, 121, 128, 139, 141	15:16	15		
		16:11-15	58, 60, 63, 68, 69	**Lamentations**	
66:3-4	59, 63, 121, 189, 193	16:19-21	49, 68, 111	2:14	111
		17:1-2	3, 16	4:17	111
66:14-15	16	17:9-10	16	4:21-22	125
		17:23	115		
Jeremiah		ch. 18	131-133	**Ezekiel**	
		18:1-6	129-130		
1:16	11, 57, 110-111	18:8	180	1:5-13	164
		18:12	3	1:24, 28	164
2:5	49, 59, 72, 110-111	19:3-5	42, 188-189	2:3-8	3, 20-21, 164
		19:12-15	58, 115	3:7-9	3, 20-21, 164
2:7-8	110-111	22:5-9	58, 91	3:10-11	14, 164
2:11	110-111	22:17	15	3:18-21	164
2:19-23	58, 110	23:17	60	3:27	164
2:27-30	57, 69, 110	23:20	69	5:11	58
3:1-9	58, 110	24:7	70-71	6:4-6	68, 73
3:11-17	116	25:3-9	58, 65	6:8-14	58, 60-61, 64, 68, 73, 135
4:1-4	115-116	29:11-14	68, 70		
4:19	15	30:9	76		
5:3	20	30:17	70	8:10	111
5:7	58	30:24	69	9:8-11	135
5:18-25	3, 9-11, 58, 63-67, 65-66, 72, 87, 89, 152, 155, 165, 173	ch. 31	76, 108, 114, 150, 178	11:13-21	16, 59, 71, 75, 89, 106, 136
		31:9	107		
		31:10-14	68	12:2	60-61, 65, 89
		31:33-34	16, 71, 80, 107-108, 178	13:9	111
7:1-11	59, 90-91, 193			13:19	111
7:16-34	3, 11, 21, 57, 65, 90-91, 116, 189	32:18-19	9	13:22	14
		32:28-30	10	14:1-8	3, 16, 56, 59-60, 69
		32:35	46, 188-189		
8:19	49, 57, 111	32:38-42	70-71, 146	16:16	13
9:13-16	3, 58, 60	ch. 33	76, 178	16:30	15-16, 58
9:24	76	33:14-26	71, 76, 178	16:38	58
9:26	101	35:15	65	16:60-63	71-72, 75, 176
10:1-5	57, 111	36:3-7	69		
10:8-9	49, 57, 111	42:22	69	18:30-32	69, 75
10:14-16	49, 57, 111-112	44:2-5	58, 65, 189	20:5-8	5, 32, 35
		46:28	76	20:16	3
10:19-22	112	48:7	45	20:37-44	58, 68-69, 73, 175
11:2-4	112	48:46	45		
11:7-10	60, 65	49:3	45	21:29	111
11:8-17	112, 148, 152	49:7-22	16, 125	22:15	68
			137	22:28	111
11:12	69	50:4-5	69, 71	23:28-31	58
11:20	16	50:20	70	24:24	71
12:3	16	50:38	61	24:27	71
12:14-17	64	50:40	137	25:12-14	125
13:10	3	51:15-18	49, 62, 111	29:3	166

30:13	32		135, 181	*Obadiah*	
32:2-3	166	2:13-14	14, 64		
33:31	15	2:16-23	71, 74, 107,	8	126
35:3-5	125		108, 133,	10-11	125
35:14-15	125		135, 181	15	125
ch. 36	71-72, 74,	3:1	82	17-18	125-126
	103, 108,	3:5	69		
	114, 150,	4:6	134	*Jonah*	
	178	4:10-19	15, 57, 61,		
36:18-38	16, 58, 68,		64, 134	2:8	49, 111, 181
	74-75, 95,	5:4	61		
	106-108,	5:15	69	*Micah*	
	127, 131,	6:6	59, 135		
	135, 146-	7:11-12	134	3:2	190
	147, 176,	7:16	134	4:6-8	71, 74, 136
	178, 184	8:4-10	57-58, 134	5:12-15	73
ch. 37	71, 74, 178	9:3	134	6:8	194
37:13-14	68, 107, 147	9:7	134	7:19-20	76
37:21-24	12, 179	9:17	134		
37:27	107	10:1-2	3	*Nahum*	
38:10	191	11:2	57		
38:23	186	11:5	134	2:1	139
39:27	68	13:1-9	16. 57, 134		
40:4-5	15	14:4	70	*Habakuk*	
44:5-10	65, 101				
		Joel		2:18-20	
Daniel					
		2:12-13	69		
ch. 3	57	3:19	125	*Zephaniah*	
chs. 4-5	67-68	3:5	139		
4:30-37	176			1:4-6	73
5:4	102			2:10-11	58, 73
5:21-23	16, 102	*Amos*		3:11-14	15, 58
ch. 7	166-167				
11:31-45	13, 191	1:5	45	*Zechariah*	
12:11	13	1:11-12	125		
		4:11	137	7:11-14	21, 25, 75
Hosea		5:15	190	8:12-23	136, 190
		5:21-25	59	10:2	111
1:9	134	8:11-14	64	10:7	14, 16
1:10-11	107, 133,	9:14-15	68, 146		

II. New Testament

Matthew		5:31-32	194	11:4-6	82, 86
		6:9	81	11:15	85, 165
3:7-10	122	6:21	81	11:25-27	82, 86-90
4:8-10	77, 82	6:24	77, 85	12:34	79
5:8	81	6:33	186	12:39	81
5:27-28	79, 194	11:2-4	179	13:3-23	56, 79, 81,

Index of Biblical and Other Ancient Sources 209

	83-86, 165		147, 179	10:31-39	92
13:43	85, 165	7:30	128, 147	11:8	92
15:7-9	78	7:34	179	11:53-57	92
15:29-31	179	8:4-15	83-86, 165	ch. 12	96
16:13-23	89	9:44-45	89	12:3	93
18:35	80	10:21-22	82, 86-90	12:7	94
19:26	192	10:30-37	194	12:12-13	93
21:12-13	90	11:2	81	12:16	92
22:37-40	78	11:20	80	12:24-34	94
23:16-26	87	13:29	180	12:32	94
23:37-38	88, 91	13:34-35	144	12:35-45	79, 81, 92-93,
24:15	81	11:46-53	91, 99, 144		94, 173, 180,
26:26-29	106, 179	14:16-24	180		181
27:34, 48	144	14:35	85	13:2-7	79, 92
		15:11-32	179	13:19-21	191
Mark		16:14-15	78-79, 81	14:1	79
		18:18-27	192, 194	14:26-27	79, 94
3:5	88	18:31-34	89	15:25	144
4:3-20	83-86	19:45-46	90	16:3	92
4:9	165	21:34	80, 89	16:8	94
4:10-12	56, 81, 87,	22:14-20	76, 95, 106,	16:13-18	92, 94
	89, 93, 143,		184	16:22	79
	151	23:36	144	17:9	94
4:11-20	165	24:25-26	89	17:21	94
4:23	85, 165	24:38	79	18:37	93
6:51-52	88			19:29	144
7:1-23	88	*John*		19:38	92
7:6-8	78, 81			20:8-9	92, 94
7:16	85	1:2-5	91	20:28	92
7:18-19	89	1:9-14	91-92, 95	20:30-31	91, 95
8:17-21	66, 85, 89	2:17-22	92		
8:27-33	89	3:1-8	91, 94, 144	*Acts*	
10:27	192	3:16	91, 188, 191		
11:15-17	90-91	3:18-19	92, 95	1:8	97
12:1-12	179	4:24	195	1:20	144
12:13-17	81, 95	5:16-18	92	1:24	81
12:28-34	78, 81	5:19-36	86, 91	2:26	79
14:24-25	106, 179	6:29	91	2:37	79
14:30	191	6:41-43	92	2:46	81
16:14	79	6:47	91	4:32	80
		6:52	92	5:4	79
		6:60	92	5:32	103
Luke		6:64	192	7:37	102
		7:1	92	7:39	79, 99-100
1:37	192	7:35-39	92, 94	7:41	97, 99-102
1:51	79	8:12-13	91-92	7:43	46, 78, 99-102
1:71-75	102	8:43-47	92, 188	7:48	97, 100-101
4:5-8	77, 82	9:22	92	7:51	79, 81, 100,
5:30-32	179	9:39	174		173
6:20-23	87, 91, 144	10:6	92	7:52-53	100, 173
6:45	79, 81	10:17-18	188	11:23	80
7:22-23	82, 86-87,	10:20	92	14:15	98, 111

15:8-9	79, 81, 103	4:9	119		127, 128, 130, 131, 133, 137-140, 147, 150
15:20	78, 99	4:13-16	119, 123-124		
15:29	78, 99	4:17	147		
16:14	79	4:18-24	120, 123		
17:16	78, 97	5:5	80, 106, 138-139		
17:23-29	97-98, 101			10:16	127, 140
17:30-31	98	5:8	125, 188	10:18-21	121-128, 140, 141, 144, 147
19:9	102	5:10	7		
19:26-29	97-98, 101	5:12	190		
21:13	79	6:17	80	11:1-3	121-122, 141, 151
21:25	78, 99	7:12-14	140		
26:9-11	104	8:3-4	136, 140	11:4-6	123, 127, 131, 135, 137, 139, 141, 143
26:18	103	8:14-15	106, 123, 139		
28:24-28	56, 79, 93, 102-103, 174	8:17	144, 147		
		8:27	81, 139	11:7-10	121-122, 127, 141-142, 143-144, 147, 180
Romans		8:28	119, 121, 138		
1:1-7	105, 107-108, 112, 120, 144, 180	8:29-30	107, 139, 191		
1:16-17	119-121, 127-128, 138-139, 148-149, 151	8:32	188	11:11	126
		8:36	144	11:13-14	122, 141
		9:1-7	122	11:15	147, 152
		9:2	79	11:17-25	119-121, 123, 128, 131, 134, 138, 148, 151-152
1:18-32	79, 100, 105-106, 108-110, 112, 114, 117, 125, 127, 134, 137, 144, 151-152, 173-174	9:3	128, 180		
		9:4-5	151		
		9:6	119-120		
		9:8	119, 122		
		9:9	123	11:23	95-96, 119, 131, 135, 138, 147-148, 180-181
		9:10-13	123-126, 138		
		9:14-15	127		
2:5-9	79, 115-116, 127, 131, 134, 138, 140, 147	9:15-19	19, 81, 119, 127-128, 131, 137, 144		
				11:25	122, 127, 147, 152
2:11-12	119, 127, 147, 151	9:20-24	119, 122, 127, 129-131, 132, 135, 143, 180	11:26-28	122, 141, 149, 150-151, 175
2:15	80, 107, 139				
2:21-24	116-117				
2:28-29	81, 94, 107, 115, 119, 123, 130, 135, 138-139, 147, 150, 183			11:32	119, 122, 151
		9:25-26	74, 108, 122-123, 135, 138, 152, 181	12:1-2	195
				15:3	144
				15:25-28	107
3:10-12	112	9:27	123	16:25-26	149
3:21-26	106, 137, 147, 150	9:30-33	119-120, 122-123, 128, 134-135, 137-138		
				1 Corinthians	
3:27	118			3:20	111
3:28	128			5:9-11	113
3:31	140			6:9-10	113
4:3	119, 126	10:1-15	75, 79, 103, 119-123,	8:4	78
4:6	127			8:10	162
4:7	123				

Index of Biblical and Other Ancient Sources

8:13-9:7	162	6:19	149	**Hebrews**	
10:7-8	162				
10:14-22	78, 99, 162,	**Philippians**		3:8-19	19, 79, 173, 181
11:25	76, 106, 179			4:7	19
12:2	78	1:7	79	4:12	81
13:12	185, 192	2:1-4	184	8:10	80
15:17	111	2:21	183	10:16	80
		3:20-21	138, 152, 180, 195	10:22	79, 81
2 Corinthians		4:3	144	11:26	144
				12:16	124
1:22	80	**Colossians**			
2:4	79			**James**	
ch. 3	113-114, 150, 180	1:25-29	149		
3:3	80, 106	2:1-3	80, 149	1:26	111
3:6	106, 152, 184	3:5	778	1:27	195
3:14-16	107, 118, 152, 153	3:15	79		
		3:22	81	**1 Peter**	
3:18	107, 138, 194-195	4:3	149		
				1:18	111
4:1	107	**1 Thessalonians**		1:22	79
4:4	181			2:9	194
4:6	80	1:9	78, 103	3:4	81
5:12	81	2:4	81	3:15	79
5:17-18	107, 120, 138, 152	2:13	129		
		2:14-16	144	**2 Peter**	
6:11	80-81	2:17	79		
6:16-18	78, 107	3:13	79	1:19	80
7:3	79			2:14	79
		2 Thessalonians			
Galatians				**1 John**	
		1:6-10	133	1:5	190
3:2-5	140	2:4-12	19, 21, 133	2:2	191
3:6	126-127	2:14	134	3:5	190
3:21-29	123, 150, 152	3:5	79	5:21	78
4:6	79, 107-108				
4:8-11	113-114, 121	**1 Timothy**		**2 John**	
4:21-23	122				
5:19-21	78	1:5	81	7	192
6:15	107	2:6	191		
		4:10	191	**Revelation**	
Ephesians					
				1:5	157
1:4-5, 11	191	**2 Timothy**		1:9	157, 160
1:9-23	79, 149			chs. 2-3	156, 161, 163-165
3:1-12	149	2:20	132		
3:14-19	80	2:22	81	2:2	161
3:17	79			2:3	157, 160
4:17-20	79, 113, 114	**Titus**		2:5	163
5:5	113-114			2:6	161
6:5	81	3:9	111	2:7	85, 86

2:9	157, 160	5:12-13	195	14:9-13	160, 170-171
2:10	161	6:9-11	157, 160	15:2-3	170-171
2:11	85-86	9:20-21	78, 154-155,	16:1-2	144, 170-171
2:13	156-157, 160-161		163, 167, 171-172, 174	16:8-10	155, 171
2:14	78, 162	10:8-11	164	16:21	155, 171
2:15	161	11:7	157-158	ch. 17	83
2:17	85-86	ch. 12	83	17:3	166
2:20	78, 157, 162	12:1-6	166	17:6	157-158, 160
2:21	171	12:7-9	158, 166, 190	17:9	164
2:23	81, 155	12:10-17	166	17:12	166
2:26	86	ch. 13	83, 157	17:17	80, 155
2:29	85	13:2-4	154, 166, 167, 169, 171	18:7	79, 155
3:1	163	13:7	158	18:24	157, 160
3:5	86, 144	13:8-9	85, 154, 167, 171, 174	19:2-3	157, 160
3:6	85			19:10	195
3:8-9	157, 160-161			19:20	171
3:12-13	85-86	13:12	167, 171	20:4	157, 170-171
3:16	163	13:14-15	167-169, 171	21:1-4	167
3:17-18	163	13:18	164, 168-169, 171, 174	21:7	86
3:21-22	85-86			22:9	195
4:11	195	14:7	170	22:11	164

III. Second Temple Jewish Writings

Old Testament Apocrypha:

Tobit

14:5-6   176

Judith

8:18   102

Wisdom of Solomon

13:5, 15   98
14:8   102
14:12   113
14:22-31   129
15:7   132
15:14-17   62
33:13   129

Sirach

15:14-17   129
16:11   101
27:5   129

33:7-13   129
38:29   129

Baruch

1:19-22   101, 145
2:3-3:7   115, 145-146
2:30-33   101, 115, 176
2:35   146
3:5-8   146
3:30-33   73
4:5-7   146

2 Maccabees

9:2   116-117
13:6-7   90, 117

1 Esdras

1:46-58   115-116, 125

Pseudepigrapha:

Jubilees

1:22-25   176
12:5   3

Psalms of Solomon

2:29-30   166

Pseudo Philo (L. A. B.)

32:5   124

Testament of Judah

23:1   113

Testaement of Naphtali

2:2   129

Testament of Reuben	*Josephus: Jewish Antiquities*	*1 QH*
4:6 113	17.163 116	12:14-17 60, 67
Testament of Zebulun	*Qumran Writings:*	*1QS*
9:5-9 149, 176	*Damascus Document* (CD)	11:22 129
Philo:	2:7-8 124	*4Q521* 86
Multiple Works Cited on p. 124	3:10-16a 125 20:8-10 60, 67	

IV. Church Fathers and Roman Sources

Eusebius		*Dio Cassius* LXVII 5, 7	159
Ecclesiastical History 5.30.3	156	*Juvenal* 4:38	170
Irenaeus		*Martial* 11:33	170
Against Heresies 5.30.3	156	*Suetonius*	
Clement		*Domitian* 13	159
1 Clement	124	*Tacitus*	
		Annals 3.63; 4:55-56	156

V. Egyptian Sources

The Book of the Dead
"Spells of Emerging in Daytime"

Spell 17	28
Spell 30	24
Spell 30A	24
Spell 30B	25
Spell 125	23
The Instruction of Ptahhotep	26
Shabaka Stone	28

Index of Modern Authors

Allen, Leslie A. 3
Allen, Thomas George. 25
Andrews, Carol. 23-24, 32
Aune, David. 156-157, 160-161, 166, 170-171
Barrick, W. Boyd. 46
Barth, Karl. 134
Bauckham, Richard. 168-170
Beale, G.K. 2, 9, 25, 60, 64-65, 156-158, 166, 168
Betz, Hans Dieter. 107
Calvin, John. 11, 152
Charles, R. H. 162
Childs, Brevard. 9
Clifford, Richard J. 3
Craig, William Lane. 189
Cranfield, C. E. B. 116, 126-127, 134-135, 140
Currid, John D. 22-23
Cuss, Sr. Dominique. 168
Davis, John J. 2, 29
Day, John. 4, 38
Deissmann, Adolf. 156
Dunn, J. D. G. 116-118, 152
Edwards, Jonathan. 1, 9
Eichrodt, Walter. 1, 14
Eisenmann, R. 86
Evans, Craig. 64, 66, 73-74, 81
Fabry, H. J. 3, 14, 15
Faulkner, Raymond. 13, 25
Finegan, Jack. 4, 38
Fitzmyer, J.A. 100, 118, 127, 151
Frankfort, Henri. 30
Furnish, Victor P. 106
Garlington, D. B. 118
Goelet Jr., Ogden. 13, 14
Greenfield, J. C. 4
Grudem, Wayne. 187-188, 190
Guinness, Os. 85, 182
Guthrie, Stan. 194
Harris, Murray J. 138

Hays, Richard B. 129-130, 180
Healy, J. F. 4
Heider, George C. 46
Hemer, Colin. 156-157
Herion, Gary A. 5
Herrmann, W. 4, 54
Hoffmeier, James K. 22, 30-31, 34
Hort, Greta. 34
Huddelstun, J. R. 24
Hübner, Ulrich. 124
Kaiser, Otto. 181
Kaufmann, Yehezkel. 2
Kitchen, Kenneth A. 22, 24, 32, 33, 34
Kutsko, John F. 58, 65, 72
Lewis, C. S. 182-183
Lichtheim, Miriam. 23, 26
Lincoln, Andrew. 114
Longenecker, R. 107
Martin, Ralph P. 106, 152
Matera, Frank J. 106
McCarthy, Dennis J. 5
Meeks, D. and C. F. 29, 31
Mendenhall, G. E. 4-5
Mettinger, Tryggve N. D. 8
Metzger, Bruce. 156, 165
Miller, Patrick D. 8
Moo, Douglass. 116-117, 127, 130
Morenz, Siegfried. 26, 29
Moreland, J. P. 189
Müller, Hans-Peter. 45
Packer, J. I. 184
Petrie, W.M.F. 32
Piper, John. 1, 2, 129, 187
Plantinga, Alvin. 189
Price, S. R. F. 156
Puech, Emile. 45
Ramachandra, Vinoth. 182
Redford, Donald B. 22
Rignell, L. 60
Sadek, A. I. 24
Sandelin, Karl-Gustav. 81-82
Scherrer, Steven J. 168
Schlossberg, Herbert. 182

Schreiner, Thomas R. 116-117, 152
Scott, James M. 106
Shupak, Nili. 13-14, 21-22, 24
Sider, Ronald J. 193
Slater, Thomas B. 159-160
Strand, K. A. 158
Stuhlmacher, Peter. 110, 120, 135, 139, 150, 175
Swete, H. B. 170
Swinburne, Richard. 189
Talbot, Mark. 187-188
Tanner, J. Paul. 108
Theissen, Gerd. 83
Thielman, Frank. 107, 179
Thompson, Leonard L. 158-159, 162
Thorsell, Paul R. 108
Thrall, Margaret. 106-107
Tozer, A. W. 184-185
Vermes, Geza. 124
von Rad, Gerhard. 8
Ware, Bruce. 190-191
Watts, Rikk E. 62, 64-65
Wente, Edward. 28, 30, 33
Whitney, J. T. 46
Wilson, Robert R. 20, 21
Wolff, Hans Walter. 108
Wright, N. T. 152, 179
Wyatt, Nicholas. 45
Yamauchi, E. 38
York, Terry. 194